BLOUNT COUNTY TENNESSEE

DEEDS

1819–1833

ABSTRACTED BY

Jane Kizer Thomas

HERITAGE BOOKS
2011

HERITAGE BOOKS

AN IMPRINT OF HERITAGE BOOKS, INC.

Books, CDs, and more—Worldwide

For our listing of thousands of titles see our website
at
www.HeritageBooks.com

Published 2011 by
HERITAGE BOOKS, INC.
Publishing Division
100 Railroad Ave. #104
Westminster, Maryland 21157

Other Heritage Books by the author:
CD: *Blount County, Tennessee Deeds, 1819–1833*

International Standard Book Numbers
Paperbound: 978-1-55613-768-6
Clothbound: 978-0-7884-8914-3

TABLE OF CONTENTS

INTRODUCTION

The deeds of this period reflect the hard circumstances following the Panic of 1819 and the business crisis of the early 1820's which it caused. Within months of the panic's onset, prices fell by 50 percent, and the average wage of a dollar a day deflated proportionally. Markets collapsed, and the farmer as well as the businessman was saddled with debts that overnight had doubled in real-dollar values. Bank notes (the government did not issue paper money until the Civil War) depreciated in value. Banks refused to redeem their paper notes in specie, and credit contractions left both large and small farmers land-poor. Farmers could live off their land and stock, but there simply were no markets from which to acquire bank paper or hard money. Taxes could be paid in coin only; thus, when hard money could not circulate, even the smallest of land taxes could not be paid. Large farms were lost to the sheriff's sale for want of fifteen or twenty dollars' worth of hard money. The farmer's hatred of paper banks and their rag money would last for the next several generations.

The Tennessee General Assembly passed an act on 19 October 1819, entitled "An Act to provide for payment of the interest and monies due from the citizens residing south of French Broad and Holston and between the rivers Big Pigeon and Tennessee and for other purposes." This Act allowed citizens who had purchased land under a grant to pay only the interest due the State, the principal remaining as a lien on the land. Interest due for 1818 was to be paid on 1 November 1820, and for 1819 by 1 November 1821. Those who failed to pay the interest had their lands exposed to public sale. Sales under the provisions of this act will be indicated as "under 19 Oct 1819 Act."

EXPLANATION

These deeds were abstracted from microfilm copies in the Blount County Public Library, 301 McGhee Street, Maryville, TN 37801.

In the mid-1800s, Blount County officials found deed books of the county in a state of deterioration, and they voted to have the books copied into new ledgers. After being copied, the original books were destroyed. Books were not copied consecutively, but according to the condition of the original book. Thus, the deeds in Book 4 actually were registered in an earlier year than those found in Book 3.

The handwriting of the transcribers was often difficult to read. At times it was apparent that the clerk who registered the deed and copied it for the first time could not decipher a name and thus spelled it as it looked to be. In Deed Book 2, in particular, an "a", "o", or "u" looked alike, as did "er" and "on". It was impossible sometimes to determine just what a name should be. "McCully" might appear to be "McCally" or "McColly", "Burnes" might be "Barnes". Was it "Simens" or "Simons"? Or even "Simms"? A name may also have been shown in several different ways within a deed; this is indicated by a "slash" [/]. In case of doubt, the name is followed by a question mark. It also appeared that the copier frequently skipped, omitted, or repeated phrases within the deed.

The researcher is advised to request a copy of the deed from Blount County Public Library if he wishes to verify names or facts.

As a convenience for the researcher, EACH DEED *is* SEQUENTIALLY NUMBERED *and* INDEXED *by* DEED NUMBER, *not the page on which the deed appears.* Following the deed number, the book and page number for each deed is shown in parentheses; (2:20-21) indicates Deed Book 2, pages 20 and 21. This is followed by the date the deed was written; the consideration for which property was conveyed; description of the property, including location and adjoining property owners, where shown; names of witnesses; and date of registration by county clerk. (Deeds were often not registered until several years after they were made.) If any signature was by "mark" that fact is indicated "(X)". Deeds had to be acknowledged or proven at the county court before they could be registered. This acknowledgment is not shown unless it contained special information.

Land Grants were issued by the State of Tennessee unless otherwise stated. Small amounts of land (rods, poles, chains, etc.) over and above the acreage are not shown.

ABBREVIATIONS

ac	acres
ack	acknowledged
admin	administrator
adj	adjoining
atty	attorney
Co.	County
cor	corner to
decd	deceased
execr	executor
orig	original(ly)
Sig	Signature
Wit	Witness

Blount County, Tennessee, Deeds
Deed Book 2

1. (2:1) Samuel ROWAN/ROIN to Benjamin JAMES: 20 Mar 1819, $300, 90 ac on west fork of Lackey's Creek, part of Grant to Samuel Roin by TN, cor to Josiah PATTY, crossing creek, adj Martin BONHAM, Henry WHITTENBURGER. Wit: Joseph HART, Thomas HENDERSON. 5 May 1819.

2. (2:1-2) Joel McCORKEL to Samuel FRAZIER: 23 Sep 1817, $300, 71 ac on waters of Gallaher's Creek, adj Nehemiah BONHAM, James MOORE, Paul COCHRAN, the spring. Granted by TN to William H. RAY and conveyed to FRAZIER. Wit: Parks FRAZIER, William MONTGOMERY, Joseph HACKNEY. 5 May 1819.

3. (2:2-3) Henry BOWERMAN to William DAVIS: 12 Mar 1819, $250, 112 ac on waters of Holston River, surveyed 16 Dec 1806. Wit: John GAUTT, James YOUNG. 6 May 1819.

4. (2:3-4) Samuel FRAZIER to James MURRAH/MORRAH: 11 Mar 1810, $150, 70 ac on waters of Cloyd's Creek formerly belonging to William H. RAY; cor to John ALLEN, adj Widow READ. Wit: John M. RANKIN, James LOVE. 6 May 1819.

5. (2:4) Samuel WINTERS to Mary CARTER and each of her children (not named), heirs of Richard CARTER, decd: (date omitted) Nov 1816, $400, 95 ac on waters of Cloyd's Creek, cor to Isaac HARE. Wit: Henry STEPHENSON, Solomon DIXSEN. 6 May 1819.

6. (2:4-5) Samuel FRAZIER to James LOVE: 10 Mar 1819, $75, 23 ac on waters of Gallaher's Creek, part of Grant #2409 to Frazier, 2 July 1812. Wit: John M. RANKIN, Samuel W. WILLIAMS. 7 May 1819.

7. (2:5-6) Robert HUGHES, executor of Aleson/Allison WASHUM, decd, to Jesse CARTRIGHT: 30 Dec 1811, $320, 160 ac adj Samuel MONTGOMERY, Thomas CARTRIGHT, David PARKINS' old line. Wit: Henry RON, Robert WILSON. 7 May 1819.

8. (2:6-7) Thomas WEBB to Abraham HEARTSELL: 12 Jan 1818, $650, 109 ac on Holston River, cor to Elizabeth (BOY?) adj GILLESPIE and HOUSTON, Charles McCLURE, being occupant claim surveyed by James SLONE and conveyed by John CARSEN to Thomas WEBB. Sig: Thomas (X) WEBB. Wit: William (X) WEBB, Willis WEBB. 7 May 1819.

9. (2:7-8) Edward HOLLOWAY to Sarah HAMMONTREE: 28 Nov 1818, $100, 47 ac on Six Mile Creek, part of Grant to Jeremiah HAMMONTREE, adj Edward BURNET, George SNIDER. Wit: Joseph HOLLOWAY, John HOLLOWAY. 30 May 1819.

10. (2:8-9) Samuel HACKNEY to Francis HENDERSON: 27 Sep 1815, $250, 40 ac on waters of Holston River, part of survey made for James WALKER and conveyed to William WILLIAMS, adj Francis JONES. Wit: Joseph HENDERSON, Alexander HENDERSON. 30 May 1819.

11. (2:9-10) Abel R. CHENEY to John NORWOOD: 2 Oct 1818, $255, 106 ac on waters of east fork of Pistol Creek, Grant #1371 by State of TN to John HANNAH, decd, and   conveyed to Moses HANNAH, heir of John; to CHENEY on 11 Jun 1818, cor to William HARRIS, adj John DUNCAN, Robert GAUTT, John WILKINSON, James DONOHOO. Wit: William WALLACE, Jesse WALLACE. 29 Jun 1819.

12. (2:10) Jonathan HENDERSON to (son) Samuel HENDERSON: 30 Mar 1818, power of atty to make a deed of conveyance for 24 ac of land which I sold to Moses HANNAH adj "the plantation whereon I now live"; also to convey "all my other land...including the plantation whereon I now live." Wit: Mathew McGHEE, John WILKINSON. 15 Jul 1819.

13. (2:10-11) William AYLETT "at present of County of Blount" to Thomas TURK, "late of Augusta Co., VA": 22 Oct 1818, $5000, 444 ac on west fork of Pistol Creek; the state is owed $444.375 with interest; adj McCALLAN and John McCULLY, Felix KENNEDY, Jack HOUSTON, land the property of the estate of William HOUSTON, decd, James WEAR, land sold by A. WEAR to Aylett, crossing the creek. Also a tract of 225 ac adj above tract; the state is

owed $225.0625 with interest, cor to James WEAR, adj Thomas HENDERSON, ALLEN, (MALLER?). Wit: Jacob FOUTE, Jno. TOOL. Proven at June session of court by witnesses. 15 Jul 1819.

14.   (2:11-14)   Charles DONOHOO, Sheriff, to John MONTGOMERY and James BERRY: 5 Apr 1819, undivided moiety of four lots in Maryville; public sale 1 Apr 1818. $500 for lot #60, $500 for lots #85 and #86 together; $21 for lot #108; total $2,021 (sic). Levied upon to satisfy judgment issued by court of Greene Co. on behalf of Francis PRESTON "in a certain action of covenant..prosecuted against Lilbourn L. HENDERSON, executor of William TRIGG, decd, who was surviving executor of William KING, decd..[and] recovered $20,433 for his damage and costs of $4.69...It appears of record that L. L. HENDERSON fully administered all the [estate] of William KING and William TRIGG, decd...Preston may have execution of his damage and cost with interest on the damage from 1 Aug 1817 till paid, of the real estate of William KING which was devised or descended to the heirs; namely, Thomas CLEBOURN and Sarah, his wife, late Sarah King, relict of James KING; William, Thomas, and Eliza KING in fact children of James King; John, Polly, and Rachel in part children of John MITCHELL by his wife Elizabeth, decd; William, James, and Thomas KING, infant children of Samuel KING, decd, by Alexander BROWN, their guardian; John MITCHELL, William HESKELL, and Eliza his wife; (Wavaley?) FINDLY and Nancy, his wife; Joseph TRIGG and Elizabeth his wife, late Elizabeth FINLEY; John ALLEN and Hannah, his wife; William CONNALLY, Daniel and Lilburn TRIGG, infant children of William TRIGG, decd, by his wife Rachel by Lilburn L. HENDERSON, their guardian. Plaintiff should recover further sum of $15.84 for costs of prosecution. .." "[Greene Co. Court] command you as we have heretofore commanded the Sheriff of Washington Co. and the Sheriff of Greene Co. that of the real estate and lands..which were of the will of William KING, decd...descended to the heirs...you cause to be made $14,489.29, the residue of the damage to which plaintiff may be entitled..and have monies ready to deliver to the Court House in Greeneville on the fourth Monday in April." Sig: Andrew PATTERSON, clerk of Greene Co. court, 4th Mon Jan 1819, by M. PAYNE, deputy. Wit: Thomas CAULDWELL, Hambright BLACK. 16 Jul 1819.

15. (2:14-15) John MONTGOMERY and James BERRY, trading as MONTGOMERY AND BERRY, and Charles DONOHOO to Isaac ANDERSON, Jr.: 27 Mar 1817, $230, all right, title and interest vested in them by virtue of a purchase and deed of conveyance from Thomas HENDERSON, who purchased at Sheriff's Sale from David RUSSELL, Sheriff, 1 Aug 1800, as property of John LOWERY, Samuel WEIR, and William MACLIN, lot #42 in Maryville, adj Main Street, being known as the front end on which there is a small shop and cold house, a line being run across the lengthwise of the lot so as to divide it equally, the back end or other half being heretofore conveyed to Trustees of MARYVILLE FEMALE ACADEMY. Wit: James TEDFORD, William M. BERRY. 17 Jul 1819.

16. (2:15-16) David NIMON to William ANDERSON: 11 Nov 1818, $275, 50 ac, adj John COULDWELL, McCULLOM's corner, original grant #2830. Wit: James GILLASPEY, James A. McCULLEY. 19 Jul 1819.

17. (2:16-17) John GILLESPIE and wife Anne and Thomas F. COLEBURN/COULBURN and Isabella his wife of Murray (sic) Co., TN; William WALLACE and Mary his wife; William WALLACE, Sr. and Margaret, his wife, of Blount Co., heirs of John CHAMBERLAIN, decd, to William CORLEY: 28 Jun 1817, $450, 102 ac on waters of Holston River, part of survey made for heirs of John Chamberlain, cor to Josiah PATTY, adj William YOUNG, cor to Robert YOUNG, adj Edward GORELY/GOURLY. At Oct session 1818, Murray Co. court appointed John LINDSEY and John MARSH to privately examine Anne Gillespie and Isabella Coleburn. James GILLESPIE and George EWING, of Blount Co. court, examined Mary and Margaret Wallace separately. 22 Jul 1819.

18. (2:18) John S. BENNETT to Elliott GRILLS of Knox Co.: 20 Aug 1818, $3000, two town lots and improvements, one on Main St. adj John GARDNER, being the lot where Josiah DANFORTH now lives, and the lot immediately in back of it whereon stables stand. Bennett to pay in twelve months the sum of $3000 which he owes to Grills. Wit: Enoch PERSON, W. K. PERSON. Proven in Knox Co. court by witnesses, Jul 1819. 27 Jul 1819.

19. (2:18-20) Charles DONOHOO, Sheriff, to John MONTGOMERY: 5 Apr 1819, $10, public sale 4 Apr 1818 to satisfy judgment obtained in Greene Co. [writ shown in #14 above is repeated], a tract of land levied on as property of William KING's heirs; Grant #64 to William King and John Montgomery 13 Jul 1818. Adj Samuel McGAUHEY, James EDINGTON, David CAMPBELL, Robert HOOKS, William LOWERY, John SWART, Samuel WEAR. Wit: Jacob F. FOUTE, James BERRY, Thomas COULDWELL. 5 Aug 1819.

20. (2:20-21) John HICKLAND to Samuel TORBET: 12 (mo omitted) 1819 (sic), $100, 19 ac on waters of Holston River, Grant #71. Wit: James GILLESPIE, Alex ISH, Hugh TORBET. Proven at June court 1819 by ISH and "Hugh TORBET, Jr., the subscribing witnesses." 6 Aug 1819.

21. (2:21-22) John HICKLAND to Samuel TORBET: 12 Apr 1819, $1150, 276 ac on waters of Holston River, Grant #160. All other details same as in #20 above. 6 Aug 1819.

22. (2:22-23) John HICKLAND to Samuel TORBET: 12 Apr 1819, $1750, 430 ac, Grant #154. All other details same as in #20 above. 6 Aug 1819.

23. (2:23-24) Charles DONOHOO, Sheriff, to John LOWERY: 4 Aug 1819, $5000, 330 ac on waters of Pistol Creek, adj Bartley McGHEE, John B. CUSICK, John MONTGOMERY, and others. Wit: William LOWERY, James L. BOGLE. 7 Aug 1819.

24. (2:24-25) Joal TUCKER to John PICKENS, Sr. (Blount Co.) and James KENNEDY, Knox Co.: 28 Jun 1819, $500, 135 ac on waters of Nails Creek at foot of Bays Mountain, "tract I now live on"; adj James McCLURG/McCLARY. No witnesses. 20 Aug 1819.

25. (2:25) Miles and David CUNNINGHAM to James TURK: 25 Aug 1813, $100, lot #16 in Maryville. Sig: Miles (X) CUNNINGHAM. David (X) CUNNINGHAM. Wit: Enoch PARSEN, Jas. H. PACK. 30 Aug 1819.

26. (2:25-27) Charles DONOHOO, Sheriff, to Jacob F. FOUTE: 26 Jun 1819, $1.57, 60 ac on waters of Gallaher's Creek; public sale 13 Mar 1819 to satisfy two judgments: one obtained by Josiah BEALL against Lenna RHEA and William MONTGOMERY; another obtained by Josiah PAYN against Lenna RHEA. Adj Isaac BROOKS, M. BENNETT, W. ADAMS. Wit: Azaciah SHELTON, Jesse THOMPSON. 4 Sep 1819.

27. (2:27) Charles DONOHOO, Sheriff, to Doctor Edward GAULT: 12 Dec 1818, $200, land on waters of Nine Mile Creek "whereon David CUNNINGHAM now lives." Public sale 12 Dec 1818 to satisfy six judgments: one by John McGHEE, one by LOWERY & PERSON, one by James SCHRIMSHER against David CUNNINGHAM, also McGHEE AND BROTHERS Thomas HENDERSON (sic) against Miles and David CUNNINGHAM; also Joel CAMPBLE against Miles CUNNINGHAM, Jr. No witnesses. 30 Sep 1819.

28. (2:27-28) William BEASLEY to John G. BROWN: 25 Feb 1819, $2601, 282 ac on Baker's Creek, cor to surveys made for Samuel COWAN and William GRAY, adj surveys made for John MILLAR, Wiley LASSATER, Hugh KELSO. Sig: William (X) BEASLEY. Wit: Robert WEAR, Wiley LASETER. 1 Oct 1819.

29. (2:28-29) Philip FOUST to Henry WHITTENBURGER, Jr.: 13 Jun 1814, $650, 165 ac on waters of Lackey's Creek, part of survey made for John COX "whereon Henry COX, decd, formerly lived"; adj WHITTENBURGER, cor to John COX's occupant survey, Ambrose COX. Wit: Josiah PATTY, Henry WHITTENBURGER. 14 Oct 1819.

30. (2:29-30) John BUNDY to Josiah ROWAN: 5 Dec 1816, $300, 107 ac on waters of Cloyd's Creek, adj Samuel SHAW, Joseph DUNCAN. Wit: Samuel JOHNSTON, William JOHNSTON. 17 Nov 1819.

31. (2:30-31) Russell BATES to William MACKEY: 5 Sep 1819, $200, 67 ac on Little River, Grant #5464, adj survey of John (PINTER?). No witnesses. 29 Nov 1819.

32. (2:31) Russell BATES to William MACKEY: 25 Sep 1819, $100, all [Bates'] rights as heir of John HESS, decd, to a tract in Miller's Cove. No witnesses. 29 Nov 1819.

33. (2:31-32) William DURHAM to Isaac HAIR: 25 Oct 1816, $500, 118 ac in Hickory Valley, surveyed by William GRIFFITH and assigned to Benjamin BAILY; adj John MORDUK, MATHEW heirs, Nicholas STEPHENSON. Wit: Aucher JOHNSON, Thomas DURHAM. 29 Nov 1819.

34. (2:32-33) Samuel HENDERSON to Thomas RHENOLDS: 28 Jun 1819, $500, 150 ac on waters of Pistol Creek, part of Grant #1766 to James DONOHOO. Wit: Jonathan HENDERSON, Thomas HENDERSON. 13 Dec 1819.

35. (2:33-34) George EWING, Alexander B. GAMBLE, Robert McTEER, and Carson COULDWELL to William HUTCHISON: 16 Aug 1819, $2500, 331 ac on Little River, adj James EWING, Henry McCULLY's line at present William WALLACE; Grant #1295 to Andrew KENNEDY. Wit: Gordon WHITE, James GILLESPY. 13 Dec 1819.

36. (2:34-35) James WALKER to John WATERS: 18 Aug 1819, $70, 72 ac on waters of Little River in Miller's Cove. Sig: James (X) WALKER. Wit: John PANTER, Henry DAVIS. 13 Dec 1819.

37. (2:35) Russell BATES and Joseph BURNET to John WATERS: 25 Sep 1819, $200, 79 ac in Miller's Cove on Reed's Creek, north side of Little River Grant #1794? Wit: John PINTER, William MACKEY. 13 Dec 1819.

38. (2:35-36) John PANTER, Sr. to Thomas HICKS: 6 Sep 1819, $600, 50 ac on Little River, Grant #2576, surveyed 14 Jun 1818. Wit: Joseph PRATER, James (X) WALKER. 14 Dec 1819.

39. (2:36-37) Henry BAIRD/BARD to William BAIRD: 24 Apr 1818, 30 ac "being part of tract I now live on [and] the place where William BAIRD now lives" adj Richard DAVIS. Sig: Henry (X) BAIRD. Wit: Thomas MORISON, David FIRE/FARR. 14 Dec 1819.

40. (2:37-38) John RHEA to James and John KINCANNON: 16 Sep 1819, $1600, 400 ac including the Blue Spring, adj John WILLIAMS. Sig: John (X) RHEA. Wit: Hugh BOGAL, Edwin HODGE, Samuel BOGAL. 14 Dec 1819.

41. (2:38) Thomas WOODEN to Thomas COPPOCK of Jefferson Co.: 18th day of 8th month 1818, 173 ac, $600, adj south side Holston River, granted to Wooden. Sig: Thomas (X) WOODEN. Wit: William GRIFFITH, John CRYE, John COULSEN. 15 Dec 1819.

42. (2:38-39) Benjamin TAYLOR to James DELZELL: 7 Aug 1816, $150, 12 ac on waters of Six Mile Creek adj McGHEE. Granted to William MEANS. Wit: Robert DELZELL, William DELZELL, George HOGE. 15 Dec 1819.

43. (2:39-40) Mail McPHAIL to John EDINGTON: 4 Apr 1812 (sic), $800, 198 ac adj Joseph JOHNSTON, Samuel SHAW, Holston River, John SHADLE. Surveyed 17 May 1817. Wit: Thomas (X) WOODEN, Samuel EDINGTON. 15 Dec 1819.

44. (2:40-41) John EDINGTON to George and Benjamin FORD: 9 Nov 1812, $800, 198 ac adj John SHADOE/SHADLE, Joseph JOHNSTON, Samuel SHAW, Holston River Edington covenants..that the "before Rented Land"..he will warrant, etc. Wit: Samuel STEEL, Robert PARKS. 15 Dec 1819.

45. (2:41-42) Robert GILLASPY/GILLESPY to Josiah PATTY: 27 Jun 1817, $147, 42 ac on Lackey's Creek, part of the occupant survey made by James HOUSTON, James, John and Robert GILLESPY, adj Obed PATTY, William SAFFELL, crossing a neck of the Iron Works dam. Wit: (M?) HOUSTON, John SAFFELL. 16 Dec 1819.

46. (2:42-43) Edward HODGES to Henry G. HODGES (both of Sevier Co.): 22 Sep 1819, $600, 207 ac on waters of Nails Creek, part of tract granted to Samuel DAVIS, adj Thomas (BRECKINRAGE?). No witnesses. 18 Dec 1819.

47. (2:43-44) John WHITE to Gardner MAYS: 6 Sep 1819, $700, 182 ac on waters of Nails Creek, adj MARTIN, north to foot of Bays

Mountain, SHARP, (BRAKEBILL?). Wit: Jeffie JOHNSTON, James BERRY. 18 Dec 1819.

48. (2:44-45) Samuel DAVIS of Madison Co., AL Territory, to Thomas BUCKANAN: 26 May 1818, $300, 100 ac on waters of Nails Creek. Wit: Edward HODGES, Henry G. HODGES, John HOOK. 18 Dec 1819.

49. (2:45) Joseph GASTON to Thomas DAVIS: 27 Sep 1819, $300, 37 ac in Miller's Cove. Wit: Jac F. FOUTE, A. SHELTON. 18 Dec 1819.

50. (2:45-46) Samuel DAVIS of Madison Co., AL Territory, to Edward HODGES of Sevier Co.: 26 May 1818, $600, 207 ac on waters of Nails Creek, adj Thomas BUKANAN. Wit: Thomas BOKANAN, Henry G. HODGES. 20 Dec 1819.

51. (2:47-48) Rebeckah REED, widow of Alexander REED, and others to William TAYLOR: 25 Apr 1816, $300, 164 ac laid off by John WILKINSON for William TAYLOR, Grant #880 dated 11 May 1810 to Rebecka Reed for 315 ac, being "upper end of said tract on north side of Little River...where Taylor now lives." Sig: Rebeckah (X) REED. James C. REED. John W. REED. Jacob HUNTER and Sally D. (X) HUNTER, his wife, lately Sally D. REED.   Samuel R. (X) REED and Elizabeth (X) REED. Heirs at law of Alexander Reed, all of Rhea Co., TN. Wit: (J. RUE?), David RAWLINGS/RALINGS, Alexander B. GAMBLE, John (REN/RICE/REA?. 20 Dec 1819.

52. (2:48-49) Samuel HACKNEY to Alexander HANNAH: 31 Aug 1819, $800, 160 ac on waters of Holston River adj Francis HENDERSON. Wit: John PICKENS, F. HENDERSON. 20 Dec 1819.

53.   (2:49-50) James CUNNINGHAM, admin of John CUNNINGHAM, decd, of Campble Co., to James PITNER: 15 Oct 1818, $150, 86 ac on Ellejoy Creek, adj MOORE. Wit: Benjamin TIPTON, Robert MURRIN. 21 Dec 1819.

54. (2:50-51) Charles LOCKHART to William EVERETT: 21 Feb 1818, $300, 116 ac on waters of Crooked Creek, Grant #1042. Wit: Robt. EVERETT, William GAY. 30 Dec 1819.

55. (2:51) William HUGHES to [son] David HUGHES: 22 Sep 1817, "natural love and affection" and $1.00, 181 ac on waters of Little River whereon is a Grist Mill, surveyed by John WILKINSON. William reserves the mill and water works, with necessary timber for firewood and repairing and completing the mill and sawmill already begun.   Wit: Ignatius WILSON, Samuel M. GAUTT, John WILKINSON, Jno. GARDNER, William WILKINSON. Proven at Sept court 1819 by Ignatious Wilson and John Wilkinson.   30 Dec 1819.

56. (2:51-52) Jesse KERR to David KERR: 17 Mar 1819, $1000, 168 ac on Nine Mile Creek, adj Cullinas MILLER, George COOP, Charles HENRY, Grant #1446 to John HANNA 18 June 1810. Wit: Daniel KERR, John KERR, Jr. 13 Jan 1820.

57. (2:52-53) Jesse KERR to David KERR: 15 Aug 1818, $1000, 284 ac on Nine Mile Creek, adj John HANNAH, Charles HENRY, William WOODS, John McGEE. Grant #1071 to Cullinas MILLER, 14 May 1810 and conveyed to Jesse KERR on 26 Mar 1816. Wit: David THEU, Isaac OAKS. 14 Jan 1820.

58. (2:53-54) Robert FINDLEY to Alexander SHADDEN: 22 Dec 1818, $1,000, 271 ac on waters of Nails Creek. Wit: William C. CRESWELL, Joseph McMURRY. 14 Jan 1820.

59. (2:54-55) James THOMPSON to [brother] William THOMPSON: 26 Nov 1819, power of atty to sue for and recover of John McCALESTER and Thomas BRABSEN of Washington Co., TN, adminr of estate of Ephraim BRABSEN, decd, of Washington Co., all sums of money, etc..that now is or may be coming to me as one of the heirs at law. Wit: Jack F. FOUTE, Azaciah SHELTON. 18 Jan 1820.

60. (2:55) William CAMPBLE to Grinsfield TAYLOR: 1 Jul 1819, $600, 120 ac, adj Nathaniel HOOD, Charles McCLAIN and William

MAXWELL, Samuel GEORGE. Wit: Andrew THOMPSON, William KEITH. 3 Feb 1820.

61. (2:55-56) Charles DONOHOO, Sheriff, to George MISER:12 Dec 1818, $72, 85 ac on waters of Nine Mile Creek, adj William ARMSTRONG, public sale 20 Dec 1818 to satisfy two judgments, one obtained by John McCALESTER and another by Abner GARNER against Andrew VAUGT and David CUNNINGHAM. 16 Feb 1820.

62. (2:56) Charles DONOHOO to John GLASS: 12 Dec 1818, $68.50, 181 ac; public sale 12 Dec 1818 to satisfy five judgments obtained by John GLASS against Harvey KING, Peggy KING, Isaac KING, Nancy KING, and Adam KING, heirs of Adam KING, decd. 16 Feb 1820.

63. (2:56-57) John McCOOL to Henry BOWERMAN: 22 Mar 1819, $300, 77 ac on waters of Holston River part of occupant survey for Luke and Thomas HAIL, adj Henry PESTERFIELD, Daniel BONINE. Wit: (? MYERS?), John (X) HICKS. No reg date.

64. (2:58-59) William EARLY to John B. ELLIS: 10 Feb 1819, $600, 121 ac on west fork of Pistol Creek, adj Edward BUCKINGHAM, Polly POSEY, Hezekiah POSEY, James POSEY, E. DeBUSK, Andrew YOUNG, John EDMONSON. Wit: Archable TURK, Samuel LOVE. 17 Feb 1820.

65. (2:59-60) Enoch PERSONS to Thomas HENDERSON: 10 Apr 1817, $4725, 743 ac on Pistol Creek; one tract of 191 ac, Grant #2264 to Henry PARRAT; one tract 13 ac Grant #1218 to Josiah PAIN; one tract 108 ac Grant #618 to Cornelius ALEXANDER; one tract 309 ac Grant #3451 to Cornelius BUCK and James BRAUDER; one tract 120 ac part of grants #1746 and #1818 to David EAGLETON. Crosses Rankin Road, adj OWENS, PAYN, WOODS, James WEAR, WORLDLEY, HOUSTON, RUSSELL, leaving a lime kiln, WALLACE. Wit: David M. HUNTER, Samuel BLACKBURN. 17 Feb 1820.

12   Blount County, Tennessee, Deeds 1819 - 1833

66. (2:60-61) George SNIDER, Sr. to Elihue HICKS: 9 Aug 1817, $250, 89 ac on waters of Crooked Creek, Grant #841, adj William WAKER (sic). Wit: Isaac WHITE, Robert EVERETT. 17 Feb 1820.

67. (2:61) William COKER to Thomas SPRADLING: 10 Jan 1816, $200, 40 ac on waters of Nine Mile Creek, part of 139 ac granted to James CONNATSER, assignee of Elizabeth STEEL, execr of Joseph STEEL, decd, adj "lands then belonging to R. CHAWS by Samuel THOMPSON and by SPRADLING"; sold by David THOMPSON to COKER. Wit: [three marks?: SL LB RTS], Jacob COLE. Ack in court Sep 1817. 18 Feb 1820.

68. (2:61-62) William H. RAY to Samuel FRAZIER: 13 Mar 1817, $400, 167 ac on waters of Cloyd's Creek, granted to Ray, adj John ALLISON, FRAZIER, James CRAWFORD, James WATSON, REED. Wit: "RZZ" [possibly a mark] CULLY, Alex McKEE. 18 Feb 1820.

69. (2:62-63) John RAGON, Sr. to Thomas HICKS: 27 Dec 1819, $1000, 150 ac, residue of a tract of 315 ac, Grant #883 to Rebeckah REED on 11 May 1810, on Little River including tract where HICKS now lives. Wit: William WILLIAMSON, David GREENWAY. 18 Feb 1820.

70. (2:63) John NEAL to Barney COCHRAN: 22 Nov 1819, $300, 120 ac on south side of Baker's Creek, part of 158 ac grant to Samuel TUCKER, 21 Dec 1811; adj William HAMMONTREE, William McCLUNG. Wit: William McCLUNG, George TOWNSLEY. 18 Feb 1820.

71. (2:64) William McCLUNG as guardian of heirs of Polasky WALLACE, decd, to William GAUTT, Jr.: 27 Dec 1819, $400 paid to Wallace in his lifetime, 84 ac on Crooked Creek, adj Henry THOMAS, BLACK's heirs, Joal WALLACE, being Grant #794 dated 4 May 1810. Wit: [appears to be several marks], Alexander STUART. 19 Feb 1820.

72. (2:64-65) Thomas STUART to Jacob McGHEE: 14 Sep 1819, $475, two tracts in Tuckaleechee Cove on Little River and its waters; one tract adj William DAVISON, Little River, Isaac

GIDEONS/GIDDENS, Smith Branch, surveyed 6 Mar 1807 and granted to Barbry MORE on 16 May 1810, Grant #1119 of 87 ac; other tract adj Michel TALER, William McCRUG?, surveyed 8 Apr 1807, granted to Barbry More 17 May 1810, 65 ac. Wit: Samuel C. DAVIDSON, John BROWN. 19 Feb 1820.

73. (2:65-66) John SHARP and Polly, his wife, to Magness TULLOCH: 4 Aug 1818, $300, 116 ac whereon SHARP now lives. Wit: Addison SHARP, James CLARK. 21 Feb 1820.

74. (2:66-67) John HOUSTON and Samuel HOUSTON to Moses McCONNAL, Hawkins Co.: 31 Aug 1819, $1039, 343 ac on waters of Crooked Creek, Grant #2556 dated 6 Aug 1812, adj James McGINLEY, Robert BELL, Jacob THOMAS, Robert GAUTT. Wit: Jacob F. FOUTE, A. SHELTON. 21 Feb 1820.

75. (2:67-68) William McCAMEY/McKAMY to Good CLAMPETT: 1 Sep 1817, $50, 31 ac adj William KEBBAL. Sig: William (X) McKAMY. Wit: W. (SLENSON?), William SIMERLY. 21 Feb 1820.

76. (2:68-69) John RAGON to James RAGON, Knox Co.: 27 Dec 1819, $5 per ac, 42 ac north side of Little River adj the river, Alexander NORTON, Nicolas NORTON, the Big Road leading from Maryville to Sevierville, Samuel READ. Wit: (?) ROBERTSON. 21 Feb 1820.

77. (2:69-70) Philmer GREENE to Augustin/Agustin/Austin BOWERS: 8 Oct 1819, $775, 153 ac on waters of Ellejoy Creek, adj HOUSTON, HUGHS, CUNNINGHAM, James DAVIS, BENJAMINS. Wit: Joseph HOLLOWAY, William JEFFRIES. 22 Feb 1820.

78. (2:70-71) Samuel H. BOGAL to Jonathan McCHURCH: 17 Dec 1819, $800, 179 ac on waters of Ellejoy Creek. Wit: Hugh BOGLE, James UPTON. 22 Feb 1820.

79. (2:71) Philmer GREEN to Augusten BOWERS: 25 Sep 1819, $25, 6 ac on waters of Ellejoy Creek. Wit: Joseph HOLLOWAY, William (X) JEFFRES. 22 Feb 1820.

80. (2:71-72) Winford/Winiferd WARD/WORD (female) of Knox Co. to John VICKS and George McKENRY: 14 Dec 1816, $300, 52 ac. Wit: Robert (LONEY?), John McCORY, Benjamin EDMENSTON. 22 Feb 1820.

81. (2:72-73) Josiah P. SMITH to Bartley McGHEE and (third party) John EWING and Samuel LOVE: 29 Mar 1819, $600, one tract of 500 ac on waters of Nine Mile Creek described in deed of conveyance executed this day by Bartley McGHEE to SMITH, and another tract of 105 ac on waters of Pistol Creek, being Grant #242 to James EDINGTON. EWING and LOVE are endorsers and securities for SMITH in the sum of $600 to the Bank of TN in Knoxville. Wit: John WILKINSON, John TOOL. 23 Feb 1820.

82. (2:73-75) Ransom PERRY and Katherine, his wife, to John MARTAIN: 28 Nov 1817, $300, an undivided moiety in 583 ac on waters of Nails Creek, a grant to Waring MARTAIN, decd, adj John KELLY's heirs, Lewis SHROYER, Joseph COULDWELL, John MARTAIN, James CLARK.   Katherine is an heir to Henry MARTAIN, decd, who was heir to Waring MARTAIN. Wit: Isaiah THOMPSON, Isaac THOMPSON. 23 Feb 1820.

83. (2:75) Meshack TIPTON to John KITCHEN(S): 24 Dec 1816, $100, 48 ac in Miller's Cove on south side of Little River. Sig: Meshack (X) TIPTON. Wit: William TAYLER, John GLASS. 16 Mar 1820.

84. (2:75-76) Charles DONOHOO, Sheriff, to Bartley McGHEE of Maryville: 8 Jun 1819, $325, 218 ac adj land of David MILLER situated on Tellico Road near Tennessee River. Public sale 5 Jun 1819 to satisfy judgment obtained 13 Apr 1817 by Jacob SHARP against Cullinas MILLER, Joseph RODGERS, and Robert DOUGLASS for $56.75; and eight judgments against Cullinas MILLER issued 15 Apr 1819, totaling $129.85: two in favor of Thomas SPRADLING, two in favor of John HAMMENTREE, one each in favor of McCROSKEY, BERRY; Amos BARNETT; Samuel THOMPSON; John BOYD. Wit: Jac. F. FOUTE, Azariah SHELTON. 21 Mar 1820.

85. (2:76-77) Charles DONOHOO, Sheriff, to Bartley McGHEE: 24 Jan 1818, $50, two ac on northwest side of the Great Road leading to

Tellico on McGHEE's original line. Wit: (Jno?) McGHEE, David M. HUNTER. 31 Mar 1820.

86. (2:77) Stephen ANDERSON, Jr. to Thomas GIBBS: 29 Nov 1819, $250, 68 ac on waters of Nine Mile Creek, cor to John BALL. Sig: Stephen (X) ANDERSON. Wit: James DENTEN, Alexander (X) DOWNEY. 6 Apr 1820.

87. (2:77-78) William L. TAYLOR to MONTGOMERY & BERRY: 20 Apr 1816, 21 ac on waters of Crooked Creek claimed and held by right of occupancy, part of Grant #1074 to Thomas McMURRAY, adj David WHIGHT, Robt CAMPBLE. Wit: Wm. W. BERRY, Jefferson COULDWELL. 18 Apr 1820.

88. (2:78-79) William BURTON to George MISER: 29 Dec 1819,$100, 40 ac on waters of Holston River, part of Grant #2166 to heirs of Thomas CONNER, decd, dated 1 Aug 1812 and conveyed by heirs to BURTON, adj George MISER. Sig: William (X) BURTON. Wit: James LOVE, Henry MISER. 18 Apr 1820.

89. (2:79-80) James and Nancy PARKS to George MISER: 16 Jul 1819, $64, 32 ac on waters of Holston River part of Grant #2466 to heirs of Thomas CONNER, decd, adj George Miser. Sig: James PARKS. Nancy (X) PARKS. Wit: John M. RANKIN. [Deed does not indicate relationship of James and Nancy PARKS.] 18 Apr 1820.

90. (2:80) John THORNBURY to James TURK: 23 Mar 1820, $300, lot #14 in Maryville, adj lot #15 belonging to James TURK and back lot #13 belonging to BOAZ AND TOOL and the Commons. Wit: James BERRY, Wm. M. BERRY. 18 Apr 1820.

91. (2:80-81) David OGLEBY to Abednego BOAZ: 28 Apr 1819, $600, 127 ac on Knoxville Road adj John THORNBERRY, Thomas McCULLOCK, Benjamin ALEXANDER, William WALLACE, David EAGLETON. Grant #1225 to OGLEBY, 21 May 1810. Sig: David (X) OGLEBY. Wit: Jno. THORNBERRY, Obediah BOAZ. 13 Apr 1820.

92. (2:81-82) John WEIR to David W. McREYNOLDS: 27 Mar 1820, $1600, 275 ac on Crooked Creek, Grant #789, adj William

McCAMPBLE, William L. TAYLOR, LOWERY heirs, John (BIDDAL?), John McREYNOLDS, Thomas LURKINS. Wit: James TEDFORD, William L. TAYLOR. 19 Apr 1820.

93. (2:82-83) Thomas ADAMS to John BOGART: 2 Nov 1819, $800, 135 ac on Baker's Creek granted to ADAMS on 15 Jun 1809, adj Matthew WALLACE, David EDINGTON, Charles LOGAN, Joseph ORR, David RITCHEY, Samuel VARNER, Henry WILLIAMS. Sig: Thomas (X) ADAMS. Wit: Wm. McCLUNG, Thos. MONTGOMERY. 19 Apr 1820.

94. (2:83-84) John and Matthew McGHEE to Ephraim LEE: 31 Dec 1819, $1000, all right...Bartley McGHEE at the time of his decease had in and to...133 ac on waters of Gallaher's Creek, Grant #163, adj Joseph JOHNSTON and others [not named].   Wit: A. B. EMMUNSEN, Enoch PERSENS. Sig: John McGHEE.   A. M. McGHEE. Mat McGHEE. 19 Apr 1820.

95. (2:84) George and William HENDERSON to [brother] James HENDERSON: 14 Mar 1820,"love, good will and affection", 86 ac on waters of Pistol Creek, a moiety of a tract of 173 ac granted to Robert HENDERSON and willed by him to George and William. Wit: Robert LOVE, John HUNTER, Adam DINSMORE. 21 Apr 1820.

96. (2:84-85) Charles ALFORD to John ALFORD: 26 Nov 1818, $325, an undivided moiety of 48 ac on Holston River deeded to John and Charles ALFORD by John McCLURG on 23 Feb 1818, and 21 ac adj it, deeded the same date. Wit: Matthias PARR, James PARR, William LEVINE. 21 Apr 1820.

97. (2:85-86) James CLARK to Stephen PLUMLEE: 2 Nov 1819, $2100, 367 ac in District South of French Broad and Holston River on the river, cor to KELLEY's heirs, adj Warner MARTAIN, south side of Nails Creek near a spring, (HARDAM?).   Wit: William MONTGOMERY, John MARTAIN. 21 Apr 1820.

98. (2:86-87) Elihu HICKS to Samuel JOHNSTON: 20 Jan 1820, $245, 89 ac on waters of Crooked Creek, adj vacant land, William WALKER. Sig: Elihu (X) HICKS. Wit: Joseph JONES, David JOHNSTON. 22 Apr 1820.

99. (2:87-88) Isaac BROOKS to William BROWN: 23 Nov 1819, $350, 100 ac, an undivided moiety of Grant #2580 to Samuel JONES dated 20 Jan 1809 for 147 ac, being southwest end of the survey, on head of east fork of Gallaher's Creek. Adj George MISER, Alexander STUARD, Samuel and Even WALLACE, William BOMAN. Wit: James W. LACKEY, Alexander STUART. 22 Apr 1820.

100. (2:88-89) John MARTAIN to William GARNER: 24 Oct 1818, $800, 241 ac on waters of Nine Mile Creek, part of Grant #2824 to John WALLACE, adj William WALLACE, Wm. ARMSTRONG, John MARTAIN, George WEAR, Robert HAMBLE, James MARTAIN now James HENRY's. Wit: William WILLIAMSON, William ARMSTRONG. 26 Apr 1820.

101. (2:89) John MONTGOMERY and James BERRY, partners, trading as MONTGOMERY & BERRY, and Charles DONOHOO to Trustees of MARYVILLE FEMALE ACADEMY: 24 Apr 1816, $100, one- half of lot #42 in Maryville, the part on the back street considered the back end of said lot, reserving to ourselves the half which joins Main Street. Purchased by Thomas HENDERSON at Sheriff's Sale 1 Aug 1804, being sold as property of John LOWERY, Samuel WEIR, and William MACKLIN; conveyed to MONTGOMERY & BERRY by HENDERSON. Wit: Thomas WEIR, Wm. TOOL. 26 Apr 1820.

102. (2:89-90) John G. BROWN, Jacob F. FOUTE, to John ALEXANDER, Matthew McGHEE and William BLAIR, trading as McGHEE & BLAIR: 13 Mar 1820, $559.43, 282 ac on waters of Baker's Creek, Grant #166 to Wm. BEASLEY, adj lands granted to Burten BEASLEY and others; security for payment of a note from BROWN to McGHEE & BLAIR by 1 Oct next. Wit: Chas. DONOHOO, Daniel RAGON. 1 Jun 1820.

103. (2:90-92) John THORNBURY (first party), Jacob F. FOUTE (second party), and John ALEXANDER and Mathew W. McGHEE (third party): 27 Mar 1820, $620.24 due McGHEE & BROS. by a note of this date and to secure payment of note and payment of $1.00 to Thornbury by Foute "and for other divers good causes and considerations," several tracts contiguous to each other now occupied

by THORNBURY: One of 97 ac, Grant #760 dated 4 Mar 1810 to John WOODS; another of 224 ac, Grant #753 to THORNBURY dated 2 May 1810; another of 205 ac, Grant #1702 dated 22 Jun 1810 to Benjamin ALEXANDER; 255 ac, Grant #280 to David CAMPBLE and conveyed to William MACLIN, Sr., decd, and afterwards purchased by THORNBURY from John MONTGOMERY, one of the execrs of MACLIN; 225 ac, Grant #1827, 27 Jun 1810, to Thomas McCULLOCH, with grist mill, cotton gin, and stills and distillery..belonging to Grant #280 dated 17 Oct 1818. THORNBURY to pay the note, plus interest, to McGHEE within three months. In case of failure to pay, FOUTE may sell all or part of the lands except about 100 ac of the tracts of Grants #737 and #1702 heretofore sold by THORNBURY to Benjamin KILBURN. Wit: John L. BURNETT, A. B. EMMENSON. 1 Jun 1820.

104.   (2:92-93) William HARRIS (first party), John WILKINSON (second party) and John ALEXANDER and Mathew M. McGHEE (third party): 31 Dec 1819, $559; John McGHEE & BROS. are surety for HARRIS to the Bank of the State of Tennessee at Knoxville for $559, and also ..in consideration of the further sum of $1.00 paid by WILKINSON to HARRIS and the further sum of $250.93 and for other divers good causes and considerations,170 ac on waters of Nine Mile Creek described in Bill of Sale from DAVID Martain to HARRIS adj Amos BELL and others. Also a negro boy named HIRAIM about 20 yrs of age. HARRIS to pay note within twelve months. Wit: A. B. EMMESON, Jesse THOMPSON. 2 Jun 1820.

105.   (2:93-94) James PAUL to Thomas RANKIN: 28 Sep 1818, $230, 115 ac on waters of Holston River. (No further identification) Wit: Jac F. FOUTE, Arch TURK. 6 Jul 1820.

106.   (2:94-95) John CRAIG of Limestone Co., AL, to COMMISSIONERS OF MARYVILLE: 5 Apr 1820, power of atty to Jacob F. FOUTE to make a deed of conveyance to Commissioners of Maryville for 52 ac on which the town of Maryville now stands. Wit: M. M. HOUSTON, Samuel MOORE. 31 Jul 1820.

107.   (2:95) John THORNBURY to BOAZ & TOOLE: 28 Mar 1820, $350, lot #13 in Maryville, adj lot #14 conveyed by THORNBURY to

James TURK on the southwest and the main cross street on the northeast. Wit: James BERRY, Isaac ANDERSON. 5 Aug 1820.

108.   (2:95-96) John WILLIS to Isaac YEAROUT: 1 Mar 1820, $350, 114 ac on waters of Pistol Creek, part of Grant #176 to John EDMISTON, adj John WILKINSON, Mary PASEY, Robert HENDERSON, Wm. JACKSON, MAYORS, decd, Andrew YOUNG. Wit: A. EARLY, Thos. E. BROWN. 1 Aug 1820.

109.   (2:96-97) Hugh and Charles KELSO to Thomas PAIN: 29 Mar 1819, $1400, 160 ac on Tennessee River and Baker's Creek adj Warehouse Lot on the riverbank in Morganton, Eli HICKS, formerly Richard DEARMOND's, Hugh KELSO's survey granted 25 May 1818 which tract of 463 ac has been divided into three separate tracts; HALL, LOWERY formerly Wiley LASSETER's. Wit: Robert WEAR, Samuel McCROSKY, Ambrose R. HUNTER. 9 Aug 1820.

110.   (2:97-98) Robert SLONE to William DAVIS: 1 Mar 1819, $800, 96 ac on Nine Mile Creek, Grant #2534 to SLONE, adj Joseph PASY, James COOK, McMAHAN.   Wit: William DAVIS, Amos RICHARDSON, William ASLER, John (STRAIN?), Jefferson YOUNG. 15 Sep 1820.

111.   (2:98-99) Thomas SPRADLING to Willeby ROGERS: 15 Jan 1820, $225, 40 ac on waters of Ellejoy Creek.   Sig: Thomas (X) SPRADLING. Wit: Hugh BOGAL, James HICKLAND.15 Sep 1820.

112.   (2:99-100) Ephraim LEE to John BEALL: 3 Jan 1820,$560, 80 ac on waters of Rock Creek, part of Grant #181 for 136 ac, adj Humphrey MONTGOMERY, Margaret OWN, Francis JOHNSTON. Wit: Josiah ROWAN, Samuel JOHNSTON. 15 Sep 1820.

113.   (2:100-01) Athiel? McCALESTER to David and Ambrose HUNTER: 17 Apr 1820, $400, 111 ac on waters of Baker's Creek adj on west by Robert BUKEY's, on north by Richard JONES, on east by James McCONAL, on south by John LUKEN, David RICHEY now LUKEN's, Samuel VANCE now Isaac ADNEY.   Wit: John McCROSKEY, James (MONNUAS?). 22 Sep 1820.

114. (2:101) John T. GARNER to William LOWERY, Jr.: 6 Jan 1820, $271, negro girl MARY aged 6 yrs. Wit: (David?) I. FREEMAN, Joseph R. HENDERSON. 25 Sep 1820.

115. (2:101-02) George TOWNSLEY to John TOWNSLEY: 23 Sep 1816, $100, 130 ac on waters of Baker's Creek adj main road, John BLACK, George TOWNSLEY; part of 271 ac granted to George on 1 Oct 1808. Wit: Jesse BEEN, William (HARRIS. 14 Nov 1820.

116. (2:102-03) Francis SHAW to James I. GREEN: 1 Apr 1820, $2500, 286 ac on Cloyd's Creek, adj WALKER, Josiah JOHNSTON. SHAW reserves right to use a ditch cut by himself and William GRIFFITTS for conveying water to machinery and the privilege of raising a dam 4-1/2 feet high at head of the ditch. Wit: Nathaniel MORRISON, William GRIFFITTS, Joe PRIGMORE. 29 Oct 1820.

117. (2:103) Francis SHAW to John MONTGOMERY, merchant: 17 Apr 1820, deed of trust to secure to GREEN BRABSON AND COMPANY the payment of $3,269 by 1 Sept 1821, negro man named PETER, negro boy named ANDREW, negro girl named SALLY, negro girl named POLLY, negro boy named NEWTON and negro boy named BEN. Wit: Nathaniel MORRISON, Jos. (Jas.?) PREGMORE. 24 Oct 1820.

118. (2:103-04) William AYLETT to Andrew S. MORRISON: (date omitted), $900, 364 ac on waters of Baker's Creek, part of Grant #719 to Joseph B. LAPSELY, 120 ac of which has been lately sold by AYLETT to Ephraim DUNLAP; original survey made by Josiah PATTY, deputy for Robert WEAR, Surveyor General. MORRISON to pay $364 with interest due the state. Wit: Wm GAUT, Wm. McCLUNG, Wm. THOMPSON. 20 Nov 1820.

119. (2:104-06) John LOWERY (first party), John WILKINSON and Jacob F. FOUTE (second party), to John McGHEE, Alexander and Mathew M. McGHEE(third party): 14 Apr 1820, $3,000 borrowed by John LOWERY from and now due to John, Alexander, and Mathew McGHEE and in consideration of further sum of $5.00 to WILKINSON and FOUTE, LOWERY conveys to WILKINSON and FOUTE 320 ac in Monroe Co. on south side of Tennessee River at Blair's ferry including the ferry and also the mouth of Tellico River

being that part of 640 ac reserved to Cabbin SMITH, a Cherokee Indian, by the terms of the late treaty made and concluded between John W. CALHOUN, Secretary of War, and a deputation of the Cherokee Nation of Indians in behalf of said nation at the city of Washington on 27 Feb 1819; adj fort Loudon, crossing Tellico River. Also LOWERY's claim to 320 ac on north side of Tennessee River directly opposite the above mentioned land, including the north side of the ferry now in the possession of John, Alexander and Mathew M. McGHEE. LOWERY shall pay within two years and seven calendar months from date of this indenture. Wit: William LOWERY, Azaciah SHELTON. 24 Nov 1820.

120. (2:106) John NORWOOD to James and Ignatius WILSON: 27 Jun 1820, one red wagon, six sets of gears and all apparatus belonging to wagon, six horses, to secure payment to them of $417.87 within three months. Wit: John WILKINSON, Robert MORRIS. 24 Nov 1820.

121. (2:107) John WILKINSON to John NORWOOD: 13 Aug 1820, $300 in horses paid on 22 Dec last past by John NORWOOD, 129 ac on waters of Crooked Creek, adj Thomas WALLACE. Wit: John (DENNING/DEMMING?), Nathaniel HUNT, Jno. GARDNER. 24 Nov 1820.

122. (2:107-08) Ann BEARD formerly Ann KELLEY, James COULDWELL, William COULDWELL and Betsey KELLY to Gordon WHITE, late of Augusta Co., VA: 5 Jan 1818, $3000, 413 ac on Little River, part of Grant #1300 for 640 ac to heirs of John KELLY, decd, adj William EWING. Sig: John (X) BEARD. James (X) COULDWELL. Wit: William EWING, William HUTCHESEN, James GILLASPEY. 7 Mar 1819.

123. (2:108-09) Jacob THOMAS to Andrew COWAN: 25 Nov 1820, $1200, 400 ac on waters of Pistol Creek, where THOMAS now lives, adj Morgan THOMAS, David CUP, Robert BELL, John HOUSTON, Grant No. 244 to Thomas, 5 Aug 1808. Wit: James BERRY, J. MONTGOMERY. 25 Nov 1820.

124. (2:109-10) John THORNBURY (first party), to John WILKINSON (second party) and James TURK, James HOUSTON

and Jesse WALLACE (third party): 7 Feb 1820, to secure TURK, HOUSTON, and WALLACE, who are endorsers and sureties for THORNBURY to the State Bank of Tennessee for $200 to be paid by (third parties) to the execrs of William MACKLIN, decd, and also in consideration of the further sum of $1.00 paid to THORNBURY by WILKINSON and for other considerations; THORNBURY conveys to WILKINSON several tracts on waters of Pistol Creek contiguous to each other and occupied by THORNBURY; 224 ac, Grant #753, 2 May 1810; 225 ac, Grant #1702, 22 Jun 1810, to Benjamin ALEXANDER and conveyed by him to THORNBURY; 255 ac, Grant #280 to David CAMPBLE and conveyed by him to William MACKLIN, since decd, and afterwards purchased by THORNBURY from John MONTGOMERY, one of the execrs of MACLIN for which THORNBURY has MONTGOMERY bound to make a title when the $200 and interest shall be paid, it being the balance of the price of the last mentioned purchase of land; 25 ac, Grant #1827 to Thomas McCULLAH, 27 Jun 1810; also the grist mill, cotton gin and distillery on tract mentioned in Grant #280, dated 15 Oct 1808. THORNBURY to pay within two months the debt of $630 to the Bank and to Execrs of MACLIN $200 with interest. If not paid, property may be sold except for about 110 ac of tracts granted by Grants #753 and #1702 sold by THORNBURY to Benjamin KILBURN. Wit: Obediah BOAZ, William TOOLE. 27 Nov 1820.

125. (2:110-11) John TOWNSLEY of Marion Co., TN, to James TOWNSLEY: 22 Jul 1820, $100, 130 ac on waters of Baker's Creek, adj main road, John BLACK, George TOWNSLEY's old line, being part of 271 ac granted to George TOWNSLEY on 2 Oct 1808. Wit: John GOULD, Joseph S. TAYLOR. 27 Nov 1820.

126. (2:111-13) John THORNBURY (first party) to John WILKINSON (second party), and David COULDWELL, John AMBRISTER, Joal CHANDLER, Charles DONOHOO and Jonethan TRIPET (third party): 27 Mar 1820, to secure and indemnify David COULDWELL who is THORNBURY's security for payment of debt of $130 to execrs of Jeremiah ELLIS, decd, and to indemnify John AMBRISTER who is also John's security to a note executed and due to David BURKE of about $100 and to indemnify Joal CHANDLER who is THORNBURY's security for a note to the execrs of William

HENRY, decd, for about $100, also for indemnifying Charles DONOHOO and Johnathan TRIPPET who are THORNBURY's surety in a bond payable to the United States for about $85 for internal duties and also in consideration of the further sum of $1.00 paid by WILKINSON to THORNBURY and for divers other good considerations; several tracts on waters of Pistol Creek: one tract of 224 ac Grant #753 dated 2 May 1810; another of 205 ac Grant #1702 to Benjamin ALEXANDER, 22 Jun 1810; one tract of 255 ac Grant #280 purchased by THORNBURY from John MONTGOMERY, one of the execrs of William MACLIN, decd, MACKLIN having the title for which John THORNBURY has sued MONTGOMERY to make a title as soon as the purchase money is all paid; one other tract of 25 ac Grant #1837, 27 June 1810, to Thomas McCULLOH; one tract of 37 ac Grant #780 to John WOOD, 4 Mar 1810, conveyed by Wood to THORNBURY. THORNBURY shall pay within six months to execrs of J. M. ELLIS the sum of $132 and costs and damages, and will pay Daniel RINKLE $100, and the heirs of William HENRY $100, and the U.S. $85 with all costs charges and damages. Wit: John S. BURNETT, Isaac ANDERSON. 8 Dec 1820.

127. (2:113-14) William WALLACE to Andrew THOMPSON: 28 Dec 1818, $2,500, 437 ac on waters of Pistol Creek, adj road from Maryville to Knoxville, David COULDWELL, KING, MONTGOMERY, David OWENS, David EAGLETON, David OGLEBY. Wit: Josiah PATTY, Thomas DURHAM. 9 Dec 1820.

128. (2:114-15) Isaac CASNER to Josiah JOHNSTON: 28 Jan 1818, $300, 87 ac on waters of Cloyd's Creek, adj Samuel SHAW, Joseph JOHNSTON, Michal BOWERMAN. JOHNSTON to pay money yet due the state. Wit: Ja I GREEN, B. H. MAYO, Nathe MORRISON. 25 Dec 1820.

129. (2:115) John NORWOOD to James BERRY, merchant of Maryville: 17 Dec 1819, $507.05, household furniture (10 feather beds with covers and furniture complete, ten bed steads for same, 10 tables and bureau, one clock and case, one cupboard and furniture, two dozen chairs with whole of the kitchen furniture now in use by me), three milk cows, and three sows. Wit: J. Houston GILLASPEY. 26 Dec 1820.

130. (2:115-16) James BERRY to John NORWOOD: 17 Dec 1819, household furniture (10 feather beds with bedsteads and furniture, two dozen chairs with a quantity of kitchen furniture), three milk cows and three breeding sows, $15.00 per month for whatever time he may have the same in use. NORWOOD further agrees to take good care of the whole of said property and return it in good order whenever BERRY demands it; NORWOOD responsible for any injury done to property. Wit: J. Houston GILLESPIE. 26 Dec 1820.

131. (2:116) William BERRY of Sevier Co. to James BERRY: 10 Sep 1820, $550, negro woman slave named HARRIET, aged about 18 yrs, together with her child, a female aged about 8 months named SARAH or SALLY, slaves for life. Wit: William LOWERY, William TOOL. 26 Dec 1820.

132. (2:116) William BURNES of Sevier Co. to James BERRY: 15 Feb 1820, $425, negro boy about 14 yrs of age named PHILIP, slave for life. Wit: John SHARP, Rufas I. DAVIS, William LOWERY, William TOOLE. 15 Feb 1820.

133. (2:117) Gideon BLACKBURN of Williamson Co. to Samuel BLACKBURN:30 Sep 1820, power of atty to liquidate all such accruants as may at this date be unsettled within Blount County, sell lands in my name. Wit: Tho HARDEMAN, E. L. HAIL. Proven at court October 1820 by Elisha L. HAIL and Thomas HARDEMAN. 11 Jan 1821.

134. (2:117-18) Charles DONAHOO, Sheriff, to [William] HENDERSON AND LOWERY: 21 Dec 1818, $120, to satisfy judgment obtained on 8 April 1818 by John MARTAIN against Miles and David CUNNINGHAM and two judgments dated 8 Jul 1818, one by Edward GAUTT against Miles and David CUNNINGHAM, and one by Jesse WALLACE issued for Alexander AKIN against Cunninghams and John GOULD; another dated 22 July 1818 by William LOWERY against Miles CUNNINGHAM; public sale 1 Aug 1818, 100 ac on waters of Nine Mile Creek whereon Miles CUNNINGHAM now lives. William HENDERSON was high bidder on behalf of HENDERSON & LOWERY. 16 Jan 1821.

135. (2:118-20) Charles DONOHOO, Sheriff, to John, Alexander and Mathew M. McGHEE, merchants   trading as McGHEE AND BROTHERS 18 Dec 1820, $301, 575 ac in several tracts on waters of Pistol Creek and Crooked Creek, public sale 25 Sept 1819 to satisfy judgment issued against Jacob NEYMON for $376.325, which Bartley McGHEE assignee of John S. BENNETT lately recovered of NYMAN. One tract of 236 ac adj Joseph STUKS, WEIR, WALLACE, Jonethan HARRIS, Grant #252 to John PATE heirs, 4 Aug 1812; one tract of 209 ac, adj Henry THOMAS, PATE orphans, William HARRIS, Grant #2547, 5 Aug 1812, to NEYMON; tract of 80 ac purchased by NEYMON of WALLACE adj SCROGGS, William ANDERSON and one or both of the above tracts; one tract of 50 ac purchased by Joe (sic) NEYMAN of Sarah ELLIOT adj SCROGGS, Wm. ANDERSON and one or both of the tracts above. Wit: Jac F. FOUTE, A. SHELTON. 19 Jan 1821.

136. (2:120-21) Charles DONOHOO, Sheriff, to John McGHEE AND BROTHERS: 25 Nov 1820, $33, 23 ac on waters of Nine Mile Creek, adj William HARRIS; public sale 21 Mar 1818, to satisfy three judgments amounting to $65.35 in favor of McGHEE & BROTHERS against David COOK, returned by Joseph ALEXANDER, Deputy Sheriff; also two judgments in favor of William LOWERY, Jr. for $179.935. Wit: A. SHELTON, Jac F. FOUTE. 19 Jan 1821.

137. (2:122) William FORESTER to Samuel SHAW: 23 Jun 1818, $500, 200 ac on south side of Holston River adj survey made for Benjamin PRATER, being part of survey made for John MITCHEL. Wit: Wm. GRIFFITS, Samuel JOHNSTON. 2 Feb 1821.

138. (2:123) Thomas HARPER to William HARPER: 25 Dec 1820, $375, 62 ac on Crooked Creek, adj George BERRY, heirs of William REAGON, LOWERY. Wit: John W. LOWERY, Thomas BROWN. 3 Mar 1821.

139. (2:123-24) James COURRIER to Thomas HENDERSON: 15 Apr 1820, "I...convey and confirm at my decease and my wife Mary unto..Thomas HENDERSON all my property consisting at this time one negro wench ABEGAL, about 40 years of age; two head horses, five head of cattle, wagon and number of hogs with all household

furniture belonging to the premises at our decease...unto Thomas HENDERSON and his wife Christan/Christeen?. Sig: James (X) COURRIER. Mary (X) COURRIER. Wit: Mathew HENRY, James HENDERSON, James MARTAIN. 3 Mar 1821.

140. (2:124) James COURRIER to Thomas HENDERSON: 15 Apr 1820, $400, 62 ac on waters of Crooked Creek, adj Richard CURRIER, John WEIR, Henry LEESTER. Sig: James (X) COURRIER. Wit: Mathew KAY. 3 Mar 1821.

141. (2:124-25) John M. LOWERY and William LOWERY to John KEYS: 14 Mar 1820, $1235.50, 247 ac on waters of Crooked Creek, adj James MOOR, PATERSON heirs, George BERRY, THOMPSON and Abraham WALLACE, THOMPSON and Thomas WALLACE. Signed by John M. and William LOWERY 22 Nov 1820. Wit: Thomas I. COULDWELL, Ignatius WILSON. 5 Mar 1821.

142. (2:125-26) Abraham UTTER to Samuel UTTER: 29 Apr 1820, $200, 67 ac. Wit: William ARMSTRONG, Samuel THOMPSON. 5 Mar 1821.

143. (2:126) William BURNES of Sevier Co. to Samuel HOUSTON of Maryville: (date omitted), $525, negro boy named LEWIS? about 14 years of age. Wit: Jesse THOMPSON, William KEITH. 5 Mar 1821.

144. (2:126-27) William DUGLESS to Jacob F. FOUTE: 21 Nov 1820, "whereas John HUNTER has married my daughter Phoebe DOUGLESS..and I had given to my daughter and her husband on their marriage, a negro girl slave named PATSY now aged seven or eight years..and HUNTER has sold to FOUTE the girl for the sum of $275...". Wit: Wm. E. ANDERSON, J. TIPTON, Richard G. DUNLAP. 5 Mar 1821.

145. (2:127) Thomas MORRISON of Monroe Co. to Jesse RAY: 25 Dec 1820, $300, 61 ac on the waters of Murphy's Creek in Miller's Cove, adj John BLAIR, whereon Zackeries HICKS now lives. No witnesses. 5 Mar 1821.

146. (2:128) James I. GREEN to Isaac HAIR: 2 Nov 1820, $3000, 286 ac on Cloyd's Creek, adj WALKER, Josiah JOHNSTON. So much of land as has been appropriated to a ditch cut by William GRIFFITTS for a dam 4-1/2 feet high at head of ditch is excepted. Wit: Nathaniel MORRISON, Josiah JOHNSTON, Jas. PREGMORE. 5 Mar 1821.

147. (2:128-29) Isaac COSNER to Francis SHAW: 3 Sep 1819, $4,000, 287 ac on Cloyd's Creek, adj E. WALKER, Josiah JOHNSTON. Wit: Ja I. GREEN, Josiah JOHNSTON, Nath'l MORRISEN. 5 Mar 1821.

148. (2:129-30) James I. GREEN to Francis SHAW: 3 Apr 1820, $1000, 67 ac on waters of Cloyd's Creek, adj William GRIFFITTS. Wit: Nathaniel MORRISON, Wm. GRIFFITTS, Jas. PREGMORE. 6 Mar 1821.

149. (2:130-31) William B. WARREN of Monroe Co. to Joseph HURLY of Greene Co.: 7 Feb 1820, $500, 117 ac on Baker's Creek, Grant #582 to Samuel CAMPBLE, adj James SCOTT, William MORE, Jos. B. LAPSLEY, Robert McGILL, Joseph M. RANDLES. Wit: John CATCHING, Bryant HURLY, Joseph MATTHIS, William W. HENRY, James HENRY. 6 Mar 1821.

150. (2:131) Samuel BOND to Obediah MORGAN: 14 Nov 1820, $450, 49 ac on waters of Cloyd's Creek, adj John MERDECK, William GRIFFITTS, Thomas DURHAM, William DURHAM. Sig: Samuel (X) BOND. Wit: James JONES, Joseph JONES. 6 Mar 1821.

151. (2:131-32) John B. McLIN to Gilbert BLANKENSHIP: 12 Feb 1819, $172, 43 ac, part of grant to John ORR. Wit: William BRADBRY, John (X) LAIN. 6 Mar 1821.

152. (2:132-33) Gilbert BLANKINSHIP to John B. McLIN: 15 Feb 1819, $250, 63 ac, part of tract granted to Mark LOVE. Wit: William BRADBURY, John (X) McLAIN. 6 Mar 1821.

153. (2:133) Jonethan TIPTON to Gilbert BLANKENSHIP: 26 Dec 1818, $700, 236 ac part of tract granted to Mark LOVE, adj John

ORR, William JAMES. Wit: John B. McLIN, Paten LANE. 7 Mar 1821.

154.   (2:133-34) Mathew SAMPLES to James and Charles BEVERLY/REVELY of Knox Co.: 28 Oct 1818, $630, 253 ac on Nine Mile Creek, Grant #375 to SAMPLES, 28 July 1808, cor to John CLEMENTS and Abraham UTTER, William ARMSTRONG, John WALLACE, Samuel McCAMMON. There remains $227.925 due with interest on the land. Wit: Jacob F. FOUTE, Wm. F.GILLASPY. 7 Mar 1821.

155.   (2:134-35) Spencer BLANKINSHIP to Gilbert BLANKENSHIP: 7 Jan 1815, $950, 178 ac on waters of Gallaher's Creek, adj John ORR, Alexander FEMSTER/FOSTER?. Wit: Hugh FORGUSEN, Nehm. BONHAM. 10 Mar 1821.

156.   (2:135-36) John MATHEWS to Joseph JONES: 23 Dec 1820, 55 ac on waters of Cloyd's Creek , adj JONES, a line formerly William DURHAM's, Obediah MORGAN , a line formerly John MURDOCK's. Wit: James JONES, Obediah MORGAN. 10 Mar 1821.

157.   (2:136) James SMITH to David CARSON: 22 Nov 1819, $500, 92 ac on waters of Baker's Creek, adj McCLERKEN's line, THOMPSON. Wit: John C. BATENY?, Joseph CARSON. 12 Mar 1821.

158.   (2:136-37) John BOWERMAN, Sr. to John HUBBARD: 18 Sep 1820, $150, 152 ac on waters of Little River., adj Shadrick MOORE, McCALEN. No witnesses. 12 Mar 1821.

159.   (2:137-38) Aaron WALLER to William DAVIS and Isaac WHITE: $131, four horses, a black bull with a bald face, one bay colt, several cows, two feather beds, one chest, six bed quilts, 12 sheets and 9 counterpins, 2 blankets, one big kettle, one pot, two ovens, two skillets, two dishes, 8 plates, one bousher plow, one shovel plow, one pair hawes and chains, two clevers and corn and father [fodder] all that he has, one wheel, one cotton wheel, two flax wheels, one walnut table, twelve dozens of flax yarn, four cuts each, 22 hunks of cotton yarn, four cuts each 14 hunks of wool yarn three .?.each, one looking glass, one check reel, and 3 sheep. WALLER is to pay DAVIS and

WHITE the sum of $131 on 10 Dec 1822 with interest for redemption of property. Wit: George SNIDER, Henry HACKWORTH, John LOWERY. 12 Mar 1821.

160. (2:138-39) Thomas SPRADLING/SPRAGUE/SPRAGAN to Vincent ROGERS: 22 Sep 1820, $200, 40 ac on waters of Isle of Joy (Ellejoy) Creek adj Willeby ROGERS, John REED now Shadrick ROGERS. Wit: Benjamin TIPTON, James DAVIS. Sig: Thomas (X) SPRAGAN. 12 Mar 1821.

161. (2:139) Adam GRAVES to Thomas DUN: 8 Jul 1820, $260, on waters of Harris Creek, ac omitted, adj Jacob MOORE. Wit: Hugh BOGLE, Augustine BOWERS. 12 Mar 1821.

162. (2:139-40) James McGEHERRON/McILHERRIN to Henry BOWERMAN: 10 Jun 1813, $400, 100 ac on Walker's Mill Creek, part of occupancy claim surveyed for Daniel BONINE and conveyed to George LOW, then to McGHERON, adj Francis CONNER, WALKER. Wit: Wm. LOWRY, Thos. HENDERSON. Proven Sep 1820 court by William LOWRY, Jr. and Thos. HENDERSON. 13 Oct 1821.

163. (2:140-41) John JONES of Roane Co. to David PAULSELL: 4 Feb 1820, $800, on waters of Gallaher's Creek, cor to JONSEN's original survey, cor to MOORE's survey, (Smith OAR's?) survey, PAUSELL. Wit: Jas. LOVE, Francis JONES, W. LACKY. 13 Mar 1820.

164. (2:141-42) Andrew GAMBLE of Warren Co. to John REAGAN, Jr.: 4 Nov 1818, $500, ac not stated, on Little River, adj Richard COULTER, Mrs. GAMBLE. Grant #2887. Wit: Alex B. GAMBLE, (Saml/Saul/Sanb?) C. DAVIDSON. 13 Mar 1820.

165. (2:142) Stephen GRAVES to Adam GRAVES: 13 Jul 1820, $500, 92 ac, on Harris Creek. Wit: Jac F. FOUTE. Sig: Stephen (X) GRAVES. 14 Mar 1821.

166. (2:143) Samuel JOHNSTON, Sr. and William ORR, execrs of Robert ORR, decd, to Robert WILSON: 11 Apr 1818, $350, granted

to Robert Orr, 120 ac on waters of Cloyd's Creek, adj David WILSON. Wit: David WILSON, Wm. McLIN. 14 Mar 1821.

167. (2:143-44) Mathew SHARP to Samuel WHELER: 18 Oct 1818 , $100, on waters of Little River, 10 ac, part of Grant #1819. Wit: Wm. WHELER, Jonethan SHARP. 14 Mar 1821.

168. (2:144) John G. BROWN to William (S. or I.) BLAIR: 29 July 1820, $350, a negro boy named LEWIS about 15 yrs of age. Wit: Charles DONOHOO, Ignatius WILSON. 27 Mar 1821.

169. (2:144-45) Henry M. RUTLEDGE of city of Charleston, SC, to Bartley McGHEE: 25 Aug 1814, $2500, 400 ac within the lands to which the Indian title is not yet extinguished on north side of Tennessee River, NC Grant #830 to Isach BOMAN?, adj John COWAN, mouth of Nine Mile Creek, same land sold to Henry M. RUTLEDGE by McGHEE on 25 Aug 1805. Wit: John WILKINSON, Samuel COX. Proven in court March 1817 by Wilkinson, who swore that COX is out of the state. 31 Mar 1821.

170. (2:145-46) Henry LOGAN to Bartly McGHEE: 22 Aug 1818, $450, 135 ac, adj Hugh KELSO, the Indian boundary line, vacant land. Wit: Wm. LOGAN, William S. BLAYER. 31 Mar 1821.

171.   (2:146) Andrew GIFFIN and John GIFFIN to Robert DEARMOND: 22 Mar 1821, $600, 108 ac on Little River. Wit: John DEARMOND, David GIFFIN. 15 May 1821.

172. (2:146-47) John LAIN to Gilbert BLANKINSHIP: 9 Jan 1820, $100, 30 ac part of land deed to LAIN by David PAULSELL on Gallaher's Creek, adj Edward MORE, ORR. Wit Peter LAIN, Elisha (X) FARMER. Sig: John (X) LAIN. 12 May 1821.

173.   (2:147-48) Charles DONOHOO, Sheriff, to Robert MONTGOMERY: 23 May 1820, $62, 71 ac, public sale 23 May 1820, to satisfy judgment obtained by Samuel HENRY against Samuel COSTNER/CARTER and Amos COSTNER/CARTER, the property of Samuel CARTER (sic), adj Barbary MOORE, John GIDDEN. 12 May 1821.

174. (2:148) Duerry JENKINS to Robert THOMPSON: 10 Dec 1820, $200, 160 ac in Territory of Missouri North, being the northeast quarter of Section 31 of Township 56 north in Range 19 west in the tract appropriated by an Act of Congress for Military Bounties. Wit: Barns HOLLOWAY, George BERRY. 12 May 1821.

175. (2:148) William YOUNG to Joseph VANPELT: 7 Apr 1819, $1500, 237 ac granted to Young, on waters of Holston River, adj Robert YOUNG and William CONLEY, GILLESPIE. Wit: J. W. LACKEY, Charles H. WARREN, Edward GOURLEY. 15 May 1821.

176. (2:149-50) Samuel M. JOHNSTON to David WALKER: 21 Feb 1820 $500, 84 ac, adj Samuel JOHNSTON, Sr., John JOHNSTON. Wit: Mary MATHEWS, Simon CAVETT. 15 May 1821.

177. (2:150-51) Nicholas STEVENSON to Leroy NOBLE: 25 Mar 1813, $300, 82 ac in Hickory Valley, adj Samuel WINTERS, David PARTLE, John SIMPSON, Henry BOND, Thomas SIMPSON. Wit: John STUKE. 16 May 1821.

178. (2:151-52) William ROOKER to Samuel SAFFELL: 28 Sep 1818, $550, 135 ac on Holston River on north side of road leading from Maryville to Townsend ferry, cor to Robert GILLESPIE. Wit: Matt M. McGHEE, John COX. 16 May 1821.

179. (2:152-53) Charles DONOHOO, Sheriff, to Magness TULLOCK: 26 Mar 1821, 124 ac on Nine Mile Creek; public sale 27 Jan 1821, as property of John SHARP, to satisfy two judgments amounting to $436.635, against John SHARP and Robert BELL, one obtained by John GLASS and John ORMUND, another obtained by Allen McCONLY, John GLASS and John ORMUND. Azaciah SHELTON was highest bidder at $2.00. Magness TULLOCK, a creditor of John SHARP, tendered SHELTON $2.00 plus interest to redeem the land, and SHELTON directed DONOHOO to convey the land to TULLOCK. Wit: Jac F. FOUTE, J. H. CHAPMAN, 16 May 1821.

180. (2:153-54) John WATERS to Adam FAGELA/FAGALA of Sevier Co.: 14 Feb 1820, $200, 79 ac in Miller's Cove on Reeds Creek on north side Little River Wit: John McMURRAY, Samuel CRESSWELL. Sig: John (X) WATTERS. 17 May 1821.

181. (2:154-55) John WATERS to Adam FAGELA/FAGALA of Sevier Co.: 9 Feb 1821, $200, 3 horses, 14 cattle (12 are marked with WATERS' mark: 2 small forks and double in the left ear and an under square in right ear); 30 hogs, all household furniture and implements. Wit: James (X) WALKER, Robert (X) MACKGIL. 17 May 1821.

182. (2:155-56) Samuel BLACKBURN to Samuel HOUSTON: 16 Jun 1821, $1300, lots 2, 3, 46, 47, 48 in town of Maryville. Lot #2 bounded on northeast by lot #1 where Rev. Isaac ANDERSON now lives. Wit: Andrew THOMPSON, Jesse THOMPSON. 4 July 1821.

183. (2:156-57) Geo. MISER to Andrew VAUGHT: 26 Dec 1820, $72, ac not stated, south side of Nine Mile Creek, adj Ruban CHARLES, Silas GEORGE, William LOGAN, purchased at public sale by MISER. Wit: Andrew THOMPSON, Gideon I. THOMPSON. 6 Aug 1821.

184. (2:157) James HENRY to John S. BARNETT/BURNETT: 23 Mar 1821, $400, a mulatto boy named NED aged 14, "warranted to be sound and sensible in every way except in one of his arms which was sprained." Wit: James McMAHEN. 6 Aug 1821.

185. (2:157) John S. BURNETT to Matthew M. McGHEE: 13 May 1821, $265.80, a mulatto boy named NED aged 14, warranted to be healthy and sound.   Wit: Jesse THOMPSON, A. B. EMMERSEN/EMMENSEN. 6 Aug 1821.

186.   (2:157-58) Thomas GAMBLE of Roane Co. to Johnston JONES: 29 Jan 1819, $700, 165 ac, on Holston River, adj Carter BRANDON, Josiah JOHNSTON, John (COLSON?). Wit: Thomas LEWIS, James JONES. 7 Aug 1821.

187. (2:158) John S. BURNETT to Mathew McGHEE and William LOWRY, Jr.: 16 Feb 1820, $500, a negro woman named JUDE and her child named LYDIA. BURNETT shall pay within four months a

note on the Bank of State of Tennessee of $500 to which McGHEE and LOWRY are securities. Wit: A. B. EMMENSON, B. W. RUSSELL. 7 Aug 1821.

188. (2:159) John WOODS to John THORNBURY: 6 Jan 1816, $500, 97 ac on waters of Pistol Creek on great road from Maryville to Sevierville cor to David COULDWELL and Samuel McGAHEY, adj Wm. HENRY, Gideon BLACKBURN. Wit: Jesse BEENE, Andw. COWAN. 7 Aug 1821.

189. (2:160) Richard and John WILLIAMS, atty for James WILLIAMS of Carter Co., TN, to Adam KOUNS (sic)/THOMAS: 25 March 1820, $461, 129 ac on waters of Ellejoy Creek, adj James DUNLAP. No wits. 7 Aug 1821.

190. (2:160-61) David RUSSELL to James WILSON: 13 Apr 1821,$533, lot #58 in Maryville where James and Ignatius WILSON now have a store. Wit: Charles DONOHOO, William KEITH. 8 Aug 1821.

191. (2:161) James ADAIR to Cynthia RUSSELL: 23 Mar 1821, $120, 108 ac on waters of Baker's Creek, adj Moses CAYWOOD, Grant #1235 to William RUSSELL; one-half part of tract which I held in my right of my wife Elizabeth S., a child and heir of William RUSSELL, decd. Wit: Azaciah SHELTON, Jac F. FOUTE. No reg date.

192. (2:162-63) Charles DONOHOO, Sheriff, to James JONES: 25 Jun 1821, $378, 205 ac on waters of Gallaher's Creek, adj Alexander HENDERSON, John HENDERSON, S. JONES, James ALLEN, Robert McCULLOH. Public sale 24 Mar 1821 to satisfy judgment against David PARKINS, Joseph HACKNEY, and Nathaniel BRADBURY for $75.75 which John COPELAND, assignee of Samuel FRAZIER, obtained for debt and costs; also three other judgments against David PARKINS, Samuel JONES, James JOHN and John CAULSON, amounting to $229.805. Sheriff levied on various articles of personal property which were insufficient to satisfy judgments. Wit: Jac F. FOUTE, A. SHELTON. 9 Aug 1821.

193. (2:163-64) Samuel FRAZIER to David PARKINS: 20 Oct 1819, $2,000, on waters of Gallaher's Creek, 205 ac, adj Alexander HENDERSON, John HENDERSON, James ALLEN, Robert MCCULLAY, Alexander HENDERSON. Wit: Samuel M. GAULT, Jesse WILLIAMS. 9 Aug 1821.

194. (2:164) George GRIGSBY of Roane Co. to James LOVE: 17 June 1816, $450, 149 ac on waters of Gallaher's Creek, adj Alexander LOGAN. Wit: Andrew JAMES, William RICHARDS. 9 Aug 1821.

195. (2:165) John and James KINCANNON of Sevier Co. to George HADDIN of Wilkes Co., NC: 29 Jun 1820, $1600, 406 ac on waters of Ellejoy Creek containing the Blue Spring, adj John WILLIAMS. Wit: John WILLIAMS, (R. HUNT?). 13 Aug 1821.

196. (2:165-66) Charles DONOHOO, Sheriff, to George MIZER: 23 Sep 1820, $43, 100 ac adj MIZER, Public Sale 23 Sept 1820 to satisfy judgment issued in favor of GILLESPIE and HOUSTON and Nathaniel BRADBURY against James PARKS for $28. No further description. Sig: Jas. ALEXANDER, deputy sheriff. 18 Aug 1821.

197. (2:166-67) State of TN to Joseph BLACK: 15 Jun 1810, Grant #1503, 628 ac on waters of Ellejoy Creek, due $628.805 with interest, adj John WILLIAMS, J. TIPTON, Benjamin TIPTON. Surveyed 24 June 1807. Surveyor Robert WEAR, S.G., 12 Feb 1808. 8 Aug 1807, George BERRY, Deputy Surveyor. Edward SCOTT, Register of East TN, 15 Jun 1810. 13 Aug 1821.

198.   (2:167-68) John GILLESPEY and Anna his wife, Thomas COLBURN and Isabella, his wife, of Maury Co., TN; William WALLACE and Mary, his wife; William CORLEY and Jane his wife; William WALLACE, Jr. and Margaret his wife, heirs of John CHAMBERLAIN, decd, to Edward GOURLEY: 28 June 1817, $450, 96 ac on waters of Holston River, part of tract surveyed for heirs of John CHAMBERLAIN, adj Benjamin BONHAM, Robert YOUNG. Proven in Maury Co. court Oct 1818 by John GILLESPIE and Thomas T. COLBURN; court appointed John LINDSEY and John MUSH, Esq., to examine Ann GILLESPIE and Isabella COULBURN. Sig: Joseph B. PORTER clerk, 16 Nov 1818. 18 Aug 1821.

199. (2:169-70) Josiah P. SMITH to James BERRY: 10 Nov 1819, $230.31, 606 ac in two tracts, one of 400 ac adj (Col.?) David HANLY survey and Nicholas AIRHART, John MISER, conveyed by Bartley McGHEE to Smith 29 Mar 1819; another of 206 ac, cor to David CAMPBLE, adj KING and MONTGOMERY, S. McGAHEY, conveyed by James EDINGTON to SMITH 3 Oct 1816. Deed of trust to secure payment on or after 11 Mar 1820 to Samuel HENRY $230.31 with interest. Sig: J. P. SMITH, James PERRY (sic), Samuel HENRY. Wit: Jac F. FOUTE, A. SHELTON. 8 Sept 1821.

200. (2:170-72) William W. HENRY (first party), Jacob F. FOUTE (second party), to John McGHEE, Alexander McGHEE, and Mathew M. McGHEE trading as McGHEE AND BROTHERS (thirty party): 17 Sep 1820, $464.76 owed by Henry to McGHEE AND BROTHERS by note and $1.00 paid by FOUTE to HENRY, 252 ac on waters of Baker's Creek, Grant #23 to HENRY, adj Samuel HENRY. HENRY shall pay by 1 Sep 1822 the $464.76 with interest. Wits: A. B. EMMERSON, Jesse WALLACE. 3 Dec 1821.

201. (2:172) Samuel STEEL to Samuel BLACKBURN: one negro man named CHARLES aged about 22, one mulatto girl named MALINDA about 13 yr and one mulatto boy named JEFFERSON about 8 yrs, $1500, 23 May 1820. Wit: J. MONTGOMERY, 4 Dec 1821.

202. (2:172-73) Joseph L. BOGLE of Dallas Co., Alabama, to Mathew BOGLE: 28 Dec 1820, $200, [Joseph's] undivided part of the landed estate of Joseph BOGLE, decd, on waters of Ellejoy Creek, adj Robert MCTEER. Wit: Wm. LOWRY, Matt M. HOUSTON. 13 Dec 1821.

203. (2:173) Samuel H. BOGLE of Dallas Co., Ala. to Mathew BOGLE: 27 Dec 1820, $500, [Samuel's] undivided part of the landed estate of Joseph BOGLE, decd, adj land of Robert McTEER. Wit: Wm. LOWRY, Matt M. HOUSTON. 13 Dec 1821.

204. (2:173-74) James BOGLE of Blount Co. to Mathew BOGLE: 21 Nov 1820, $500, [James'] undivided part of the landed estate of Joseph BOGLE, decd, adj Robert McTEER, Sr., Joseph BOGLE and Hugh BOGLE. Wit: Hugh BOGLE, Samuel BOGLE. 13 Dec 1821.

205. (2:174-75) Joseph HART to Edward HART: 25 Jun 1821, for love and natural affection and $5.00, 100 ac on waters of Pistol Creek, part of Grant #1537 to George CAMPBLE dated 18 Jun 1810 conveyed by CAMPBLE to Joseph HART, adj Thomas HART, Thomas McCULLOH, passing a branch of Mrs. Mary FRUS (FREW's?) in the field. Wit: Jeremiah DUNCAN, John HOOD. 17 Dec 1821.

206. (2:175) Joseph HART to Thomas HART: (date omitted) 1821, love and natural affection and $5.00, 111 ac on waters of Pistol Creek, same grant as above, adj Thomas McCULLOH, CAMPBEL, Joseph HART. Wit: Josiah PATTY, Hugh WEAR of James. 13 Dec 1821.

207. (2:175-78) Charles DONOHOO, Sheriff, to Jacob F. FOUTE: 18 Nov 1820, $76.12, 200 ac tract where Isaac BROOKS lived on waters of Gallaher's Creek, adj Thomas D. O'CONNOR, William BOWMAN, Alexander STUART, Stuart MONTGOMERY, William JAMES, Mark LOVE, John ORR, Alexander FOSTER; Public sale 16 Sep 1820, to satisfy six judgments issued by June 1820 term of court: one in favor of Francis JONES and James JONES, admins of Thomas JONES, decd, against Isaac BROOKS and Joseph HACKNEY for $106.55; one in favor of Nathan SHUGART for the use of Robert GILLASPEY against Zorabable PATTY, Isaac BROOKS and Andrew JAMES for $83.97; one in favor of Samuel EAKIN against Andrew JAMES and Isaac BROOKS for $18.92, the balance of a judgment of $105.29; one in favor of Jesse BUTLAR against Isaac BROOKS and William BURTON for $2.40; one in favor of Jesse BUTLAR against Isaac BROOKS and William BUTLAR for $4.17 and one in favor of McGhee HUNTER assigns of Andrew JAMES against Isaac BROOKS and James ROACH for $4.90; amounting to $220.92.   Also, two judgments issued by June 1820 court in favor of Josiah PAYNE for $42.30 with interest from 6 Jan 1820 and further costs of $5.77 against Lane RHE and Isaac BROOKS, and another in favor of John NORWOOD against BROOKS. Jacob F. FOUTE by his agent David D. FOUTE was high bidder.   Wit: Wm. LOWERY, James BERRY, Thomas CAULDWELL. 14 Dec 1821.

208. (2:178-79) James CRAFORD to James and Ignatius WILSON: 11 Feb 1820, $122.62, 256 ac, adj William GRAY, Spencer BLANKINSHIP, Robert RHEA. Grant #1545, 18 June 1810 to James Craford. Sig: James (X) CRAFORD. Wit: John WILKINSON, John NORWOOD. 13 Dec 1821.

209. (2:179-80) Jacob F. FOUTE to James and Ignatius WILSON, Merchants trading as James and I. WILSON: 9 Dec 1820, property purchased by Foute at Sheriff Sale 16 Sep 1820 as property of Isaac BROOKS. James and I. WILSON as [assignees] of Josiah PAYNE claim a balance of an unsatisfied judgment against Isaac BROOKS..."and require to render the tract of land under an act of the general assembly of TN passed 28 July 1820 at Murfreesboro entitled an act to provide security of real estate and for other purposes, and [WILSONs] agree to pay FOUTE the amount paid by him and ten percent annum on purchase money and agree to credit BROOKS with the further sum of ten percent on the amount bid at the Execution Sale"...the sum of $76.125 and the interest thereon. [See #207 above.] Wit: John LOWRY, Richard (LEWING?) Edward ROSE.

210. (2:180-81) Joseph HART to George DUNCAN: 24 Sep 1821, $650, 562 ac on waters of Pistol Creek, the tract whereon HART and DUNCAN now live, adj James WEAR. Wit: Josiah PATTY, Hugh WEARE of James. 20 Dec 1821.

211. (2:181-82) Henry STEPHENSON to John ADAMSON of Jefferson Co.: 30 Jul 1819, $450, 120 ac in Hickory Valley, part of survey purchased by George COOK of Nicholas STEPHENSON. Wit: James JOHNSON, Enos ADAMSON, Nordecus ADAMSON, Abraham ADAMSON. 21 Nov 1821.

212. (2:182) James McNUTT to Alexander McNUTT: 7 Dec 1819, $2,100, 180 ac on Little River, adj John EWING, James GILLESPEY, Archibald HITCH. Wit: James GILLESPEY, George EWING. 21 Dec 1821.

213. (2:183) William McCLOURG to Trustees of CHURCH OF BAKER's CREEK: 8 Aug 1821, $10, 4-1/2 ac on waters of Baker's Creek, adj a spring, Samuel HENRY, land granted to Hugh MONTGOMERY. Trustees: Robert THOMPSON, Samuel

MONTGOMERY, and James HOUSTON. Wit: Richard JONES, G. W. MONTGOMERY. 21 Dec 1821.

214. (2:183-84) Archy MURPHEY to George JULIAN: 20 Oct 1817 $350, 114 ac, Granted to John GIBSON and conveyed by him to Murphy. Wit: Isom JULIAN, John JULIAN. 24 Dec 1821.

215. (2:184-85) James ANDERSON to James TEDFORD: 22 Jun 1821, $100, 152 ac on a branch of Nine Mile Creek, part of Grant #2530 to ANDERSON, adj William MILLER, S. HICKSON. Wits omitted. Sig: James (X) ANDERSON. 24 Dec 1821.

216. (2:185) William MACKEY to William DEVER: 27 Feb 1821, $200, 67 ac, on Little River, adj John PANTER; Grant #5464, "the before Rented land" is warranted, etc. Wit: William HAMBY, David FARR. 25 Dec 1821.

217. (2:185-86) Alexander KELLEY and Archable LACKEY to Hugh KELSO: 16 May 1803, $600, 640 ac on Tennessee River at mouth of Baker's Creek, Grant #962 from state of NC, 26 Dec 1791. Wit: W. W. LACKEY, Valentine MAYO. 26 Dec 1821.

218. (2:186-87) James MONTGOMERY to William BREWER: 23 Mar 1816, $300, 80 ac on waters of Gallaher's Creek, part of Grant #894 dated 20 May 1810 to William MONTGOMERY, which Stuart MONTGOMERY holds by virtue of a bill of sale from William, and granted to James MONTGOMERY [by] a conveyance from said MONTGOMERY dividing said tract. Adj MACKLIN. Wit: Francis JONES, Spencer BLANKENSHIP. 28 Dec 1821.

219. (2:187-88) William BREWER to William BRADBERY: 14 Jan 1819, $300, 80 ac on waters of Gallaher's Creek, part of Grant #894, 12 May 1810 to Wm. MONTGOMERY, sold to Stuart MONTGOMERY, conveyed to James MONTGOMERY and conveyed to Wm. BREWER. Adj McLIN. Sig: William (X) BREWER. Wit John M. RANKIN, John B. McLIN. 28 Dec 1821.

220. (2:188-89) Hugh KELSO of Monroe Co. to Blackmin H. MAYS: 21 May 1821, $600, 640 ac on Tennessee River at mouth of

Baker's Creek, Grant #962 from NC, 26 Dec 1791. Wit: Nathaniel MORRISON, Wm. GRIFFETH. 29 Dec 1821.

221. (2:189) Jonathan WEAR to Charles DONOHOO: 20 Nov 1816, $400, negro girl named (GELLER?) about 18 yrs old. 3 Jan 1822. Wit: Thos. HENDERSON, James TURK.

222. (2:189-90) Josiah P. SMITH to James McMILLAN: 6 Jan 1820, $800, 240 ac on waters of Pistol Creek, adj James EDINGTON, KING and MONTGOMERY, Josiah P. SMITH, John WOODS, David CAULDWELL, part of Grant #748 to Samuel McGAUHEY, 1 May 1810. Wit: John HOUSTON, Samuel HOUSTON. 3 Jan 1822.

223. (2:190-91) Samuel WEAR of Monroe Co. to William FAGG: 4 Sep 1821, $200, 119 ac, adj the Green Pond, John WEAR, Samuel McGAHEY, KING and MONTGOMERY, John SMART.   Grant #782 to WEAR 4 May 1810. Wit: Ignatius WILSON, W. BERRY. 4 Jan 1822.

224. (2:191) George P. HOGY to James TURK & James HENRY: 9 Oct 1821, 2 feather beds and furniture, 4 bedsteads, 2 large pots, 2 ovens, 2 skillets, 6 knives and forks, 6 pewter plates, 6 delft blue-edged plates, one dining table, 7 chairs, 2 wheels, 2 plows and three hoes, "all my part of corn after paying the rent on the farm I now live on." HOGY to pay a debt to Bank of the State of Tennessee at Maryville for $80 with interest for which TURK and HENRY stand surety. Wit: A. B. EMMERSON, B. M. RUSSELL. 7 Jan 1822.

225. (2:191-92) Thomas WILKINSON of Jefferson Co. to James TURK: 12 Dec 1821, for natural love and affection...to James TURK's wife Polly, step daughter, as well as for the better maintenance and preferment of Polly, a negro woman PAT, and her three sons, JESSIE, CHARLES and WILLIAM, and two feather beds, bedstands and furniture, one bureau now in possession of Polly. Wit: Jesse THOMPSON. 4 Jan 1822.

226. (2:192-93) Charles DONOHOO, Sheriff to John McGHEE, Alexander McGHEE and Mathew W. McGHEE, merchants trading as McGHEE AND BROTHERS: 24 Dec 1821, $124.50, 108 ac on Little River adj lands of David GIFFIN and others, Grant from TN to

Andrew GIFFIN, Sr.; public sale 22 Sep 1821 to satisfy judgments against Robert DEARMOND: two totaling $4.90 and $49.30 recovered by State of TN and Polly GIFFEN, one in favor of Philip COOPER against Robert H. DEARMOND and David GIFFIN $25.675; one in favor of John NORWOOD for $6.65; one in favor of Samuel ROBERTS against DEARMOND and GIFFIN for $35.36; one in favor of Elisha HICKS against DEARMOND for $19.275. John McGHEE high bidder for McGHEE AND BROTHERS. Wit: James TURK, A. B. EMMERSEN. 8 Jan 1822.

227.   (2:193-95) James LOVE (first party), Jacob FOUTE (second party) to McGHEE AND BROTHERS: 1 Aug 1821, $400 owing by LOVE to McGHEE AND BROTHERS and $1.00 paid by FOUTE to LOVE, 149 ac on waters of Holston, Grant #1245 to Alexander PATTERSON, assignee of Alexander CRAYE, adj Alexander LOGAN. LOVE shall pay $400 on or before 1 Jan 1822 with interest. Wit: A. B. EMMERSEN, B. M. RUSSELL. 8 Jan 1822.

228.   (2:195-96) Robert MONTGOMERY to Jacob McGHEE: 27 Sep 1821, $70, 71 ac on waters of Little River in Tuckaleechee Cove, south side of Little River adj Burbury MOOR, John GIDEON. Wit: Samuel DAVIS, John RUSH. Sig: Robert (X) MONTGOMERY. 15 Jan 1822.

229.   (2:196) James CAULDWELL to Major REEDER, "late of Wythe Co., VA": 31 Jan 1821, $1350, [land] on waters of Little River, part of 224 ac granted to heirs of John KELLY; adj James CLARK, SHROYER. Wit: James GILLESPIE, J. Houston GILLESPIE. Sig: James (X) CAULDWELL. 13 Jan 1822.

230.   (2:196-97) Samuel JOHNSTON to Eli RICHIE: 13 Jun 1818, $500, 125 ac on Tennessee River, adj Hugh KELSO, "land heretofore claimed by James I. GREENE". Wit: Wm. MONTGOMERY, David CARSON, John McCROSKEY. 15 Jan 1822.

231.   (2:197-98) John TIPTON to James DAVIS: 22 Jan 1820, $300, 71 ac on waters of Ellejoy Creek, adj Joseph BLACK, David VANCE, Benjamin TIPTON. Wit: Hugh BOGLE, James DAVIS, William CHAMBERS, Jesse BROWN. 16 Jan 1822.

232. (2:198-99) George SNIDER to James MURRY: 29 Aug 1821, $500, 146 ac on waters of Six Mile Creek, adj John NEEL, John BOYD. Wit: James ROBINSON, John (X) BOYD. 16 Jan 1822.

233. (2:199) Menter HOLLOWAY to Joel BAKER: 24 Nov 1820, $160, 67 ac on waters of Six Mile Creek, adj Joseph HOLLOWAY, the Indian Boundary, Joseph HOLLOWAY. Wit: William DAVIS, Jos. ROBESON.

234. (2:199-201) William SHERRELL and Robert McTEER (first party), John WILKINSON (second party), James and Ignatius WILSON and Nelson S. WRIGHT (third party)   to John WILKINSON: 25 Apr 1821, in consideration of the debt suretyship and other matters..SHERRELL and McTEER convey 114 ac on waters of Ellejoy Creek adj Robert McTEER, Sr., Joseph BOGAL, Samuel BOGAL, Richard WILLIAMS. SHERRELL is indebted to WILSONs for $251.36 for four notes signed 23 Apr 1821 and due 3 and 4 June 1821. WRIGHT is security for SHERRELL for $158 payable 1 July 1821 to James HENRY and the further sum of $106 payable to Jesse KERR on 2 Dec 1822. Wit: Tarens CONNER?, Uriah SHERRELL, John NORWOOD, Azekiah A. BARNARD. 20 Jan 1822.

235. (2:201) Hezekiah A. BARNARD to William TOOL: 25 Dec 1821, $1500, two lots in Maryville, #59 where BARNARD now lives, by the main street, and lot #87 whereon BARNARD's stable now stands. Wit: W. W. BERRY, Joseph ALEXANDER. 29 Jan 1822.

236. (2:201-02) Nicholas STEPHENSON to George COOK: 7 Oct 1817, $1600, 473 ac in Hickory Valley, part of original occupant survey of STEPHENSON for 560 ac, adj Daniel DURHAM, Thomas SIMPSON, formerly Mahlen STEVENSON. Wit: Nathaniel MORISON, Henry STEPHENSON, James ALLEN. 4 Feb 1822.

237. (2:202-03) John BIBLE to Holbert McCLURE: 19 Nov 1816, $1000, 196 ac, part of Grant #1409 to William BARNES, 14 June 1810, adj James GREENWAY, George COOK, John FRANKS. Wit: Robert McREYNOLDS, John McCLURE, Henry FRANKS. Sig: John (X) BIBLE. 1822.

238. (2:203-04) John NORWOOD to Hezekiah A. BARNARD: 11 Aug 1821, on 25 May 1821 for $1500 NORWOOD conveyed lots #59 and 87 in Maryville,"which conveyance was stolen by sum villian (sic) from BARNARD"... Wit: Jas. R. RUSE?, Jac F. FOUTE, William FAGG. 5 Feb 1822.

239. (2:205) John S. BURNETT to Josiah F. DANFORTH: 12 Oct 1820, $800, 1 pair of tractor wheels, one log chain, one yoke of oxen, two beds with their furniture, one set china ware, one set silver, ten spoons, two sets knives and forks, one set Windsor chairs, one set half-round cherry tables, one cow and calf, one burow, one candle stand, one trunk and one walnut chest and all the kitchen furniture. Wit: I. W. LACKY, Jos. DANFORTH. 11 Feb 1822.

240. (2:205-06) John HUNTER to Jane LOVE, widow: 6 Dec 1820, $600, 187 ac on waters of Pistol Creek, adj Thomas HUNTER, Ester RICE, widow, Stuart MONTGOMERY. Granted to Hugh WEAR, Jr. 1 June 1809, and conveyed to John WEAR, and part of a tract granted to Hugh WEAR, Sr. on 2 June 1809 and conveyed by will to John WEAR, and by John WEAR conveyed to Samuel LOVE, by him willed to John HUNTER. Wit: Wm. GAULT, James HENDERSON. 12 Feb 1822.

241. (2:206-07) John PINTER/PITNER to John JONES, Jr., of Washington Co., VA: 13 Dec 1820, $600, 228 ac on waters of Ellejoy Creek, adj John McNALLEY, Benjamin TIPTON, James DAVIS, Robert MURRIN; Granted to William JOHNSTON 29 May 1810. Wit: Adam PITNER, Isaac LINDSAY, John KINCANNON. Sig: John (X) PITNER. 2 Feb 1822.

242. (2:207-08) David LOWE to John COX: 13 Sep 1815, $35.25, 11 ac on north east of the east fork of Lackey's Creek, part of survey made for John GILLASPEY now in possession of David LOWE and John COX; adj TEEL. Wit: John LOW, Josiah PATTY. 25 Mar 1822.

243. (2:208-09) Hugh KELSO to Archable CABLE and Thomas PAIN: 26 May 1818, $2500, 576 ac on Baker's Creek and Tennessee River, adj Bruce BLAIR and Joseph DOBSON, William GRAY and William BEASLY, Wyly LASETER, the upper end of the lot of

Morganton and James TORBETT, Jacob FOUTE, Joseph DOBSON. Wit: Bary ABERNATHEY, Robert WEAR. 25 Mar 1822.

244. (2:209-10) John S. BURNETT to John W. DANFORTH: 15 May 1821, $50, lots #66 and 79 in Maryville. Lot #66, Grant #216 to James HOUSTON, 3 Aug 1806. Lot #79, Grant #215 to James HOUSTON, 3 Aug 1808. Lot #66 being where BURNETT now lives and #79 being the one lying immediately in back of #66 and separated by an alley and where BURNETT's stable now stands. Wit: John McFADDEN, Josiah F. DANFORTH. 7 Jan 1822.

245. (2:210-11) William TOOLE to Obediah BOAZ: 25 Dec 1821, $800, quit claim to lot #35 in Maryville deeded 23 Feb 1816 by John THORNBURY to Wm. TOOL and BOAZ and lot #13 which THORNBURY deeded on 28 Mar 1820 to TOOL and BOAZ. Wit: W. W. BERRY, Jos. ALEXANDER. 17 Apr 1822.

246. (2:211) John NORWOOD to McGHEE AND BLAIR: 10 Jun 1820, $325, a negro girl named PHEBY about 10 years of age. Wit: A. B. EMMERSON, Nelson S. WRIGHT. 26 Apr 1822.

247. (2:211-12) John WALKER to Samuel WALKER: 24 Mar 1820, $800, 78 ac on waters of Little River. Wit: Samuel HENRY, John (X) BOWERMAN. 26 Apr 1822.

248. (2:212-13) Isaac HAIR to William HUMPHREYS[IES]: 20 Oct 1820, $4500, 378 ac in Hickory Valley. Wit: James I. GREEN, Wm. McLIN, A. HUMPHRESS. 7 May 1822.

249. (2:213) Josiah JOHNSTON to William GRIFFITH: 1822, $10, 2.7 ac on Cloyd's Creek, part of an old original survey made for Samuel SHAW. Wits omitted. 7 May 1822.

250. (2:213-14) Samuel BLACKBURN to James BERRY: 28 Dec 1820, $500, 143 ac on waters of east fork of Pistol Creek, adj John WOOD, Samuel McGAHEY, John WEAR, Joseph WEAR, G. BLACKBURN. Grant #1872 to William HENRY 26 May 1810. Wit: John WEAR, Hugh WEAR of James. 9 May 1822.

251. (2:214-15) Samuel BLACKBURN to Samuel STEEL: 28 Dec 1821, $1500, 186 ac on waters of Pistol Creek, adj David CAULDWELL, KING AND MONTGOMERY, John WOODS and William HENRY, Joseph WEAR, Bartley McGHEE. Grant #551 to Gideon BLACKBURN, 15 Jun 1809. Wit: John WEAR, Hugh WEAR of James. 9 May 1822.

252. (2:215-16) William BELLEW to William HARPER: 20 Jan 1820, $120, 50 ac on waters of Crooked Creek adj John SHARP, Samuel PORTER, GAMBLE. Wit: Isaac WHITE, John KINCANNEN. 10 May 1822.

253. (216-17) Charles DONOHOO, Sheriff, to Holbert McCLURE: 27 Feb 1822, $60, public sale 9 June 1821 to satisfy judgment against George COOK for $331.335 recovered by John BIBAL, 208 ac where COOK formerly lived, part of Grant #993 to Nicholas STEVENSON, adj lands now owned by John ADAMSON and others, Thomas WOODEN. Wit: Daniel D. FOUTE, John McGHEE. 10 May 1822.

254. (2:217-18) James HUBBARD to William DAVIS: 18 Sep 1821, $80, number of acs not given, on waters of Ellejoy Creek, adj James DAVIS, Jacob MOOR. Wit: Samuel RHEA, Hugh BOGLE. 11 May 1822.

255. (2:218-19) John MAY to Daniel TAYLOR of Grainger Co.: 29 Nov 1820, $600, 249 ac on waters of Holston River adj James PAUL and others. Wit: Greensfield TAYLOR, Samuel GEORGE. 11 May 1822.

256. (2:219) Joseph TIPTON, Sr. to Jesse DELOZIER: 25 Mar 1822, $450, 10 ac on waters of Ellejoy Creek, adj Andrew BOGLE. Wit: Jac F. FOUTE, Hugh BOGLE. Sig: Joseph (X) TIPTON. 4 May 1822.

257. (2:219-20) Archable MURPHY to Hugh HAMBLE and David HAMBLE: 3 Mar 1820, $300, 100 ac on headwaters of Nine Mile Creek, adj John DAVIS, Robert HAMBLE, David EDMENSON. Wit: Robert HOUSTON, William WALLACE. Sig: Archey MURPHY. 11 May 1822.

258.   (2:220-21) James HAMOLE, John HAMOLE, Robert HAMMELE and Samuel HAMMELE to Hugh HAMMEL and David HAMMALE: 12 Oct 1816, $200, their interest in 359 ac Grant to Robert HAMMELE and whereon he died, adj Robert TEDFERD, John TEDFERD, Esq. and others. Except the interest transferred to and vested in Jane HAMMELLE, their mother and widow of Robert HAMBLE, deceased. Wit: John WILKINSON, David McKAMEY. 14 May 1822.

259. (2:221) William SAMPLES to James EADENS, Sr. of Maury Co.: 28 June 1820, 182 ac, the land where SAMPLES now lives, to secure payment of $100 with interest from 26 May 1819, to be paid on or before 25 Dec 1820. Wit: Jason PERSEN. Isaac PENS. 14 May 1822.

260. (2:221-22) William JOHNSTON, Sr. to Peter P. DAVIS: 12 Feb 1820 $350, 31 ac on waters of Ellejoy Creek, adj Hugh BOGAL, RUSAIN. Wit: Hugh BOGAL, James (X) DAVIS. 14 May 1822.

261.   (2:222-23) Thomas SIMPSON of Monroe Co. to Samuel BOND: 18 Mar 1822, $600, 121 ac in Hickory Valley, a tract conveyed from Nicholas STEVENSON to Simpson in 1813, adj Stevenson, Henry BOND, and Mahlen STEVENSON, Samuel WEATENS?, Luroy NOLES?. Wit: John CULSON, John CARSON. Sig: Thomas (X) SIMPSON. Proven at court session 1822 by John CAULSEN and William GRIFFITS. 18 May 1822.

262.   (2:223-24) Jermiah JACK, Jr. of Knox Co. to Isaac HINES/HAINS: 18 Aug 1818, $350, 140 ac on waters of Nails Creek. Wit: William C. CARLAS, Robert (X) HEINES. 18 May 1822.

263.   (2:224-25) Jacob CAPPENBARGER to John HIX: 13 Dec 1816, $300, 87 ac on a branch of Lackey's Creek, surveyed for James RORK and by ROACK conveyed to COPPENBURGER, adj the Branch, top of the Gray Ridge, Jesse JAMES, Alexander STUART. Wit: Josiah PATTY, Nathaniel RAGAN. 22 May 1822.

264.   (2:225-26) Bacon BURWILE of Barkley Co., VA, admin of James BURWELL, decd, to Alexander McGHEE: 20 June 1818, $6000 to be paid in the manner and terms stipulated and agreed upon

between McGHEE and William C. LATTAMORE, who intermarried with Nancy BURWELL, daughter of James, decd; negro ADAM, his wife PATTY and child and their sons, JAMES and ADAM, ELIZA and child, ALICE and two children, Lucy HOLDER and two children, James and Louisa STEPHENS and Jesse...belonging to the estate of James BURWELL, decd. Wit: Wm. P. FLOOD. E. VIVENE?, B. BURWILL. Ack at Jefferson Co., VA, court 22 June 1818 by William P. FLOOD and Edwin B. BURWILL. 29 May 1822.

265. (2:226) Thomas CAPPS to Thomas McCLURKIN: 13 Oct 1815, $400, 100 ac on waters of Baker's Creek, adj James HAMMENTREE, Hugh CUNNINGHAM, James ANDERSON, Captain BIGGS, William HAMMENTREE. The "before rented land" is warranted, etc. Wit: Jeremiah HASK? (possibly a "mark"), John PARKS. 7 June 1822.

266. (2:226-27) Wyley LASSETER to John EDINGTON: 17 June 1815, $825, 240 ac on Baker's Creek, adj Hugh KELSO, William BEASLY, William GREEN, KELSO. Wit: Rob WEAR, H. THOMAS. 1 July 1822.

267. (2:227-28) Hugh W. DUNLAP to John McGHEE, Alexander McGhee, Mathew McGHEE and David M. HUNTER, partners trading under the firm of McGHEES AND HUNTER of Blount Co. and Monroe Co.: January 1822, Joseph WILSON of Monroe Co. by deed of 14 Dec 1820 conveyed to DUNLAP a negro woman named MARIA aged about 22 yrs, a boy named URIAH/WACH? aged about two years and a boy named PETER aged about three months, in trust, to secure Samuel and John McCROSKY who had become bound as security for WILSON for a debt of $490 due to McGHEES AND HUNTER payable by 14 Dec 1821 with interest from that date. Public Sale 28 Dec 1821 at courthouse in Monroe Co., where Charles KELSO lives. Negroes sold for $626, bid by Ambrose R. HUNTER, agent for McGHEES AND HUNTER. Wit: Thos. L. WILLIAMS, Dury P. ARMSTRONG. Ack in Knox County Court by Hugh W. DUNLAP. 1 July 1822.

268. (2:229) Charles McCLUNG of Knox Co. to John McGHEE of Maryville: 27 June 1821, for affection I have for John McGHEE who

intermarried with my daughter Betsey Jones McCLUNG and $1.00 paid by McGHEE, four negroes: SALLY, PATIENCE, WASHINGTON, and LIZZY. Wit: Thomas L. WILLIAMS, A. B. EMMERSON. 1 Jul 1822.

269.   (2:229) Nicholas BYERS as atty in fact for the legal representatives of John W. HOOKER, to Bartley McGHEE: 5 May 1806, all claim that was in any manner vested in John W. HOOKER at time of his decease in 400 ac on north side of Tennessee River, Grant #830 from State of NC to Hisciah BOWMAN, and as per deed of conveyance from HOOKER dated 17 Jan 1804. McGHEE is to settle and comply with all contracts that have been made between him and HOOKER and BOWMAN relating to purchase of land by HOOKER from BOWMAN. Wit: John WILKINSON, A. H. HENLEY. 3 July 1822.

270.   (2:229-32) Caleb CARTER, "late of Blount Co.", to Barclay McGHEE: 26 Dec 1799, $100, 200 ac on south side of Holston River adj east fork of Lackey's Creek, Grant #214 from State of NC, dated 22 Feb 1795; adj Edward CHISNUTT line, John GILLASPEY, William GRAY. Signed by Jacob (X) MERK? as atty in fact for Caleb CARTER. Wit: J. WILKINSON, John LOWERY. 3 Jul 1822.

271. (2:230-31) John and Mathew McGHEE to Alexander McGHEE: 27 Jun 1822, $1.00, Quit Claim to shares of lands devised to them by their father and not specifically divided in the will; title to certain tracts of land on waters of Lackey's Creek, one tract of 472 ac, Grant #230 to Barkley McGHEE adj James HOUSTON, W. HOUSTON, James TEDFERD. Another tract of 564 ac, Grant #231 to McGhee, adj James TEDFERD, Robert McCURDY. 437 ac, Grant #205 to Barkley McGHEE, adj bridge where Gillespie Mill Road crosses a branch, John GILLESPIE, William GILLESPIE, Christian McCLURE. 639 ac, Grant #228 to Barclay McGHEE, adj David FALKER?, James HOUSTON. Also town lots #69 and 76 in Maryville. Wit: Jac F. FOUTE, Daniel D. FOUTE. 9 July 1822.

272.   (2:232-33) John and Alexander M. McGHEE to Mathew McGHEE: 27 Jun 1822, $2.00, Quit Claim to tract of land on waters of Pistol Creek about two miles from town of Maryville on the Great

Road leading from Maryville to Knoxville adj Andrew THOMPSON, BOAZ, COWAN, McMILLEN, and AMBRISTER, being the land lately occupied by Col. John THORNBURY and sold under a deed of trust by John WILKINSON, Esq. to John, Alexander and Mathew W. McGHEE on 10 Jan 1822; also one other tract of 97 ac on Great Road from Maryville to Sevierville, sold under deed of trust by Jacob F. FOUTE bought by John, Alexander, and Mathew McGHEE. Wit: Jesse THOMPSON, B. M. RUSSELL. 10 Jul 1822.

273. (2:233) Hugh FORGUSON to James OLIVER: 4 Mar 1820, $200, 71 ac on waters of Nine Mile Creek, part of the tract whereon Forgusen now lives, adj William MILLER. Wit: William WHITE, John TEMPLETON. 10 July 1822.

274. (2:233-35) Banner SHIELDS of McMinn Co. to Michal GOODLINK: 13 Oct 1820: $1000, 274 ac on a branch of Pistol Creek, part of occupant claim surveyed for SHIELDS by Josiah PATTY, adj Joseph FINDLY, William SIMINS and Thomas HUNTER, Josiah PATTY. Wit: James W. STEPHENSON, Jesse E. GOODLINK, Samuel GOODLINK. 10 Jul 1822.

275. (2:235) James HENRY (first party) to Hugh KELSO of Monroe Co. (second party) and Samuel JOHNSTON (third party): 3 Aug 1821, $100 paid by Kelso as security, 291 ac on waters of Nine Mile Creek, the land where HENRY now lives, adj Major William HARRIS, Jonethan TIPTON. HENRY is indebted to JOHNSTON for $600 by note to be paid before 1 Aug 1822 with all accruing costs and interest. Wit: Josiah ROWAN, Josiah JOHNSTON, Samuel M. JOHNSTON. 10 July 1822.

276. (2:235-36) Thomas McCLARKIN to Robert THOMPSON: 3 May 1822, $175, 81 ac on waters of Baker's Creek, part of 284 ac Granted to James RICHEY adj James CONNER, James TEDFERD, David CARSON, John THOMPSON, James ANDERSON, RICHEY. Wit: Wm. McCLUNG, John CUNNINGHAM, John THOMPSON. 10 July 1822.

277. (2:236-37) John BLACK, William BLACK, Abigal BLACK and Uriah BLACK, all heirs of Samuel BLACK, decd, to Richard DEARMOND : 9 Oct 1818, $800, 164 ac on waters of Crooked

Creek, part of Grant #2552 to heirs of Samuel BLACK, adj Martain RORAX, Henry THOMAS and the Widow THOMAS, Robert GAULT. Sig: William BLACK by his attorney in fact John BLACK. Abigail (X) BLACK. Uriah BLACK. Wit: Martain ROREX, Abram WALLACE. 26 Sep 1822.

278. (2:237-38) John TORBETT to David HUMPHRYS: 25 March 1819, $765, 125 ac on waters of Sinking Creek, part of 619 ac granted to TORBETT 28 Sep 1809 by Burton PRIDE, surveyed 16 June 1807. Wit: James ANDERSON, Isaac ANDERSON, John BEGGS. 21 (month omitted) 1822.

279. (2:238-39) William SHERREL to John HOUSTON: 22 June 1818, $1200, 280 ac on waters of Pistol Creek, part of 590 ac of Grant #797, adj William BONES, Banner SHIELDS, Abraham WEIR, William HOUSTON, John SMITH, Barclay McGHEE. Wit: Obediah BOAZ, Isaac ANDERSON. 4 Dec 1822.

280. (2:239) Richard H. KING of Knox Co. to Mary G. GILLESPEY: 26 May 1822, for natural love and affection for...my daughter Mary Gibs GILLESPEY, widow of Robert GILLESPEY, decd, a negro boy named OWEN aged 12. Wit: James G. TALBUT. 4 Dec 1822.

281. (2:239-40) Richard H. KING of Knox Co. to Ignatius WILSON: 26 Mar 1822, for natural love and affection for my daughter Jane COWN who intermarried with Ignatious WILSON, negro girl MILLEY aged 16 yrs. Wit: James G. TALBUT. 4 Dec 1822.

282. (2:240) Henry HODGE to James & Ignatious WILSON: 23 January 1822, $160.50, negro woman named JUDAH, supposed to be about 50 yrs old. Wit: James TRUNDLE, Thos. WILSON. 18 Dec 1822.

283. (2:(240-41) William SHERREL to James WILSON: 23 Apr 1821, $625, a negro boy named HENRY aged 18 yrs. Wit: Nelson WRIGHT, Ignatius WILSON. 18 Dec 1822.

284. (2:241-42) Samuel WEAR of Monroe Co. to John GRISSOM: 4 Sept 1820 $1500, two tracts on east fork of Pistol Creek, one tract

260 ac lying entirely north of the east fork of Pistol Creek and adj on the north Gideon BLACKBURN, on east by John WEAR, and on south by Hugh WEAR and James BERRY; Grant #576 to Joseph WEAR, decd, 7 June 1809, and willed by Joseph Wear at his death to Samuel WEAR. The other tract containing 33 ac, adj Hugh and Joseph WEAR, John WEAR, Grant #923, 4 May 1810, to Samuel WEAR. Wit: Ignatious WILSON, Charles DONOHOO. 13 Dec 1822.

285. (2:242-43) John NICHOL of City of Nashville to James McCLANAHAN of Maryville: 31 Mar 1812, $1400, two lots of land in Maryville, #31 at the intersection of an alley and the main street, whereon McCLANAHAN now lives, and #10 lying immediately back of lot #39 at the intersection of back street and cross street adj the commons and Pistol Creek. Grant to John NICHOLS #1980 and #1979. Wit: John McGHEE, Enoch PERSONS. 21 Dec 1822.

286. (2:243-44) John GRESHAM to James and Ignatius WILSON: 5 Jan 1822, $647.67, two tracts on east fork of Pistol Creek, 293 ac, one tract of 260 ac lying entirely north of east fork of Pistol Creek, bounded on north by Gideon BLACKBURN, on east by John WEAR and on south by Hugh WEAR and James BERRY which was Grant #576 to Joseph WEAR, dated 7 June 1809, and willed to Samuel WEAR; another tract of 33 ac adj Hugh and Joseph WEAR, John WEAR, Grant to Samuel WEAR #923, 4 May 1810. Wit: Charles DONOHOO, Tarens CONNER. 21 Dec 1822.

287. (2:244-45) Richard H. KING of Knox Co. (first party), James and Ignatious WILSON, merchants t/a J & Ig WILSON of Maryville (second party) to Jacob F. FOUTE: 9 May 1822, KING is indebted to [WILSONs] for $732.50 by note dated 10 Jan 1821, for which Jacob F. FOUTE is security; negro man MILES aged 23 yrs, negro woman LUCY aged 40 yrs and her four children: NED, aged 15, SHEFFY aged 9 yrs, BETSY, 6 yrs, and RICHARD, aged 2 yrs. KING to pay $732.50 and interest within two months; if unpaid, slaves may be sold at public auction. Wit: Tarens CONNER, Thomas WILSON. 23 Dec 1822.

288. (2:246-47) John McGHEE and Alexander McGHEE to Mathew W. McGHEE: 27 June 1822, $1.00, Quit Claim to (their) shares of the

estate of their father in land in Sevier Co. on east fork of Little Pigeon River, adj James COWEN, James P. H. PORTER, Isaac THOMAS, Jerry MATHIS, James CAMRON, 564 ac Grant #33 to Barkley McGHEE; also another tract in Blount Co., 135 ac, part of David MILLER's occupant claim and sold by Miller to Henry LOGAN and by Logan to Barcley McGhee, adj Hugh KELSO. Another tract on the Tellico Road near Little Tennessee River 218 ac, adj David MILLER which was sold by Charles DONAHOO, Sheriff. Another tract of 2 ac, part of Jno. LOWERY's survey adj Bartley McGhee west of Maryville, on northwest side of the Great Road leading to Tellico. Also lots #68 and #77 in Maryville. Wit: Jesse THOMPSON, B. M. RUSSELL. 25 Dec 1822.

289. (2:248) Alexander McGHEE and Mathew McGHEE to John McGHEE: 29 Jun 1822, $1.00, quit claim to their shares of the estate of their father, a tract of land in Monroe Co. on south side of Little Tennessee River, adj Cabbin SMITH reservation. Also two lots in Maryville adj commons on the northwest known as #72 and #73. Wit: Jesse THOMPSON, R. W. RUSSELL. 46 Dec 1822. Sig: Matt W. McGHEE.

290. (2:248-49) Alexander WILSON and James STRAIN to Benjamin FORD: 14 Dec 1822, $600, 3 ac on waters of Baker's Creek, part of John EWIN's tract, adj John COULDWELL, W. WILSON. Wit: John JACKSON, William EWING. 11 Jan 1823.

291. (2:249-50) William WALLACE, Sheriff, to James I. GREEN of Roane Co.: 1 Aug 1822, $.25, to satisfy judgment from county court of Roane 23 July in favor of Robert CANNAN, 159 ac of land belonging to James LOVE, public sale 27 July in Maryville, 149 ac (sic) on waters of Holston River, Grant #1245 to Alexander PATTERSON, assignee of Alexander EWING, adj Alexander LOGAN. Wit: Samuel STEEL, James HENRY. 13 Jan 1823.

292. (2:250-52) Jacob F. FOUTE to James I. GREEN of Roane Co.: 22 July 1822, $505, 149 ac on waters of Holston River, original grant #1245 to Alexander PATTEN assignee of Alexander CRAGE, adj Alexander LOGAN. James LOVE executed deed to FOUTE on 1 Aug 1821 to secure the payment of the sum of $400 by 1 Jan 1822 with all

interest, costs..that might accrue thereon to John McGHEE, Alexander McGHEE and Matthew W. McGHEE t/a McGHEE and BROTHERS, and LOVE having defaulted in the payment of the said note, on 24 May 1822 the McGhees requested Foute to sell the land; public sale 27 July 1822 at which GREEN offered highest bid. Wit: Samuel GAULT, Will WALLACE. Certified to be registered by Daniel David FOUTE, Clerk of Circuit Court of Blount Co. at July term 1822. 13 Jan 1823.

293. (2:252) A. WILLSON of Monroe Co. to Benjamin FORD: 14 Dec 1822, $400, 119 ac on waters of Baker's Creek, adj John EWING, Andrew JACKSON, Samuel GOULD, William HUSTON. Wit: John Jackson, William Ewing. 28 Jan 1823.

294. (2:252-53) John EWING to A. WILSON and James STRAIN: 5 Apr 1820, $33, 3 ac on a branch of Baker's Creek, part of John EWING tract, adj John CAULDWELL, A. WILSON. Wit: John JACKSON, William EWING. 28 Jan 1823.

295. (2:253-54) Samuel ORR to Absolem McNABB: 29 Dec 1819, $40, 5 ac on waters of Baker's Creek, cor to McNABB, adj James McCONAL. Wit: J. Lom? ADAMS, Thomas ADAMS. 30 Jan 1828.

296. (2:254-55) Samuel ORR, Sr. to Samuel ORR, Jr.: 21 Dec 1822, for natural love and affection for his nephew and for better maintenance and prefarement of Samuel ORR, Jr., 107 ac on waters of Baker's Creek, adj James LOGAN, Robert McCABE. Wit: Absolom McNabb, James McCONNELL. 30 Jan 1823.

297. (2:255-56) John RAGON to Jeremiah HAYSE: 12 Oct 1822, $1000, 160 ac on a branch of west fork of Lackey's Creek, the occupant survey made for Martain CASTETER, whereon John RAGAIN now lives, adj Henry WHITTENBARGER, George MOORE, Thomas EATHERTON, Jacob COPERBURGER. Wit: Josiah PATTY, Nathaniel HOOD, Moses HILL. 30 Jan 1823.

298. (2:256-57) James SIMS to Wm. G. SIMS: 9 Dec 1822, 255 ac on waters of Nails Creek, adj Robert McMURRAY, Samuel McMURRAY. Wit: Ignatious WILSON, James BOYD. 30 Jan 1823.

299. (2:257-58) James BROWN of the Cherokee Nation to James R. DANFORTH of Richmond Co., GA: March 1822 (day omitted), no consideration stated, negro woman named POLLY, aged 18 yrs. Wit: Henry P. SIMMERMAN, James SMITH, John S. BURNETT. Ack 18 Apr 1822 in Hamilton Co., TN, by James SMITH, Henry R. SIMMONAIN and John S. BENNETT, before George McGUIRE and Jeremiah JONES

, acting justices of the peace for Hamilton Co. Reg Blount Co. 1 Feb 1823.

300. (2:258-59) Samuel WEAR, "late of Blount Co. and now of Monroe Co." to James BERRY: 13 Mar 1822, $400 paid by David RUSSELL and John LARKINS, 100 ac of land on waters of Pistol Creek, part of original survey granted to Joseph WEAR Sr., adj Hugh WEAR, Robert GAULT, Barcley McGHEE, Samuel STEEL. Samuel WEAR had sold [land] to David RUSSELL and bound himself by bond dated 25 Sep 1813 to make a good title thereto; RUSSELL sold to John LARKINS and obligated himself to make a good title thereto, John LARKINS sold land to James BERRY and obliged himself by bond dated 31 Jan 1821 to make a good title. Wit: Jac F. FOUTE, Josiah PATTY, Samuel STEEL. Sig: Samuel WEIR. 3 Feb 1823.

301. (2:259) Barclay McGHEE to Joseph WEAR: 24 Feb 1809. "Know all men by these presents that I...do bind myself, to make a deed of conveyance to Joseph WEAR...for 23 ac out of the tract of land claimed by me under John MEANS agreeable to lines as run by John WILKINSON...as soon after the Grant is obtained as it conveniently can be done." Sig: B. McGHEE. Wit: John LOWERY. 3 Feb 1823.

302. (2:259-60) John McGHEE, Alexander McGHEE, and Mathew W. McGHEE, execrs of Barclay McGHEE, decd, to James BERRY: 27 June 1822, $33.41, 33 ac on waters of Pistol Creek, part of Grant #252 dated 28 Sept 1809 to Barclay McGHEE, adj lands now owned by James BERRY, John MONTGOMERY and others, corner to survey originally made for Joseph WEARE. [land described in agreement above] Joseph WARE has died and bequeathed land to his

son Samuel WEAR; WEAR sold land to James BERRY. Wit: Jac F. FOUTE, David D. FOUTE. 4 Feb 1823.

303. (2:261-62) Samuel STEEL to James BERRY: 17 May 1822, $1800, 186 ac on waters of Pistol Creek, adj David CAULDWELL, KING and MONTGOMERY, crossing the creek, John WOODS and William HENRY, Joseph WEAR, Barclay McGHEE, Grant #551 to Gideon BLACKBURN dated 15 Jun 1809. Wit: Jac F. FOUTE, James H. GILLESPY. 4 Feb 1823.

304. (2:262) James STUART of Marion Co. to Samuel GOULD and James LOGAN: 21 Jan 1819, $100, 5 ac on Nine Mile Creek, adj William STUART. Grant #999 to James STUART. Wit: Samuel J. WILSON, Joseph WILSON, John GOULD. 5 Feb 1823.

305. (2:262-63) Moses COOK to James McMAHEN: 19 Feb 1818, $250, "my right...in 219 ac belonging to heirs of James COOK, decd, my claim including two distinctive shares of said land to my one and also David COOK's that I purchased from [him] and have now sold to James McMAHEN, on Nine Mile Creek including the Grist Mill and Iron Works formerly the property of James COOK, decd, which two shares of said land, viz, my own and the share purchased from David COOK, I will warrant.." etc. . Wit: James COOK, John McMAHAN. 20 Feb 1823.

306. (2:263) James HOUSTON to John MONTGOMERY: 11 Mar 1822, $1100, a negro woman named BETSEY aged about 24 yrs and her four children: FANY aged about 9 years, LEWIS aged seven years, BEN aged 5 yrs and HARIOT aged one and half years. Wit: James BERRY, John STRAIN. 25 Feb 1823.

307. (2:263-64) Jonathan WEAR to Hugh WEAR: 2 June 1820, $130, 207 ac on headwaters of Pistol Creek, part of Grant #1128 dated 26 May 1810. Wit: Jonethan WEAR, John M. RANKIN. 28 Feb 1823.

308. (2:264-65) Hugh FORGUSEN to Spencer BLANKENSHIP: 7 Jan 1815, $687.50, 138 ac on Gallaher's Creek, Grant by TN to FORGUSON, beginning at a post oak near a Grave Yard, cor to

Robert McCULLY and Isaac WHITE. Wit: Nehemiah BONHAM, Thos. MAXWELL. 28 Feb 1823.

309. (2:265-66) Alexander McKEE (first party), Alexander B. GAMBLE (second party) to Samuel HENRY (third party): 3 Sep 1821, $150, 234 ac on waters of Baker's Creek, Grant #1715 to John McKEE, Sr., a part where McKEE now lives, transferred by Abe GRESHAM to Alex McKEE on 16 Feb 1817. McKEE shall pay Alex B. GAMBLE $150 due by note of hand together with interest until paid, which payment is to be made against the first of June next. Wit: John RAGON, Hugh HENRY. Following this deed is a note: Samuel HENRY for whose benefit and use the within deed of trust was executed has this day received of Samuel STEEL full and complete payment..for the debt, interest and costs provided for...and transfer all my interest therein to Samuel STEEL. 13 Nov 1822. Sig: Sam HENRY. Wit: Jac F. FOUTE, And M. KEITH. 28 Feb 1823.

310. (2:266-67) David PAULSELL of Greene Co. to John LANE: 26 Sep 1820, $800, 311 ac on waters of Gallaher's Creek, cor to John ORR's original survey of which this is a part and cor to Alexander FOSTER, cor to Edward MORE. Wit: James LANE, Gilbert (X) BLANKENSHIP. 8 Mar 1823.

311. (2:267-68) Alexander WILSON to James SCOTT of Knox Co.: 9 May 1821, $125, 45 ac on Baker's Creek, "purchased [by Wilson] of Joseph GLENN's tract of land #160" (sic). Wit: Joseph McRANDALE, Joseph WILSON, James STEPHENSON. Ack in court June 1821 by James W. STEPHENSON and at Sept court 1822 by Joseph McRANALDS (sic) and Joseph WILSON. 8 Mar 1823.

312. (2:268-69) James HENRY to Adam R. ALEXANDER: 27 Dec 1822, power of atty to deliver to John RAGON a deed for three-fourths part of a 164 ac tract of land granted to James HENRY..on a warrant or certificate and issued in the Fall of 1820...to be laid off so as to be 3/4 of the value of the tract of land as well as of the quantity. Wit: Will WALLACE. 4 Jan 1823.

313. (2:269-70) Edward ROSE to Andrew EARLY: 26 Mar 1821, $250, 122 ac on waters of Pistol Creek, adj Elias DEBUSK. Wit: Silas F. CALDWELL, William EARLY, J. P. HOUSTON. 1 Apr 1823.

314.   (2:270-71) William TURK (first party), Jesse THOMPSON
(second party) to James TURK and Hiram TURK (third party): 12
Aug 1822, to indemnify and secure James and Hiram TURK who are
security for William TURK to John McGHEE, Alexander McGHEE
and Mathew McGHEE, trading as McGHEE AND BROTHERS for
about $370, and the further consideration of $1.00 paid to William
TURK by Jesse THOMPSON,   160 ac, Grant #1611 to Joseph
CASTEL, on waters of Holston River now occupied by William
TURK, assignee of Peter KEE, conveyed to Wm. TURK by
CASTEEL 9 June 1810; also a negro girl MARY. William TURK
shall pay within two months debt of $370. Wit: Alex HARTT, Lewis
RICE?/RESE? 1 Apr 1823.

315. (2:271-72) TRUSTEES OF PORTER ACADEMY to Jack F.
FOUTE: 28 Sep 1820, $173, tract containing one rood in Town of
Maryville, lot #110, Grant #2316 to Trustees of Porter Academy 4
Aug 1812, cor to lot #109 on a back street formerly belonging to John
WILKINSON, cor to lot #111 on which the public jail now stands, adj
the commons. Trustees sig: John McGHEE, Alexander McGHEE,
James BERRY, Andrew THOMPSON, I. MONTGOMERY, D.
CAULDWELL, James GILLESPIE, J. HOUSTON. Wit: A. B.
EMMERSON, John WOODS, Thomas CALDWELL, John
LOWERY. 5 Apr 1823.

316. (2:272-73) David BELL, by his atty John BELL, of Franklin Co.
to David LOGAN: 20 Jan 1820, $650, 235 ac on waters of Little
River adj Peggy NIMEN, Molly TIPTON, David MITCHAL, John
GIBSON. Wit: Alexander LOGAN, James LOGAN. 1 May 1823.

317. (2:273-74) David FREEMAN to John MONTGOMERY: 22 Feb
1823, $412.50, negro girl named SILVIA aged about 17 yrs. Wit:
Jesse THOMPSON. 1 May 1823.

318.   (2:274) James CLARK to Boyd McMURRAY and Hugh
BOGLE: 2 Feb 1822, to secure CLARK in debt of $350 due by bond
dated 2 Feb to John SIMS, 26 ac on waters of Nails Creek, adj Charles
KIRKPATRICK and Alexander THOMPSON, including the mill and
distillery, sorral horse and gold watch. CLARK to pay debt within a

year and three months. Wit: Andrew KIRKPATRICK, Boyd (Paahz?). 20 May 1823.

319. (2:274-75) James CALLAWAY et als to George SNIDER: "State of Tenn. High Wassee [Hiwassee] District: Agreeable to an Act of the General Assembly of the State of TN passed at Murfreesboro the 17th day of Nov 1817, I have caused to be surveyed and laid down for George SNIDER an occupant claim in Cades Cove the waters of Tennessee River..320 ac, adj William TIPTON. Surveyed 5 Sep 1820. Jas CALLAWAY, principal surveyor of High Wassee District. Recorded 28 Feb 1822." "I assign over all my write (sic), title, claim and interest of the within plat and certificate to Jesse HART for value received." 25 March 1822. Sig: George SNIDER. Wit: William TAYLOR, William (X) KINARD. 10 June 1823.

320. (2:275-76) David CAULDWELL, John MONTGOMERY, Barclay McGHEE, George BERRY, George EWING, Jonethan TRIPPET, Jonethan WEAR, William GILLESPEY, John LOWERY and James HOUSTEN to Isaac ANDERSON: 28 Mar 1817, $400, a house and lot #1 in Maryville. Wit: James BERRY, Wm. W. BERRY. 10 June 1823.

321. (2:276) John TEDFORD of Monroe Co. to Joseph NOLEN: 20 May 1822, $325, 160 ac on waters of Nine Mile Creek including the houses, whereon NOLEN now lives, part of Grant #2480 to TEDFORD. Wit: Joseph BLAIR, William TEDFORD. 24 June 1823.

322. (2:276-77) John BOGART to Mathew WALLACE: 7 Dec 1822, $800, 135 ac on waters of Baker's Creek, Grant #552 to Thomas ADAMSON dated 18 June 1809, adj Mathew WALLACE, David EDINGTON, Charles LOGAN, Joseph ORR, David RITCHEY, Henry WILLIAMS. Wit: Saml. M. GAULT, Iredell W. WRIGHT. 24 June 1823.

323. (2:277-78) Thomas HIX to Enoch WATERS: 19 Aug 1822 $600, 50 ac on Little River, Grant #2596. Surveyed 14 June 1809. The "Before Rented lands" are warranted, etc. Wit: William TATE. 25 June 1823.

324. (2:279-80) John GILLESPEY, Anne his wife; Thomas F.
COLBURN, Isabela his wife of the county of Maury, TN; William
WALLACE, Mary his wife; William CORLEY, Jane his wife; William
WALLACE, Jr. and Margaret his wife of Blount Co., heirs of John
CHAMBERLIN, decd, to Robert YOUNG: 28 Jun 1817, $600, 198
ac on waters of Holston River, part of tract of John CHAMBERLIN,
decd, adj Benjamin BONHAM and survey made for William
FORESTER, Edward GOURLEY, William YOUNG, William
HENDERSON. Robert YOUNG acknowledges that the land which
he purchased from Stephen W. BROWN, Hannah, his wife, and James
MOORE formerly the property of John CHAMBERLAIN..is
contained within [this] tract. 1 Jul 1823.

325. (2:280-81) Henry CRESSWELL of Madison Co., Al, to Carter
METTON: 29 Mar 1820, $300, 74 ac in the valley between Bays
Mountain and the pine ridge, on waters of Nails Creek, adj
MALCOM, DAVIS. Wit: John SHARP, Elisha RESE/RICE?. 1 July
1823.

326. (2:281-83) William WALLACE, Sheriff, to James FINLEY: 21
June 1823, $221, 274 ac near the line of Blount and Sevier Co. adj
Isaac HICKEY and others (not named). Public sale to satisfy a
judgment obtained by Robert FINLEY on 6 Mar 1822 against
Alexander SHADDING for $218.76. Wit: Jac F. FOUTE, I. W.
WRIGHT. 7 Jul 1823.

327. (2:283-84) Catherine SIMONS to Michal TEDFORD: 12 Jun
1823. Articles of Agreement; Catherine SIMENS, Sr. agrees to sell to
TEDFORD his wife   Ruth TEDFORD, and Andrew Simons
TEDFORD, Michal's oldest son, and ABALINE? his oldest daughter,
and John Kenneda, TEDFORD's second son and Martha Jane his
second daughter. Catherine reserves the three oldest children as her
attendants during her life; at her decease, TEDFORD..is to have the
three children as his property. TEDFORD [has] full power to till my
part of my plantation for the support of the family, and..his part of the
farming tools and property for use of tilling the plantation until
SIMONS' decease. TEDFORD is to clear land sufficient for the
support of the family and agrees to give the plantation sufficient
attendance for to raise grain for support of family and deliver grain

raised on the plantation at SIMONS' crib and barn until SIMONS' decease with the assistance of SIMONS' working hands. TEDFORD to keep plantation and house and barn in good repair during SIMONS' lifetime sufficient for comfortable living. TEDFORD to keep iron and steel for keeping the tools in good repair and pay tax for the land and taxable property on the plantation. TEDFORD has power to sell grain to get these articles with. He agrees to keep Catharine SIMONS Sr. in a comfortable living while living a single life and to give [her] one cow and two sheep, one horse valued at $50 in money in two years from date, and $5 a year during her lifetime." Sig: Catharine (X) SIMENS. Michal (X) TEDFORD.   Wit: John McCULLOH, Jr., James DELZELL, Robert STERLING, John McCULLOH. Proven at court June 1823 by John McCULLY, Jr. and James DELZELL.   7 July 1823.

328.   (2:284) Catharine SIMONS to Michal TEDFORD: 12 June 1823. Five of my slaves named as follows: Ruth, Andrew, Abaline, John, Martha, for value received of him. Sig: Catherine (X) SIMONS. Wit: James DELZELL, Robert STERLING, John McCULLY, John McCULLY, Jr. 7 July 1823.

329.   (2:284) John WOODS to John McGHEE: 19 Apr 1822, $2512, pursuant to an agreement made 12 Feb 1822, negro slaves MANY?/MONY? and HARRIET, his wife, together with their children MILLY, JULIAN, ELLENER, RALPH, JAMES and WESLEY. Wit: Matt W. McGHEE, Jas. M. ALEXANDER. 18 July 1823.

330.   (2:284-85) John BEATY of Monroe Co. to John McGHEE: 30 Jan 1822, $600, negro boy named ISRAL, slave for life. Wit: A. B. EMMERSON, Jesse THOMPSON. 18 Jul 1823.

331.   (2:285) Samuel VANCE to John McGHEE: 16 Sep 1822, $840, three islands in Little Tennessee River. containing 85 ac, Tucksegee Island containing 34 ac, Grant #7077; Tomotley Island containing 31 ac, Grant #7076; one other Tomotley Island containing 20 ac, Grant #7078, all dated 24 Aug 1822.   Wit: Obediah BOAZ, A. B. EMMERSON. 13 Jul 1823.

332. (2:285-86) Nicholas BYERS to John McGHEE: 23 Jul 1821, $3200, an equal undivided one-half moiety of a 640 ac tract on Little Tennessee River reserved to BYERS by the late treaty between the United States and the Cherokee Nation concluded at Washington city on 27 Feb 1819, on north bank of Tennessee River including Toqua Island, beginning on north bank of the river five poles above Sucoky Branch, about 50 poles below the upper point of said island, etc...Wit: A. B. EMMERSON, Jas. B.U.? RUP, Samuel LOVE. Proven in court June session 1822 by Love and further proven March 1823 by EMMERSON. 18 Jul 1823.

333. (2:286-87) William WALLACE, Sheriff, to Mathew W. McGHEE: 23 Nov 1822, $240.40, two children of a negro woman named JUDE, as property of John S. BURNETTE; public sale 19 Nov 1822. HARRIET aged about 3 yrs, BENJAMIN aged about 8 months. To satisfy two judgments issued 30 July 1822 by James TURK, Justice of the Peace, in favor of John RICHARDSON against John S. BURNETT and John RICHARDSON against John S. BURNETT and John LOWRY, attorney, in the amounts of $103.50 plus $.75 cost and $65.16 plus $.75 costs. Also a judgment issued 15 May 1822 in favour of Samuel HENRY against BURNETTE for $54.77 and $.50 costs. Wit: Jac F. FOUTE, Daniel D. FOUTE. 18 Jul 1823.

334. (2:287-88) John MONTGOMERY to Jesse THOMPSON: 14 Feb 1823, for natural love and affection for Jesse THOMPSON's wife Betsy, my daughter, and for the better maintenance and prefurement of the said Betsy, a negro girl BETSY and her two children HARRIET and ADOLPHIS. Wit: David FREEMAN. 19 July 1823.

335. (2:288) Charles DONOHOO, Sheriff, to David CUNNINGHAM: 21 June 1817, $42.60, 86 ac, the plantation where Andrew VAUGHT lives on Nine Mile Creek; public sale 21 June 1817 to satisfy judgment obtained by Thomas SPRADLING, adminr of Anthony HUGINS?, and another in favor of David BELL, each against VAUGHT. Sig: Charles DONOHOO, Shff by his Deputy John WAUGH. 28 June 1817.

336. (2:288-89) Jeffery JOHNSTON to (trustees) David LOGAN, Abraham PHILIPS, Archible MURPHY, James EDMONSTON,

Robert McCALLEY, Michal SWISHER: 23 Feb 1816, $2, 2 ac, part of tract of land owned by Johnston wherein is erected a Meeting House, for use and benefit of the Methodist Episcopal Church, "wherein all regular ministers authorized by the Methodist Episcopal Church shall have privilege to preach and expand God's Holy Word". Wit: John PHILLIPS, John FARMER. 13 Aug 1823.

337. (2:289-90) John BOWERMAN, Sr. to John BOWERMAN, Jr.: 23 Jun 1823, $60, 128 ac in Miller's Cove on Reed's Creek on north side of Little River, the occupant claim surveyed for Edward MURPHY. Wit: Jac F. FOUTE, Andrew COWAN. 18 Aug 1823.

338. (2:290-91) Robert MORRIS (first party) to William BARNHILL (second party) and Mary DEVINE (third party): 26 March 1821, $257.545 advanced to him by Mary DEVINE and further sum of $1.00 paid by BARNHILL, 76 ac on waters of Baker's Creek, cor to Robert RICHEY, adj Joseph ORR; to secure payment of that amount plus interest to DEVINE by 21 Jan 1820. Wit: Jac F. FOUTE, John F. GILLASPEY. 26 Aug 1823.

339.   (2:291-93) John WILKINSON to James and Ignatious WILSON: 5 Jul 1822, $50, public sale 14 Feb 1822, 114 ac on waters of Ellejoy Creek adj Robert McTEER, Sr., Joseph BOGAL, Samuel BOGAL, Richard WILLIAMS.   A deed of trust tripart between William SHERRELL and Robert McTEER of the first part, John WILKINSON of second part, and James and Ignatious WILSON and Nelson WRIGHT of the third part dated 25 Apr 1821, [was made] to secure payment of $250.36 by 1 Jan 1822 due from SHERRELL to WILSONs. The several debts being due and unpaid, at the request of James and Ignatious WILSON, John WILKINSON exposed to public sale the tract of land; Grant #537 from TN to Robert McTEER. Wit: William TOOL, James CANNON. 13 Sep 1823.

340. (2:293) James P. NELSON of town of Louisville, KY, or Robert BOGAL his atty in fact, to Nancy SCOTT: 24 Dec 1816, $846.31, 404 ac, adj George EWING on Little River, up to mouth of Crooked Creek, George BERRY, George CAULDWELL. Wit: James BERRY, Robert BOYD. 6 Oct 1823.

341. (2:293-94) Samuel SHAW to John TAYLOR: 15 Aug 1822, $500, 100 ac on waters of Baker's Creek, adj (Holden SHANK?), James DUNKIN, Rebecca MONTGOMERY, Thomas MONTGOMERY, part of 622 ac Granted to MONTGOMERY 14 May 1810. Wit: Wm. GRIFFITTS, Nathaniel MORESON, Peter D. WILSON. 9 Oct 1823.

342. (2:294-95) Isaac HAIR to William GRIFFITTS: 7 Apr 1821, $500, 118 ac in Hickory Valley, part of tract conveyed from William DURHAM to HAIR in 1816, adj John MURDOCK, MATHEWS heirs, Nicholas STEVENSON. Wit: John P. CHAPMAN, Isaac W. HAIR, Wm. LEE. 9 Oct 1823.

343. (2:295) James ANDERSON to Samuel JONES: 14 Jun 1823, $57, 20 ac on waters of Gallaher's Creek, adj land formerly John GIBSON's. Wit: James JONES, Mordecai ELLIS. Sig: James M. ANDERSON. 10 Oct 1823.

344. (2:295-96) James JONES to Samuel JONES: 14th day of sixth month 1823, $100 paid by Samuel JONES to David PERKINS, 10 ac, a part of the tract of land sold by Charles DONOHOO, Sheriff, to James as the property of David PERKINS, adj Samuel JONES, a line formerly James ALLEN's. Wit: Mordecai ELLIS, James ANDERSON. 10 Oct 1823.

345. (2:296) Martha ELLIS to Samuel MONTGOMERY: 21 Aug 1823, $14, five negro slaves: DORKAS, AARON, WASHINGTON, EDWIN and ELIZABETH. Wit: Elijah ELLIS, William HART. S: Martha (X) ELLIS. 16 Oct 1823.

346. (2:296-97) John SIMONS to James and Charles REVELY: 21 Apr 1819, $300, 100 ac on waters of Baker's Creek, part of 220 ac granted to Abraham UTTER 7 June 1809, adj Robert THOMPSON. Wit: Wm. McCLUNG, Jas. DICKSEN. Sig: John (X) SIMONS. 11 Nov 1823.

347. (2:297-98) COMMISSIONERS OF MARYVILLE to James WILSON: 24 Sep 1823, $30, lot #9 in Maryville. Wit: Jac F. FOUTE, Josiah DANFORTH. Sig: John MONTGOMERY, Samuel LANE,

Andrew THOMPSON, James HOUSTON, John LOWERY (merchant), Commissioners of Maryville. 8 Dec 1823.

348. (2:298-99) Nicholas BORING to Alexander S. COULTER: 1 Feb 1821, $350, 42 ac on waters of Crooked Creek, adj a line formerly WALLACE's, RANSBURGER. Wit: John B. CUSICK, Ignatious WILSON. 8 Dec 1823.

349. (2:299-300) Alexander S. COULTER to John COLTER, James COLTER, Andrew COLTER, and Maryann COLTER: 26 July 1823, $200, 104 ac on Little River, Grant #2349 to William WILLIAMSON, assignee of Isiah WALKER, adj James TAYLOR, Richard COULTER. Wit: John REAGAN, Thomas (X) HARPER. 8 Dec 1823.

350. (2:300-01) Alexander S. COULTER to John COULTER, James COULTER, Andrew COULTER, and Mary COULTER: 26 Jul 1823, $200, 94 ac on Little River, adj Isaac WALKER, Moses GAMBLE, Andrew GAMBLE, surveyed 14 Mar 1817 for Richard COULTER on Grant #2350. Wit: John RAGON, Thomas (X) HARPER. Sig: Alex S. COULTER. 9 Dec 1823.

351. (2:301) Elizabeth GAMBLE to Jesse WALLACE: 6 Aug 1823, $450, a negro girl named PHILLIS? about 32 yrs of age and her child aged about 6 weeks (a girl). Wit: Daniel D. FOUTE, John WOODS. 9 Dec 1823.

352. (2:301-02) John WEAR of McMinn Co. to Richard GAY: 10 Oct 1820, $200, 42 ac on Crooked Creek. Wit: James McGINLY, Samuel GAY. 9 Dec 1823.

353. (2:302-03) Alexander HENDERSON and John PICKINS, execr of Francis HENDERSON, decd, to Joseph JOHNSON: 20 Sep 1823, by virtue of contract made by Francis in his life in consideration of $100, 25 ac on waters of Rocky Creek, part of Grant #181 containing 136 ac, adj Nathaniel MORRISON. Wit: Wm. McLIN, S. HUMPHRIES. 9 Dec 1823.

354. (2:303-04) Henry WHITTENBURGER, Sr. to Samuel SAFFEL, Charles WARREN, John NORWOOD, Henry WHITTENBURGER,

Jr., Ambrose COX, Benjamin BONHAM, and Henry WHITTENBURGER, Sr., trustees: 22 Feb 1821, $20, 6 ac, on a branch of Lackey's Creek, adj the meeting house, near a spring; trustees shall build a house or place of worship for use of members of the METHODIST EPISCOPAL CHURCH IN USA. Sig: Henry (X) WHITTENBURGER. Wit: Moses HILL, Michal BRIGHT. 10 Dec 1823.

355. (2:304-05) Samuel FRAZIER of Jackson Co., Alabama, to Alexander HENDERSON: 6 Mar 1822, $500, on waters of Gallaher's Creek, all the rest of a tract of 206 ac granted to Frazier except a small piece of land not exceeding 20 ac which FRAZIER conveyed to Major James LOVE, being the north east corner of the land, adj lands granted to Joseph WELDEN, assignee of Joshua PERSENS, John WELDEN and James McWILLIAMS. Wit: John P. THOMPSON, Joel McCORKEL, John J. HENDERSON. 10 Dec 1823.

356. (2:305-06) John HARRELL (first party), to Daniel D. FOUTE (second party), Hugh WEAR and John M. RANKIN (third party): 8 Mar 1823, $1.00 paid by FOUTE to HARRELL and for the purpose of indemnifying WEAR and RANKINS who are sureties for HARRELL in a note executed by HARRELL, WEAR, and RANKIN for $100 payable to the Branch Bank of the State of Tennessee at Maryville; 389 ac on Pistol Creek in the occupation of John HARRELL, Grant #2554 to William HARRIS and conveyed to George DOUGLASS by deed dated 29 Mar 1814, from him to Wm. and Matthew C. HOUSTON, 22 Sept 1817, and to HARRELL, 30 Dec 1822. HARRELL to pay, within 12 months, $100 and damages of the state as the law directs. Wit: David HAMMONTREE, Mury (X) McCONNAL, John T. GILLESPIE, Andrew COWAN. 11 Dec 1823.

357. (2:306) Allen STRAIN and Jane STRAIN to John HENRY: 18 Apr 1823, $500, 91 ac on waters of Nine Mile Creek, adj James HENRY, Robert HAMBLE, heirs of John HENRY, and John PATEN. Wit: David McCAMEY, (Jos. or Jas). ALEXANDER. 11 Dec 1823.

358. (2:307) Samuel JOHNSTON to William DUNWIDDIE of Greene Co.: 13 Aug 1822, $300, 89 ac on Crooked Creek, Grant #841

to George SNIDER on 9 May 1810, adj Wm. WALKER. Wit: James McGINLEY, Joseph R. McGINLEY. 11 Dec 1823.

359. (2:307-09) John EDINGTON of Monroe Co. to Joseph DUNCAN: 22 Feb 1820, $850, 163 ac on Baker's Creek, part of 241 ac granted to Wiley LASSETER, adj lands surveyed for Hugh KELSO, William BEASLEY, Jesse BUTLER and James HALL, Joseph and John LAMBERT. Wit: David M. HUNTER, David RAGON. Proven at March 1820 court by David REGON who made oath that David M. HUNTER signed his name and that HUNTER is not now an inhabitant of the state or so he is informed and believes. 12 Jan 1824.

360. (2:309-10) Heirs of James COOK to Thomas WALLACE: 10 May 1823, $1124, 100 ac on Nine Mile Creek, including the Iron Works, Grist Mill of the estate of James COOK, decd, part of the old tract held by the heirs by right of [sonship?], adj Richard MARTAIN, Ann COOK's dowry line. Wit: Robert HOUSTON, Charles REVES, M. HOUSTON.   Sig: James COOK, Joseph COOK, John McMAHEN, James McMAHEN, Jane McMAHEN, Mary McMAHEN, J. H. BRIGHT, Ann Delea WRIGHT, Elizabeth COOK, Wm. COOK, Robt. COOK, Margaret SLOAN, Alexander COOK. Acknowledged by Robert SLOAN and Margaret his wife 17 May 1823 in presence of John WILKINSON, John HOUSTON. Ack by Alexander COOK 21 May 1823 in presence of M. HOUSTON, Charles REEVES, Robert HOUSTON. [The certification by clerk includes the name "I.A. WRIGHT."] Certified for registration 1 July 1823; registered 12 Jan 1824.

361. (2:310) Thomas WALLACE to Robert HOUSTON: 23 May 1823, $1400, 100 ac on Nine Mile Creek, including the Iron Works and Grist Mill formerly of the estate of James COOK, decd, part of the old tract held by James; adj Richard MARTIN, Ann COOK dowry line. Wit: Wm. McCLUNG, Samuel MONTGOMERY. 12 Jan 1824.

362. (2:310-11) Isaac WILBOURN to Robert HOUSTON: 26 Mar 1823, $350, 24 ac on north side of Nine Mile Creek, part of Grant #2455 of 213 ac to Jesse CONDRAN, adj Sarah LEATHERDALE,

Thomas HART, Ann THOMPSON. Sig: Isaac (X) WILBURN. Wit: John HOUSTON, John HOUSTON, Jr. 13 Jan 1824.

363.   (2:311-12) Thomas and Hiram K. TURK to Dread J. FREEMAN: 28 Mar 1823, $2500, 124 ac, part of Grant #720 to Bonner SHIELDS, cor to the part conveyed to Michael GOODLINK. Wit: Josiah PATTY, Alex HART. 13 Jan 1824.

364.   (2:312-13) Thomas TURK of Blount Co. and Hiram K. TURK of Marion Co. to Dread I. FREEMAN: 28 Mar 1823, $2500, 330 ac on Pistol Creek, part of Grant to William AYLETT, cor to James WEAR. Wit: Josiah PATTY, Alexander HART. 13 Jan 1824.

365.   (2:313-14) Archable JOHNSTON and John B. CUSICK, guardian of the heirs of James WILLIAMSON, decd, to John ADAMSON: 26 Mar 1821, $300, 160 ac in Hickory Valley, being tract granted to WILLIAMSON as assignee of David PARKINS; cor to Allanson WASHAM and Thomas CARTWRIGHT, adj Nicholas STEPHENSON, Samuel WINTERS. Sig: Archer JOHNSTON. John B. CUSICK. Wit: Samuel M. GAUTT, Wm. W. BERRY. 20 Jan 1824.

366.   (2:314-15) Alexander MALCOM to Charles KIRKPATRICK: 22 Dec 1823, $120, 40 ac on Nails Creek, near Alexander THOMPSON's Mill, John McCALLIN. Wit: Jac F. FOUTE, Daniel D. FOUTE. 17 Feb 1824.

367.   (2:315-16) James OLIVER to Rebecca DODD, Elizabeth WHITE, Chapman WHITE, and Catherine WHITE: 20 Aug 1823, $24, 71 ac on waters of Nine Mile Creek, a part of tract whereon Hugh FERGUSEN now lives; adj William MILLER. OLIVER conveys all his title, etc. in the land..."except any supermenry [supplementary] claim..." except the support of William WHITE and Jemimah WHITE his wife, the father and mother of the heirs of the land; they are to have it in their possession during their lifetime and after their demise then it shall fall to the.. heirs, Rebeckah DODD, Elizabeth WHITE Chapman WHITE and Catharine WHITE". Sig: James (X) OLIVER. Wit: John TEMPLETON, Jas. DICKSON. 17 Feb 1824.

368. (2:316) Henry FRANKS to James MITCHEL: 30 Sep 1823, $800, 94 ac on Tennessee River. Wit: George R. (X) BENETT, Jim (X) CARTRIGHT, Moses (X) ROBINETT. 17 Feb 1824.

369. (2:316-17) Joseph ALEXANDER to Jonethan POLAND: 9 Nov 1823, $160, 75 ac on waters of Nine Mile Creek on the dividing ridge between the waters of Nine Mile and Baker's Creek, adj Joseph Josiah HUTTON and others, known by the name of the dry land place, there being no spring on the land. Conveyed by William WALLACE, Esq. Sheriff, by a deed made on 25 Oct 1823. Wit: James HENRY, Jesse KERR. 17 Feb 1824.

370. (2:317-18) Charles DONOHOO, Sheriff, to Josiah CHILDERS: 3 May 1821, $20, 50 ac on Sinking Creek, adj John SIMONS, and land formerly Adam CARUTHERS; public sale 12 Dec 1818 to satisfy judgment for $73.22 recovered by Robert McCULLY against Robert COOPER. Wit: Samuel GAUTT, A. SHELTON, Jac F. FOUTE. 18 Feb 1824.

371. (2:318-19) Joseph HARMEN, by his agent Adam HARMEN of Washington Co., to John McCALL: 8 Mar 1822, $65, 67 ac on south side of Nine Mile Creek, adj the old Indian Line. Sig: Adam (X) HARMEN. Wit: Andrew COWAN, Alfred COWAN. 18 Feb 1824.

372. (2:319) Henry FRANKS to Moses ROBBINETT: 24 Sep 1823, $330, 50 ac on Tennessee River. Wit: Wm. GRIFFITT, George ROBNET, Benjamin ROBNETT. 18 Feb 1824.

373. (2:320) William AYLETT to Francis HICKMAN of Jefferson Co.: 15 Sep 1819, $250, two tracts on waters of Nine Mile Creek; one tract of 151 ac Grant #1654 to Ruben CHARLES, 20 June 1810, and another of 303 ac, Grant #1547 to CHARLES, 18 Jun 1810; conveyed to AYLETT by deed of Charles DONOHOO, Sheriff, 27 Aug 1819. Wit: Robert BOGLE, James McWILLIAMS. 19 Feb 1824.

374. (2:320-21) James McCALLEN to John WOODS: 19 Feb 1821, $500, 133 ac on waters of the west fork of Pistol Creek, cor to Abraham WEAR and Josiah DANFORTH, adj Thomas PRIDE, Robert WILSON; Grant #1629 to Miles and David CUNNINGHAM,

19 June 1810, and conveyed by them to McCALLEN on 20 Oct 1815. Wit: Archible FREEMAN, John WILKINSON. 24 Feb 1824.

375. (2:321-22) Mathew NELSON, Treasurer of East Tennessee, to John TORBET of Marion Co.: 19 Nov 1823, $48.095, 619 ac on Sinking Creek, Granted to Burton PRIDE, public sale 4 Sep 1821 at Maryville, to satisfy the interest and costs on land, by virtue of an act of the General Assembly of the State of Tennessee passed October 19th, 1819, entitled an act to provide for the payment of the interest or monies due from the citizens residing south of French Broad and Holston and between the Rivers Big Pigeon and Tennessee and for other purposes... Wit: Wm. WALLACE, Jac F. FOUTE. 27 Feb 1824.

376. (2:323) John WEAR to Esther RICE, "lately a citizen of Grainger Co.": 22 Mar 1820, $1500, 330 ac on waters of Pistol Creek, "there being 30 ac more contained in the original Grant which was sold to Samuel LOVE and not included in this agreement", cor to James HENDERSON and Thomas HUNTER, adj Robert LOVE, Robert SCOTT, John JAMES, Hugh WEAR, Sr. Originally granted to Hugh WEAR. Wit: James TURK, Thomas TURK. 10 Mar 1824.

377. (2:324) William TIPTON to Joshua JOBE: 3 Dec 1821, $1600, 426 ac on waters of Tennessee River, part of Grant #6730 to TIPTON. Wit: David B. TIPTON, Levinia TIPTON. 12 Mar 1824.

378. (2:324-25) (Reverend) Andrew S. MORRISON to Robert C. and James FULKERSON, all of Lee Co., TN: 18 Apr 1823, $900, 364 ac, part of Grant #719 to Joseph B. LAPSLEY which originally contained 486 ac but out of which 122 ac have been sold to Ephraim DUNLAP. Wit: Wm. GAUTT, P. W. CULTON, John GAUTT. 26 Mar 1824.

379. (2:325-26) Hugh KELSO to Moses SCRUGGS: 9 Mar 1823, $1000, 200 ac on waters of Tennessee River, cor to Thomas SHADDEN. Wit: Joseph DUNCAN, James (X) HAMMONTREE, John R. DUNCAN. 14 Apr 1824.

380. (2:326-27) Henry G. HODGES to William EVANS of Knox Co.: 17 Jan 1824, $275, 207 ac on waters of Nails Creek, part of

Grant to Samuel DAVIS; adj Thomas BUCKANON. Wit: William E. CRESSWELL, Joseph McMURRAY. 13 Apr 1824.

381. (2:327-28) Halburt McCLURE to John COOK: 24 Jul 1823, $340, 280 ac purchased at Sheriff Sale as property of George COOK, conveyed to McCLURE by Charles DONAHOO, Sheriff, on 27 Feb 1822. Wit: Daniel D. FOUTE, Andrew M. KEITH?. 13 Apr 1824.

382. (2:328-29) Aaron HACKNEY to Ephraim LEE: 25 Mar 1822, $100, 9 ac near Gallaher's Creek, part of occupant survey made for John HACKNEY, Sr., adj Ewin ALLEN, cor to survey made for Barclay McGHEE originally. Wit: John HACKNEY, Thos. HACKNEY. 23 Apr 1824.

383. (2:329-30) Thomas HACKNEY to Aaron HACKNEY: 25 Mar 1822, $1000, 31 ac land on Gallaher's Creek, part of occupant survey made for John HACKNEY, Sr. and by him bequeathed to Thomas HACKNEY, adj the Mill Dam, cor to original survey and land conveyed to Aron HACKNEY by Samuel HACKNEY surveyed by John RANKIN....plus one-fourth part of the grist and saw mills which John HACKNEY bequeathed to Thomas HACKNEY. Wit: Ephraim LEE, John HACKNEY. 23 Apr 1823.

384. (2:330-31) John SIMMS to Charles KIRKPATRICK: 20 Mar 1824, $330, 26 ac on Nails Creek, part of Grant #1302, 24 May 1810, to KIRKPATRICK, cor to KIRKPATRICK's original survey, crossing the creek...Wit: Hugh BOGLE, Andrew KIRKPATRICK. 24 Apr 1824.

385. (2:331) Robert THOMPSON to William TIPTON: 21 Feb 1824, "in pursuance of an Article of Agreement entered into for himself and the heirs of David THOMPSON and lodged in the hand of Jonethan TIPTON of Monroe Co. and also the further sum of $100 paid to the treasury of the State," 160 ac, being the north west quarter of Section first of Township fifth of Range first west of the Meridian in the county of McMinn in the Highwassee District". Wit: George HENDERSON, Nancy A. HENDERSON. 24 Apr 1824.

386. (2:331-32) Dorcas WYLIE of Greeneville, TN, admin of Robert WYLY, decd, to Jacob PACK: 24 Apr 1823, $500, undivided half

interest in 282 ac on Little River, cor to Nicholas BARTLET, as described in a Grant to James PEARCE, being the [same] land. Wit: Wm. McCLURE, James W. WYLY. 21 Apr 1824.

387. (2:332-33) State of North Carolina to James GILLASPIE, assignee of Martain ARMSTRONG: 4 Feb 1795, Grant #1326, in consideration of the services of Col. Martin ARMSTRONG, Surveyor of the lands alloted to the officers and soldiers of the Continental line of said State, 640 ac in Greene Co. on Little River, adj John CLARK. Sig: Richard Dobbs Spaight, Governor Captain General and Commander in Chief, at Newburn. Surveyed 15 Nov 1794 by Stockly DONELSON, D.S. Wit: Natl. EWING, John EWING. 28 Apr 1824.

388. (2:333-34) David CAULDWELL, now of Monroe Co., to James TRUNDLE: 19 Mar 1824, $4000, Grant #599, 376 ac on Pistol Creek, adj KING and MONTGOMERY, William WALLACE, Adam SAFLEY,   Samuel   McGAUGHEY,   John   WOODS,   Gideon BLACKBURN. Wit: A. B. EMMERSEN, Wm. THOMPSON. 4 May 1824.

389. (2:334-36) James TURK (first party), Jacob F. FOUTE (second party) and James WILSON, surviving partner of the late firm of James and Ignatious WILSON, merchants (third party): 12 July 1823, for the purpose of securing payment of $1104.01 now owing by James and the late firm of James and Archible TURK to the late firm of James and I. WILSON as evidenced by a note of this date given by James TURK to James WILSON and a note by James and A. TURK 19th May 1819 for $120.87, and 28 April 1820 for $57.33, and 16 July 1821 for $30.87, the first credited with $50 22 June 1820, and the further consideration of $2.00 paid by Jacob F. FOUTE to James TURK; lots #14, 15, and 16 in town of Maryville, where TURK now lives and has his tannery and on which he has his stable. James TURK to pay the sum of $1104.01 plus interest on or before 1 May 1824. Wit: Tarns CONNER, Thomas WILSON. 5 May 1824.

390. (2:336) James TURK to James WILSON: 10 Sep 1823, $500, a negro boy named BILL aged 16 yrs. Wit: A. B. EMMERSEN, Tho. WILSON. 5 May 1824.

391. (2:336-37) Jacob PECK, by his atty in fact, Seth J. W. LACKEY of Jefferson Co., to Andrew McBATH of Knox Co.: 26 May 1823, $1000, 282 ac, an undivided half of a tract on Little River, cor to N. BARTLET, cor to John WHEELER, adj Joseph McFADDEN, Robert PEARCE. Surveyed 11 June 1807. Wit: John R. NELSON, Jno. BOYD, Samuel BOYD. Ack at Knox Co. court 18 Aug 1823. 28 Jun 1824.

392. (2:337) James McMILLAN to William TOOL: 7 July 1823, $400, a negro girl slave named ANNEY aged about 15 yrs. Wit: Jac F. FOUTE, Daniel D. FOUTE. 16 July 1824.

393. (2:337-38) Joseph TIPTON to John SIMINS/SIMMS: 28 Dec 1818, $200, 60 ac on waters of Nails Creek, adj James McCLURG. Sig: Joseph (X) TIPTON. No witnesses. 16 July 1824.

394. (2:338-339) James McCLURG to John SIMMS: 20 Jun 1824, $420, 68 ac on waters of Nails Creek, adj McCLURG's corner. Wit: John PICKINS, William C. McMURRAY. 17 Jul 1824.

395. (2:339) Eboner BIRD to Bennet JAMES: 23 Feb 1824, mortgage, a certain negro boy now belonging to me called JACK, as security for $75 and interest for three years. BIRD to hold the negro boy in his possession until the three years have expired. Wit: Enoch G. LOWERY?. 17 July 1824.

396. (2:339-40) David GIFFIN to Alexander MALCOM: 24 Mar 1822, $520, 108 ac on waters of Little River, adj Andrew GIFFIN, John and David GIFFIN. Wit: John DEARMOND, David DEARMOND. 17 July 1824.

397. (2:340) James MITCHELL to Bennett JAMES: 5 Feb 1824, $800, 94 ac on Tennessee River. Wit: Elijah MITCHAL, Fielder WOODWARD, Benjamin (X) ROBART. 17 Jul 1824.

398. (2:341-42) Thomas CAMPBLE to Daniel DUNN of Greene Co.: 9 Oct 1822, $300, 14 ac in Tuckaleechee Cove, part of Grant #1727. Wit: William HEADRICK, John REAGON. 21 Jul 1824.

399. (2:341-42) Thomas CAMPBLE to Daniel DUNN of Greene Co.: 9 Oct 1822, $300, 33 ac in Tuckaleechee Cove on north side of Little River, adj Fleet MANUEL. DUNN to pay installments not yet paid. Wit: William HEADRICK, John RAGON. 21 July 1824.

400. (2:342-43) Thomas CAMPBLE to Daniel DUNN of Greene Co.: 9 Oct 1822, $300, 28 ac in Tuckaleechee Cove, north side of Little River, adj Thomas CAMPBLE, Patan MANUEL. DUNN to pay installments that are not yet paid. Wit: William HEADRICK, John RAGON. 21 July 1824.

401. (2:343) Bennet JAMES to Fielder WOODWARD: 8 Feb 1823, $400, 117 ac, adj Aaron ALLEN, Henry BOND. Wit: John FRANKS. 21 Jul 1824.

402. (2:344) Jabes THURMAN to Hezekiah FORESTER: 7 Dec 1822, $300, 74 ac on waters of Ellejoy Creek, adj Robert MURRAY, John JOHNSTON, Benjamin TIPTON, Joseph BLACK, Michael McCHOLLEY [McCALLEY?]. Wit: Jesse BARTLETT, Elisha DIXSON. 26 Jul 1824.

403. (2:344-45) James RODDY to Alexander RODDY: 20 Jul 1822, $250, 43 ac, part of Grant #1626 to Samuel COWAN, surveyed 11 Jun 1807, adj James HANNAH. Wit: John JORDON, James HARRIS. 18 Aug 1824.

404. (2:345-46) Samuel WHEELER to John RODDY: 6 Sep 1822, $80, 2 ac on waters of Little River, part of Grant #819. Wit: Samuel RODDY, Edwind McCOY?. 18 Aug 1824.

405. (2:346) Martha FOSTER and Andrew CAULDWELL to William ADAMS: 1 Mar 1815, $33, 127 ac on waters of Gallaher's Creek, part of Grant #3478 to Alexander FOSTER. Sig: Martha (X) FORSTER. Andw. CALDWELL. Wit: John DUNLAP, Spencer BLANKINSHIP. Proven in court Mar 1824 by John Dunlap and June 1824 by Spencer Blankenship. 18 Aug 1824.

406. (2:346-48) David LOWE to John NORWOOD, Sr.: 23 Sep 1816, $500, 100 ac on east and west forks of Lackey's Creek, part of surveys made for John GILLASPEY and Wiley WINFROE, adj Jacob

DYER, Josiah PATTY, Daniel REAGON, John COX. Wit: Andw.
THOMPSON, Jesse THOMPSON, John LOVE. 19 Aug 1824.

407.   (2:348) Josiah PATTY to John NORWOOD: 13 Sep (year
omitted). Patty purchased from David LOWE 55 ac on the east fork
of Lackey's Creek on the north side of the tract made for John
GILLASPEY.. for which LOWE made a deed bearing date 1811 or
1812, which was acknowledged in court but has been misplaced and is
not found on any of the books; the right of the land is vested in LOWE
by contract, and PATTY does not claim any right or make use of the
land; the deed is...to be nul and void and the title remains with LOWE
as though the deed had never been made. Wit: John COX, John
LOVE. Ack at court Sep 1816. 19 Aug 1824.

408.   (2:348-49) Alexander SHADDEN to William McMURRAY: 10
Feb 1824, $666, 221 ac on waters of Nails Creek. Wit: Hugh
BOGLE, William E. CRESSWELL, Thos. HENDERSON. 19 Aug
1824.

409.   (2:349-50) William JONES (first party) to William GRIFFITTS
(second party), Robert JOHNSTON (third party): 11 Nov 1822, $224,
140 ac adj John HANNAH, Alexander FORD; GRIFFITTS is security
for JONES of a debt owed to JOHNSTON. Jones to pay Johnston on
or before 11 Nov 1820 with all accruing costs. Land to remain in
possession of Jones until 11 Nov 1820. Wit: Josiah JOHNSTON, J. H.
HAIRE. 7 Jul 1824.

410.   (2:351-52) Mathew NELSON, Treasurer of East Tennessee, to
James WILSON, surviving partner of the late firm of James and
Ignatious WILSON: 18 May 1824, $30.34, the amount of interest and
costs due, for 184 ac on waters of Holston River, adj Thomas D.
O'CONNER, William BOWERMAN, Alexander STEWARD, Stewart
MONTGOMERY, William JAMES, John ORR, Alexander
FORSTER. Grant #138 to Evan WALLACE 3 May 1810. Public sale
(among others) to satisfy the interest and costs as required by act of
assembly, the same being due and unpaid, on 3 Sept 1821. Ignatious
WILSON, one of partners, was high bidder in behalf of the firm.
"Since the day of sale, Ignatious WILSON...hath departed this life".
Wit: Jacob F. FOUTE, Samuel M. GAULT. 6 Jul 1824.

411. (2:352-53) Isaac TATE to Richard DAVIS: 10 Mar 1823, $200, 35 ac on Little River. Wit: Thomas HARE, William TATE. 4 Dec 1824.

412. (2:353-54) William GILLESPIE to John COX: 2 Nov 1821, $400, 100 ac on waters of Lackey's Creek, a part of the tract whereon William GILLESPIE lives, adj John GILLESPIE, Henry LEE's survey now John COX's, Nathaniel HOOD, McGHEE. Cox to pay State demands of $1 for each acre. Wit: James BERRY, Jac F. FOUTE. 4 Dec 1824.

413. (2:354-55) Mathew NELSON, Treasurer of East Tennessee, to Barkley M. RUSSELL: 18 May 1824, $37.155, the amount of interest and costs due to the state, 388 ac adj [Mary/Mury?] LACKEY, William GREEN, LASSETER, Tennessee River. Grant #2827 to RUSSELL. Public sale 3 Sep 1821. Wit: Jac F. FOUTE, Saml. M. GAULT. 13 Dec 1824.

414.   (2:355-56) William WALLACE, Sheriff, to Joseph ALEXANDER: 29 Oct 1823, $7.25, 75 ac on dividing ridge between waters of Baker's Creek and waters of Nine Mile Creek, adj Josiah HUTTON and others, "lands known by the name of the Dry Land place having no spring thereon". Public sale 22 Mar 1823, to satisfy judgment issued 4 Jan 1823 in favor of TN against James HENRY and William McCAMY, his security. Jesse WALLACE, agent for Joseph ALEXANDER, Esq., was high bidder. Wit: Samuel STEEL, Jesse WALLACE. 13 Dec 1824.

415. (2:356-57) David WILSON of McMinn Co. to John W. WILSON: 24 Sep 1824, $600, 138 ac, adj John WALKER, Samuel JONES, Thomas GIBSON, Michael BOWERMAN. Surveyed 18 May 1807. Wit: Hugh P. WILSON, Samuel DIXSON. 13 Dec 1824.

416. (2:357) James BADGETT, Jr. to Betsey DONCARLAS: 8 Jul 1823, $600, 100 ac, on Little Tennessee River adj Samuel JOHNSTON, James HART. Wit: Samuel BADGETT, Carter McCARLASE, William C. CARLASE. Reg omitted.

417. (2:357-59) Mathew NELSON, Treasurer of East Tennessee, to John McGHEE, Alexander McGHEE and Mathew McGHEE, trading

as McGHEE & BROTHERS: 18 May 1824, $49.55, 512 ac on Baker's Creek, being Grant #2491 to John GLASS assignee of James LOGAN; adj Edward DIXSON, MONTGOMERY, JOHNSTON, ORR, Samuel JOHNSTON, WILSON/MELSON?, Samuel DIXON, John WOODY. Public sale 4 Sep 1821 to satisfy the unpaid interest and costs on the grant. Wit: Jacob F. FOUTE, Samuel M. GAULT. 21 Dec 1824.

418. (2:359-60) Thomas STANFIELD to David GRULBS: 20 Jul 1824, $2,000, 276 ac on Gallaher's Creek, Granted by TN to James McCLANAHAN, assignee of John HANNAH, adj the Creek, William JONES, David GRULBS. Wit: John STANFIELD, Edwin G. STANFIELD. 22 Dec 1824.

419. (2:360) James BADGETT, Sr. to Bestey DONCARLAS: 8 Jul 1823, $610, 89 ac on Little Tennessee River adj Robert WEAR, James HALL, cor to tract formerly owned by James I. GREEN. Wit: Carter M. CARLAS, Samuel BADGETT, William C. CARLAS. 24 Dec 1824.

420. (2:360-61) Jesse KERR to John THOMPSON: 18 Mar 1824, $400, negro girl named MATILDA. Wit: William AULD?, Archabald SLOAN. 24 Dec 1824.

421. (2:361-62) Enos ADAMSON of Jefferson Co. to Thomas STANFIELD: 6 July 1824, $2400, 276 ac on Gallaher's Creek, grant #1159 to James McCLANAHAN, assignee of John HANNAH, adj John COPLAND, Wm. JONES, William WATKINS. Wit: Samuel LOVE, Jesse WALLACE. 6 Jan 1825.

422. (2:362) James CREWS to Tobler VINYARD: 27 Mar 1824, $244, 85 ac on waters of Little River, adj Robert CHILDERS, Nathaniel WATSON, ALLISON. Wit: James GILLESPEY, Alexander SHADDEN. 7 Jan 1825.

423. (2:363) John HOUSTON to Nathaniel TORBET: 27 Dec 1824, $804, 225 ac on waters of Pistol Creek, adj John HANLEY, cor to heirs of William HOUSTON, decd, Thomas TURK, Banner SHIELDS, John MONTGOMERY, Doctor WRIGHT's ferry road, the

road that leads from John HANLEY's to Benjamin JAMES. Wit: J. HOUSTON, A. EARLY. 11 Jan 1825.

424. (2:363-64) David H. CRAIG and Elen CRAIG, his wife, of Limestone Co., AL, to William TOOL, of town of Maryville: 13 Oct 1824, $100, the undivided one-fifth part of the following property: one-half of an undivided interest in lot #33 on Main Street; lot #83, a middle lot on the plat of town of Maryville; an undivided one-half of a parcel containing two ac lying near the town of Maryville, adj the Great Road leading from Maryville to Tellico on a line of original survey made for Barcley McGHEE and John LOWERY. ..being our interest as devised of the estate of John TOOL, lately decd, which property was held by John TOOL before his death and Samuel LOVE jointly together. Wit: Daniel D. FOUTE, Joseph McCLURE. Sig: Elen (X) CRAGE. 11 Jan 1825.

425. (2:364-65) James TOOL of Lincoln Co., TN, to William TOOL: 14 Sep 1824, $100, my undivided one-fifth part of lots #33 and #81 in Maryville; also a tract of land containing two ac [same description as in deed above]. Wit: Daniel D. FOUTE, George W. FOUTE. 11 Jan 1825.

426. (2:365-66) Polly WHITE, relict and widow of [name omitted] WHITE, decd, formerly Polly TOOL, now of Madison Co., AL: 14 Oct 1824, whereas John TOOL lately departed this life.. possessed of an undivided one-half of lots #33 and #81, also two ac, [same as deeds above]. John TOOL, having made his last will and testament which was proven and admitted to record in County Court of Blount County, [and] appointed that his interest in the aforesaid premises should descend in fee to his brothers James TOOL, Mathew TOOL and William TOOL, and sisters Eleaner CRAGE and Polly WHITE. Wit: Daniel D. FOUTE, Joseph McLANE. Sig: Polly (X) WHITE. 12 Jan 1925.

427. (2:366) Samuel LOVE to William TOOLE: 20 Nov 1824, $250, one half of lot #81 in Maryville. Wit: James BERRY, Wm. W. BERRY. 12 Jan 1825.

428. (2:366-68) Benjamin McCOOL and Margaret McCOOL, his wife, formerly Margaret V. O'CONNER, widow and relict of John

O'CONNER, decd, to William TOOL: 27 Dec 1824, $100, the undivided one-sixth part of the share or bequeath of Thomas CONNER, being the share inherited by John CONNER, decd. Tarrence O'CONNER, Sr. decd, late of Blount Co. was possessed of 240 ac on waters of Gallaher's Creek, Granted to Tarrance O'CONNER by TN; [in his will] he directed that the farm on which he lived at the time of his death descend equally to seven of his sons: James, Thomas, Joseph, Tarrance, John, Jeremiah, and Patrick B. O'CONNER. Thomas O'CONNER, one of the legatees, died intestate without issue and his undivided share descended to the other brothers and sisters in common. John O'CONNOR intermarried with Margaret V. HURDLEY and her issue of one daughter, named Ann, died intestate as a minor. Margaret has since married Benjamin McCOOL. Sig: Benjamin (X) McCOOL. Margaret McCOOL. Wit: Jac F. FOUTE, Joseph ALEXANDER. Proved as to Benjamin at Dec session 1824 and court appointed Jr. NORWOOD and George EWING, Esqs., two of their own body to take the privy examination of Margaret. 12 Jan 1825.

429. (2:368) James TURK to Edward MITCHELL: 29 Nov 1824, consideration omitted, lots #14, 15, and 16 in Maryville; adj #13 belonging to Obadiah BOAZ, lot #17 belonging to John SHARP, the commons. Wit: David A. MAUGH, Alexander HABE, Jr. The following note is appended: "MITCHELL is to have privilege of conveying the water from my spring on my farm in pipes to his Tanyard if he thinks proper in a way to do the least injury to my meadow." 14 Jan 1825.

430. (2:368-69) *Isham BLANKINSHIP to James I. GREEN of Roane Co.: 25 Jun 1824, $400, 149 ac, adj Alexander LOGAN. Original Grant #1245 to Alexander PATERSON assignee of Alexander CRAGE, and purchased by GREEN under a Deed of Trust made by James LOVE to John McGHEE AND BROTHERS, and also under three executions of Robert CONNER against James LOVE and James I. GREEN. Wit: Spencer BLANKINSHIP, Miller BRADBERY. 14 Jan 1825. [*This is a clerical error. The land is conveyed by GREEN to BLANKINSHIP.]

78   Blount County, Tennessee, Deeds 1819 - 1833

431. (2:369-70) Dread I. FREEMAN to James FREEMAN: 1 Feb 1824, $3000, 330 ac, on Pistol Creek, part of a Grant to William AYLETT, cor to James WEAR. Wit: Jesse THOMPSON, Baniss/Burriss? E. BORING. 15 Jan 1825.

432. (2:370-71) Dread FREEMAN to James FREEMAN: 21 Feb 1824 $1000, 125 ac , part of Grant #720 to Daniel SHIELDS, adj Michal GOODLINK. Wit: Jesse THOMPSON, James E. BORING. 15 Jan 1825.

433. (2:371-72) "State of Tennessee, Highwassee District: Agreeable to an act of the General Assembly of State of TN passed at Murfresboro on 17 Nov 1819, I have caused to be survaied (sic) and laid down for George SNIDER an occupant claim in Cades Cove...320 ac, adj William TIPTON, surveyed 5 Sep 1820. William PENNINGTON, Daniel RAGON, CC. Sig: Jas. CALLAWAY, principal Surveyor, Highwassey District (sic). 9 July 1825." Registered 28 Feb 1825. Following the above is: "I assign over all my ...title [to] the within plat and certificate to Isaac HART for value received. 25 Mar 1822. George SNIDER." Wit: William TAYLER, William KNARD. Followed by: "I assign my..title..[to] the within plat and certificate to John and William HENDERSON for value received. 27 Dec 1824. Sig: Isaac (X) HART." 15 Jan 1825.

434. (2:372) John LOCKIN to John EAKIN: 5 Feb 1824, $600, 96 ac on waters of Baker's Creek, part of Grant #1272 to David RICHY for 311 ac dated 28 May 1810, adj land granted to Joseph ORR. Wit: David REED, William BARNHILL. 17 Jan 1825.

435. (2:372-73) Moses ELLIOT to John EAKIN: 27 Jan 1824, $225 , 76 ac on waters of Baker's Creek, part of Grant #1273 to David RICHEY for 311 ac dated 23 May 1810, cor to Robert RICHEY, Joseph ORR. Wit: Thomas MONTGOMERY, William BARNHILL. 17 Jan 1825.

436. (2:373-74) Samuel COWAN, Sheriff, to William COLEBURN: 30 Nov 1811, $50.06, Public Sale to satisfy judgment against Robert EAKIN obtained by Robert McCULLY. Wit: Samuel EAKIN, J. B. HENDERSON. Followed by: "Know all men by these presents that I Wm. COLBURN, do assign the within Sheriff Deed to the said Robert

EAKIN, Jr., the son of Samuel. Given under my hand and seal 20th Dec 1811. Wit: John HICKEY, Joseph HACKNEY, James O'CONNOR. 17 Jan 1825."

437. (2:374-75) William WALLACE to Arthur B. CAMPBLE: 28 Dec 1824, $35, 11 ac on waters of Lackey's Creek, part of land whereon WALLACE now lives, adj survey made for James HOUSTON, James John Robert GILLESPIE (sic), tract previously conveyed to Arthur B. CAMPBLE, John GILLESPIE. Wit: James GILLESPIE, J. GILLESPIE. 18 Feb 1825.

438. (2:375-76) Alexander STUART to Philip DAVIS: 9 Sep 1824, $500, 93 ac in Tuckaleechee Cove on south side of Little River, adj Robert MONTGOMERY, Steven STAFORD. Wit: Peter SNIDER, Samuel DAVISON. 18 Jan 1825.

439. (2:376) John HENRY to James DUNLAP: 13 Sep 1824, $500, 91 ac on waters of Nine Mile Creek, adj James HENRY, Robert HAMMEL, heirs of John HENRY, decd, and John POLAND; part of tract granted to Michal HIGANS and left by will to Allen and Jane STRAIN and conveyed by them by deed to HENRY on 18 Apr 1823. Sig: John (X) HENRY. Wit: John DUNLAP, Samuel McCLARG, Henry DUNLAP. 18 Jan 1825.

440. (2:376-77) John ROGERS to William McCAMY: 21 Sep 1816, $65, 31 ac on waters of Ellejoy Creek, adj William KEEBLE. Sig: John (X) ROGERS. No witnesses. 22 Jan 1825.

441. (2:377-78) William HARTGRAVE to Archible HITCH: 22 Aug 1823, $300, 52 ac on waters of Little River, beginning at top of the ridge between John EWING and HITCH, cor to small tract containing six ac ..conveyed by Wm ANDERSON to HITCH, adj Adison SHARP, John EWING. Wit: Billey HOLLOWAY, Alex McNUTT. Sig: William HASTINGS (sic). 22 Jan 1825.

442. (2:378-79) William W. HENRY of Baker's Creek (first party) to Alexander B. GAMBLE (second party) and Samuel HENRY of Little River (third party): 3 Feb 1824, $648.69 borrowed from and due on 28 June next by William HENRY to Samuel HENRY, and the further sum of $5 by GAMBLE to Wm. W. HENRY, 252 ac on Baker's

Creek, cor to Samuel HENRY; cor also to 56 ac of land purchased by Wm. W. HENRY from Robert McCABE, part of Grant #1056. Wit: James HENRY, Moses GAMBLE. 31 Jan 1825.

443. (2:379-80) James WILLIAMS to Markee TIPTON: 22 Mar 1825, $260, negro boy named FORNEY, between 8 and 9 yrs of age. Sig: James (X) WILLIAMS. Wit: Jessee RHEA, John CETCHEN? 2 May 1824.

444. (2:380) James MARTIN to William TOOLE: 31 Mar 1825, $67, land on waters of Crooked Creek entered at the Entry Taker's Office, Entry #13 dated 7 Apr 1824, and granted to him by Grant #9719 on 24 Nov 1824, adj John MEARS survey, Henry LUSTER, John B. CUSICK. Wit: John WILKINSON, James BERRY. 14 Apr 1825.

445. (2:381) William WALLACE, Sheriff to William TOOLE: 11 Feb 1825, $10, 257 ac on waters of Gallaher's Creek adj lands of William DAVIS and others; public sale 25 Dec 1824 to satisfy judgment issued against estate of Joseph O'CONNER obtained by William TOOL for $98.67 damages plus $13.005 for costs. Wit: Wm. W. BERRY, Jonas BERRY. 14 Apr 1825.

446. (2:382) William RAPER of Monroe Co. to William THOMAS of Maryville: 20 Dec 1824, $102, 61 ac in the Long Hollow, adj Mark LOVE, John JAMES. Wit: J. G. CHAMBERS, Daniel D. FOUTE. 15 Apr 1825.

447. (2:382-83) Shadrick HICKS of McMinn Co. to William THOMAS: 28 Mar 1825, $200, 92 ac in the Long Hollow, being the residue of tract which HICKS sold to William RAPER which was Grant #1812 to William JAMES dated 24 May 1810, adj Mark LOVE, John JAMES, MONTGOMERY. Wit: William CHANDLER, Daniel D. FOUTE. 15 Apr 1825.

448. (2:383-84) Shadrick HICKS to William RAPER: 21 Jun 1816, $200, 61 ac, part of tract surveyed for William JAMES in the Long Hollow, adj Mark LOVE, John JAMES. Wit: James DOYEL, Talbert HIX. 15 Apr 1825.

449. (2:384-85) William JAMES of Monroe Co. to Shadrick HICKS of McMinn Co.: 29 May 1820, $150, 153 ac in the Long Hollow, being a survey made for William JAMES in the year 1807, adj Mark LOVE, John JAMES, MONTGOMERY. Wit: Jac F. FOUTE, John LOWERY. 15 Apr 1825.

450. (2:385-86) William WALLACE, Sheriff, successor to Charles DONOHOO, to Jacob F. FOUTE of Maryville: 5 Apr 1824, $170, 97 ac on waters of Baker's Creek, on which Wm. THOMPSON formerly lived, cor to James LOGAN and William W. HENRY, John McKEE, James EDMISTON. Grant #1152 to Alexander McKEE. Public Sale 6 July 1822 held by former Deputy Sheriff William FAGG to satisfy judgment against William THOMPSON for $13.0075 recovered by Tarrence CONNER. Wit: John F. GILLESPEY, Daniel D. FOUTE. 16 Apr 1825.

451. (2:386-87) Taylor SNEED to Archible STONE: 11 Apr 1823, $95, "a tract of land being the south east quarter of Section 31 of Township 3 north in range 10 west in the tract appropriated by the Act of Congress for Military Bounties in the Territory of Arkansas due me...for my services in the Late War between the United States of America and Great Britain as a Corporal in Clinche's Company of the Seventh Regiment of Infantry." Sig: Taylor (X) SNEED. Jeremiah LANE/LOVE? Wit: James (X) BELL, Archible SLONE, Terns CONNER. 24 Apr 1825.

452. (2:387) James McDONAL to Michal BOWERMAN: 9 June 1824, $800, negro woman and two children by name CATHERINE, JO and GEORGE. Wit: Henry BOWERMAN, James MAXWELL. 24 Apr 1825.

453. (2:387-88) James FREEMAN to John DEVER: Mar 1825, $3000, 246 ac on waters of Little River, part of Grant #1966 to Samuel GLASS, adj Richard KIRLY, James TRICE?, Isaac BOWMAN, Richard CHANDLER. Witnesses omitted. 28 Apr 1825.

454. (2:388-89) Alexander MALCOM to John STEPHENS: 23 Mar 1825, $600, 108 ac on waters of Little River, beginning at a line between 7th and 8th cor of tract granted to Andrew GIFFIN, on the

conditional line between John and David GIFFIN. Wit: James LUSK, Joseph GRASTON. 29 Apr 1825.

455. (2:389-90) James HENDERSON to Thomas HUNTER: 26 Feb 1825, $100, 30 ac on waters of Pistol Creek, part of tract surveyed for Edward BUCKHANHAN, adj HUNTER, Hugh WEAR. Wit: Alexander McKEE, Joseph CALL. 30 Apr 1825.

456. (2:390) William WALLACE, Sheriff, to John S. BURNETT*: 15 May 1822, $370.25, negro woman, property of John S. BURNETT, public sale to satisfy two judgments against BURNETT, one in favor of Jesse KERR for $205, the other in favor of Thomas WEAR for $274. 3 May 1825. [*Error; property was sold to William TURK.]

457. (2:390-91) John WEAR, Sr. to Daniel D. FOUTE: 28 Jan 1825, $415, and the further consideration of the bond by me executed to FOUTE to make title to land by me sold to James WEAR and by the said JAMES sold to FOUTE, cor with land formerly owned by Joseph WEAR and William HENRY. Wit: Wm. WALLACE, Wm. ANDERSON. Proved in court by Wm. WALLACE and William W. ANDERSON Mar 1825. 14 May 1825.

458. (2:391-92) James MONTGOMERY to Benjamin BINGHAM: 20 Sep 1823, $277.03, 64 ac on Baker's Creek adj Mathew WALLACE, Thomas ROACK, John WILSON, Charles LOGAN, Thomas ADAMS; Grant #1505 dated 15 June 1810. Wit: Joseph B. LOGAN, John MILLER. 17 May 1825.

459. (2:392-93) Peter P. DAVIS, Sr. to William TIPTON: 28 Feb 1825, $400, 31 ac on waters of Ellejoy Creek, adj Hugh BOGLE, SIMMONS?. Wit: John SIMMONS, Thomas (X) DAVIS. 17 May 1825.

460. (2:393) Holburt McCLURE to John McCLURE: 28 Mar 1825, $500, 112 ac on waters of Little Tennessee River, beginning on the bank of river below a bluff, adj Joseph LAMBERT. Wit: Joseph McRANDLES, John McCOOL. 17 May 1825.

461. (2:394) James HENRY to Jesse KERR: (day omitted) March 1820, $150, 91 ac on waters of Nine Mile Creek, adj James HENRY, Robert HAMIL, John HENRY. Wit: William HARRIS, Rebacer LOFTAS. 18 Jul 1825.

462. (2:394-95) David THOMPSON to Samuel THOMPSON: 1 Nov 1824, $400, 185 ac on Nine Mile Creek, adj Silas GEORGE, William MORE, William CRANSHERE, Ruben CHARLES. Wit: William TOOLE, Joseph McCLAIN. 22 Jul 1825

463. (2:395-96) John LOWERY of Monroe Co. to William TOOLE of Maryville: 7 Jun 1825, $175, 2 ac on Pistol Creek, adj the commons of Maryville, John RUSSELL, John WOODS, Jacob DANFORTH. Wit: James BERRY, Wm. W. BERRY. 23 Jul 1825.

464. (2:396) Holburt McCLURE to Joseph McREYNOLDS: 27 Jun 1825, $1,000 (mortgage), 196 ac where McCLURE now lives, on waters of Little Tennessee River, adj James GREENWAY, George COOK, John BIBAL, John FRANKS. McCLURE is to pay to McREYNOLDS the full sum of $1000 before seven years after date. Wit: James HENRY, Martin ROWIN. 25 Jul 1825.

465. (2:396-97) Holburt McCLURE to Sally McREYNOLDS: 27 Jun 1825, $100, negro girl JANE. Wit: Jesse THOMPSON, John NORWOOD. 23 Jul 1825.

466. (2:397) Benjamin TIPTON to James DAVIS, Sr.: 25 Oct 1824, $400, 192 ac on bank of the Creek (not named), the 11th corner of original survey of 341 ac made for TIPTON. Wit: Jac F. FOUTE. 25 Jul 1825.

467. (2:397-98) William AYLETT to Ephraim DUNLAP: 11 Sep 1819, $260, 122 ac on waters of Baker's Creek part of tract originally surveyed and Granted to Joseph B. LAPSLEY. There is due to the state on the land the sum of $222 with interest. Wit: John DUNLAP, William EDMUNDSON. 25 Jul 1825.

468. (2:398-99) Jesse KERR to Joseph COOK: 4 Jul 1823, $305, 270 ac on waters of Nine Mile Creek including the house where Joseph BLAIR lives, part of Grant #2485 to Robert FERGUSON; adj John

TEDFORD. Wit: George (X) DAVIS, Arch SLOAN, David (X) KERR.

469. (2:399-400) Dorcas WYLEY, by her atty Jas. W. WYLEY of Green Co., to Andrew McBATH of Knox Co.: 3 May 1823, $1000 "in Tennessee bank notes of good currency", an undivided half of 282 ac on Little River   adj N. BARTLETT, John WHEELER, Joseph McFADEN, Robert PEARCE, surveyed 11 Jun 1807. Wit: John B. NELSON, Jno. BOYD, Samuel BOYD. 29 Aug 1825.

470. (2:400-01) William WALLACE, Sheriff, to Enoch PERSONS of Alabama: 4 Jan 1825, $120, 76 ac on waters of Pistol Creek, Grant #877 to George   WORLEY dated 11 May 1810 adj James HOUSTON, the land whereon John McNEELY formerly lived, James WEAR, Worley's Branch, surveyed January 22, 1807. Public sale 24 Jan 1825 to satisfy judgment issued 13 Sep 1824 in favour of James TURK, Chairman for Blount County,   against John LOWERY, merchant, John NICHOL and Enoch PARSONS, for $1700.85 together with interest.   Silas PARSONS as agent for Enoch PARSONS became high bidder. Wit: Jesse WALLACE, Wm. THOMPSON. 6 Jan 1826.

471. (2:401) Enoch PARSONS of AL to James WEAR: 23 Sep 1825, $300 ($275 of which has been paid to Parsons and $75 paid by Wear to State of TN), 76 ac adj James HOUSTON, cor to James HOUSTON and John McNEELY, James WEAR, Worley's branch; last sold upon execution in favor of the Chairman of Blount County against John LOWRY former Trustee and Enoch PARSONS and John NICHOLS his securities and purchased by PARSONS. Tract is yet liable to a redemption. Wit: J. MONTGOMERY, J. HOUSTON. 5 Jan 1826.

472. (2:402) Enoch PARSONS of AL to James WEAR: 22 Sep 1825, "for divers good causes", power of atty, "if John LOWERY, merchant, or any creditor of his or creditors, should hereafter offer to redeem a tract of land by me purchased in January last being sold as the property of said LOWERY allow any credit and enter the same, which shall not be above the sum which I paid over and above the price of said land upon said execution as one of the securities of said

LOWERY and discharge LOWERY for such sum hereby ratifying and confirming whatsoever my said attorney shall for me and in my name do"... Wit: J. MONTGOMERY, J. HOUSTON. 5 Jan 1826.

473. (2:402) John BLACK to Daniel D. FOUTE: 21 Jan 1825, $500, a mulatto boy named JAMES, about 21 or 22 years of age. Wit: Andw. THOMPSON, John SAFFELL. 6 Jan 1826.

474. (2:402-03) John STRAIN to Andrew EARLY: 20 Jul 1825, $600, two tracts on waters of Pistol Creek, one tract of 56 ac cor to James PAULY, adj John McCULLEY, crossing the creek four times, DeBUSK. The other of 43 ac cor to DeBUSK's original survey, then with a direct line formerly made between James McCOLLUM, Sr. and James McCOLLUM, Jr., John McCulley, LONG?.   Wit: James BERRY, John HOUSTON. 6 Jan 1826.

475. (2:403-04) Samuel HOUSTON to John STRAIN: 23 Jul 1825, release of deed of trust made by STRAIN on 16 June 1825 of [his] plantation ...to secure the payment of $157.75 due to James and William W. BERRY. STRAIN has made payment. Wit: William TOOL, John HOUSTON. 6 Jan 1826.

476. (2:404) John REAGON to Alexander S. COULTER: 2 Oct 1824, $500, 133 ac on Little River, adj Richard COULTER, Moses GAMBLE, "on a great road to John REAGON from Andrew GAMBLE bearing date 4 Nov 1818" (sic) [there is an omission in the clerk's transcription]. Wit: Samuel HENRY, James HENRY. 7 Jan 1826.

477. (2:405) Jas. McCLURG to Jas. HAMBLE: 13 Dec 1824, $400, 96 ac on waters of Nails Creek, land Gelly CROWS now lives on, adj John SIMS and James BOYD, "the land I live on", John PICKINS and Boyd McMURRAY. Wit: George TEDFORD, John TEDFORD. 20 Jan 1826.

478. (2:405-06) Samuel GOULD and John LOWERY to John BURT and William GARNER: 17 Sep 1825, $700, 220 ac on Nine Mile Creek. Witnesses omitted. 23 Jan 1826.

479.   (2:406-07) Alexander NORTON to David VANCE: 13 Oct 1823, $800, 122 ac on Little River, Granted to Benjamin ROGERS, adj John REAGON. Wit: Hugh BOGLE, Nicholas MORTON. 23 Jan 1826.

480.   (2:407-08) George HADDEN to Jacob M. HADDEN: 16 Apr 1824, $453, 88 ac on waters of Ellejoy Creek containing the half of a small spring, adj George HADDEN, John WILLIAMS. Wit: Nathaniel JEFFARS, John WILLIAMS. 26 Jan 1826.

481.   (2:408) John KENNEDY to William EWING: 7 Nov 1825, $600, 197 ac on west fork of Baker's Creek, adj Michel H. MARTIN and   John   KENNEDY,   Alexander   McKEE,   heirs   of   Samuel BLACKWELL. Wit: Alijah CONGER, Wm. N. EWING.   26 Jan 1826.

482.   (2:408-09) William TOOL to Samuel LOVE, both of Maryville: 20 Nov 1824, $200, an undivided half of 2 ac near the town of Maryville on east side of the great road leading from Maryville to Tellico on the line of original survey made for Barcley McGHEE and John LOWRY. Wit: James BERRY, Wm. W. BERRY. 27 Jan 1826.

483.   (2:409-10) John RANKIN to James DUNCAN: 2 Dec 1825, $200, 67 ac on Holston River, Granted to RANKIN, corner to survey made for David VAUT. Wit: Saml. U. RANKIN, James W. EWING. 27 Jan 1826.

484.   (2:410) James McGINLEY to "his Reputed Son" (sic) Joseph McGINLEY: 25 July 1822, "in consideration of Joseph being a dutiful son", 100 ac on Crooked Creek, part of Grant #1719 to James, 22 June 1810, taking in Joseph's house. Wit: William ALEXANDER, Isaac WELLS, James BROWN. 27 Jan 1826.

485.   (2:410-11) Samuel M. GAUTT of McMinn Co. to Jacob F. FOUTE of Maryville: 13 Jan 1826, $782.50, 260 ac on Pistol Creek, cor to John WILKINSON, adj Hugh and Joseph WEAR, Barcly McGHEE, John DUNCAN, Grant #2385 to Robert GAUTT dated 29 June 1812, surveyed 23 July 1807. Wit: James BERRY, Campble WALLACE. 9 Feb 1826.

486. (2:411-12) Sarah ELLIOT, Administrator of estate of West ELLIOT, decd, to Martain ROREX: By virtue of an act of the General Assembly passed at Knoxville on 5 Nov 1817 empowering her to sell such part of the real estate of West ELLIOT as may be necessary for the payment of debts and in consideration of $150 paid by ROREX in discharge of a debt due from the estate to the state of TN, 73 ac on waters of Crooked Creek, adj BLACK's original grant, WALLACE, Henry THOMAS' original grant, corner to a ten acre piece of said Grant sold by Henry THOMAS, the original Grant to Jacob NIMON, being a part of the tract originally granted by Tennessee to Henry THOMAS and sold by him to West ELLIOTT. Wit: Samuel M. GAUTT, James M. ALEXANDER, Jr. 9 Feb 1826.

487. (2:412-13) Jonethan TRIPPET to John POLAND: 27 Sep 1824, $360, 150 ac on waters of Nine Mile Creek, part of an original tract now occupied by William HARRIS also being that part whereon John POLAND now lives, cor to James HENRY. Wit: Jesse WALLACE, S. W. WALLACE. 11 Feb 1826.

488. (2:413-15) Isaac ANDERSON, James BERRY, David CALWELL, Andrew THOMPSON, James HOUSTON, Dr. Alexander McGHEE, Thomas HENDERSON, John MONTGOMERY and John LOWERY, all TRUSTEES of MARYVILLE FEMALE ACADEMY, to John A. McKAMY of Hawkins Co., Joseph HAMBLETON of Jefferson Co., Hugh L. WHITE of Knox Co., John McGHEE of Blount Co. and David RAWLINS of Rhea Co., trustees for the SOUTHERN AND WESTERN THEOLOGICAL SEMINARY: 26 Apr 1820, $600, one half of lot #42 in Maryville with the brick house thereon. Public sale 1 Apr 1820. Joseph TEDFORD was high bidder on behalf of the trustees. Wit: Jacob F. FOUTE, Arthur B. EMMONSON, Daniel D. FOUTE, Azaciah SHELTON. 10 Feb 1826.

489. (2:415) Archey MURPHY to David NIMON: 19 Feb 1825, $200, 62 ac on waters of Little River, part of Grant #2567 to Joseph NICHOLSON, conveyed by him to Murphey on 28 Sep 1818, cor to HAFLEY, adj INGRAM. NIMON is surety on a note for MURPHY for payment of $96 to Thomas HICKS and also for the stay of an execution for $60 on a judgment obtained by Hugh BOGLE,

administrator of the estate of Henderson McMURRAY before
Alexander B. GAMBLE, Esq., a Justice of the Peace, and for the stay
of execution on a judgment obtained by John F. GARNER against
MURPHY for $55. Wit: John WILKINSON, John WILKINSON, Jr.
17 Apr 1826.

490. (2:416-17) John KING of Morgan Co. to William BURNES: 30
Oct 1824, $1000, 243 ac on waters of Sinking Creek. Wit: John L.
McKINSEY, George ROGERS, M. C. HOUSTON. 17 Apr 1826.

491.   (2:417) Daniel D. FOUTE to John HENCLE and Lott
HENCLE: 9 Sep 1825, $300, 97 ac on road leading from Maryville to
Sevierville , grant #780 to John WOODS, cor to James TRUNDLE
and William WALLACE, adj James BERRY.   Wit: James
TRUNDLE, Peter LANDER. 18 Apr 1826.

492. (2:418) Samuel TORBET to John TORBETT: 24 Mar 1826, for
"natural love and affection unto his son", 233 ac deeded by John
HICKLAND, beginning at lower end of survey cor to Peter
BOWERMAN, cor to Hugh TORBET. Wit: Samuel TORBETT. 19
May 1826.

493. (2:418-19) Samuel TORBETT, Sr. to Samuel TORBET, Jr.: 24
Mar 1826, "for natural love and affection unto his son", part of tract of
235 ac deeded by John HICKLAND, Sr.; on Holston River above the
ferry landing, cor to William GILLESPEY, Sr., cor to John
GILLESPEY, cor to Hugh TORBETT. No witnesses. 20 May 1826.

494. (2:419-20) Samuel TORBETT to John BOWERMAN: 10 Aug
1822, $200, 19 ac on waters of Holston River, Grant #71 to John
HICKLIN in 1808. Wit: Henry BOWERMAN, John (X) ROBISEN.
20 May 1826.

495. (2:420-21) Isaac WHITE to Moses GAMBLE, Sr.: 8 Oct 1821,
$20, 51 ac on Crooked Creek. Grant #2503 to Moses GAMBLE, Sr.
Wit: Robert EVERETT, John REAGAN. 2 May 1826.

496. (2:421-22) Isaac WHITE to Moses GAMBLE, Sr.: 8 Oct 1821,
$400, 84 ac on Crooked Creek, Grant #2489 to Moses and Alexander

B. GAMBLE. Wit: Robert EVERETT, John REAGAN. 23 May 1826.

497. (2:422-23) John RUSUM?RUSAIN? to William JEFFERIES: 1826, $12.375, 33 ac on waters of Ellejoy Creek, adj land granted to Michael McNEELY. Wit: James McNEELY, James JEFFERES. 23 May 1826.

498. (2:423-24) Peter BOWERMAN to John BOWERMAN: 25 July 1820, $1150, 230 ac near Holston River, part of occupant survey made for Peter on which he lives, cor to survey made for John HICKLAND now TORBET, adj small survey made for John Hickland. Wit: Wm. COLBURN, James McCLURG, John McCLURG. 23 May 1826.

499. (2:424-25) Edward DELOZIER of Sevier Co. to John RUSAM: 15 Sep 1825, $32, 100 ac on waters of Ellejoy Creek, cor to John McNEELY, William JEFFRIES, John RUSAM, John WILLIAMS, James McNEELY. Wit: Benjamin TIPTON, Sr., Benjamin TIPTON. 24 May 1826.

500. (2:425-26) John RUSAM to James McNEELY: 6 Feb 1826, $14.87, 39 ac on waters of Ellejoy Creek, adj John McNEELY, William JEFFERIES.   Wit: James JEFFERIES, William (X) JEFFERIES. 24 May 1826.

501. (2:426-27) Edward ROSE to James RUSSELL and Robert CUNNINGHAM: 12 Sep 1823, $400, 122 ac on waters of Pistol Creek. Wit: Robert HOUSTON, A. EARLY. 25 May 1826.

502. (2:427-28) Alexander McKEE to Samuel STEEL: 3 Nov 1822, $250, 234 ac on waters of Baker's Creek, Grant #1815 to John McKEE dated 23 Nov 1809, cor to Joseph B. LAPSLY and David and William EDMISTON, adj Joseph McCONAL.   Wit: Pat McCLUNG, Henry DUNLAP. 25 May 1826.

503. (2:428-29) Samuel GOULD and Joseph WILSON to Robert/ Raeben/Rueben? DAVIS: 19 Jan 1825, $100, 150 ac on Nine Mile Creek, Grant #1536 to James McTEER, cor to James COOK. Wit:

Richard WILLIAMS, Newton WILLIAMS, William DAVIS. 25 May 1826.

504. (2:429-30) Jane POSEY and Hezekiah ROUTH to Samuel COPE: 20 Mar 1826, 186 ac on waters of Nine Mile Creek adj Robert WILSON, cor to Fredrick YOWIN?. Wit: Brian C. MORSE, Newton WILLIAMS. 25 May 1826.

505. (2:430-31) William McGHEE to Joseph NOLEN: 30 May 1825, $600, 200 ac, part of tract of 635 ac on Nine Mile Creek granted to the late John McGHEE, decd. Land is laid off on the upper end of the original tract of land as willed to William McGHEE by John McGHEE. Adj Robert FERGUSON, Thomas COOPER, Robert COOPER. Wit: John McGHEE, Thomas ROSS. 29 May 1826.

506. (2:431) John McGHEE to William McGHEE: 11 June 1825, Quit Claim to 71 ac on Nine Mile Creek, part of Grant to the late John McGHEE, decd, cor to Joseph NOLEN, Robert FERGUSON. Wit: C. W. GEORGE, William GAY, Sr. 2 June 1826.

507. (2:431-32) John McCALLIE to John VINYARD: 10 Apr 1824, $123, 25 ac on Nails Creek, part of grant to John McCALLIE, cor to John VINYARD and Henry DUPES on south side of Nails Creek. Wit: William McMURRAY, Andrew KIRKPATRICK. 3 June 1826.

508. (2:432-33) William HENRY to William WEST: 19 Oct 1824, $400, 130 ac, part of grant of 186 ac to Robert McCABE on waters of Baker's Creek, cor to Samuel HENRY, adj Samuel MONTGOMERY claiming under James MONTGOMERY, adj Samuel ORR, James LOGAN. Sig: Wm. H. HENRY. Wit: Absolom McNABB, Samuel ORR. 3 June 1826.

509. (2:433) Michael H. MARTIN to Jonethan TIPTON: 1 Oct 1818, $800, 197 ac on waters of Baker's Creek, adj John CONNEL, James and Joseph McCONNELL, Alexander McKEE. Wit: Wm. THOMPSON, Samuel ORR. Acknowledged in court March 1826 by Samuel ORR who stated that William THOMPSON is not an inhabitant of the state. 5 June 1826.

510. (2:433-35) John McCallie DAVIS of Knox Co. to William E. CRESSWELL: 29 Nov 1825, $400, 96 ac, Grant #155 to John McCallie DAVIS, on waters of Nails Creek adj land of Susanna DAVIS, Samuel DAVIS, Robert DAVIS. Wit: William EWING?, William McCUREY. 15 June 1826.

511. (2:435) Jane PASY/POSY and Hezekiah ROUTH to Richard WILLIAMS: 20 Feb 1824, $300, 60 ac on waters of Nine Mile Creek. Sig: Jane (X) PASY. Wit: James TEDFERD, James DICKSEN. 15 June 1826.

512. (2:435-36) Joseph ALEXANDER, Sr. to Joseph M. ALEXANDER, Jr.: 25 Mar 1826, $450, negro girl named PHILLIS? about 33 yrs of age and her child MERIAH about 2 yrs. Wit: J. ALLAN, I. CALDWELL, W. D. CUSIC. 1 Jul 1826.

513. (2:436) Robert EAKIN to William and John McGHEE: 1 Mar 1825, relinquishment of [Robert's] claim to 50 ac lying in the bounds of William and John McGHEE's old original survey. $75. Wit: Wm. BURNS, Josiah JOHNSTON. 29 Jul 1826.

514. (2:436-37) Jacob H. HADDEN to John WILLIAMS: 18 Dec 1825, $20, 50 ac on waters of Ellejoy Creek near the Clear Spring, cor to John WILLIAMS, adj John RASAM, HADDEN's survey. Wit: Math H. BOGLE, Nathaniel JEFFRIES. 26 Jul 1826.

515. (2:437-38) Robert THOMPSON to Arthur GREER: 21 Dec 1820, $900, 213 ac on waters of Baker's Creek, adj Abraham UTTER, Samuel HANDLEY, Robert THOMPSON, Samuel McCAMEN, James SCOTT, part of 217 ac surveyed for Samuel THOMPSON. Wit: David THOMPSON, Joseph GREER, Robert A. THOMPSON. 29 Jul 1826.

516. (2:438-39) James MOORE of Greene Co.(sic)[should be Grainger Co.], admin with the will annexed of Ninian CHAMBERLAIN, decd, and Stephen McBROOM/McBROWN and Hannah, his wife, formerly Hannah CHAMBERLAIN, widow and relict of Ninian CHAMBERLAIN, now of Madison Co., MS Territory, to Robert YOUNG: 23 Nov 1814, $215, one undivided sixth part of 395 ac near the Holston River, being the land whereon

John CHAMBERLAIN,decd, father of Ninian, formerly lived, and which undivided sixth part..descended from John to Ninian. Wit: Jno. H. BROWN, Jno. HOWELL. Sig: Stephen McBROWN. Hannah McBROWN. Following the deed is an order from two Justices of the Peace of Grainger Co. TN requesting that Hannah McBROWN be privately examined since she "is so indisposed that she cannot attend said court for Grainger Co." to be privately examined. This order was signed by John COOK, Clerk of court, in Rutledge 24 Nov 1814. Hannah McBROOM (sic) was examined on 24 Nov 1814 by Isaiah Medkeff and James Jackson, two Justices of Grainger Co. The deed was acknowledged in open court by John McBROOM and John HOWELL, and was ordered to be certified to Blount County for registration.

517. (2:439-40) James EDINGTON, Sr. to Moses SCROGGS: 10 June 1824, $350, 70 ac on waters of Baker's Creek, adj Samuel COWAN, William BEASLEY, being part of original survey made for John MILLER. Wit: John LOWERY, John F. GILLASPEY. 15 Aug 1826.

518. (2:440-41) James EDINGTON, Jr. of McMinn Co. to Moses SCROGGS: 10 Jun 1824, $350, 89 ac on waters of Baker's Creek, cor to Brice BLAIR and William GRAY, adj John BEATY, John MILLER, William BEASLEY. Surveyed 7 July 1807. Sig: James (X) EDINGTON. Wit: John LOWERY, John F. GILLASPY. 15 Aug 1826.

519. (2:441-42) James HOUSTON to John ELLIOT: 26 Apr 1824, $600, 237 ac on waters of Pistol Creek, part of 341 ac tract Granted to Daniel FALKNER. Wit: James ELLIOT, John McNUTT. 15 Aug 1826.

520. (2:442) Mark LOVE to Jonethan TIPTON: 14 Aug 1814, $600, 286 ac, a tract granted to LOVE, cor to John ORR. Wit: John GLASS, James LOVE. 8 Sep 1826.

521. (2:442-43) Robert McGILL of Maury Co. to Jonethan TIPTON: 9 Aug 1811, $150, 50 ac on Baker's Creek, part of a grant to McGILL, cor to Solomon McCAMBLE and Robert MAGILL's survey. Wit: Wm. GAULT, Samuel McCONNEL. 8 Sep 1826.

522. (2:443-44) Dorcas WILY, by her agent James W. WILY/WYLY of Green Co., to Jonethan TIPTON: 27 Sep 1816, $450, 225 ac on Nine Mile Creek, adj Mathew SAMPLES, James MARTIN, Joseph ROGERS, Wm. Rich---?. Wit: Wm. GAUTT, John GAUTT. 5 Sep 1826.

523. (2:444-45) Daniel DEARMOND to John DEARMOND: 4 July 1826, $200, 100 ac on Little River, part of tract whereon Daniel now lives; cor to David DEARMOND's original survey. Wit: Edward GEORGE, Thepher HERRICK. 26 Sep 1826.

524. (2:445-46) Jacob M. HADDEN to Peter FRENCH of Knox Co.: 18 Sep 1826, $300, 88 ac on waters of Ellejoy Creek containing the half of a small spring, adj George HADDEN, John WILLIAMS. Wit: Michal FRENCH, Jacob FRENCH. 19 Oct 1826.

525. (2:446-47) William CARSON to John MILLER: 13 Nov 1824, $200, 60 ac on Baker's Creek, cor to David EDINGTON and Mathew WALLACE, adj Samuel HANLEY, Magness TULLOCH, John WILSON. Was a 62 ac Grant to Betsy RUSSELL, assignee of Thomas ROORK. Wit: John KENNEDY, John W. PRITCHARD. Acknowledged in Monroe County court 21 Dec 1826.

526. (2:447-48) Samuel HATHAWAY to Francis SHAW: 12 Aug 1826, $50, 32 ac, Grant #8759 to Hathaway. Sig: Samuel (X) HATHAWAY. Wit: Josiah JOHNSTON, Leeroy NOBLE. 27 Sep 1826.

527. (2:448) John RUSUM to William TIPTON: 26 Sep 1826, consideration omitted, 12 ac on waters of Ellejoy Creek, adj Hugh BOGLE. Wit: John R. NELSON, Michael FRENCH. 24 Jan 1827.

528. (2:448-49) Ephraim DUNLAP to Alexander KENNEDY: 26 Dec 1825, $400, 122 ac on waters of Baker's Creek, cor to John GOULD and William MOORE. Wit: William EWING, Wm. MEANS. 24 Jan 1827.

529. (2:449-50) William WALLACE, Sheriff, to Joel BAKER: 10 May 1826, $30, 31 ac on Six Mile Creek adj Jeremiah HAMMONTREE, Indian Boundary, James HOLLAWAY. Public sale

14 Feb 1824, as property of James ROBERTSON/ROBINSON and William ROBERTSON/ROBINSON to satisfy judgment issued 16 Dec 1823 in favor of John SHARP against James and William ROBERTSON/ROBINSON for $325.23. Wit: Wm. W. BERRY, Jas. GILLISPEY. 25 Jan 1827.

530. (2:450-51) William WELDEN to John CRYE: 15 Aug 1821, $600, 94 ac on south side of Nine Mile Creek adj Reuben CHARLES. CRYE to pay installments and interest that have or may become due the State. Wit: John COCHRAN, Wm. M. HENDERSON. 25 Jan 1827.

531. (2:451-52) Morris, James, and Jessee MITCHELL to David WILLIAMS: 29 April 1826, $600, 179 ac, part of survey made for Benjamin PRATER and part of an entry made by Jesse and Stephen MITCHELL, cor to Samuel D. WARREN. Wit: Samuel D. WARREN, Stephen MITCHELL. 26 Jan 1827.

532.   (2:452) Jonathan TIPTON of Monroe Co. to David EDMONDSON: 13 Sep 1826, $600, 197 ac on waters of Baker's Creek, part of Grant to James LOGAN, cor to John CANNADAY, adj James and Joseph McCONNEL, McKEE. Wit: Samuel STEELE, James RUSSELL. 27 Jan 1827.

533. (2:452-53) James TEDFERD to John GAULT: 18 Sep 1826, $300, 60 ac on waters of Pistol Creek, cor Nathaniel TORBET and John HOUSTON, adj Doctor McGHEE, cor Nelson WRIGHT and heirs of William HOUSTON. Wit: Wm. C. RANKIN, Wm. (X) B. WRIGHT. 27 Jan 1827.

534. (2:453-54) William IRWIN to James WITHERSPOON: 5 Mar 1811, $500, 118 ac on waters of Cloyd's Creek, adj Isham BLANKENSHIP on west, Joseph DOBSON on south, Paul COCHRON on east, William BAIN on north. Wit: Thos. W. SMITH, Benjamin IRWIN. Proven in Shelby Co., AL, by Thomas W. SMITH and certified by James ESTELL, Clerk of County Court of Shelby Co., 7 Feb 1826. Reg Blount Co. 29 Jan 1827.

535. (2:454-55) Henry LONG to Joseph LOPASSER of Washington Co.: 21 Jun 1825, $500, 141 ac on waters of Nails Creek. Wit: Samuel M. GAULT, John BOETH. 30 Jan 1827.

536. (2:455) William WALLACE, Sr., to James BERRY of Maryville: 27 Aug 1826, $550, a negro slave named ARCHY, a slave for life. Wit: Jac F. FOUTE, Thos I. FOUTE. 13 Feb 1827.

537. (2:455-56) Jacob McGHEE to Christopher WINDERS: 22 Feb 1826, $300, 171 ac in Tuckaleechee Cove on north side of Little River adj Robert McMURRY. Sig: Jacob (X) McGHEE. Wit: William DAVIDSON, Richard (X) McBREAN. 13 Feb 1827.

538. (2:456-57) Moses ELIOTT to .James Russell and Robert CUNNINGHAM: 28 Sep 1826, $114, 37 ac on waters of Pistol Creek, part of land whereon Moses ELLIOTT now lives, near the Morganton Road. Wit: James TRUNDLE, John LANGFORD. 13 Feb 1827.

539. (2:457-58) John McCLURE to William McKISACK: 8 Mar 1826, $450, 112 ac on waters of Little Tennessee River, adj Joseph LAMBERT. Wit: John McCLAIN, Hiram (GUNNISON?). 14 Feb 1827.

540. (2:458) John ALFORD to William SMITH, both of Knox Co: 5 Oct 1826, $400, 70 ac on Holston River. Wit: John S. SMITH, James PERRY, John FINLEY. 14 Feb 1827.

541. (2:458-59) Edward HART to John EAGLETON: 29 Dec 1826, $40, 43 ac on waters of Pistol Creek, cor to HART, Grant #10901 part of entry of #64 made in Entry Taker's Office of Blount County dated 30 June 1824 at rate of 12-1/2 cents per ac. Wit: Andrew C. MONTGOMERY, James WILSON. 14 Feb 1827.

542. (2:459-60) Milton BRADBURRY to James BASHERS: 12 Mar 1824, $300, 127 ac on waters of Gallaher's Creek, part of Grant #2478 to Alexander FORSTER. Wit: B. D. CLIFT, Wm. BROWN. 15 Feb 1827.

543. (2:460) Wm. ALEXANDER to A.ISH: 8 Dec 1825, $450, 70 ac on Gallaher's Creek, being all the right, etc. of William ALEXANDER and his wife Phoebe ALEXANDER, to 618 ac tract patented to Elizabeth ISH, decd, and heirs of John ISH, decd, adj Peter BOWERMAN, Alexander FORD's old survey, John DEAVIES, Wm. WALKER. Wit: Thomas STANFIELD, Adam DUNSMORE, David BEALL. 15 Feb 1827.

544. (2:461) Robert WEAR to Joseph NOLEN: 25 Dec 1826, $50, 50 ac on Nine Mile Creek, Grant #12119 to WEAR 9 Dec 1825, adj McGHEE's heirs, cor to Andrew BAKER, adj William COOPER. Witnesses omitted. 15 Feb 1827.

545. (2:461-62) Jacob McGHEE to Fredrick EMET (sic) of Sevier Co.: 15 Feb 1826, ac omitted, in Tuckaleechee Cove on Little River, adj William DAVIDSON, Isaac GIDDENS. Wit: Ephream GREEN, James (X) STEPHENSON. Sig: Jacob (X) McGHEE. 19 Feb 1827.

546. (2:462-63) Jacob McGHEE to Fredrick EMET of Sevier Co.: 15 Feb 1826, $500, 71 ac in Tuckaleechee Cove, adj Barbara MOORE, John GIDDENS. Wit: Ephriam GREEN, James (X) STEVENSON. Sig: Jacob (X) McGHEE. 19 Feb 1827.

547. (2:463-64) James RUSSELL and Robert CUNNINGHAM to Jacob GARST, Sr. of VA: 27 Jan 1827, $250, 89 ac by a survey made by John HARREL, on a prong of Pistol Creek, cor in the edge of the Morganton road. Wit: Daniel D. FOUTE. 19 Feb 1827.

548. (2:464) James TEDFORD to Nelson WRIGHT: 25 Sep 1826, $300, 60 ac on waters of Pistol Creek, adj William HOUSTON, decd, John GAUTT, McGHEE, Samuel HARVEY/HARRY?. Wit: Jas. ALEXANDER, John MEANS. 20 Feb 1827.

549. (2:464-65) James L. WARREN to Samuel GEORGE: 7 Jan 1826, $300, 24 ac on waters of Holston River, part of Grant #9711 to James L. Warren, cor John SINGLETON and Samuel GEORGE. Wit: Edward GEORGE, Sr., Edward GEORGE, Jr. 20 Feb 1827.

550. (2:465-66) Thomas WALKER to William WALKER: 10 Feb 1826, $400, 138 ac on north side of Little River in Tuckaleechee

Cove, cor to William WEAR, adj Thomas CAMPBELL, Barbury MOORE. Surveyed 5 Mar 1807. Wit: Benjamin BENSEN, Jacob (X) McGHEE, Ephraim GREEN, Fredrick EMET. 21 Feb 1827.

551. (2:466-67) John F. BURNETT, for himself and as agent for the other heirs [not named] of Edward BURNETT, decd, to David COOPER: 8 Sep 1826, $100, 49 ac on waters of Six Mile Creek, Grant #1201 to John McNEEL, adj Jeremiah HAMMONTREE, Patrick MURRY. Wit: John WILKINSON, John B. CUSICK. Sig: John S. (sic) BURNETT. 22 Feb 1827.

552. (2:467-68) Samuel GOULD to James MOOR: 5 Feb 1823, $600, 110 ac on waters of Walker's Creek, cor to Andrew JACKSON, HOUSTON, Robert (surname omitted), John JACKSON. Surveyed April 2, 1807. Wit: James BERRY, W. W. BERRY. 26 Feb 1827.

553. (2:468) Thomas WALLACE to John M. RANKIN: [date omitted] 1825, $911, 237 ac on waters of Baker's Creek, adj Samuel HENRY, James MONTGOMERY, (Armstrong?) WEIR. Wit: Robert TEDFORD, Andw. COWAN. 27 Feb 1827.

554. (2:468-70) William I. MILLER (first party) to Jacob F. FOUTE (second party) and William A. SCOTT (third party): 20 Sep 1825, 223 ac on waters of Nine Mile Creek whereon Miller now lives, part of Grant #2530 to Nicholas AIRHART and part of a tract sold by Isaac WOODS to AIRHART, cor Samuel DICKSON. On 20 May last MILLER became indebted to William A. SCOTT in sum of $200 for which FOUTE is security. Also conveyed is one dun horse. MILLER to pay SCOTT $200 before 1 March 1826 with interest from 21 May 1825. Wit: Daniel D. FOUTE, James TEDFORD. 3 Apr 1827.

555. (2:470-71) Peter BRICKEY to Thomas JONES: 10 Feb 1827, $1000, 640 ac in Cades Cove being the occupant claim held by heirs of James SMITH, adj William McCAGG. Wit: Samuel DAVIDSON, Jesse DALIKEN? Sig: Peter (X) BRICKEY. 17 May 1827.

556. (2:471-72) Richard WILLIAMS to Newton R. WILLIAMS: 24 Mar 1827 $600, 267 ac on waters of Nine Mile Creek, cor to Joseph PASEY in WILSON's line, adj HOUSTON, Charles HENRY. Wit:

James McCONNELL?, Samuel COPE, Robert (X) DAVIS. 17 May 1827.

557.   (2:472-73) John LOWERY of Monroe Co. to John MONTGOMERY, James HOUSTON, Alexander McGHEE, Andrew EARLY, Jacob F. FOUTE and James BERRY, TRUSTEES OF SOUTHERN AND WESTERN THEOLOGICAL SEMINARY: 3 Jun 1826, $2500, 339 ac on Pistol Creek adj the town of Maryville, Granted to John LOWRY, adj John MONTGOMERY, Mathew W. McGHEE, except two ac conveyed to David TOOLE, about 3/4 ac conveyed to David RUSSELL, 1/2 ac conveyed to Mathew W. McGHEE and a part sold to Caleb M. NORWOOD between 80 and 130 ac lying east of the road leading from Maryville to Tellico and between said road and Pistol Creek and West of the road leading from Maryville to Six Mile between last mentioned road and Samuel W. McGHEE's land. Wit: (?) I. CALDWELL, Campble WALLACE. 7 June 1827.

558. (2:473-74) John LOWERY of Monroe Co. to James BERRY: 29 Mar 1827, $300, lot #55 in town of Maryville on Main Street. Wit: Jac F. FOUTE, Robert H. HAYNES. 8 June 1827.

559. (2:474) Isaac TIPTON to Benjamin HARRIS: 10 Feb 1827, $600, 100 ac, part of a survey Granted to Joseph McFADDIN. Wit: Leven WHEELER, William HARRIS, John RODY. 8 Jun 1827.

560. (2:474-75) Andrew MILLER to Jesse CARR: 2 Feb 1826, $300, 53 ac on waters of Baker's Creek, part of grant to Mathew WALLACE on his occupant right, cor to William HARRISON, Mr. E. MOORE, Robert THOMPSON. Wit: Robert THOMPSON, Josiah F. DANFORTH. 12 Jun 1827.

561. (2:475) Caleb M. NORWOOD to David DOWNS: 1 Apr 1828, $325, negro girl named MARY about eight yrs of age. Wit: William WALLACE, Thos. F. McMURRAY. 12 Jun 1827.

562. (2:475-76) Andrew COWAN to Robert BOGLE: 26 Mar 1827, $1000, lots #88, 89, and 90 in town of Maryville. Wit: Campble WALLACE, Wm. THOMPSON. 12 Jun 1827.

563. (2:476) John McCOOL to Abijah CONGER: 17 Feb 1827, $100, two cows, one horse, two sows and pigs, two feather beds and furniture, all house and kitchen furniture, to hold until 1 June 1830, McCOOL to pay CONGER $100 on or before 1 June 1830. Wit: Alex McKEE. 12 Jun 1827.

564. (2:476-78) Mathew NELSON, Treasurer of East TN, to Robert BOGLE: 13 Jan 1827, $51.685, 444 ac on Little River adj Crooked Creek, George BERRY, granted by State of TN to heirs and widow of William SCOTT. Public Sale 4 Sep 1821 under the Act of 19 Oct 1819 entitled an act to provide for payment of the interest on monies due from the citizens residing South of French Broad and Holston and between the rivers Big Pigeon and Tennessee and for other purposes. Wit: Robert M. ANDERSON, Pryor LEN?LEE?. 12 Jun 1827.

565. (2:478-79) John S. BURNETT (first party) to John F. GILLESPIE (second party) and Martin ROREX and Josiah F. DANFORTH (third party): 1 Jan 1827, ROREX and DANFORTH have been security for BURNETT for the sum of $200 on bond dated (day and month omitted) 1826 payable 88 days thereafter to the branch bank of the State of TN at Knoxville payable at the Agency for Blount County at Maryville and renewable by the regulation of the bank upon payment of the interest and discount thereon at the expiration of each 88 days thereafter. ROREX and DANFORTH paid and advanced to the bank the sum of $65 for interest and discount on BURNETT's debt. BURNETT has appointed GILLESPIE a Trustee.. and conveys in trust one yoke of young red steers, one bay horse, one dun pony, one black cow now in possession of David COOPER, fifteen head of stock hogs, two sheep, two calves. BURNETT to pay (amount omitted) by 25 Jan 1827 and regularly and punctually pay the interest and discount on his debt as it shall become due and be required by the bank. If not, GILLESPIE may, after giving 30 days public notice, sell the property to the highest bidder at the courthouse in Maryville. Wit: Jesse WALLACE. 13 June 1827.

566. (2:479-80) James JULIAN to James DUNLAP: 15 Jan 1827, $5, 40 ac on waters of Ellejoy Creek, adj James DUNLAP's old line. Wit: John JULIAN, Samuel McTEER. 15 June 1827.

567. (2:480) Lewis BRANDON of Rhea Co. to Benjamin MILLS of Jefferson Co.: 22 Mar 1827, $600, 129 ac, cor to Henry and Mitchal BOWERMAN, adj John SHADLE and vacant land, George MONTGOMERY. "N.B. This deed is given in place of one that...Lewis BRANDON gave to Enos ELLIS and..ELLIS traded to John HARRIS, and HARRIS traded to Benjamin MILLS...deed given by Lewis BRANDON to E. ELLIS is lost or misplaced so that ..E. ELLIS can't find it and never has been recorded to which Thomas LEWIS and Henry LEWIS is subscribing witnesses." Wit: Enos ELLIS, Thomas LEWIS. 15 June 1827.

568. (2:480-81) Isaac HART to John OLIVER: 22 Sep 1826, $100, 45 ac in Cades Cove adj JOBES. No witnesses. 15 June 1827.

569. (2:481-82) John COPLAND to Audly PAUL: 9 Dec 1826, $1,000, 159 ac on waters of Gallaher's Creek, adj ISH's corner, HENDERSON's line. Wit: Wm. COPELAND, Robert CLARK. 15 June 1827.

570. (2:482-83) Thomas STANFIELD and David GRUBS to Enos ADAMSON of Jefferson Co.: 8 Nov 1825, $2500, 276 ac on Gallaher's Creek, Grant #1159 to James McCLAHEN [McCLARKEN?] assignee of John HANNAH, cor to COPLAND land on William JONES line, William WALKER, ISH's line. Wit: Aaron COPPOCK, John STANFIELD, John HACKNEY. 15 June 1827.

571. (2:483-85) Mathew M. HOUSTON to John GILLASPEY and James GILLESPEY: 22 May 1826, $198.43, several tracts of land which HOUSTON purchased on 13 June 1825 at Sheriff's Sale, sold to satisfy a judgment Margaret RAMSY, guardian of John, Mary, Eliza, Thomas and Andrew HANES?/HUMES?, minor heirs of Thomas HANES?/HUMES?, decd, recovered against John GILLESPEY and James GILLESPIE, administrators of estate of Robert GILLASPEY, decd, and Mathew HOUSTON, surviving partner of the firm of GILLESPEY AND HOUSTON, and John GILLESPEY, James GILLESPEY, Samuel HOUSTON and John HOUSTON. John and James GILLESPEY as creditors of Robert GILLESPEY, decd, are entitled to redeem the land sold and purchased any time within two years; on 28 June 1825 [they] paid to Mathew M.

HOUSTON the sum of $198.43, plus interest at ten percent. One tract of 138 ac cor to Samuel SAFFELL, one of the original corners to mill tract, cor to John GILLESPIE. One tract on bank of Holston River, 178 ac, being a tract originally granted to heirs of Cornelius BOGARD. Another tract on Holston River below mouth of Lackey's Creek, cor to Samuel SAFFELL, cor to Robert GILLESPIE, containing 3 ac. Also one third part of an undivided tract granted by TN to James GILLESPIE, John GILLESPIE, Robert GILLESPIE, 156 ac on Holston River. Wit: John F. GILLESPIE, Wm. WALLACE. 18 June 1827.

572. (2:485-86) Robert BOGLE to William THOMPSON: 27 Mar 1827, $2300, 404 ac on Little River and Crooked Creek, cor to survey of George EWING, cor to George BERRY, vacant land, George CALDWELL. Wit: J. MONTGOMERY, Nancy SCOTT. 18 June 1827.

573. (2:486-88) John COPLAND to William COPLAND: 23 Mar 1827, $500, 159 ac on Gallaher's Creek, part of original occupant survey made for Alexander FORD, cor to David GRUBB. Wit: Alexander ISH, Joseph BROWN. 18 June 1827.

574. (2:488-91) Caleb M. NORWOOD (first party), Jacob F. FOUTE (second party) and Francis and John IRWIN and John IRWIN and William DAVISON and John IRWIN of Mecklenburg Co., NC (third party): 29 July 1826, lots #13 and 35 in Town of Maryville. Lot #35 adj John B. CUSICK. Also 5 ac on waters of Pistol Creek, adj B. McGHEE, Gideon BLACKBURN, commons of Maryville. Another tract of 132 on waters of Pistol Creek, part of a grant to John LOWERY and A. MURRY and sold to James TURK then to NORWOOD, being all of the original tract granted except two ac belonging to LOVE AND TOOL and one lot of ground belonging to David RUSSELL adj Mathew W. McGHEE, Tellico road and the crossing to Six Mile adj the church and graveyard. Another tract of 77 ac on waters of Pistol Creek granted to John WILKINSON and sold to NORWOOD, adj lands now owned by John DUNCAN, Sr., Jacob F. FOUTE and the tract originally granted to James DONAHOO. One tract on waters of Pistol Creek on which Henry FINGER now lives adj lands of John DUNCAN Sr. and others, being land originally granted

to DONAHOO. Also 200 head of hogs, 10 head of cattle and one horse. NORWOOD is indebted to the firm of Francis and John IRWIN for four notes for $430 each dated 9 Nov 1822, due in one, two, three, and four years after date, bearing interest from 1 July 1823; also for one note of $2000 dated 1 Jan 1823 due one day after date; also for one note for $358.57 dated 29 Mar 1824 due one day after date, also for one note for $297.88 dated 27 Aug one day after date; also for one note for $276.18 dated 16 June 1826 due one day after date. He is also indebted to John IRWIN for one note for $434.00 dated 24 Mar 1825 due one day after date; also for one note for $50 dated 4 Feb due one day after date drawn payable to the Trustee of Charlotte Academies; also for one order drawn by Absolem HOLBROOK at one day after sight on Doctor D. R. DUNLAP and Caleb M. NORWOOD and accepted by NORWOOD dated 29 Apr 1823 for the sum of $72.94. William DAVIDSON and John IRWIN have become the bail of NORWOOD on a Capeas ad (situfainendum?) issued against him in favor of George BOWERS from the Circuit Court of Ashe County, North Carolina, for the sum of $1205.785 and Sheriff costs and are bound in a bond with a penalty of $3000 conditioned for the appearance of NORWOOD before the court of Ashe Co. on the third Monday of September 1826 and then render to BOWARS the amount mentioned in the writ or take an oath for the benefit of insolvent debtors prescribed by statutes, etc. NORWOOD is to pay before the first day of January 1827 to Francis and John IRWIN and John IRWIN the several debts due them as before mentioned and discharge the bond given on the capias ad satisfaunadam. Wit: Brittan GARRARD, Jas. WALKER. 22 June 1827.

575. (2:491-92) Ambras COX to Charles H. WARREN: 5 Sep 1822, $300, 48 ac, part of occupant survey made for William YOUNG, cor to survey made for James BOGLE and one made for the heirs of CHAMBERLAIN.   Wit: Enoch   M.   MOOR,   Henry WHITTENBURGER. 25 Jun 1827.

576.   (2:492-93) James FREEMAN to John FREEMAN: (day omitted) Sep 1825, $1000, 125 ac, part of Grant #720 to Bonner SHIELDS, cor to part conveyed to Mike GOODLINK. Wit: William TURK, Hiram TURK. 16 July 1827.

577. (2:493-94) James FREEMAN to John FREEMAN: (day omitted) Sep 1825, $2000, 330 ac, part of orig tract granted to William AYLETT on Pistol Creek, cor to James WEAR. Wit: Hiram K. TURK, William TURK. 16 July 1827.

578. (2:494-95) James FREEMAN to John FREEMAN: (day omitted) Sept 1825, "for the natural love and affection which I have and bare (sic) unto my beloved son John Freeman", negroes Jack GILL and there (sic) family LYNTH? about 16 yrs of age, LYUCH? about 8 yrs of age, LYDEA about 5 yrs of age, WILLIAM about 2 yrs of age, BAILEY a negro fellow about 30 yrs of age, MATT about 22 yrs of age. Wit: Hiram TURK, William TURK. 16 July 1827.

579. (2:494-96) Mathew NELSON, Treasurer of East Tennessee, to John McLAIN: 5 May 1827, $21.35, the amount of interest and principal unpaid and due the state on 1 May 1825, property in the name of Edward CASTEEL, the Grantee, on Tennessee River adj James GREENWAY, Robert HUGHS. Surveyed 24 June 1807. Public sale 21 July 1825 at Maryville. McLAIN to pay all future installments and interest due and unpaid. Wit: Pryor LEE, Will B. REES/RICE. 16 July 1827.

580. (2:496) William BARNHILL to Samuel RITTER: 29 June 1827, $50, 108 ac on Baker's Creek, Granted to William RUSSELL, adj Moses CAWOOD, William MALCOM?. Wit: Caswell HEALL, Will B. RICE. 17 July 1827.

581. (2:496-97) Martin MORGAN to Meshack TIPTON: 10 Mar 1827, $20, 75 ac in Miller's Cove on Reed's Creek, cor to original survey of John WATERS. Surveyed 31 Dec 1825 in the late entry number of Grant #12849. Sig: Martain (X) MORGAN. Wit: James HENRY, Jr. Samuel HENRY. 18 July 1827.

582. (2:497-98) William TIPTON to Martha HART: 2 April 1825, "for..natural love and affection...and the better support and further maintainance (sic) of my daughter Martha and her children," 80 ac, part of 640 ac granted to William TIPTON, assignee of Aaron CRAWSON, on 23 March 1820, on north side of Abrams Creek adj JOBE, HENDERSON. The iron ore and privileges of working it

excepted. Wit: Jesse BARTLETT, James WILLIAMS, David B. TIPTON. 18 July 1827.

583. (2:498) Samuel SLONE to Archable SLONE: 1 Jan 1824, $55, all Samuel's right...to the one-sixth part of 228 ac tract Granted to John SLONE on waters of Nine Mile Creek adj George COPE and Richard WILLIAMS. Wit: Jesse KERR, Samuel McTEER. 9 July 1827.

584. (2:498-99) William W. BERRY of Roane Co. to Simon HINKLE and Jacob D. HARTMAN: 3 Nov 1826, $275, 107 ac adj KING and MONTGOMERY, Robert HOOK, William LOWRY, James MOORE, S. WEAR. Wit: Jacob F. FOUTE, Dnl. HANKEL. 27 July 1827.

585. (2:499-500) William WALLACE, Sheriff, to Daniel D. FOUTE: 24 Jan 1825, $237, town lot #45 in Maryville, whereon John LOWRY now lives. Public sale 24 Jan 1823 to satisfy a judgment issued on 13 Sep 1824 against John LOWERY, John NICHOL and Enoch PARSONS for $1,007.85 "recovered by James TURK, Chairman etc. of Blount County" for damages and costs. Wit: John SAFFELL, W. H. ANDERSON. Proven by William H. ANDERSON at March session 1825 and at June session 1827 by John SAFFLE. 27 July 1827.

586. (2:500-01) Elija WEAT, attorney for Abednego BOAZ, to Daniel D. FOUTE: 23 Feb 1827, $20, 17 ac, BOAZ' undivided interest as heir and son of Abed BOAZ decd, land whereon Abednego formerly lived, granted to David OGLEBY and conveyed by Ogleby to Abed, decd. Sig: Elijah (X) WROT (sic). Wit: William KEETH, Alexander RICE. 30 July 1827.

587. (2:501) Robert DONALSON to Ben CUNNINGHAM: 10 Apr 1827, $150, one sorrel horse three years old, one red and white spotted cow and calf, one white cow except a few small black spots and young calf, one black and white spotted cow and young calf, two beds and furniture consisting of 64 pounds of feathers, five seats, ten? blanketts, one double coverlead blue and white, one singel (sic) coverled blue and white, one stuff (sic) quilt, one calico quilt, and burow [bureau], one note of hand on Andrew KIRKPATRICK for a saddle to be worth $25.00. Donalson to pay Cunningham the sum of

$150 on 1 April next for redemption of the bargained premises. Wit: Alexander LOGAN, Lafon Camp MOORE. 1 Sep 1827.

588. (2:501-02) Mashac BOAZ to Daniel D. FOUTE: 18 June 1827, $25.00, "my share and interest in a tract of land granted to David OGLEBY adj lands of A. MONTGOMERY and Andrew THOMPSON and others on waters of Pistol Creek, being the land on which my father Abednego BOAZ formerly lived. Wit: Edward HART, Thomas HART. Sig: Mashac (X) BOAZ. 1 Sep 1827.

589. (2:502) Mizner BOAZ of Bartholomew, Indiana, to Daniel D. FOUTE: 18 Jan 1827, Boaz in his own right and as attorney in fact of Josua SIMONS/SIMS of IN, $40, the interest and share..of a certrain tract of land of 177 ac on waters of Pistol Creek, adj And. C. MONTGOMERY, Andrew THOMPSON, John and D. EAGLETON and John CLARK and Samuel COWAN, being the share of the said Mizner and of Joshua by virtue of his intermarriage with Agnes, his wife, formerly Agnes BOAZ, left to them with others as the heirs of Abednego BOAZ, decd.   Original tract was granted to David OGLEBY. Sig: Mizner (X) BOAZ. Wit: Edward HART, Thomas HART. 1 Sep 1827.

590. (2:502-03) James CURRIER, Jr. to Daniel D. FOUTE: 26 Jan 1827, $24, 24 ac of Grant #1087 originally granted to James MOORE, cor to John WEAR's original tract. Wit: Alexander RICE, William KEITH. 1 Sep 1827.

591. (2:503-04) William TIPTON to Jacob TIPTON: 26 Apr 1824, $500, 107 ac on waters of Little Tennessee River in Cades Cove. Wit: James CALLAWAY, Jesse BARTLETT. 3 Sep 1827.

592. (2:504-06) William WALLACE, Sheriff, to Daniel D. FOUTE: 30 July 1827, $485, 176 ac whereon David DEARMOND now lives and granted to Joshua HANNAH on Little River, cor to John WHEELER, adj Thomas COULDWELL, James HANNAH, Joseph McFADDEN. Also 50 acres unimproved which was grant #10936 to David DEARMOND, adj John RODDY. Public sale 26 Sep 1826 to satisfy judgment issued 4 Aug 1826 against David DEARMOND, Robert DEARMOND, Joshua HAMILTON (sic) and David GIFFIN

for $468.97. Wit: John F. GILLESPEY, Robert M. ANDERSON. 3 Sep 1827.

593. (2:506-07) Mathew NELSON, Treasurer of East Tennessee, to Daniel D. FOUTE: 10 Mar 1827, $46.26, a tract on waters of Pistol Creek, Grant #185 to John WEAR, cor to Joseph WEAR and William HENRY. Surveyed July 6, 1807. Public sale 22 July 1825 in Maryville under the Act of 19 Oct 1819; on 1 May 1825 the installments of one sixth with interest thereon remained due and unpaid. Wit: Will B. REESE, Pryor LEE. 4 Sep 1827.

594. (2:507-08) William FAGG to Daniel D. FOUTE: 26 Mar 1826, $300, 119 ac adj John WEAR, Samuel McGAUGHEY, KING and MONTGOMERY, John STUART. Grant #782 to Samuel WEAR. Wit: John WILKINSON, Jo F. GILLASPEY. 4 Sep 1827.

595. (2:508-09) Richard CURRIER to Daniel D. FOUTE: 24 Nov 1826, $150, a tract on waters of Crooked Creek whereon CURRIER now lives, Granted #1187 to James MOOR, adj William LOWERY, PATERSON heirs, Thomas WALLER, John WEAR. Sig: Richard (X) CURRIER. Wit: Peter LANDERS, Benjamin J. HINKLE. 5 Sep 1827.

596. (2:509-10) John WEAR and John RIDDLE/BIDDLE to Daniel D. FOUTE: 20 Apr 1825, $21.50, 34 ac on waters of Crooked Creek, Grant #9737 to Biddle and Wear, entered by them in the entry office of Blount County by Entry #135 dated 13 Aug 1824 and surveyed 20 Sep 1824, cor to original survey made for John WEAR, John BIDDLE, adj Richard CURRIER. Wit: Andw THOMPSON, William KEITH. Sig: John WEAR. John BIDWELL. 5 Sep 1827.

597. (2:510) Jesse BEENE and James HOUSTON to Isaac ANDERSON in trust for the use and benefit of the SOUTHERN AND WESTERN THEOLOGICAL SEMINARY so long as the same shall remain located at Maryville, Tennessee: 28 Apr 1827, $10, lot #5 in Maryville. If the said institution shall be removed from Maryville or dissolved, the lot shall belong to ANDERSON. Wit: Daniel D. FOUTE, Sall DYER. 5 Sep 1827.

598. (2:510-11) John McGHEE of Monroe Co. to Jacob F. FOUTE: 25 Sep 1827, $460, lots #82 and 83 in town of Maryville opposite to lots occupied by BERRY and WALLACE and Jesse WALLACE. Wit: James BERRY, Thos. I. FOUTE. 3 Nov 1837.

599. (2:511) William TOOL to Jacob F. FOUTE: 24 Sep 1827, "whereas TOOL and FOUTE have lately erected at their joint expense a two-story frame Spring House on the northeast corner of TOOL's lot on the south bank of Pistol Creek adj the Town of Maryville and in which John LOWRY now lives and FOUTE has paid TOOL the sum of $42.50, one-half the costs and expense of the spring house and desires a title to the one-half"; the one- half of the spring house, being the end next the creek in the lower story, which is divided by a partition and also the right hand or eastern one-half of the upper story of said house. Wit: Samuel PRIDE, Thos. I. FOUTE. 3 Nov 1827.

600. (2:511-12) Daniel D. FOUTE to Jacob F. FOUTE: 24 Aug 1826, $500, negro slave named JAMES. Wit: John CARPENTER, Josiah F. DANFORTH. 3 Nov 1827.

601. (2:512-13) William HARRISON of Monroe Co. to Jesse KERR: 13 Jan 1826, $500, 105 ac on waters of Baker's Creek, part of occupant survey made for Mathew WALLACE, adj Robert THOMPSON, Samuel HANLEY's survey now Thomas HENDERSON, Thompson ROAK, Mathew WALLACE, Isom ADDAMS. Wit: Samuel MONTGOMERY, John MILLER. 6 Nov 1827.

602. (2:513-14) Thomas HENDERSON of Monroe Co. to Jesse KERR: 19 Jun 1827, $3,000, 454 ac on waters of Baker's Creek adj Robert THOMPSON, Abraham UTTER, Mathew WALLACE, Samuel THOMPSON, William MORE, John CARSON, John NEEL?, Wm. McCLUNG, Magnes TULLOCH, Thomas KARRICK, surveyed 13 July 1807. Wit: Archd. SLONE, J. GOULD. 6 Nov 1827.

603. (2:514) Jno. CAMPBLE to Jesse KERR: 23 Feb 1821, $287.50, 262 roods and 37 poles on Nine Mile Creek, adj vacant land, I. Thomas COOPER, John DALZELL. Wit: Thomas WILCOX, David CARSON. Proven by Wilcox at June 1821 court. 6 Nov 1827.

604. (2:514-15) Jonathan WEAR to Jesse KERR: 5 Feb 1817, $700, 267 ac on Nine Mile Creek adj Thomas COOPER, John DALZELL. Wit: Wm. GAULT, Wm. B. WARREN. 6 Nov 1827.

605. (2:515-16) Nathaniel EWING to Jeremiah DUNCAN: 23 Oct 1826, $1350, on waters of Little River whereon EWING now lives, cor to BOWERMAN/BOWMAN and CHANDLER, adj McCALLOCH, Key WOODS, Andrew GIFFIN. Wit: Thos. McCULLOCH, J. EWING, Thos. McCALLOCH. 7 Nov 1827.

606. (2:516-17) Samuel JONES to George MISER: 21 Sep 1827, $70, 25 ac on waters of Gallaher's Creek, adj Robert McCALLEY, Alexander LOGAN, Alexander FOSTER, Francis JONES, Wm. BAKER, the sawmill creek, Wm. HENDERSON and HACKNEY, Francis JONES, George MISER, BASHEAR's line. Wit: Thomas HACKNEY, Henry MISER. 7 Nov 1827.

607. (2:517-18) Elizabeth and Henry McCURDY to Benjamin JAMES: 19 Sep 1825, $800, (ac not given) on west fork of Lackey's Creek being the occupant claim surveyed for Robert McCURDY by Josiah PATTY, cor to surveys made for Wm. MONTGOMERY and Samuel ROAN, the Gray Ridge, Bartley McGHEE, Gideon BLACKBURN, William MONTGOMERY. Sig: Elizabeth (X) McCURDY. Henry (X) McCURDY. Wit: Josiah PATTY, Joseph DOBSON. 7 Nov 1827.

608. (2:518) James DUNCAN to Moses L. SWAN of Knox Co.: 8 Nov 1826, $300, 67 ac on Holston River, granted to John RANKIN and conveyed to DUNCAN; adj David VAUT. Wit: John? A. SWAN, Alexander SWAN. 22 Dec 1827.

609. (2:518-19) John McCLURG to George MISER: 25 May 1827, $200, 103 ac on waters of Gallaher's Creek, part of occupant survey made for Alexander HENDERSON, adj Joseph HENDERSON, Michael BOWERMAN. Wit: Wm. HENDERSON, Alexander HENDERSON. 22 Dec 1827.

610. (2:519-20) Jesse WALLACE to Campble WALLACE, both of Maryville: 7 Dec 1827, $1500, lot #63 in Maryville at intersection of Main Street and an alley, adj lot #60 belonging to BERRY and

WALLACE formerly to John LOWERY, being the lot granted to Miles and David CUNNINGHAM #314. Wit: John F. GILLESPY, Andw. COWAN. 17 Feb 1828.

611. (2:520-21) James McCAULE et al to John P. KERR et als: (deposition) "State of Ohio, Montgomery County, personally appeared before.. James EARLY, a Justice of the Peace for said county, James McCAULE and Margaret his wife...who deposeth and saith that they were well acquainted with Ann PAYNE who intermarried with a certain Joseph KERR, both of York County, PA, who are both dead some years past. The said Ann had three children born of her body (to wit) William, Mary and John KERR. William and Mary are now residents in Montgomery Co., OH. Ann, wife of Joseph KERR, was a full sister of Josiah PAYNE who removed to the state of TN from the state of PA who is now dead as we are informed, and also we know that Thomas M. CATHCART who now resides in Montgomery Co., OH, is a half-brother of the said Josiah PAYNE, decd". 8 Feb 1828.

612. (2:521) Joseph CATHCART to John KERR: 15 Nov 1827, power of atty, "whereas Josiah PAYNE of the State of East Tennessee, Blount Co., did by his last will and testament ..bequeath a part of his real estate to Joseph KITHCART, appointed executor of the same William KITHCART. Mary KITHCART intermarried with Joseph BURLEY of Harford County, State of Maryland. ..The said heirs Joseph KITHCART, William KITHCART, Joseph BURLEY and Mary his wife appoint John KERR of York Co., PA, their atty to sell or devise the real estate." Wit: Vincent NORRIS. Sig: Joseph CATHCART, William CATHCART, Joseph BURLEY.

613. (2:521-22) (deposition) York Co., PA: 5 Nov 1827. "Before me a Justice of the Peace..came Joseph JORDAN and Henry MANSFELD, who..saith that John Pain CARR of York County is the son of Joseph and Ann CARR, late of York County, PA, the said Joseph and Ann having been dead more than eight yrs and further that the deponants were connections and neighbors of Joseph and Ann CARR from his childhood". Sig: P. ROBINSON.

614. (2:522) (deposition) York Co., PA: "Before me, a Justice of the Peace for said county, came John BROWN and John PAIN,

who...saith that the facts contained in the above deposition is true of their own knowledge and further that the above named Ann CARR, late Ann PAIN, was the sister of Joseph PAIN, late of Blount Co., TN." 19 Nov 1827. Sig: P. ROBINSON. Reg 27 Mar 1828.

615. (2:522-23) Thomas M. CATHCART to John P. KERR: Power of atty (same as that on page 521 above). Wit: John FALKERTH, James STEEL. Sig: Thos. M. CATHCART. William KERR. Mary McCAULE. James McCAULE. 9 Feb 1828.

616. (2:523-24) James CURRIER to Christian HENDERSON: 22 Mar 1828, "in consideration of services to me and my wife during her lifetime and the care attention and support given us in our old age by Thomas HENDERSON in his lifetime and wife Christian HENDERSON and for and in consideration of work and labour done for myself and wife whilst she lived and for me since her death by the said Thomas HENDERSON during his lifetime and by the said Christian HENDERSON the wife of the said Thomas since his death and for the purpose of indemnifying the said Christian HENDERSON for time, labour and money by her laid out and expended for my use and benefit, I ...set over to her a negro girl named ROADDY about 5 years old". Wit: Jacob SHADELLE, Peter CLEMENS. 2 Apr 1828.

617. (2:524) Isaiah MANKIN of City of Baltimore, by his atty in fact Thomas L. WILLIAMS, to James BERRY: 5 Feb 1828, $450, lot #56 and #57 in Maryville, the lot on which BERRY now lives at the intersection of the Main St. and an alley, adj lot #65 belonging to John VAUGHT, being Grant #887 to John LOWERY dated 11 May 1810. Wit: Samuel PRIDE, Thomas I. FOUTE. 28 Apr 1828.

618. (2:524-25) James RUSSELL and Robert CUNNINGHAM to Daniel D. FOUTE: 30 Oct 1827, $150, 83 ac on waters of Pistol Creek, on east side of the Morganton road. Wit: James BERRY as to Russell, A. J. McFARLAND as to both, Samuel PRIDE as to both. 27 May 1828.

619. (2:525-26) John HINKELL/HINKLE to Daniel D. FOUTE: 10 Nov 1827, $150, one half of an undivided tract of land of 97 ac on waters of Pistol Creek on the great road leading from Maryville to Little River, Grant #780 to John WOODS, adj James TRUNDLE and

William WALLACE, James BERRY. Wit: John C. CAMPBLE, John R. W. HALL. 27 May 1828.

620.   (2:526) Cody BOAZ, for himself and as atty in fact for Zadkedjah BOAZ of Bible County, AL, to Daniel D. FOUTE: 29 Aug 1827, $40, the interest and share of Cody and Zedkedjah BOAZ in 177 ac, lying near Maryville on waters of Pistol Creek adj And. THOMPSON, Andrew C. MONTGOMERY and others, being the same Granted to David OGALBY. [The] two interests are one-tenth of the tract, each making about 35 ac, as children and heirs of Abednego BOAZ, decd. Sig: Cody BOAZ for Zed BOAZ. Wit: Wm. TOOL, William KEITH. 26 Apr 1828.

621.   (2:526-27) Lott/Lutt? HANKLE to Daniel D. FOUTE: 24 Oct 1827, $150, one-half of a tract on the waters of Pistol Creek and on the great road from Maryville to Dandridge within two miles of Maryville, being Grant #780 dated 4 May 1810 to John WOODS, adj James TRUNDLE, William WALLACE, John MONTGOMERY and James BERRY. Wit: James BERRY, Thomas J. FOUTE.

622.   (2:527-28) William THOMPSON to Daniel S. DOWNS: 3 Feb 1828, lots #70 and 71 in Maryville on the Main Street. Wit: Caleb M. NORWOOD, Andrew McCLAIN. 3 Jun 1828.

623.   (2:528-29) Robert CAULDWELL (first party) and Daniel D. FOUTE (second party) to James WILSON (third party), all of Maryville: 29 Feb 1828, a negro girl called JENNY about 26 or 27 yrs of age and her child called HANNAH MINERVA? aged about two years. CAULDWELL is indebted to WILSON for $240.47 by note dated 29 Feb 1828 due one day after date; FOUTE is security therefor. Wit: John SAFFELL, William KEETH. 9 June 1828.

624.   (2:529-30) William WALLACE, Sheriff to Daniel D. FOUTE: 27 Dec 1827, public sale 27 Aug 1825 to comply with a writ of vendition exponas issued 27 April 1825 by county court directing the sale of properties for taxes due and owing for the years 1822, 1823, and 1824. FOUTE was high bidder for these properties: 40 ac in name of William GRINY/GRIVY? on waters of Nine Mile Creek for taxes due for 1824, bid $4.35. Tract of land in name of Henry HALL, 63 ac on waters of Nine Mile Creek for taxes 1823 and 1824, bid $9.92.

One tract in name of William HARMON of 10 ac formerly belonging to William P. REED on which taxes are due for 1822 and 1823, bid $9.32. One tract in name of Samuel MONTGOMERY of 59 ac on waters of (omitted), taxes due for 1823-24, bid $9.89. One tract of 50 ac on waters of Nine Mile Creek, in name of Isom CORDEAL, taxes for 1822, bid $4.83. One tract of 20 ac in name of Josiah CASNER on Cloyd's Creek, taxes due for 1822, bid $4.20. Wit: Saml. STEEL, I. D. WRIGHT. 9 June 1828.

625. (2:530-31) Arthur CAMPBLE to Barton HENRY and Robert WARREN: 5 July 1826, $1,000, 36 ac on Lackey's Creek, being the whole of a tract Granted to William LACKEY and a part of one Granted to Andrew THOMPSON now in possession of William WALLACE, cor to James HOUSTON, adj James, John and Robert GILLESPIE, William WALLACE.   Wit: Josiah PATTY, W. DUNNINGTON. 9 Jun 1828.

626. (2:531-32) James and Elizabeth HENDERSON of Monroe Co. to William THOMAS: 18 Dec 1827, $300, a negro girl named AMANDA about 17 yrs of age. Wit: David HAMBLE, Joseph DUNCAN. 9 June 1828.

627. (2:532) James BADGETT of Knox Co. to William HENDERSON: 12 Nov 1827, $400, negro boy ZACH, blacksmith, "aged somewhere about 30 years", a slave for life. Wit: Jesse THOMPSON. 10 June 1828.

628. (2:532-33) John TEDFORD to Elizabeth HENDERSON: 3 Dec 1827, "I have given...a certain black girl by the name of AMANDA to my daughter Elizabeth, alias Elizabeth HENDERSON, now of Monroe Co." Wit: William THOMAS, Samuel E. SHERRELL. 10 June 1828.

629. (2:533-34) Jane McKENZIE relict of Daniel McKENZIE, decd, John McKENZIE, Nancy MALLET/MULLET/NOLLET? formerly McKENZIE amd Jane McKENZIE, Jr., heirs of Daniel McKENZIE, to John MALLET, Kallianne MULLET, Sally MULLET and Lausen MALLET, heirs of Thomas MALLET, decd: 9 Oct 1826, Daniel McKENZIE in his lifetime did bargain and sell unto Thomas MALLET on 10 Jan 1817 for $50 one acre adj MALLET's line. Sig: Jane (x) McKENZIE. John L. McKENZIE.   Wit: James JONES, James

BARNES, James GLASS. Sig: Nancy NOLL. James McKENZIE. 10 Jun 1828.

630. (2:534-35) Robert SLOAN of McMinn Co. to Richard WILLIAMS: 30 Apr 1825, $800, 207 ac in Nine Mile adj Joseph POSEY, WILSON, Charles HENRY. Wit: John WILLIAMS, Wm. COOK, Joseph COOK. 24 July 1828.

631. (2:535-36) Abraham UTTER to Robert THOMPSON: 17 July 1826, $263, 73 ac, part of two tracts of land, one Granted to Abraham UTTER and the other to John CARSON on waters of Baker's Creek, adj a Still House, cor to Samuel UTTER, cor to Wesley NORWOOD and Joseph KENNEDY, Tellico Road. Wit: Robert THOMPSON, John THOMPSON, A. UTTER, Jr. 10 Sep 1828.

632. (2:536-37) William WICK to Abraham HARTSELL: 2 Nov 1824, $500, 100 ac on waters of Lackey's Creek, cor with Nathaniel HOOD and Robert GILLESPIE, H. MOFIT, a conditional line between William WICK and Live WICK, adj Grenfield TAYLOR. HARTSELL to pay the state the balance due on the land with interest. Sig: William (X) WICK. Wit: Wm. GILLESPIE, Alexander GILLESPIE, Thomas GILLESPIE. 15 Sep 1828.

633. (2:537) Samuel McCULLOCH to Elias HITCH: 10 Nov 1824, $200, 32 ac on waters of Little River, being a part of McCULLOCH's land. Wit: Thos McCULLOCH, Thomas CALDWELL. 15 Sep 1828.

634. (2:538) William A. SCOTT to Andrew MILLER: 2 Feb 1826, $812.50, 198 ac on waters of Baker's Creek, part of Grant to James SCOTT, adj John SCOTT and cor to Jonathan TRIPPET. Wit: Robert THOMPSON, John THOMPSON, Josiah F. DANFORTH. 15 Sep 1828.

635. (2:539) John SCOTT to Andrew MILLER: 28 Dec 1827, $200, 14 ac on Baker's Creek, part of occupant survey made for James SCOTT, cor to Jonathan TRIPET. Wit: Alex MALCOM, Adam BALL, Alexander KENNEDY. 15 Sep 1828.

636. (2:539-40) Morris MITCHELL to William B. LENOIR of Roane Co.: 12 Apr 1819, $150, land lying east of and joining the tract

of 31 ac heretofore conveyed by MITCHELL to LENOIR beginning at upper corner of that tract at stake on south bank of Holston River...to near the head of Mitchell's Island. 17 ac. Wit: Wash NORWOOD, William (X) MOIL?, James MERPPA. 17 Sep 1828.

637. (2:540-41) George EWING and James EWING to Robert PORTER: 26 June 1826, $1200, 70 ac on Little River, adj John CAMPBLE, part of original survey of 120 ac Grant #553 to John EWING. Also a tract of 111 ac on waters of Little River, adj John STEPHENS, William EWING, part of original survey of Grant #1090 of 150 ac to John EWING. Witnesses omitted. 17 Sep 1828.

638. (2:541-42) Thomas G. DEARMOND to Robert PORTER: 9 Sep 1826, $700, 104 ac on Little River, cor to land granted to John EWING, adj Bays Mountain, William EWING. Another tract of 50 ac adj the aforesaid tract, cor with John EWING. Reference to Grant No. 1623 and No. 10898. Wit: James GILLESPIE, Campble GILLESPIE. 17 Sep 1828.

639. (2:542) George HADDEN to Peter FRENCH, Jr.: 20 Mar 1828, $582.82, 194 ac on waters of Ellejoy Creek, part of original Grant to John RHEA including the Blue Spring, cor John WILLIAMS, adj Morey/Mary HADDEN. Wit: Nathaniel JEFFRIES. 18 Sep 1828.

640. (2:544) Robert REEED of McMinn Co. to Arthur GREER: 5 May 1828, $425, 51 ac on waters of Cloyd's Creek, part of land Granted to heirs of Samuel REED, decd, containing 51 ac, adj Silas COCHRAN, John HENDERSON and Alexander HENDERSON and Francis GRAVES, Robert COCHRAN. Wit: Frances GREER, Eli (X) JONES, John GREER. 18 Sep 1828.

641. (2:544-45) Morris MITCHEL of Roane Co. to James W. RUSSELL/BUSSELL: 23 Mar 1828, $900, 222 ac about a mile from the mouth of Holston, near where the upper cor of Morris MITCHEL's old tract stands on south bank of Holston, passing William B. LENOIR's corner, part of 296 ac Granted to Morris MITCHEL on July 1808 and also one other tract containing 5 ac including the Island opposite the mouth of the above mentioned tracts and being the first island in Holston River below the mouth of Fork Creek. Wit: Wm. B. LENOIR, James MITCHELL. 19 Sep 1828.

642. (2:545-46) William B. LENOIR of Roane Co. to James W. BUSSELL: 23 Mar 1828, $20, 95 ac adj Morris Mitchal's old tract, cor to Lenoir's 300 ac survey, adj Maryville road near a pond. Wit: James MITCHEL, Morras MITCHEL. Proven at court 24 Mar 1828 by James MITCHAL and Moses (sic) MITCHAL 19 Sep 1838.

643. (2:546-47) Morris MITCHELL to John STALEY: 22 Mar 1828, $400, 85 ac on Holston River, part of survey made for Benjamin PRATER. Witnesses omitted.19 Sep 1828.

644. (2:547-48) William W. HENRY of Monroe Co. to James HENRY: 24 June 1828, $2100, 308 ac on waters of Baker's Creek, Grant to William Henry #23 containing 252 ac, adj Samuel Henry, the other part (containing 56 ac) was Granted to Robert McCABE lying on east of said tract and on the west of the tract above specified adj Samuel Henry, William West and William Ewing. Wit: A. Utter, Wm. Early. 19 Sep 1828.

645. (2:548-49) Alexander B. GAMBLE, Trustee, to James HENRY Jr.: 9 June 1828, $846, two tracts of land, 250 ac on waters of Baker's Creek, cor to Samuel HENRY, the other a tract of 56 ac purchased by Wm. W HENRY from Robert McCABE joining the above described, a part of Grant #1036. On 3 Feb 1820 Wm. W. HENRY by his deed appointed Gamble his Trustee and conveyed to him the two tracts in trust for the use and benefit of a certain Samuel HENRY..to secure the payment of $648.69 due from Wm. W. Henry on a promissory note dated 3 Feb 1824. Wm. W. Henry failed to pay and property was sold at public sale 21 June 1828.   Wit: Jesse WALLACE, James H.GILLISPIE. 20 Sep 1828.

646. (2:549-50) Arabenn/Roben/Raeben/Rueben? DAVIS to William DAVIS: 1 Feb 1838, $150, 140 ac on Nine Mile Creek, Grant #1536 to Little James McTEER, cor to James COOKE. Sit: Arabenn (X) DAVIS. Wit: Morgin DAVIS, Solomon Arthur WILLIAMS, Sherwin COOPER. 23 Sep 1828.

647. (2:550-51) Daniel D. FOUTE to John W. WILSON: 25 Dec 1828, $10, 20 ac on waters of Cloyd's Creek which Foute purchased on 29 Aug 1825 at Sheriff's Sale for taxes which [land] was in the

name of Jacob CASNER. Wit: Thomas HUNT, Jacob SHADLE. 23 Sep 1828.

648.   (2:551) James THOMPSON to Thomas R. McCLUNG/McHENRY: 31 Jan 1828, $14, 20 ac on waters of Little River adj William TIPTON, James TIPTON, McHENRY, Joseph RAMSEY. Surveyed 5 June 1824. Wit: Robert McCAMy, J. W. COWAN. Proven in court March 1828 by witnesses. 23 Sep 1828.

649. (2:551-52) Thomas UPTON to Joseph SCOTT: 24 July 1827, $400, 90 ac on a branch of Pistol Creek, part of the occupant survey made for Robert HENDERSON. Sig: Thomas S. UPTON. Wit: A. EARLY, Hamilton FRAZIER. 23 Sep 1828.

650. (2:552-53) Samuel M. REED to John GREER: 5 May 1828, $125, 51 ac, adj Silas COCHRAN on south, John HENDERSON on north, lot #6 on south, lot #4 on west, being lot #5. Wit: Ather GREER, Eli (X) JONES. Proven by wits 27 June court 1828. 23 Sep 1828.

651.   (2:553-54) James SHADDING/SHADDEN from John STERLING: 1828 (date omitted), $500, 75 ac on waters of Baker's Creek, adj Samuel MONTGOMERY, John BEYS, HUMPHREYS, Moses SCRUGGS. Wit: Joseph L. GOULD, Jno. WALLACE. Ack at court 28 June 1828. 24 Sep 1828.

652. (2:554) John SCOTT to Adam BALL: 24 Dec 1825, $500, 101 ac on Baker's Creek, part of survey made for James SCOTT, decd, by Josiah PATTY, adj Samuel HENRY, William MORE, John EWING, Robert BOYD. Wit: Wm. HARRIS, Jonethan TRIPPET. 24 Sep 1828. Proven at June court 1828 by witnesses.

653. (2:555) James THOMPSON to Joseph RAMSEY: 11 June 1827, $300, 140 ac on waters of Little River, adj Alexander LOGAN, cor to ten ac Grant to Robert WARE conveyed to James THOMPSON. This 10 ac is now included within the lines to make 140 ac. Adj Peter BRAKEBILL, William UPTON, Thomas McHENRY. Surveyed 5 June 1824. Wit: William McTEER, Samuel HENRY. 24 Sep 1828.

654. (2:555-56) Samuel HOUSTON to Hugh WEAR: 27 Nov 1820, $775, 389 ac on waters of Pistol Creek, being held and claimed by right of occupancy and preemption and Granted to William Harris, Grant #2554, then sold to George DOUGLASS by deed 29 Mar 1814 and from DOUGLESS to COWAN and Mathew C. HOUSTON 22 Sep 1817, and from them to John HARRELL 31 Dec 1822 and from HARRELL to HOUSTON 10 Dec 1823. Wit: John HARRELL, Samuel CUNNINGHAM. 24 Sep 1828.

655. (2:556-57) James McGINLEY to Isaac WELLS: 28 Aug 1823, $100, 73 ac on Crooked Creek being part of tract James McGINLEY now lives on. 28 Aug 1823. Wit: Ebenezer McGINLEY, Benjamin PIOTT?. 26 Sep 1828.

656. (2:557-58) John, Alexander, and Mathew W. McGHEE to Abraham WALLACE: 26 Mar 1828, $300, 156 ac on waters of Crooked Creek, adj Abraham WALLACE, M. ROREX, McGHEE and SCRUGGS, William ANDERSON. Wit: Campble WALLACE, Joseph JOHNSTON. 26 Sep 1828.

657. (2:558-59) James HOUSTON to Joseph LAMON: 24 Mar 1828, $1200, the undivided half of 1200 ac on Pistol Creek, adj James WEAR. Wit: James WEAR, Hugh WEAR of James, Henry LAMON. 26 Sep 1828.

658. (2:559-60) William TURK to Hugh CARTER, Jr. of Greene Co.: 1 June 1828, $200, 104 ac, Grant #312 to Jacob CAPPENBURGER 28 Sep 1808, adj Peter KEY, Al CASTETTER, F. ETHERTON. Wit: Campble WALLACE, Wm. GRIFFITTS. 26 Sep 1828.

659. (2:560-61) Daniel D. FOUTE to Samuel STEEL: "I [FOUTE] am firmly bound to STEEL...for the sum of $500.... 18 Dec 1827. FOUTE has sold to STEEL 83 ac on the Morganton Road about 3 or 4 miles from Maryville..in part consideration STEEL has this date executed his promissory note to FOUTE for 50 bushels of good sound corn delivered on the premises on or before 25 Nov 1828. Also for 100 bushels of good sound dry corn delivered on the premises on or before 15 Nov 1829, also for 100 bushels of good sound dry corn delivered on or before 15 Nov 1820 and 100 bushels on 15 day of Dec

1831. FOUTE to make a good title to the land on payment of the last mentioned 100 bushels of corn." Wit: Jesse THOMPSON, Hugh TORBET. 27 Sep 1828.

660. (2:561) Thomas McCULLOCH to William THOMPSON and Isaac CAMPBLE: 17 Feb 1824, $1775, 152 ac on waters of Little River and Pistol Creek, Grant #2335 to McCULLOCH, adj Alexander McCULLOCH, Thomas CLARK. Wit: William WALLACE, Samuel GEORGE. 27 Sep 1828.

661. (2:561-62) Andrew CUMMINS to Thomas UPTON: Jan 1826, $307, 90 ac on a branch of Pistol Creek, a part of the occupant survey made for Robert HENDERSON. Wit: Nathaniel KING, Daniel YEAROUT. 27 Sep 1828.

662. (2:562-64) William WALLACE, Sheriff, to Samuel HENRY: 4 Sep 1827, $200, 240 ac, orig Grant #748 dated 1 May 1810 to Samuel McGAHEY on waters of Pistol Creek, cor to James EDINGTON, adj KING and MONTGOMERY, Josiah P. SMITH, John WOODS, David COULDWELL. Public Sale 28 Aug 1824 to satisfy a judgment recovered by HENRY against James McMILLAN before Alexander B. GAMBLE, a Justice of the Peace for Blount County, on 15 June 1824, in the amount of about $293. Judgment execution was issued and put into the hands of James Henry, Jr? then a Deputy Sheriff, who finding no goods or chattels levied on one tract of land containing 240 ac adj the lands of James TRUNDLE, Samuel HENRY, Jr. Wit: Eleven HITCH, John F. GILLESPIE. 6 Oct 1828.

663. (2:564-65) Samuel HENRY to William WALLACE: 4 Sep 1824, "whereas James HENRY, Deputy Sheriff, did by virtue of four orders of sale issued from Blount County Court exposed to public sale on 28 Aug 1824 a certain tract containing 240 ac levied on as property of James McMILLAN to satisfy four judgments obtained by Samuel Henry against McMillan for $293, [and] Henry became the purchaser of tract; WALLACE being a creditor of James McMillan to the amount of $100 and McMillan being wholly insolvent and not able to pay Wallace his debt...according to the act of assembly in such case made and provided and on the day above mentioned [Wallace] redeemed the tract of land from Henry; Henry conveys for $331.95 (it

being the amount of my debt against the said James McMillan including the costs of suit, etc. ...$60.80 of the above sum was paid by Wallace to Henry in silver and the residue in Tennessee bank notes." [Tract described in deed above.]. Wit: Eleven HITCH, John F. GILLESPIE. 6 Oct 1828.

664. (2:565-66) Joseph NOLEN to William WALLACE: 4 Aug 1824, $400, 106 ac on waters of Nine Mile Creek, being the tract which Nolen purchased of John TEDFORD including the house wherein NOLEN now lives, being part of Grant #2425 to Robert FERGUSEN. Wit: Samuel M. GAULT, John NORWOOD. 6 Oct 1828.

665. (2:566) John DOUGLESS of Anderson Co. to William WALLACE: 25 July 1828, $400, negro woman named NINSAY about 21 years, and negro girl, MINSY, aged about 3 yrs, both slaves for life. Wit: B. M. WALLACE, Campble WALLACE. 8 Oct 1828.

666. (2:566-67) James AUSTIN of Washington Co., VA, to William WALLACE: 18 July 1828, $230, negro girl VILET about 9 or 10 yrs old. Wit: B. M. WALLACE, Jesse WALLACE. Proven at court Sept 1828 by Campble and Jesse WALLACE. 7 Oct 1828.

667. (2:567) James BERRY to Jacob F. FOUTE: 8 Oct 1827, on 15 Jan 1819 BERRY sold to Jacob F. FOUTE for $1500 lots #84 and #109 in town of Maryville, Foute has fully performed the requisition of said obligation; #84 immediately back of the court house and corner at the intersection of the main cross street and a back alley. #109 immediately in the rear of the first lot #84 and corner at the interesection of the main cross street and a back street and James on the southwest by the old Academy lot, being the lots whereon Jacob F. FOUTE now lives and has since the date of said sale." Wit: A. J. McFARLAND, Daniel D. FOUTE. 16 Oct 1828.

668. (2:568) Jesse DUN to Samuel PICKINS of Sevier Co.: 13 Sep 1828, $300, 50 ac on waters of Ellejoy Creek, adj Larkin BOLING. Wit: William SHAMBLIN, Lott SHAMBLIN. 31 Jan 1829.

669. (2:568-69) Josiah F. DANFORTH to James BERRY and Jacob F. FOUTE: 26 Jan 1829, $1200, 10 ac adj town of Maryville on Pistol

Creek, cor to the Grant made to KING and MONTGOMERY on northwest side of Pistol Creek and the Commons. [In one place the name is shown as James HENRY and Jacob F. FOUTE is shown as Josiah F. FOUTE.] Wit: Daniel D. FOUTE, Uriah SHERRELL. 9 Feb 1829.

670. (2:569-70) Charles W. C. NORWOOD to Jacob F. FOUTE: 24 Dec 1828, $300, negro girl slave named CHALOTE, aged about 28 years and her increase. Wit: Andrew McALLEN?, Robert McNUTT. 9 Feb 1829.

671. (2:570) Eburn? BIRD to Jacob F. FOUTE:5 Dec 1828, $250, a yellow girl slave named LUCY aged about 13 years. Wit: John (X) ADKINS, Daniel D. FOUTE. 9 Feb 1829.

672. (2:570-72) Jesse THOMPSON to John MONTGOMERY, James HOUSTON, Alexander McGHEE, Andrew EARLY, Jacob F. FOUTE and James BERRY, Trustees appointed by the Board of Directors of the SOUTHERN AND WESTERN THEOLOGICAL SEMINARY: 20 Dec 1828, $50, for lots $50 and #4 in Maryville at intersection of South Broad Street and an alley. 9 Feb 1829.

673. (2:572-73) John FREEMAN to Campble WALLACE: 3 Dec 1828, $1,000, 125 ac being part of Grant #720 to Bonner SHIELDS, adj Michael GOODLINK. Wit: John TEMPLE, Thos. L. LOCKET. 10 Feb 1829.

674. (2:573) John FREEMAN to Campble WALLACE: 3 Dec 1828, $2500, 330 ac on Pistol Creek, part of tract granted to William AYLET, cor to James WEAR. Wit: John TEMPLE, Thos. L. LOCKET. 10 Feb 1829.

675. (2:573-74) William WALLACE to Jacob F. DANFORTH: 15 July 1828, $650, a negro woman named DELY about 30 or 35 yrs old, slave for life; also negro girl named ELIZA about 4 months old, a slave for life. Said negroes warranted "to be sound and clear of any local disease so far as I know altho I do not warrant the said negro woman DELY to have as firm and strong a constitution as some others but is liable to take cold when exposed." Wit: Wm. TOOL, Jac F. FOUTE. Sig: Will WALLACE. 10 Feb 1829.

676. (2:574) Thomas B. ADAM of the Cherokee Nation to Josiah F. DANFORTH: 6 Mar 1828, $325, a negro girl slave, SUSAN, about 23 years old. Wit: Edward ADARE?, John H. RUNLEY/RUNBY? 10 Feb 1829.

677. (2:574-75) Nathaniel TORBETT to Alexander McGHEE: 16 Jan 1829, $400, 225 ac on waters of Pistol Creek, adj John HANLEY's former residence which is at present occupied by the Widow GAUTT on the original corner of the land belonging to the heirs of William HOUSTON, decd, cor to Thomas TURK, John MONTGOMERY, Bonner SHIELDS now GOODLINK, I. RIGHT's ferry road, at or near the road that leads from John Hanley's former place to Benjamin JAMES. Wit: A. MARTEN, Wm. EARLY. Proven at court Jan 1829 by Alford MARTIN and William EARLY. 11 Feb 1829.

678. (2:575-75) Aaron COPPOCK to A. ISH: 1 Dec 1828, $200, 76 ac on Holston River, adj KELLY's vacant land, adj James Thos. LEWIS. Wit: John BLACK?, John FINDELEY?. 11 Feb 1829.

679. (2:576) Aaron COPPOCK to A. ISH: 18 Dec 1824, $25, 27 ac adj Thomas LEWIS? entry, adj BOWERMAN. Wit: Edward (X) TURK, John BIBLE. 11 Feb 1829.

680. (2:576-77) Daniel D. FOUTE to John AMBRISTER: 13 Dec 1828, $320, 177 ac on waters of Pistol Creek, being Grant #1225 to David OGLEBY, adj Knoxville road, cor Andrew MONTGOMERY, Ben ALEXANDER's old place, William WALLACE old place, David EAGLETON. Wit: John F. ADKINS, Alexander RICE. 11 Feb 1829.

681. (2:577-78) Samuel SHAW to Elias BRIANT: 22 Dec 1828, $450, 100 ac on south side of Holston River, cor to SHAW, cor to WILLIAMS. Wit: Wm. GRIFFITS, David WALKER. 11 Feb 1829.

682. (2:578-79) Dread J. FREEMAN of Knox Co. to James BADGETT: 2 Feb 1829, $534, 15 ac on Stock Creek, adj THURMAN. Wit: Elisha DUNN, William KIDEL. 12 Feb 1829.

683. (2:579) Margret DAVIS of Madison Co., AL, to John COCKRAN: 8 Nov 1828, $200, 180 ac on waters of Cloyd's Creek, adj James WESDEN, Joseph McCONNEL, Isom BLANKENSHIP,

granted to William IRWIN assignee of Stephen ANDERSON. Wit: William McCLUNG, Pat McCLUNG. 12 Sep 1829.

684. (2:579-80) Andrew CROMWELL and Mary CROMWELL to Francis GREER: 29 Mar 1828, $100, one sorrel mare, one black mare, one bay horse colt, one sorrel yearling, fifty two milk cows, four young head of cattle, three sows and pigs, two feather beds and furniture, [one liven and aprates?], one man's saddle, one side saddle, one barsheer plow and one shovel plow, two pair of drawing chains and harness and two collars, two blind brindles, two axes, one pot, one writing desk, one cutting box and knife, and all the crop growing on the plantation where CROMWELL now lives. Andrew and Mary CROMWELL are indebted to GREER on several notes dated March 22, 1827 and other notes of deferred date with legal interest, which may be paid on or before 22 Apr 1828. Sig: Andrew (X) CROMWELL, Mary (X) CROMWELL. Proven June 1828 court. 12 Feb 1829.

685.   (2:580) Thomas CROWDE/CROWELE to Carter DONCARLAS: 10 Jan 1826, $500, negro girl named MARY about 5 yrs of age and negro boy named NOAH about 4 years old. Wit: Robert WEAR, Jacob FULKERSON. 12 Feb 1829.

686. (2:580-81) Ezra BUCKNER of Grainger Co. to Daniel D. FOUTE: 15 Sep 1828, $400, "FOUTE purchased of Wm. McCUBBINS two lots in Maryville on 21 Aug 1828, which was confirmed by articles of agreement on that day entered into, and FOUTE having performed his part of the contract, the said McCUBBINS, in performance of his part, hath requested Ezra to convey said lots, #11 and #38 to FOUTE." Wit: William KEITH, John F. ADKINS. 13 Feb 1829.

687. (2:581-82) William LOWERY of McMinn Co.to Daniel D. FOUTE of Maryville: 28 June 1828, $4 525, the undivided one half of lot #27 in Maryville, being the corner lot southeast of the Publick Square, adj Main Street on the north, the main cross street on the west and a back street on the south, and on the east by lot #88 (sic) owned by Wm. McCUBBIN? Wit: James CUSICK, A. B. CAMPBLE. 13 Feb 1829.

688. (2:582-83) Robert HOUSTON (first party), Daniel D. FOUTE (second party) to James BERRY and Jacob FOUTE: 5 Feb 1829, HOUSTON is indebted to BERRY by note of hand amounting to $28, and to James BERRY and Josiah F. FOUTE by notes and back account amounting to $90.51; Daniel D. FOUTE is his security therefor; 75 ac on north side of Nine Mile Creek, part of a 213 ac tract orig Grant #2435 to Jesse COUNDRY, adj Sarah LEATHERDALE and Thomas HART, cor to Anna THOMPSON's field. Also personal property: 4 head of horses (one large brown horse and small black pony, one chestnut sorrell mare, one year old sorrell colt) one yoke of oxen, two head of cattle and fifteen head hogs. Houston to pay within six months the notes with interest.   Wit: Wm. LOWRY, Robt McNUTT. 14 Feb 1829.

689. (2:583-84) Wm. B. McCAMPBLE to Abijah CONGER: 24 Dec 1828, $562, 194 ac on a small branch of Baker's Creek where McCAMPBLE now lives, adj CONGERr's Plantation on the north east, cor to GAUT and Solomon McCAMPBLE, adj James EDMUNDSON, William GAULT. Wit: Iredell D. WRIGHT, John P. KERR. 14 Feb 1829.

690. (2:584-85) John P. KERR, for himself and as atty for Joseph CATHCART, William CATHCART, Joseph BUSBY and Mary BUSBY his wife formerly Mary CATHCART of the County of Hartford, MD, and also as atty in fact of Thomas M. CATHCART, William KERR, James McCANDLES and Mary McCANDLES, his wife formerly Mary KERR, of Montgomery Co., OH, all devisees of Josiah PAIN, decd; to Abijah CONGER: 21 Apr 1828, $650, Josiah PAIN by his Last Will and Testament devised all his real estate in Blount County to the [sellers]. The real estate was condemned to sale by the court to satisfy a judgment and costs recovered by Alexander McKEE against the estate of Josiah PAIN, and all the real estate except the tract of land upon which William McCAMPBLE now lives was sold by the Sheriff to satisfy judgment and costs. Abijah Conger bid $825. [It appears that there are several omissions in this deed.] Wit: John F. GILLASPY, Wm. B. CAMPBLE, Caleb M. NORWOOD. 11 Feb 1829.

691.   (2:585-86) John and Samuel HOUSTON to Thomas BLACKBURN/BLANKENSHIP: 16 Jan 1829, $900, 49 ac on Sinking Creek, part of Grant to Eli DIXON. Wit: M. HOUSTON, John HOUSTON. 16 Feb 1829.

692.   (2:586-87) Jonethan McCHURCH to Jesse BROWN of Washington Co., VA: [date omitted] 1820, $800, 179 ac on waters of Little River. Wit: John E. KINCANNON, Andrew KINCANNON. 16 Feb 1829.

693.   (2:587-88) Amos LOVELADY and Cluryence? LOVELADY formerly Cluryence BOAZ daughter of Abednego BOAZ, decd, as heirs and distributees, to Daniel D. FOUTE: 2 Dec 1828, $20, about 17 ac, their undivided interest or share in a tract formerly owned by Abednego BOAZ, decd, Granted to David OGLEBY and by him sold to BOAZ, adj Andrew C. MONTGOMERY, Samuel COWAN, James CLARK, Andrew THOMPSON and others. Sig: Amos (X) LOVELADY.   Claryence (X) LOVELADY.   Wit: Enoch UNDERWOOD, Berry HOLLAND. Following: I George M. CLEW, Clerk of the Court of Pleas and Quarter Sessions of Sevier County, do hereby certify that at the December Session 1828 of said court, the foregoing deed was duly proven in open court by Enoch UNDERWOOD and Berry HOLLAND...and on motion Enoch Underwood and Berry Holland, Esquires, are appointed commissioners to take the privy examination of Claricy LOVELADY.... Given under my hand and seal of office at office in Sevierville 2 Dec 1828. George McCOWN by S. R. BRADFORD.

694.   (2:588-89) Thomas HENDERSON of Monroe Co. to Daniel D. FOUTE: 5 Feb 1829, on 2 Sep 1828 HENDERSON sold to FOUTE one half of lot #37 in Maryville for $550, for which Foute has now paid, lot #37 being the corner lot south east of Publick Square. Wit: A. FINOL , I. D. WRIGHT. 17 Feb 1829.

695.   (2:589) John DEARMOND to John F. GILLESPIE: 16 July 1828, for "divers good causes and considerations," [I] "nominate GILLESPIE as attorney in fact for me to appear in any circuit court to be held in Blount County after the expiration of 12 months from the 26 day of Sep 1828 and in my name confess judgment for me in action of

judgment or of forcible entry and deliver either before a Justice of the Peace or in Court in favor of Daniel D. FOUTE in any action he may bring for lands by me this day released and conveyed to the said FOUTE and being the same conveyed by David DEARMOND to the said John by deed dated July 1826 and registered 26 Sep 1826 and for me and in my name and on my behalf to do and perform any and every act, things or thing that may be necessary to eject me and give the said Daniel D. FOUTE...possession of the said premises". Wit: Jesse THOMPSON, William KEITH. 18 Feb 1829.

696. (2:589-90) David DEARMOND et als to Daniel D. FOUTE: "Whereas I, Daniel D. FOUTE, on the 26th day of Sept 1826 purchased at Sheriff Sale the lands of David DEARMOND one tract containing 176 ac and the other containing 50 ac adjoining thereto and to give and settle disputes of all description about the land I agree to continue the rite [right] of redemption 12 months from the expiration of the time allowed by law, and the said David DEARMOND, John DEARMOND, Robert DEARMOND, Joshua HAMBLETON who now live on the land are at the expiration of said 12 months upon failure to pay the sum which may be lawfully due at the expiration of the time of redemption by law with legal interest to the expiration of the time herein further given...it is hereby expressly declared and understood between the parties that there is nothing herein contained that is to be construed or understood to vest any right or claim either legal or equitable in said David, John, Joshua, or Robert against FOUTE..in any manner or form whatsoever....at the expiration of the twelve months all equity shall cease and possession be given, and it is agreed that if the law authority in the redemption of one or either of the tracts separately..the said Daniel is expressly understood to have it and every other right that the said redemption law gives." Sig: Daniel D. FOUTE, John F. DEARMOND, Joseph J. HAMILTON, Robert DEARMOND, David DEARMOND. Wit: Jesse THOMPSON, William KEITH. 18 Feb 1829.

697. (2:590-91) David DEARMOND to John F. GILLESPIE: "we David DEARMOND, Joshua HAMILTON, Robert DEARMOND ..."for divers good causes and considerations...nominate John G. GILLASPIE, Esquire, of Monroe County our true and lawful atty in fact ...to appear [same as power of atty shown on page 589] Sig:

Joseph (sic) H. HAMILTON, Robert DEARMOND, David DEARMOND. Wit: Jesse THOMPSON, William KEITH. 18 Feb 1829.

698. "State of Tennessee, County of Blount: We, J. C. HUTTON, Register, and A. P. THOMPSON, Deputy Register of Blount County, Tennessee, do hereby certify that we have faithfully collated the foregoing part of Transcript with the original Book "I" of the Registers Office of Blount County. 31 Aug 1878."

Here ends Volume 2, Blount County Deeds.

Blount County, Tennessee, Deeds
Deed Book 3

699. (3:1) John F. DEARMOND to Daniel D. FOUTE: (deed of release) 16 July 1828, "having a deed of conveyance executed to me by David DEARMOND dated 4 July 1826, one for 100 ac being part of original grant to Joshua HANNAH on Little River, the other fifty acres late entry adj the above [and] John RODDY. The above described lands were sold at Sheriff Sale on 26 Sep 1826 at which time FOUTE became purchaser and in consequence we have conflicting claims and to settle all disputes..I hereby release to FOUTE all my right , etc. in consideration of which FOUTE agrees to extend the right of redemption to DEARMOND for the term of twelve months from the 26th day of Sept 1828. Wit: Jesse THOMPSON, William KEITH. 18 Feb 1829.

700. (3:1-2) State of Tennessee (Grant #11806) to William TIPTON, assignee of John SMITH: 9 Sep 1825, "In pursuance of an act of the General Assembly passed 23 Nov 1809 and also an act passed the 17th July 1820 for the benefit of Aaron CROWSON and John SMITH and those claiming under them", 640 ac, being occupant claim in the Highwasee District in Cades Cove on waters of Tennessee River, cor to TIPTON's middle survey, crossing Abram's Creek. Surveyed 4 May 1820. 23 Feb 1829.

701. (3:2-3) State of Tennessee (Grant #6731) to William TIPTON, assignee of Aaron CROWSON: 23 Mar 1821, [cites same Acts as above] 640 ac in Cades Cove, cor to his other survey...a conditional line with Mary LINVILL? Surveyed 3 May 1820. 23 Feb 1829.

702. (3:3) State of Tennessee (Grant #6730) to William TIPTON assignee of Aaron CRAWSON: 23 Mar 1821, [cites same Acts as above, 640 ac, an occupant claim lying in Highwassey Distr in Cades Cove, conditional line between Wm CRAWSON and James SMITH. Surveyed 2 May 1820. 23 Feb 1824.

703. (3:3-4) Daniel D. FOUTE to Joseph BLACK: (date omitted) Oct 1823, $10.66, "On 21 June 1823 FOUTE purchased 75 ac at Sheriff Sale being lived on and sold as the property of William BLOUNT by

writ of an order of sale issued at the instance of John WALKER from the Court of Pleas and Quarter Sessions of Blount County and the land being conveyed by William HUGH, Sheriff, to FOUTE by deed dated 4 Aug 1823; BLACK being desirous to redeem the land by virtue of the statute in such case provided". Wit: Andrew M. KEATH, George W. FOUTE. 3 Mar 1829.

704. (3:4-5) John COOK to Josiah JOHNSTON: 23 Apr 1825, $380, 170 ac in Hickory Valley, being a part of Nicholas STEPHENSON old original survey which contains 561 ac, cor to ADAMSON, adj MERREATT, COOK known by Hollys STEPHENSON part of said survey, MARTIN, GRIFFITTS. John (X) COOK. Wit: William GRIFFITH, Leroy NOBLES.

705. (3:5) Richard GAY of Monroe Co. to John RANSBURGER: 5 Sep 1828, $90, 42 ac on Crooked Creek. Witnesses omitted. 3 Mar 1828.

706. (3:5-7) Joseph BLACK, Sr. to Joseph BLACK, Jr. of Anderson Co.: 23 Jan 1823, 473 ac claimed by right of occupancy and preemption and Granted to Joseph BLACK, Sr., on waters of Ellejoy Creek, adj David VANCE, John TIPTON, John Benjamin TIPTON..being all the land contained in Grant #1503..except 150 ac I have heretofore granted to the executors of William HOUSTON. Wit: James McNELLY, Joseph W. HADDEN. Proven by witnesses June 1825 and June 1826. 12 Mar 1829.

707. (3:7-8) James BADGETT, Sr. to James BADGETT, Jr.: 19 Apr 1823, $3,000, 207 ac on Stock Creek and Little River, beginning on south side of Stock Creek a small distance from the first bend..adj BARTLETT survey, James PERCE, James and Robert PERCE, being Grant #272 to Nickolas BARTLETT by patent bearing date 5 Oct 1808. "Included and taken on to the above survey the privy on the bank of Stock Creek on south side below the Grist Mill of Nicholas BARTLETT". Wit: William CARLAS, Sterling (X) SMITH. 29 Apr 1829.

708. (3:8-9) John S. BURNETT to James R. DANFORTH of Richmond Co., GA : 10 Oct 1820, $1,000, 340 ac on waters of Pistol Creek adj John WOODS, Barkley McGHEE, John LOWERY, Abram

YEAROUT, Jas. McCALLEN and Thos. HENDERSON, Thos. TURK. Wit: Jonethan WEIR, Samuel ROWAN, J. W. DANFORTH. Proven Sept 1821 by John W. DANFORTH, a witness and continued for further proof. Proven Monroe County court, May term 1829, by Jonethan WEIR; certified for registration by John B. TIPTON, Clerk of the court in Monroe Co., by his deputy John A. COWAN.

709. (3:9) William WALLACE, Sheriff, to Robert THOMPSON: (date omitted) Mar 1829, $1100, 130 ac adj Abraham HITCH, Arthur GREEN. Public sale 8 July 1826 as property of Daniel MOORE to satisfy judgment for $77 with interest and costs of $5.50, recovered 22 May 1824 by John McALESTER against MOORE. Wit: D. D. FOUTE, John NORWOOD. 16 May 1829.

710. (3:10) Joseph COOKE to William ASHER: 22 Jan 1822, $650, 114 ac on a branch of Nine Mile Creek. adj John RAUPH and Archabald STRAIN, Robert STRAIN, John ROUTH, being the same tract purchased by LOVE and FOUTE from Nickolas BYERS. Two installments having been paid thereon [to the state], Asher to pay the balance. Wit: Samuel CARUTHERS, William COOK, William HOOPER. 21 July 1829.

711. (3:10-11) Joseph JONES to James TIPTON: 22 Dec 1828, $975, 88 ac on waters of Crooked Creek, adj Robert CAMPBLE. Wit: Alsop Y. FAGG, John (X) HUTCHENS. 21 July 1829.

712. (3:11-12) George HADDEN to Jacob M. HADDEN and George HADDEN, Jr.: 21 Feb 1829, $800, "the plantation whereon I now live known by the name of the Blue Spring, containing 130 ac; my negro boy BERRY aged about 20 or 21 years; my roan mare Ned, three milk cows and two yearlings, eight head of sheep, twenty four head of hogs, one feather bed and furniture, one pair of tongs and fire shovel, one pair fire dogs, one table, five chairs, two pots, two ovens, one skillet, one spider, one pot rack, one cotton wheel, one douser, one pashear plough, two shovels, two (cullirgees?), one pair (stitchers?), one log chain, three chains, two pair hens and two pair chains, one blend Bridle; seven puter (pewter) plate, one pewter dish, one pewter basin, one brass candlestick, one pair of stilyards, one coffee mill, one adze, one iron wedge, one mattock, two (hens Rock Tuguspul?) plow,

one Bible, two sad irons, one chest, one tea kettle, two bolls (bowls) one four hundred (illegible word) one six hundred (same illegible word), one shawl, one pitchfork, and all the bacon which I have at this time and all the corn, hay, and fodder which I have on the plantation, six head of geese and one (illegible phrase)...which property is to be equally divided between Jacob and George." Wit: Hugh BOGLE, Nathanel JEFFRIES . 21 July 1829.

713. (3:12-13) John TORBET to Benjamin PRATER of Roane Co.: 17 Aug 1826, $1500, 233 ac on Holston River, cor to Peter BOWERMAN's occupant survey, cor to Hugh TORBET. Wit: Hugh TORBET, Alexander ISH. 21 July 1829.

714. (3:13) John LAMBERT to Thomas BLACKBURN: 2 Jan 1823, $400, 97 ac on waters of Sinking Creek, being part of a tract Granted to Henry SHIELDS and conveyed by SHIELDS to Samuel SHAW and from SHAW to Smallwood CAYWOOD and to LAMBERT. Wit: John GOINS, Larkin THOMPSON. Proven at March 1829 court by Larkin THOMPSON who further swears that John GOINS is not an inhabitant of the state. 21 July 1829.

715. (3:14) Thomas CROWDER to Betsey DONCARLAS: 10 Jan 1826, $400, one negro woman named AEGG? about 21 years of age. 21 July 1829.

716. (3:14-15) Thomas DEAN to William JOHNSTON: 11 Sep 1826, $260, 31 ac on waters of Carr's Creek, adj Jacob MOORE. Sig: Thomas (X) DEAN. With: Lot (X) ROGERS, Willoughby (X) ROGERS. 2 July 1829.

717. (3:15) David CARSON to Milton H. CARSON: 28 July 1828, "in consideration of the good will I have to my son Milton Henderson CARSON,... the tract of land that I now live on. Also two head of horses...only that I have the use of them to work and ride when I need them; also three head of milk cows and calves..also one corner cupboard." Wit: Mathew (X) SAMPLES, David CARSON, Jr., Joseph (X) CARSON, William (X) HAMMONTREE. 21 July 1829.

718. (3:15-16) John HENDRIF to Thomas CARNER/CARNES/ CARVER?: 23 Mar 1827, $400, 160 ac on waters of Tennessee River,

adj William TIPTON, being the west half of an occupant claim laid down for George SNIDER, surveyed 5 Sept 1820. Wit: Wm. HENDRIF, William DAVIS. 21 July 1829.

719. (3:16) Thomas SPRAGGINS, Sr. to Lot ROGERS: 11 Sep 1826 $200, 73 ac on Carr's Creek, adj James HUBBARD, Christian BOGLE. Sig: Thomas (X) SPRAGGINS. Wit: Wm. JOHNSON, Willoughby (X) ROGERS. Proven Sept 1828 by witnesses. 21 July 1829.

720. (3:16-17) James BADGETT, Jr. to William BOWEN of Knox Co.: 14 Mar 1829, 207 ac on north side of Stock Creek a small distance from the first bend, adj BARTLETT's survey, Little River, cor to James PERCE, cor to James and Robert PEARCE, Robert GREEN?. Another tract of 15 ac on Stock Creek where THURMAN's line crosses, containing in all 222 ac. Wit: Moses ARMSTRONG, C.G.N. BOWEN. 22 July 1829.

721. (3:18) Joseph JONES to James TIPTON: 25 December 1828, $100, a parcel of land held as Patentee from the State, 50 ac on waters of Crooked Creek, cor to JONES' original survey. Wit: Alsop Y. FAGG, John (X) KITCHENS. 22 July 1829.

722. (3:18-19) Halbert McCLURE to Joseph McREYNOLDS: 1 Feb 1826, $400, negro boy DAVID about 16 yrs old. Wit: John D. McREYNOLDS, David McREYNOLDS, John McCLURE. 22 July 1829.

723. (3:19) James KNIGHT to Jeffrey JOHNSON: 24 Jan 1815, $183.50, 183 ac on waters of Nails Creek, Grant #1351 cor to HARDIN and NORMAN, adj HAFLEY, cor N. FARMER, A. PHILLIPS, HADDEN's corner. Surveyed July 8, 1807. Wit: John REAGON, Elizabeth (X) DAVIS. Proven March 1816 court by John REAGON and afterwards by Elizabeth DAVIS, and ordered to be registered 15 May 1817 by James HOUSTON, Clerk. 22 July 1829.

724. (3:20) Mathew H. BLACKBURN to Thomas BLACKBURN: 8 Jan 1820, $250, 165 ac on Sinking Creek, Granted to Eli DIXON..beginning ...by a sink near the mill...[to] a stone by the still house, being the same tract of land that Mathew H. BLACKBURN

purchased of David HUNTER and HUNTER purchased at Sheriff Sale on 16 July 1814. Wit: Nathan THOMSON, Spencer THOMSON. Proven at March 1829 court by Spenser THOMSON, who also stated that Nathan THOMSON is dead. 22 July 1829.

725. (3:20-22) William WALLACE, Sheriff, to Jacob F. FOUTE: 2 Sep 1824, $3.25, 40 ac on waters of Crooked Creek, "adj Thomas WALLACE's corner of the survey where he did live", a tract levied on as property of John NORWOOD, to satisfy judgments issued on 30 Jan 1826: one in favor of David NEYMAN against John GOULD and John NORWOOD, one in favor of John WEIR against John NORWOOD and Josiah P. SMITH, one in favor of Archy MURPHEY against John NORWOOD. Public Sale on 21 Mar 1821 by Deputy Sheriff Joseph ALEXANDER then a deputy to Charles DONAHOO, DONOHOO [has] gone out of office and also removed not having executed any deed while in office. Wit: Wm. THOMSON, Obediah BOAZ. 23 July 1829.

726. (3:22-23) Daniel KARR to William DAVIS: 31 July 1828, $50, 75 ac on waters of Ellejoy Creek, adj Jacob MOOR, except 8 ac adj the land granted by TN to Jacob MOORE. Wit: Hugh BOGLE, Mathew H. BOGLE. 23 July 1829.

727. (3:23-24) Edward DELOZIER to Larkin BOLIN: 3 Mar 1828, $100, 50 ac on waters of Ellejoy Creek, adj L. BOLING's land. Wit: Benjamin TIPTON, Edward A.[or W]. BASS. Proven March 1828 court by Benjamin TIPTON who swears that Edward BASS is not a citizen of the state as he believes, that he saw the said ROSS (sic) witness the deed. 24 July 1829.

728. (3:24-25) Edward DELOZIER to Larken BOLEN: 3 Mar 1828, $30, 10 ac on waters of Ellejoy Creek, adj Lot ROGERS. Wit: Benjamin TIPTON, Edward BASS. 25 July 1829.

729. (3:25-26) William HARPER of Crooked Creek (first party) to James HENRY (second party) and Samuel HENRY, Moses GAMBLE and Josias GAMBLE of Little River (third party): 2 Feb 1828, $148.88 due to Samuel HENRY, one note of $19.55 due on 28 Dec 1827, one note $47.57 due 28 June 1829, one note bearing even date with this indenture for $33.15 due 25 Dec next, a judgment for Josias

GAMBLE before Samuel HENRY, Esq., balance on the same 418.82 rendered on 30 Jan last, part against Wm. HARPER and Robert R. KINCANNON, one in favor of Moses GAMBLE for $29.90, judgment also rendered by HENRY, Esq. on 3 Jan last past and owing by Wm. HARPER in hand paid. Wm. HARPER sells to James HENRY a tract of 62 ac on Crooked Creek, cor to George BERRY, adj heirs of William REGUN, LOWERY. HARPER shall pay on 25 Dec next to HENRY, Moses and Josias GAMBLE the sum of $158.88. Wit: W. W. GARNER, Philip DAVIS. 8 Oct 1829.

730. (3:26-27) Campble WALLACE to John FREEMAN: 3 Dec 1828, $3500, lot #63 in Maryville, Grant #314 to Miles and David CUNNINGHAM, adj lot #62 belonging to Campble WALLACE. Wit: Jake TEMPLE, Thos. L. LUCHETTE. 9 Jan 1829.

731. (3:27-28) William W. BERRY of Roane Co. to James BERRY: 13 October 1828, $10,000, a house and lot #40 in Maryville. Wit: Jacob F. FOUTE, Robert McNUTT. 9 Oct 1829.

732. (3:28-29) William WALLACE, Sheriff, to Robert HOOK and Elizabeth HOOK, formerly Elizabeth KILBURN: 20 Dec 1828, $58, 164 ac adj lands of Robert HOOK, John CALDWELL, cor James McCAWLLY on a line of survey made by Samuel McCAWLLY, John CALDWELL, Oliver ALEXANDER, THORNBURY, Samuel McCULLOCH. Land descended from James KILBURN, decd, to William KILBURN, Benjamin KILBURN, Elizabeth KILBURN, Hannah CAMPBELL wife of Arthur B. CAMPBELL formerly Hanah KILBURN, Mary CRAFT, widow and relict of Elias WRIGHT, decd, formerly Mary KILBURN, Nancy KILBURN, John KILBURN, and Sally KILBURN, lawful heirs at law. Public sale 4 Oct 1823 to satisfy a judgment recovered by Solomon McCAMPBELL against the estate of James KILBURN, decd, for $35.00 with interest from 31 July 1822 and $10.35 for costs. James EWING was agent of Elizabeth HOOK, then Elizabeth KILBURN, in the bidding. Wit: Campbell WALLACE, A. B. WALLACE. 10 January 1829.

733. (3:29-30) Samuel HOUSTON to Jesse THOMPSON: 16 June 1821, $1200, lot #2 thru #46, #47,and #48 in Maryville; lot #2 bounded on northeast by lot #1 whereon the Reverend Isaac

ANDERSON now lives, on the southwest by lot #3, on north by a back street, and on south end by the Commons. Lots 46-48 adj each other on which HOUSTON now lives and has a blacksmith shop, bounded on northeast by Commons. Wit: Andrew THOMPSON, Samuel BLACKBURN. 23 Nov 1829.

734. (3:30-32) The deed and court orders on these pages contain several obvious clerical errors and omissions, and they are recopied on pages 32-34.

735. (3:32) Court order to William TOOL and George EWING, Justices of the Peace, requiring the private examination of Elizabeth HOOK, wife of Robert HOOK, as to her free consent in executing a deed of conveyance to Diana KILBURN. Sig: Jacob F. FOUTE, Clerk, by his deputy D. D. FOUTE. 10 Jan (year omitted).

736. (3:32-34) Robert HOOKS et ux to Diana KILBURN: 20 Dec 1828, $300, a tract cor to James McCULLY on a line of survey made for Samuel McCULLOCH, adj John CALDWELL, Oliver ALEXANDER, Ben ALEXANDER, THORNBURY survey, Samuel McCULLOCH. Wit: A. B. CAMPBELL, J. H. HOOK. Ack at Dec 1828 session of court by Robert HOOKE. At March session 1829 the court appointed David McKAMY and Wm. GAUTT, Esqrs. to take the private examination of Elizabeth, who made their report on 23 March 1829. 19 June 1829.

737. (3:34) Samuel HOUSTON to Jesse THOMPSON of Maryville: 20 Oct 1821, $425, a negro boy slave of yellow complexion named ELIAS about the age of 15 years. Wit: A. R. LOGAN. 9 July 1822.

738. (3:34-35) John HAMMONTREE to John WOODS: 28 Sep 1829, $18.50, 9 ac on Baker's Creek, adj HAMMONTREE. Sig: John (X) HAMMONTREE. Wit: John WOOD, Joseph LOGAN. 20 Nov 1829.

739. (3:35-36) James HOUSTON to Joseph LAMON: 2 Sep 1829, $1200, an equal undivided half of 12 ac on Pistol Creek, adj James WEAR, together with the privilege of raising the mill dam where it now stands as high as it is now planked. Wit: Samuel PRIDE, Wm. TOOL, J. E. MONTGOMERY. 11 Dec 1829.

740. (3:36) James HOUSTON to James H. GILLESPIE: 28 Mar 1829, $38.74, lot #80 in Maryville. Wit: Jno. TEMPLE, James GILLESPIE. 10 Nov 1829.

741. (3:36-37) John MILLER to William McCLUNG: 17 Sep 1829, $250, 86 ac on Baker's Creek, adj McCLUNG, Thomas WEIR, John WILSON. Granted to Magnes TULLOCH and conveyed by him to MILLER. Wit: Samuel MONTGOMERY, Samuel STEEL. 20 Nov 1829.

742. (3:37-38) John WOODS to John HAMMONTREE: 25 Sep 1829, $2.50, 1 ac on Baker's Creek, cor to land of Wm. WOODS and HAMMONTREE. Wit: John WOODS, Joseph LOGAN. 12 Dec 1829.

743. (3:38) Thomas L. UPTON to Joseph WILSON, Jr.: 4 Sep 1829, $300, 100 ac on waters of Baker's Creek and a branch of the Tennessee, being part of Grant #2194 to William HOWELL and by him conveyed to Robert and James STRAIN, then to John B. HARRIS, and by Nancy HARRIS, the relict and widow of John B. HARRIS, decd, to Thomas L. UPTON; adj Isaac YEAROUT, Thomas MAXWELL. Wit: Robert CALDWELL, Wm. GAUTT. 20 Nov 1829.

744. (3:39-40) Jacob F. FOUTE to James HENRY of Baker's Creek: 1 July 1828, 252 ac on waters of Baker's Creek, adj Samuel HENRY, Grant #23 to Wm. HENRY. On 17 Sep 1821 William W. HENRY conveyed to FOUTE in trust to secure to McGHEE AND BROTHERS the payment of $464.66; on 17 May 1828 James HENRY paid $659.26 in full payment and satisfaction of the principal, interest and costs. On 10 June 1828 Wm. W. HENRY requested FOUTE to release and convey all the claim... Wit: Daniel D. FOUTE, Wm. M. LOWERY. 18 Dec 1829.

745. (3:40) Daniel D. FOUTE to David DEARMOND: 21 Sep 1829, $630 the amount of redemption money due, Quit Claim to 176 ac whereon David DEARMOND now lives, Granted to John HANNA, and another tract of 50 acres late Entry Granted to DEARMOND. FOUTE purchased at Sheriff Sale the land of David DEARMOND and

by agreement dated 11 July 1828 DEARMOND has a right to redeem the land. Wit: James TRUNDLE, Samuel HENRY. 20 Nov 1829.

746. (3:40-41) David DEARMOND to John RODDY: 21 Sep 1829, $850, 176 ac on Little River, adj John WHEELER, Thomas COULDWELL, James HANNAH, Jno McFADDEN. Another tract of 50 ac cor to DEARMOND's original survey above described, thence with John RODDY. DEARMOND is to give possession on 1 March next. Wit: Daniel D. FOUTE, Sam HENRY. 9 Dec 1829.

747. (3:42-43) Daniel D. FOUTE (first party) to James WILSON (second party) and John B. CUSICK (third party): 9 Feb 1829, 8 ac adj Town of Maryville, cor to John LOWRY now the Seminary land, McGHEE, Pistol Creek, the Commons of Maryville, KING and MONTGOMERY. FOUTE is indebted to CUSICK by notes bearing this date, one for $318, due on or before 1 Sept 1830; one for $169 due on 1 Mar 1832, and the other due on 1 Feb 1835 for $170; for which WILSON is security. Wit: James H. GILLESPIE, John SAFFEL. 20 Nov 1829.

748. (3:43-44) Joseph LAMON/LAYMON (first party) to James H. GILLESPIE (second party) and James HOUSTON (third party): 3 Sep 1829, 12 ac known by the name of HOUSTON mill place. LAYMON has made several promissory notes for $200 each payable in property, the first to be due on 1 Jan 1831, the second on 1 Jan 1830 (sic), the third to be due on 1 Jan 1833, the fourth to be due on 1 Jan 1834, fifth on 1 Jan 1835. LAYMON appoints GILLESPIE his trustee in fact to secure payment of these notes. Wit: Wm. TOOLE, Samuel HENRY. 20 Nov 1829.

749. (3:44-45) Samuel PRIDE, as atty in fact on behalf of Mathew TOOL of Mississippi, to William TOOL: 7 Sep 1827, $100, the undivided one-fifth part of following property: one half of an undivided interest in lot #33 on Main Street and lot #81, being a middle lot in the town of Maryville, and also an undivided half of a tract of 2 ac near the town of Maryville, adj the Great Road leading from Maryville to Tellico on a line of original surveys made for Barkley McGHEE and John LOWRY; the same being the interest of Mathew TOOL as a devisee of the estate of John TOOL, lately

deceased, which property was held by John TOOL before his death and Samuel LOVE fourthly together. Wit: Thos. J. FOUTE, Joseph JOHNSTON. 31 Dec 1829.

750. (3:45-46) Jacob GARST?/GURST?/GUEST and Magdalene, his wife, of VA, to Daniel D. FOUTE: 23 Mar 1829, $100 paid by FOUTE to Christopher GARST, son of Jacob, 89 ac on west fork of Pistol Creek adj Morganton Road. Sig: Jacob GURST. Magdaline (X) GURST. Ack in Botetourt Co. VA and certified 25 Mar 1829.

751. (3:46-47) John COLWELL (first party) to James HENRY (second party) and Samuel HENRY (third party): 4 July 1826, $503.36 borrowed from and owing by John and Samuel COLWELL to Samuel HENRY, due on 4 July 1827, 476.5 ac on waters of Little River adj lands of James EWING on the northeast, vacant land on the northwest, Oliver ALEXANDER and John McCULLOCH on the southwest, George CALDWELL'S Grant #1788 dated June 1810 on southeast. COLDWELL shall pay $503.36 within one year from the date of this indenture. Wit: Samuel COULDWELL, Alexander CALDWELL, Washington CALDWELL, John (X) ADKINS. 7 Jan 1830.

752. (3:48) John CALDWELL to Robert P./D.? CHANDLER: 21 Oct 1829, $600, tract on waters of Little River, part of Grant #1718 containing 288 ac to John COULDWELL, adj Jno S. DUFF. Wit: Theo WILKENSON, William L. CALDWELL. Proven at court 28 Dec 1829 by Theophilas WILKENSON and William L. CALDWELL. 7 Jan 1830.

753. (3:49-50) William WALLACE, Sheriff and Collector of the Public Taxes, to William TOOLE: 26 Dec 1829, $63.20, town lots #113 and #114; public sale 20 Sep 1828 as the property of Gideon BLACKBURN, for taxes for the years 1822 through 1826..."the [property] was liable to double tax and the double taxes were unsatisfied and...the owner of lots had not goods or chattels within the county on which he could destrain for taxes." Wit: Campble WALLACE, Sam WALLACE. 12 Jan 1830.

754. (3:50-51) Mathew NELSON, Treasurer of East Tennessee, to John SHARP: 7 July 1826, "Whereas by an Act of the General

Assembly of the State of Tennessee passed at Murfreesborough on the fourteenth day of November 1823, it is made the duty on or before the first of May 1824 of all persons claiming land within the District South of French Broad and Holston and west of Big Pigeon River, to pay to the Treasurer one-fifth part of the whole debt and interest ascertained to be due and owing after making the deduction allowed and authorized by said Act, and whereas it is also made the duty of said persons to pay to the said Treasurer one-sixth of the remainder together with the interest thereon accrued on the first day of May next following the one last above mentioned on the whole quantity contained within the Grant under which they respectively claim ... whereas default has been made by nonpayment of the installment interest and costs due on Grant #951 dated 3 May 1810 issued to Thomas WALLACE for 226 ac.." public sale 20 July 1825, John SHARP bid for the whole of said land $74.98. Land adj Thomas WALLACE, Jr., John WILLIAMSON, Abram WALLACE, Jesse WALLACE, Samuel WEAR, BELL. Wit: John F. GILLESPIE, John O'CONNER. 25 Feb 1830.

755. (3:52-53) William LOWERY and wife Polly, formerly Polly McGHEE, daughter of Barckley McGHEE, decd, of McMinn Co., to Jesse THOMPSON for Daniel D. FOUTE: 2 Mar 1830, $750, "whereas on 25 July 1823 William LOWERY sold to Daniel D. FOUTE six lots in the town of Maryville and bound himself to convey the lots to FOUTE upon certain conditions..which FOUTE on his part has performed..and in consideration of $1000..and whereas FOUTE transferred the said 6 lots to Jesse THOMPSON and requires title to be made to THOMPSON..lots #52 and 53 in front, #92 and 93 in the middle, and #100 and #101 on the back range of lots in the original plan of Maryville, being the same now occupied by THOMPSON and the same one purchased by B. McGHEE of Josiah P. SMITH and given by McGHEE to his daughter Polly LOWRY. Wit: Samuel McCONNELL, John MILLER, Commissioners appointed by County Court of McMinn Co. 25 Mar 1830.

756. (3:53-54) William THOMPSON to James THOMPSON: 13 Aug 1825, $500, 111 ac on Crooked Creek, part of Grant #1050 to John McREYNOLDS adj vacant land, the Pine Mountain. Wit: Wm. THOMAS, D. D. FOUTE. 25 Mar 1830.

757. (3:55) John LOWERY of Taladega Co. AL, to Samuel PRIDE:
11 Aug 1835, $659.40, 132 ac on waters of Pistol Creek in the vicinity
of Maryville, "all that part of original tract Granted to John LOWRY
except one acre lot known by the name of the Libera [library?] lot and
two ac belonging to Samuel LOVE and one acre lot of ground
belonging to David RUSSEL and all that on the left hand from town
on the east side of the road passing between LOVE and RUSSELL's
lots and McGHEE's field to the Creek, Mat McGHEE's, Tellico Road,
road to Six Mile at or near the corner of McGHEE's field adjoining the
church and grave yard land." Wit: Wm TOOL, C. H. SAFFELL. Ack
by TOOL and "Clemmon C. SAFFLE" (sic) 16 Sep 1835. 20 Sep
1835.

758. (3:55-57) Jane LOWERY (first party) to Samuel PRIDE (second
party) and Andrew C. MONTGOMERY and John EAGLETON (third
party): 25 Sep 1835, LOWERY is indebted to MONTGOMERY and
EAGLETON on a note of $643.83 due one day after date and
MONTGOMERY and EAGLETON having required further security;
[tract] on waters of Crooked Creek whereon Jane LOWERY now
lives, adj GRISSOM, KEY, William LOWERY, George BERRY,
John M. BERRY. Being the same that John M. LOWERY, husband
of Jane LOWERY, died possessed of that was lived on by virtue of a
deed of the county court sold at Sheriff Sale on 13 May 1835 to satisfy
claims executed against estate of John M. LOWERY and purchased by
Jane LOWERY. LOWERY to pay within 12 months with interest.
Sig: Jane R. LOWERY. Wit: John KEYS, Thomas J. HARPER. 30
Sep 1835.

759. (3:57-58) John STEPHENS to George DUNKIN/DUNCAN: 27
June 1831, $10, 30 ac adj John SINGLETON, DUNKIN's survey,
Thomas HART. Wit: James HUMPHREYS, Benjamin DUNCAN.
10 Oct 1835.

760. (3:58) Levi MAYS to Joseph McREYNOLDS: 1 Oct 1835,
MAYS is indebted to McREYNOLDS for $200; one chestnut sorrel
mare, 15 hogs, 2 beds and furniture, one side board, one walnut table,
six chains, one big wheel, one little wheel, one looking glass, one large
pot, one small pot, one oven, one skillet, one reel, three axes, three
hoes, two plows, two pair of drawing chains, one hand saw, one

drawing knife, one plow, one iron wedge, and 15 head of geese. Wit: Conrad EASTERLY?, David A. McKAMY. 13 Oct 1835.

761. (3:58-59) Hugh HENRY to William RAGAN: 10 Apr 1832, $45, 18 ac adj John HENRY's lot #7, cor to James HENRY, Sr., the river bank. Wit: Robert WEAR, James HENRY, John HENRY, John HENRY. Sig: Hugh (X) HENRY. 2 Oct 1835.

762. (3:59) Henderson CONNER to Mary, Temperance, Hannah, and Margaret CONNER: 28 Sep 1835, $200 "which we severally and jointly pay". "To Mary, bed and furniture and cow and two yearlings and one sow and her pigs. To Temperance one bed and furniture and one horse and one cow and calf and six head of hogs. To Hannah one bed and furniture, one cow and calf and 100 bushels of corn in the field. Margaret, one bed and furniture, one cow and calf, and one horse and 9 head of hogs and the corn of 50 ac of land." Wit: John McLINN, Alford B. CONNEY?. 10 Oct 1835.

763. (3:59-60) Michel TEDFORD to James HENRY: 9 Oct 1835, $22.25, one sorrel mare as security for $22.25 to be paid within six months. Sig: Michael (X) TEDFORD. Wit: James COX, Henry C. SAFFELL. 9 Oct 1835.

764. (3:60-61) James THOMPSON to John COULTER: 20 Dec 1834, $450, 111 ac on waters of Crooked Creek, part of Grant #1053 to John McREYNOLDS,   adj the Piny Mountain. Wit: John McLAIN, John FALKNER. Proven by witnesses 15 Oct 1855 before Nathaniel RAGAN, Clerk of the Court of Pleas and Quarter Sessions. 20 Oct 1855.

765. (3:61-62) John ROGERS (first party) to John WILSON (second party) and Joseph B. HOUSTON (third party): 21 Oct 1835, ROGERS is indebted to HOUSTON for $30 by note dated 21 Oct 1835 due one day after date, for which WILSON is security; one mare four years old, one cow, ten head of hogs, two beds and furniture and all the household and kitchen furniture, 150 bushels corn, 600 bundles fodder, two ploughs. ROGERS to pay within six months with interest. Wit: Samuel PRIDE. Sig: John (X) ROGERS. 23 Oct 1835.

766. (3:62-63) Hugh J. REED to James LANKFORD of Sevier Co.: 25 Sep 1835, $275, [a total of] 199 ac on waters of Nails Creek, one tract of 99 ac, adj Samuel McMURRY; second tract of 50 ac; third tract of 32 ac cor Joseph McMURRY's occupant survey, Robert READ; fourth tract 18 ac adj David HICKEY, Joseph McMURRY. Wit: Hugh BOGLE, James H. DONALDSON. 20 Oct 1835.

767. (3:63-64) John JONES of Washington County, Virginia, to Wm. D. DAVIS: 26 Aug 1835, $500, 228 ac on waters of Ellejoy Creek, adj land Granted to John McNEELY, Benjamin TIPTON, James DAVIS, Robert MANNEN?. Wit: James ROBINSON, Jesse BROWN. Proven at court Sept 1835 by Jesse BROWN, who testified that James ROBISON now resides in the State of Virginia. 21 Oct 1835.

768. (3:64-65) John HUNT to John F. HENRY: 9 Oct 1835, $29.50, one bay mare and colt, two cows, 16 hogs, 16 geese, two beds and the furniture, 2 pair bedsteads, 400 bushels corn, 1000 bundles fodder, 3 pots, 2 ovens, 2 lids, 1 skillet, 2 ploughs. HUNT to pay $29.50 within five months. Sig: John (X) HUNT. Wit: John P. LOVE/LANE?, Joel STONE. 27 Oct 1835.

769. (3:65-66) William WALLACE, Sheriff, to John CHAMBERS: 27 Oct 1835, $4.77 the amount of tax, costs and charges unpaid for year 1830, 137 ac in or near Tuckaleechee Cove belonging to John BREWER/BROWN. Public sale 16 Nov 1833. "Twelve months has expired since the day of sale and the said tract of land remains unencumbered." Wit: John SAFFELL, Sam WALLACE. 28 Oct 1835.

770. (3:66-67) John SIMERLY to James COULTER: 31 Oct 1834, $600, 228 ac on waters of Little River, on bank of Hesse Creek, adj BEARD. Wit: James RAY, Manley (X) KEEBLE. 29 Oct 1835.

771. (3:68-69) James JULIAN of McMinn Co. to Lorenzo DONALDSON: 12 Sep 1835, $700, three tracts on waters of Ellejoy Creek adj Thomas McFEE on east, James DUNLAP on the south and west, the first tract containing 129 ac. Second tract containing 50 ac corner to his original survey, cor with William CUMMINGS. Third 140 ac excepting 40 ac of the last tract which was conveyed to

DUNLAP by JULIAN "agreeable to a condition made between [them]." Wit: Hugh BOGLE, James H. DONALDSON. 29 Oct 1835.

772.   (3:69-71) William HUTCHESON (first party) to Campbell GILLESPY (second party) and Andrew COWAN (third party): 17 Oct 1835, COWAN is security for HUTCHESON in the stay of two executions obtained against him before William TOOL, Esq, an acting justice of the peace for Blount County, one in favor of Alexander GILLESPY, execr of estate of William GILLESPY, Jr., decd, for the use of John F. GILLESPEY, execr of the estate of William GILLESPY, Jr., decd, which judgment was rendered the 2nd day of May last for the sum of $74.55; and for becoming security for him in a promissory note executed to Samuel TORBIT on 5 Sep last for $210 and become due one day after date. Appoints GILLESPIE his trustee..and conveys as security all the live stock now in his possession, consisting of 6 head of horses and 8 head of cows, 13 head of hogs and 20 head of sheep, also all the household and kitchen furniture, farming utensils, and all grain. Wit: Robert HADSEN?. 30 Oct 1835.

773.   (3:71-72) Alexander ISH to Trustees of METHODIST EPISCOPAL CHURCH [Samuel BROOK, Bolen BROOK, John McCULLOUGH, Burrell BOUAM and William BROOK]: 15 Dec 1834, $4.00, about one half acre, beginning at southeast corner of land which ISH bought of COPELAND, corner that connects ISH's and John TUCK's land, adj HOOVER. Trustees shall erect a house or place of worship for the use of the members of the Methodist Episcopal Church in the United States of America ... and when unoccupied by the Methodist to be open for all other Gospel Ministers. The parties mutually agree that where it will not interfere with the Methodist appointments the meeting house is to be open to all other denominations. Wit: Thos. TUCK, Bowling BROOK. 30 Oct 1835.

774. (3:72-73) James WILSON, Trustee, to Samuel WALLACE and Wm. A. SPENCER: 16 Sep 1835, on 9 June 1832 Dan D. FOUTE conveyed to WILSON as Trustee lot #37 in Maryville to secure the payment of certain notes to Joseph R. HENDERSON, assignee of Thomas HENDERSON. FOUTE having failed to pay the debts..and WILSON having been requested by J. R. HENDERSON to sell the

lot...public sale 15 Nov 1836 to highest bidder, Joseph R. HENDERSON, for $460.55. Thomas HENDERSON, as agent of Jos. R. HENDERSON, requested WILSON to make a title of the lot to Messrs. WALLACE and SPENCER. Wit: John MONTGOMERY, James MORTON. Ack by James WILSON before Daniel D. FOUTE, Clerk of the Circuit Court for Blount Co., 16 Sept 1835. 4 Nov 1835.

775. (3:74-75) John BROOK to John J. HOOVER: 9 Aug 1834, $210, 60 ac on waters of Holston River, cor to Boling BROOK, John HENDERSON. Sig: John (X) BROOK. Wit: James GRIFFITTS, James M. JOHNSTON. 7 Nov 1835.

776. (3:75) Eli McCLURE to John CHANDLER: $300, 100 ac, part of a Grant to Charles McCLURE, cor to Alexander McGHEE, Grinsfield TAYLOR. 3 Nov 1835. Wit. Andrew SINGLETON, Edward GEORGE. 9 Nov 1835.

777. (3:76) John McMAHAN, Robert L. CUMMINGS (second part) and D.D. REID (third party): 7 Nov 1835, one sorrell horse, one bay mare, 20 hogs, wagon and gearing, one clock, 100 bushels of corn, 6 wagon loads of hay, all household and kitchen furniture, one thousand bundles fodder. John McMAHAN shall pay within six months to CUMMINGS for the use of Emanuel BEST the sum of $45 with costs and interest of a judgment BEST recovered against McMAHAN, James McALLEN, Stephen S. COULTER. Wit: Will FAGG, Jas. COX. 9 Nov 1835.

778. (3:76-77) Jeremiah M. ELLIS to James McCAMY/McKAMY: 6 Nov 1835, $250, 222 ac, an undivided interest of a tract on waters of Little River, adj George CALWELL, James MORE, Robert HOOK. Wit. Jas. H. COX, J. W. EWING. 10 Nov 1835.

779. (3:78-79) Jacob CUPP, Sr. to Peter BRAKEBILL, Sr.: 7 Nov 1835, $250, 162 ac waters of Nails Creek, adj Adam CALDWELL, Peter BRAKEBILL, John McCALLIE, Adam THOMAS, HAFLEY's line. Wit: Washington HAFLEY, George CUPP. Sig: Jacob (X) CUPP. 16 Nov 1835.

780. (3:79-80) Josiah HUTTON to William S. HUTTON of Lincoln Co., MO, an heir of Josiah HUTTON: 17 Nov 1835, 130 ac on waters

of Baker's Creek adj Webb WILSON and others, Mary WEBB, Sarah WILSON...this being the east end of my old survey, the place whereon William S. HUTTON formerly lived..his part or portion of the land I now live on agreeable to my last will and testament..[also] power to sell or dispose of said portion of land as he sees proper to do. Wit: Samuel E. COPE, James COX. 17 Nov 1835.

781. (3:80-81) William S. HUTTON of Lincoln Co., MO, to Joseph A. HUTTON: 17 Nov 1835, $500, 130 ac on waters of Baker's Creek [tract in the deed above]. Wit: Samuel E. COPE, James COX. Ack by William S. HUTTON before Nathaniel RAGAN, clerk of the Court of Pleas and Quarter Sessions, 17 Nov 1835. 18 Nov 1835.

782. (3:81) Cyris BROYLES of Greene Co. to Thomas CARPENTER: 10 Jan 1835, $100, 47 ac on waters of Nine Mile Creek, being an entry #497, made in the Entry Taker's Office of Blount, 25 May 1827, adj John GLASS, RUDD, ALEXANDER. Wit: Wm. COOPER, Washington B. CLARK. 18 Nov 1835.

783. (3:82-83) William COOPER, for himself and as atty in fact for John COOPER of Wayne Co. IN, to Thomas CARPENTER: 15 Oct 1835, consideration omitted, 157 ac on waters of Nine Mile Creek in the original survey made by Thomas COOPER, Sr. of 172 ac, in two tracts: first tract of 149 ac adj D. D. FOUTE, GLASS; second tract 7 ac. Wit: Dan D. FOUTE, Benjamin WILLIAMS. 18 Nov 1835.

784. (3:83-84) Samuel JONES to John HENDERSON: 22 Sep 1835, $50, 22 ac on waters of Gallaher's Creek, adj Robert McCULLY. Wit: Samuel HENDRICKSON, Willis HENDRICKSON. 25 Nov 1835.

785. (3:84-85) James MURRY to D. D. FOUTE: 19 Nov 1835, $600, (ac omitted) on Six Mile Creek, adj John NEAL, John BOGEL, HAMMONTREE. Wit: William McKASKLE, Alfred WHITEHEAD. 30 Nov 1835.

786. (3:85-87) Wm. WALLACE, Sheriff, to James MURRY: 13 Dec 1833, 107 ac on waters of Baker's Creek, adj Elexander McCOLLOM, being part of a 297 ac tract granted to James HAMMINTREE and John HAMMINTREE, public sale 26 Dec 1829 to satisfy judgment recovered 31 Aug 1828 by William McCLURG against James

TEDFORD for $42.78; ..James TEDFORD, Jr. became the highest bidder for $53.25, and has directed the Sheriff to make title to MURRY. Wit: Alex McNUTT, Wm. C. GILLESPY.

787. (3:87) Michael TEDFORD to John LOVE: 28 Nov 1835, $25.50, 20 head of hogs, one beaurow and bookcase, 1 set dog irons, one large kettle, two plains (sic), 1 pair of gears and saddle, one clock, two (cows?), 300 bushels corn, 3,000 feet of plank, one bed and furniture, 1 pair bedsteds. TEDFORD to pay to LOVE, the sum of $25.50 within 12 months for redemption of the property. Sig: Michael (X) TEDFORD. Wit: John C. McKAY, William S. LOVE. 3 Dec 1835.

788. (3:88-89) David D. FOUTE (first party), Samuel W. WALLACE (second party) to William W. WALLACE and Will A. SPENCER (third party): 6 Dec 1835, "FOUTE being in need of money and to obtain the same procured the names of Will WALLACE as drawer and William A. SPENCER as clerk Indorser with himself as the other indorser to a note and had the same discounted on 26 Nov 1835 at the Planters Bank of Tennessee at the office of discount and deposit at Athens and thereby obtained $1,000 payable six months after the date of discount, which money was applied to the use of FOUTE and to indemnify WALLACE and SPENCER from any costs or charges or liabilities..and for the purpose of raising the money to meet the debt, if necessary," FOUTE sells..5,000 ac of land adj James MURRAY's east corner on the old Indian boundary line, also adj William THOMPSON, HAMMONTREE, MORTON, Richard W. RAGAIN, REMINGTON, John BOYD, John SIMERLY Sr., Robert A. NEAL, including Montvale Springs, and also two wagons, 6 yoke of oxen, 8 cows and 8 calves and yearlings, 100 head of stock hogs, 20 head of sheep, ten featherbeds, bedsteds and furniture, two beaurows, two china presses, two sets of folding leaf tables and fifty chairs. Wit: Samuel PRIDE, D. W. TEDFORD. 19 Dec 1835.

789. (3:89-91) William GAMBLE and William WILSON to Harrison BOLING: 29 Oct 1835, GAMBLE and WILSON are indebted to Andrew PEERY in the sum of $200 by notes of hand, one for $150 dated 29 Oct 1835 and due the first day of Oct 1836 and one for the sum of $50 dated 29 Oct 1835 and due 29 Apr 1836, and PEERY

being willing to wait eleven months longer upon having his debts and interest secured...2 ac on waters of Little River and Ellejoy Creek, beginning near the spring of John F. GARNER, crossing the great road ...also two milk cows, one red and one pied, and one sorrel mare. Wit: Thomas R. McKENRY, Samuel McKENRY. 21 Dec 1835.

790. (3:91-92) William HANNAH to William SCOTT: 18 Nov 1835, $600, 166 ac on waters of Pistol Creek, adj Andrew F. HANNAH, John DELZELL, DAVIS. Sig: William M. HANNAH. Wit: Sam WALLACE, Fielding POPE. 22 Dec 1835.

791. (3:93-95) John WILSON, Deputy Sheriff, to John P. KERR: 15 Sep 1835, $475, 225 ac on waters of Gallaher's Creek adj Leonard RHEA, Jesse HENDRICKSON, and others. Public sale 23 May 1835 as property of Powell WILLIAMS to satisfy two judgments recovered by James McWILLIAMS against WILLIAMS before Leroy NOBLE, a justice of the peace for Blount County, for the sums of $88.88 and $314. Wit: James K. COX, Nath RAGAN. 22 Dec 1835.

792. (3:95-96) John TORBET to Nelson WRIGHT: 16 Dec 1835, $100, 24 ac, part of the tract of 590 ac granted to James TEDFORD, adj Joseph B. HOUSTON. Wit: Robert WEAR, J. B. HOUSTON. 22 Dec 1835.

793. (3:97) John TORBET to J. B. HOUSTON: 16 Dec 1835, $400, 120 ac, part of tract of 590 ac granted to James TEDFORD, cor to Nelson WRIGHT. Wit: Robert WEAR, Samuel HOUSTON. 23 Dec 1835.

794. (3:98-99) Alexander S. COULTER to William WALLACE: 12 Nov 1835, $566, 189 ac at the head of the Long Hollow, Grant #1297 to John JAMES, cor to Robert LEATHERDALE, Mark LOVE, William JAMES, Hugh WEAR. Wit: Ransom P. BOWERMAN, T. J. WALKER. 23 Dec 1835.

795. (3:99) James N. HADEN/HAYDEN to John CUMMINGS: 14 Dec 1835, $100, lot #72 in Maryville on north side of Main Street at the upper end of the town, joining the commons on the west and the lots now owned by Samuel LOVE on the east, being the same lot on which John CUMMINGS has erected a wagon maker's shop and

dwelling house in which CUMMINGS now lives. Wit: Sam WALLACE, Wm. A. SPENCER. 26 Dec 1835.

796. (3:100) James N. HADEN/HAYDEN to Will TOOLE: 14 Nov 1835, $250, one ac adj town of Maryville beginning on the commons, adj Matt McGHEE. Wit: J. A. FAGG, Will L. BRAUDER. 26 Dec 1835.

797. (3:101) James FROW to Richard RAGAN: 28 Dec 1835, $4.00, 2 ac on the road leading from Maryville to Morganton adj land where RAGAN now lives and Moses ELLIOTT. Wit: Moses ELLIOTT, John RAGAN. 28 Dec 1835.

798. (3:102-03) Martin BONHAM (first party) to William KEITH (second party) and James WILSON (third party). 25 Dec 1835, 168 ac on headwaters of Lackey's Creek, Grant #554 to James KENDRICK, adj Shadrack HICKS, G. BLACKBURN. BONHAM is indebted to WILSON for $162.90 due 26 Dec 1835 and also to WILSON and SAFFELL/SAFFLE for $251.10 due 26 Dec 1835, for which KEITH is security. If BONHAM fails to pay, it shall be the duty of Keith to advertise tract of land in the MARYVILLE INTELLIGENCER or in some other careful manner and in 30 days to sell the tract at the courthouse door in Maryville. Wit: Clement H. SAFFELL, Jas. COX. 30 Dec 1835.

799. (3:103-04) John STANFIELD to Uriah HINSHAW of Jefferson Co.: 8 Oct 1827, $50, 35 ac on the draughts of Gallaher's Creek, being a tract Granted by State of TN to STANFIELD, adj John HANNAH, David BROWN, surveyed 30 Sep 1825. Wit: Joseph JONES, Will GRIFFITTS. 1 Jan 1836.

800. (3:104-05) John COPELAND "formerly of Blount Co." to Uriah HINSHAW of Jefferson Co.: 8 Oct 1827, $150, 25 ac on Gallaher's Creek, part of the occupant survey made for Alexander FORD, adj John HANNAH. Wit: John HACKNEY, Jr., Eally (X) PALMER. 1 Jan 1836.

801. (3:105-06) John LACY to Nathan ROSE: 6 Feb 1835, $300, 160 ac in Cades Cove, lot #16. Wit: James SPARKS, Robert BURCHFIELD. 2 Jan 1836.

802. (3:106-07) Johnson SUIT to James SPARKS: 19 Jan 1835,
$150, 43 ac in Cades Cove, part of the occupant survey granted to
William TIPTON, adj Samuel SUIT. Sig: Johnston (X) SUIT Wit:
Moses Y. BURCHFIELD, Robert BURCHFIELD. 2 Jan 1836.

803. (3:107-08) Thomas TIPTON to James SPARKS: 3 Jan 1835,
$700, 160 ac on waters of Abram's Creek, adj the Creek, corner to
lots #21, 22, 23, cor to A. B. WISEMAN.   Wit: Robert
BURCHFIELD, John DAVIS. 2 Jan 1836.

804. (3:108-09) James Y. COLDWELL to Robert M. COLDWELL:
23 Nov 1835, $428, undivided half of 214 ac on the headwaters of
Baker's Creek conveyed to David COLDWELL, decd, by John
NORWOOD, to include the buildings. The tract was willed to James
Y. COLDWELL by his father David COLDWELL, decd. Wit: Wm.
McKAMY, Joseph WILSON. 2 Jan 1836.

805. (3:109-10) Wm. COPELAND to Alexander A. ISH: 24 Feb
1834, $600, 159 ac on Gallaher's Creek, one half of an old survey
made to Alexander FORD, adj David GRUBB, SHAW's Mill dam,
David KEY. Wit: Samuel PRATER, David KEY. 6 Jan 1836.

806. (3:111-12) Miles SCROGGS to George HUTSELL, Sr.: 16
May 1834, $250, 100 ac on waters of Crooked Creek adj HUTSELL,
Sr. Wit: Nathaniel RAGAN, Hugh HAMILL. 8 Jan 1836.

807. (3:114) Robert REED to Adam FAGALA of Sevier Co.: 15 Dec
1835, $300, several tracts on waters of Nails Creek: 50 ac Grant
#10935 to John McMURRY 12 May 1825, and a 10 ac tract of
McMURRIE's, adj R. REED, J. VANCE, John SHARP. 46 ac Grant
#13973 to Robert REED 7 Feb 1827, adj William McMURRY,
SHARP. 100 ac Grant #10931 to REED on 12 May 1825, cor to
Joseph McMURRY, John McMURRAY, J. VANCE, J. SIMS .
Another tract of 2 ac purchased by REED from Josiah JONES, adj
William McMURRIE. Wit: John BRABSON, John (X) WATERS. 20
Jan 1836.

808. (3:116-17) Joseph HOLLOWAY to Bains HOLLOWAY: 26
Jan 1813, $300, 131 ac on waters of Six Mile Creek, being Grant
#1445 to Joseph, adj John HOLLOWAY, crossing the Creek, adj

Jeremiah HAMMONTREE, James HOLLOWAY, Wit: John (X) EDMEANS, Minn?Mann? HOLLOWAY. 23 Jan 1836.

809. (3:117-18) John R. McCLURE(first party) to John CHANDLER(second party) and David CHANDLER (third party): 20 (month omitted) 1836, 100 ac on waters of Holston River to be cut off in the same manner that is specified in John R. McCLURE's father's will; to secure a note of hand given by McCLURE to David CHANDLER for $100 payable in 12 months from this date, for which John CHANDLER is security. Wit: Will WALLACE, Nathaniel RAGAN. 23 Jan 1836.

810. (3:119-20) James R. JOHNSTON (first party) to William WALLACE (second party) and William B. WILLIAMS (third party): 23 Jan 1836, a gray mare which JOHNSTON purchased from James HENRY, 18 head of hogs (two sows, the balance shoats and stock hogs) and a spotted cow and red calf. WILLIAMS is security of JOHNSTON in a note to James HENRY of William for $50 dated 22 Jan 1836, due the 25 Dec 1836, bearing interest from the date of the note. JOHNSTON is to retain possession of the property but is not permitted to remove it out of the county or dispose of any part of it without consent of WILLIAMS. Wit: N. RAGAN, Robe McCLURE. 2 Feb 1836.

811. (3:120-21) John F. GARNER to William RAGAN: 25 Jan 1836, $300, a negro woman named FERBY about 48 yrs old. Wit: John HENRY, Will WILSON. 2 Feb 1836.

812. (3:121) John COX to George WELLS of Knox Co.: 29 Apr 1835, $550, my negro man named SAM aged about 21 or 22 years. Wit: John T. KING, Abraham YEAROUT. 2 Feb 1836.

813. (3:121-22) Hugh CARTER, Jr. of Greene Co. to John BALEY: 8 Jan 1836, $235, 124 ac on waters of Holston River, adj GREEN, the Rocky Ford of the branch, CASTEEL, COLEBURN, KEE, M. COTHER?. Wit: William COLEBURN, Bazil CARTER. 3 Feb 1836.

814. (3:123) State of TN to William TIPTON, Grant #2799, [by virtue of] an entry #4004 by William Tipton dated 18 Oct 1830 made in the Entry Taker's Office of the Hiwassee District..500 ac on the

Potatoe Branch in Cades Cove. Sig: William CARROLL, Governor of TN, 15 Dec 1834. 3 Feb 1836.

815. (3:123) State of TN Grant #2811 to William TIPTON [by virtue of] an entry #4111 by TIPTON, 21 Mar 1832, made in Entry Taker's Office of the Hiwassee District..1320 ac at Rich Gap, adj old Indian boundary, SCOTT, Sig: William CARROLL, Governor, 6 Jan 1835. 4 Feb 1836.

816. (3:124-25) William RHEA (first party), Samuel SAFFELL (second party) and John SAFFELL (third party): 4 Feb 1836, 81 ac on waters of Holston River, adj Ambrose COX, Wm. DAVIS, Wm. COLBURN, as security for payment of notes. Sam SAFFELL had sold unto RHEA a tract of land, for the payment of which RHEA has executed his notes, the first executed on 1 Sept 1834 due 12 months after date for $50, the second executed same date and due two years after date, the third...due 3 years after date and fourth due 4 years...fifth due 5 years thereafter, each for $50 and each bearing interest from the date. Wit: Jesse THOMPSON, James WILSON. 5 Feb 1836.

817. (3:126) Samuel SAFFELL to William RHEA: 13 Feb 1835, $300, 81 ac on waters of Holston River, adj Ambrose COX, being the tract purchased by SAFFELL of John and James GILLESPY which they purchased of William YOUNG, Granted to Young by State of TN. Wit: Jesse THOMPSON, James WILSON. 6 Feb 1836.

818. (3:127-28) Thomas ROGERS of Cocke Co. to Benjamin F. DUNCAN: 30 Mar 1835, $1,000, 150 ac on Little River, being the lower part of Grant #1295 to Andrew KENNEDY. Wit: Jesse WALLACE, Ruben (X) HUTCHESON. "I do hereby certify that this deed is made in the place of one that was lost and is not to be binding on said ROGERS further than the deed which was lost or the original as said ROGERS does not know the courses in the original deed." Sig: B. F. DUNCAN.   Wit: James W. ROGERS, G. M. CROOKSHANKS. 10 Feb 1836.

819. (3:128-30) William M. GAMBLE and William WILSON to Hugh HENRY, Trustee: 5 Jan 1826, GAMBLE and WILSON are indebted to Josias GAMBLE for $1500 by note dated 11 Dec 1835

and due 11 Dec last past, and Josias being willing to wait 12 months longer upon having his debt and interest secured; 50 ac on waters of Ellejoy Creek, adj John F. GARNER and others; also one brown cow and one sorrel colt, two calves, one cupbord, one table, two beds with the other household furniture, one man's saddle and one side saddle, five head of hogs, one pair of drawing chains and harness. Wit: John GAMBLE, John HENRY. 13 Feb 1836.

820. (3:130-31) Abraham PHILIPS to James WOLF: 11 Jun 1828, $350, 184 ac on north side of Little River, adj James KNIGHT, Joseph COLDWELL, George EWING, original Grant #1170 to PHILIPS. Wit: James GILLESPY, Campbell GILLESPY. 13 Feb 1836.

821. (3:131-32) Robert STEPHENSON of McMinn Co. to Nicholas VINYARD of Grainger Co.: 4 Sep 1833, $450, 78 ac on Little River, adj Thomas HARDIN's old line, Abraham PHILIPS old line. Wit: Caswell L. WALKER, David (X) CUNNINGHAM, John VINEYARD, James (X) WOLF. 15 Feb 1836.

822. (3:132-33) Jacob CARPENTER to John VINYARD: 25 Sep 1820, $370, 86 ac on Nails Creek, part of a Grant to VINEYARD. Wit: Jeffery JOHNSON, Gardner MAYS. Ack 13 Feb 1836 by Gardner MAYS, who stated that CARPENTER and JOHNSTON are now living in Alabama. 15 Feb 1836.

823. (3:133-34) Nathaniel HARRIS to Rowly BROWN: 21 Feb 1835, $250, 52 ac on (omitted) Creek. Wit: Lewis KIDD, Resh (X) KIDD. 27 Feb 1836.

824. (3:135-36) John CROMWELL to Samuel X? MONTGOMERY, Jr.: 21 Dec 1835, consideration omitted, 100 ac on waters of Baker's Creek, part of 220 ac granted to Abraham UTTER, adj Robert THOMPSON. MONTGOMERY to pay one dollar per acre with the interest due and to become due to the state. Wit: John M. RANKIN, Samuel MONTGOMERY. 27 Feb 1836.

825. (3:136-37) Robert HOOK, Thomas HUNTER, William EWING, John EAGLETON, David DELZELL and Andrew EARLY, Elders of NEW PROVIDENCE CHURCH, to William TOOLE: 26 Feb 1836, $20, a lot adj town of Maryville, being part of a lot purchased by the

Elders from Caleb M. NORWOOD and adj a lot owned by James M. HAYDEN, lying on the Tellico road. Wit: F. A. PARHAM, Samuel PRIDE. 9 Mar 1836.

826. (3:137-38) James P. MONTGOMERY, Jesse THOMPSON, Samuel PRIDE and James BERRY, execrs of John MONTGOMERY, decd, to James BERRY: Sept 1833, on 3 June 1828 John MONTGOMERY, now deceased, executed to James BERRY his bond to convey to BERRY lots in Maryville, #60, 85, 86 and 108 (all had been Grants to William KING and John MONTGOMERY). Wit: Wm. A. SPENCER, H. B. LEEPER. 9 Mar 1836.

827. (3:139-40) William PUGH to William PUGH, Attorney: 8 Mar 1836, Wm. PUGH of Blount County appoints William PUGH of Carter Co. [his] lawful attorney "to rent my land in Carter Co." Wit: Will WALLACE, W. W. WALLACE. 9 Mar 1836.

828. (3:140-42) James BERRY, Jesse THOMPSON, Samuel PRIDE Executors, to John BRABSON: On 5 June 1828 John MONTGOMERY, now deceased, executed a bond to James BERRY to convey town lots in Maryville, lot #60, being the lot where MONTGOMERY formerly kept his store; lots #85 and 86 lying immediately below it, and lot #108 lying below those two lots adj the Creek where there is a small house, all Granted to John MONTGOMERY and William KING and William KING's undivided interest being purchased by the firm of MONTGOMERY and BERRY then carrying on the mercantile business in the town of Maryville, and John MONTGOMERY having departed this life and James BERRY having sold the lots of ground this 21 Feb 1835 to John BRABSON of Sevier Co., and it being requested by BERRY that the Executors of John MONTGOMERY convey title to BRABSON who has this day paid to BERRY $2145...it being further understood that James P. MONTGOMERY, one of the executors, did execute a deed of conveyance..and in consequence of him [James P. MONTGOMERY] being about to move to the Arkansas Territory..Jesse THOMPSON, Samuel PRIDE and James BERRY, Execrs, and James BERRY in his own private capacity convey all the right, etc..that John MONTGOMERY, decd, had in the lots at the time of death and at the time of executing title bond..BERRY conveys to BRABSON four lots

of ground, having title to two lots of ground in Maryville where #108 lies, being lots #107 and 106, and his own undivided interest in lots #60, 85, 86, and 108. Wit: Wm. A. SPENCER, B. D. BRABSON. Ack 21 Feb 1835. 10 Mar 1836.

829. (3:142-43) John WILLIAMS, Trustee, of Knox Co., to John BRABSON of Sevier Co.: 13 Mar 1835, "whereas James BERRY and Jacob F. FOUTE heretofore executed a deed of trust to John WILLIAMS to secure payment of debts to sundry merchants of Baltimore and Philadelphia, and [WILLIAMS] having duly advertised the real estate" and [sold it] on 23 Dec 1833...and WILLIAMS on behalf of the creditors bid the following sums for a portion of the property: lots in Maryville, #60 on which the store house and counting room stand, $500; #85 and 86 on which the stable stands, $100; lots #106, 107, 108, at $50; [and] whereas John BRABSON has paid and secured to be paid to the said creditors of BERRY and FOUTE the sum of $1500 in current money for the above lots"...[WILLIAMS conveys] to BRABSON the lots named. Wit: Joseph L. WILLIAMS, D. P. ARMSTRONG, Jo SCOTT, E. BRABSON. 11 Mar 1836.

830. (3:143-45) Jane R. LOWERY to Enoch WATERS: 20 Oct 1835, $800, 225 ac on a branch of Crooked Creek, adj KEY, William LOWRY, "William LOWRY's WEAR tract", GRISSEM. Wit: A. C. MONTGOMERY, Spencer HENRY. 11 Mar 1836.

831. (3:145-46) David VANCE to Philmer GREEN: 19 Sep 1833, $800, 122 ac on Little River, part of Grant to Benjamin RAGAN, adj John REAGAN. Wit: James HENRY, Jr., Andrew PEERY, John HENRY, Sr. Ack 23 Jan 1836. 12 Mar 1836.

832. (3:146-47) Nicholas NORTON to Philmer GREEN: 8 Feb 1832, $800, 202 ac on waters of Little River, part of tract Granted to John RAGAN under a right of improvement, occupancy and preemption, adj Benjamin RAGEN, the county road, William McKAMY, William LLOYD, John GIBSON, Benjamin RAGEN. Wit: Isom JULIAN, John HENRY Sr. 12 Mar 1836.

833. (3:148-49) Isaac THOMPSON to John CAMPBELL: 12 Mar 1836, $70, 51 ac on waters of Little River, adj James YOUNG, William ROGERS, Archibald MURPHY, Betsy HAFLEY, George

NIMAN, James YOUNG, surveyed 10 June 1824. Wit: Hiram
HARTSELL, James K. COX. 12 Mar 1836.

834. (3:149-50) Hesekiah DANLEY to D. D. FOUTE: 9 Feb 1836,
$250, lot #5 containing 80 ac, and lot #45 containing 80 ac all in
Blount Co. Hiwassee district, being Grant #2899 to DANLEY as
assignee of CALLOWAY and McGHEE on 9 Oct 1835. Wit: A. C.
KENDRICK, John MADDEN?. Sig: Hezekiah (X) DANLY. 18 Mar
1836.

835. (3:150-51) Malcom McONAGIN/McOMAGIN? to D. D.
FOUTE: 27 Feb 1836, $350, two tracts on waters of Six Mile Creek,
one of 35 ac adj lands of John BOID and others Granted to
McOMAGIN, another of 111 ac Granted to John RANEY adj lands
on the east by John PATTEN, on the north and west by George
KELLAR and touching on John BOYD's land, and the first mentioned
tract on the south and west by WHITEHEAD's land and D.D. FOUTE
on the south and east. Wit: John SHARP, William (X) EVANS? 18
March 1836.

836.   (3:151-52) William WALLACE, Sheriff, to William
HEADRICK: 27 Mar 1832, $42.62, 182 ac on waters of Little River
in Tuckaleechee Cove, being Grant #5462 dated 9 Apr 1831 to David
HUGHS; public sale 28 May 1831, to satisfy judgment against David
HUGHS and James CARNER for $144.32, which Benjamin
BENSON, assignee of William SCOTT, recovered against them for
debt, damages and costs. Wit: James HAIR, J. J. WALKER. 18 Mar
1836.

837. (3:152-53) Rolley BROWN to Donald McINTOSH of Knox
Co.: 29 Mar 1836, $125, 52 ac adj the Creek (not named), STINNET.
Wit: James W. WAYNE, Ephraim BRABSON, Peter NANCE. 30
Mar 1836.

838. (3:153-54) John McCLURG to Leonard RHEA: 5 Oct 1831,
$300, 87 ac on headwaters of Gallaher's Creek, adj Jesse
HEADRICKSON, Peyton LOVE, William BROWN, James M.
WILLIAMS. Wit: John (X) HARRIS, Robert (X) COCHRAN. 31
Mar 1836.

839. (3:154-55) Arthur H. HENLY of Monroe Co. to Henry LOGAN: 2 Sep 1833, $800, 198 ac, Grant #1689 to David HENLEY, adj James EDMONTON, McCAMPBELL, McGILL, William GRAY. Wit: A. MOORE, M. FRANCES. 31 Mar 1836.

840. (3:156-57) Leonard WOOD to John McNABB: 7 Mar 1836, $360, 50 ac on Baker's Creek, part of Grant #552 to Thomas ADAMS dated 15 June 1809, adj Charles LOGAN, Joseph ORE. Wit: Alex McNUTT, R. THOMPSON. 1 Apr 1836.

841. (3:157-58) John GILLESPIE of Blount Co. and James GILLESPIE of Shelby Co. to John HOOD: 27 Feb 1836, $80, two front lots and two half back lots in the town of Louisville, the lots on which John HOOD now lives and has inclosed containing one quarter of an acre to each lot and one eighth, a half lot as now laid off. Wit: William HENDERSON, Abram HARTSELL. 1 Apr 1836.

842. (3:158-59) John GILLESPIE of Blount Co. and James GILLESPIE, of Shelby Co., to Abram HARTSELL: 27 Feb 1836, $45, two lots in town of Louisville, the lot on which HARTSELL now lives, and another back lot adjoining it, each one quarter ac. Wit: John HOOD, William HENDERSON, Jr. 2 Apr 1836.

843. (3:159-60) John GILLESPIE of Blount Co. and James GILLESPIE, of Shelby Co., to James JOHNSTON (a free man of color): 27 Feb 1836, $60, four lots in town of Louisville, on which JOHNSTON now lives, and the lot joining where the shop stands with two back lots, all being four in square and each containing one quarter of an ac. Wit: John HOOD, William HENDERSON. 2 Apr 1836.

844. (3:160-61) John GILLESPIE of Blount Co. and James GILLESPIE, of Shelby Co., to William CORLEY: $30, two lots in town of Louisville, the lot on which Edward BROWN now lives, and the other back lot adjoining thereto, each containing one quarter of an ac. Wit: John HOOD, William HENDERSON, Jr. 2 Apr 1836.

845. (3:161-62) Andrew HOOK to Samuel HENERY and sons: 31 Mar 1836, $11.24, two sows and 7 shoats, 1 clock, 1 bed and furniture, 1 cubberd, 1 set dry irons, 1 chest. HOOK to pay HENERY and sons the sum of $11.24 within nine months for redemption of

bargained premises. Wit: Philip (M.or N.?) MORONEY, Hiram HARTSELL. 4 Apr 1836.

846. (3:162-63) Ephraim SAWTELL to Archibald GRISOM: 23 Aug 1831, $800, 275 ac on waters of Crooked Creek, part of 281 ac Grant to Samuel THOMPSON, adj heirs of John M. LOWERY, decd, John KEYS. Wit: John KEYS, William LOWERY. 4 Apr 1836.

847. (3:164) James FROW to Richard RAGAN: 1 Apr 1836, $56, 28 ac on waters of Pistol Creek, cor to land RAGAN lives on, adj Moses ELLIOTT, Andrew EARLY near the Morganton Road. Wit: Daniel YEAROUT, John RAGAN. 7 Apr 1836.

848. (3:165-66) William H. McCLURE to Grinsfield TAYLOR: 14 Apr 1836, $400, 100 ac in two tracts, part of a tract of 449 ac granted to Charles McCLURE, now deceased, which descended to William H. McCLURE as one of the heirs at law of Charles McCLURE. One tract of 71 ac adj CHANDLER; other tract of 29 ac. Wit: Hance N. RUSSELL, N. RAGAN. 16 Apr 1836.

849. (3:166-68) James GILLESPIE to Wm. C. GILLESPIE: 26 Apr 1828, in consideration of natural love and affection and $100, 150 ac on Little River, part of 508 ac Grant #2293 to James GILLESPIE, adj William WALLACE. Use of the water and the race to the still house is reserved to James GILLESPY. Wit: James H. GILLESPY, Sr., Campbell GILLESPY. 18 Apr 1836.

850. (3:168-69) William GAULT and Margaret GAULT, formerly Margaret WEAR, daughter and heir at law of Jonathan WEAR, decd, to John F. DeARMOND: 9 Apr 1836, $60, 22 ac on waters of Pistol Creek adj lands of John F. DeARMOND, Jonathan WEAR, Jr., William ANDERSON, Esq., part of 47 ac that descended to Margaret GAULT as heir of Jonathan WEAR, decd. Sig: Wm. GAULT. Margaret (X) GAULT. Wit: Wm. ANDERSON. 21 Apr 1836.

851. (3:169-70) Nathaniel HARRISON to Samuel N. MONTGOMERY: 25 Mar 1836, $250, 120 ac on waters of Baker's Creek, adj James MONTGOMERY, CROMWELL, Robert THOMPSON. Wit: John M. RANKIN, Samuel MONTGOMERY. 22 Apr 1836.

852. (3:171-72) William GAULT et ux to William ANDERSON: 9 Apr 1836, $75, 25 ac on headwaters of Pistol Creek adj John RANKIN, Margaret WEAR, William ANDERSON and John F. DeARMOND, part of 47 ac that descended to Margaret GAULT, formerly Margaret WEAR as heir of law of Jonathan WEAR, decd. Sig: William GAULT. Margaret (X) GAULT. Wit: Ake HENRY, John F. DeARMOND. 22 Apr 1836.

853.   (3:172-73) John McMAHAN (first party), Robert S. CUMMINGS (second party) to David D. READ, Trustee: 16 Apr 1836, one wagon and rigging, four horses and gearing. McMAHAN shall within six months pay to CUMMINGS for the use of Samuel HENRY and James McKAMY the sum of $85 and interest on two notes of hand held on CUMMINGS by HENRY and McKAMY, HENRY's for $25 and McKAMY's for $60. 16 Apr 1836. Wit: N. RAGAN, J. C. FAGG. 25 Apr 1836.

854. (3:173-74) John BLAIR, executor of John BLAIR, decd of Washington Co., to George BROWN of the same place: 7 Sep 1833, "in consideration of the payment of a note heretofore executed to me by John BROWN of Blount County for $400 in trade equal to corn at two shillings per bushel of corn," 237 ac on west fork of Lackey's Creek, adj Martin BONHAM, Benjamin JAMES, [the residue] of land which I sold to Benjamin JAMES. Wit: Adam BROYLES, Isaac BROYLES. 28 Apr 1836. Proven before James N. ANDERSON, Clerk of the Circuit Court for Washington Co.

855. (3:174-75) Samuel JACKSON, admr of estate of James SLOAN, to William HEISKELL: 3 May 1836, $34.75, lot #12 in town of Morganton containing one-half ac. Wit: A. HENRY, William McTEER. 11 May 1836.

856. (3:176-77) Jincy BLACK to Nathaniel JEFFERS: 17 Mar 1835, $387.50, 85 ac on waters of Ellejoy Creek, cor to Mathew H. BOGLE and Jincy BLACK. Sig: Jincey (X) BLACK. Wit: James DAVIS, Sr. James H. BLACK. 27 May 1836.

857. (3:177-78) Harris PRIVETT (first party), to Thomas HARPER trustee (second party) and James WILSON and John SAFFELL known as the firm of WILSON AND SAFFELL (third party): 30 May

1836, PRIVETT is indebted to J. WILSON and SAFFELL for $36.75 due by note of hand executed this day and due one day after date, for which HARPER is security; one cubord and all the furniture, two feather beds and steads and furniture, 6 split bottom chairs, 1 table, 1 chest, 1 set knives and forks, 1 set spoons, 1 oven, 1 pot, 1 horse, 20 geese, 2 ploughs, 1 pr gears, 2 hoes, 1 mattock, 3 axes. Wit: John MARTIN, Clemet H. SAFFELL. 3 June 1836.

858.   (3:178-80) Daniel D. FOUTE (first party), to Samuel WALLACE (second party) and William WALLACE and William A. SPENCER (third party): 2 June 1836, FOUTE has borrowed from the Planter's Bank of the State of Tennessee at Athens $1,000, for which his note was discounted at said bank on 26th day of this month, with WALLACE and SPENCER his indorsers; the Montvale Springs tract of land containing 160 ac, which was Granted to FOUTE, whereon he now lives; also the MURRAY tract of land lying at the foot of the mountain containing 150 ac, conveyed by James MURRY to David D. FOUTE; also the Sulphur Spring tract whereon Smith DELZELL now lives, which was conveyed to FOUTE by David and Robert DELZELL; two wagons, six yoke of oxen, eight cows and calves and sixty head of stock hogs, 20 head of sheep, ten feather beds, bed steds and furniture, two beauroes, two china presses, two set folding leaf tables and fifty chairs.   Wit: John MONTGOMERY, Will SINGLETON. 4 June 1836.

859.   (3:180-81)   Lewis McMILLEN (first party), to James HAMMONTREE (second party) and John WILSON, trustee (third party): 30 May 1836, 15 head of hogs, two beds and bedsteds and furniture, two tables, four chairs, spinning wheel, one set of knives and forks, one set teacups and saucers, two set plates, one looking glass, two ovens and one skillet, one frying pan, one shovel and tongs, one saddle. McMILLEN has executed to James HAMMONTREE his promissory note now due for money amounting to $18.20 [which he] shall pay before 1 March 1837. Wit: N. RAGAN, Ake HENERY. 10 June 1836.

860.   (3:182-83) Edmund WAYMAN to John WAYMAN: 6 Jun 1836, $82, lots #16 and #14 in town of Morganton. Wit: Joseph CARTER, Wilson (X) ALLOWAY. 10 Jun 1836.

861. (3:183-84) Benjamin AUSTIN (first party) to William TOOLE (second party) and William WALLACE (third party): 18 May 1836, $75, two sets of blacksmith tools complete, to wit: two anvilles (sic), 2 pr bellows or vices, 2 screw plates, 1 brace and bits, divers hammers and togs and a great variety of small tools "to teadious (sic) to mention." AUSTIN has executed his promissory note to Wallace for $75 dated 17 May 1836 due in one day after date. AUSTIN is to keep possession of the property and is prohibited from disposing of any part of it or removing it from Blount County. Sig: Benjamin (X) AUSTIN. Wit: J. J. WALKER. W. WAMPSON? 10 Jun 1836.

862. (3:184-86) Will WALLACE, Sheriff, to Thomas HUNT: 10 Jun 1836, $30, 94 ac on Cloyd's Creek, adj James LOGAN, Michael BOWERMAN, Frederick SIMMERMAN, levied upon as property of Robert GLASS on 21 Dec 1833 by Samuel LEE, a constable for the county, to satisfy a judgment obtained 9 Mar 1833 against Robert GLASS, John GLASS and Isaac GLASS in favor of James McCAMMON, for $80.88 and costs. Public sale 24 May 1834; James McCAMMON by his agent Campbell WALLACE became the purchaser for $30.00. "Two years having expired since the sale, the time given by law to redeem all lands sold by virtue of execution, and the land not having been redeemed by Robert GLASS or any other person, and James McCAMMON has sold the land to Thomas HUNT and has requested me in writing to make a deed to HUNT." Wit: W. WALLACE, R. P. BOWERMAN. Ack 20 June 1836 before Ake HENRY, Deputy Clerk of the County Court. 11 June 1836.

863. (3:186-87) William DAVIS to John F. HENERY and Co.: 28 May 1836, $56, 1 yoke of oxen, 2 cows, 3 heifers and 2 calves, 3 head of horses, all mares, 1 clock, 30 head of hogs, 1 windmill, 2 ovens and lids, 1 pot, one big and one little wheel, 12 head of geese, 2 pair horse gears, 4 plows, 1 table, 10 head of sheep, 1 loom, 3 beds and furniture, 1 man's saddle, 1 wagon. DAVIS to pay $56 within four months for redemption of property. Sig: William (X) DAVIS. Wit: Joel STONE, Matthew WHITTENBARGER. 11 Jun 1836.

864. (3:187-88) John and Henry GLASS to Eli RICHEY: 12 Nov 1833, $500, 177 ac being part of Grant #2491 to John GLASS, assignee of James LOGAN, and taken off the southwest end of said

tract; 50 ac of land is taken in adj an entry #298 made by John GLASS in the Entry Taker's Office of Blount County adj Joseph JOHNSTON. Wit: Andrew FERGUSON, Isaac GLASS. 11 Jun 1836.

865. (3:189) Richard WILLIAMS to William WILLIAMS: 17 May 1836, "for natural love and affection for my son and also for the benefit of the said William WILLIAMS", all my horses: one white mare named Beck, one 3 yr old mare, iron gray, called Snap, one year old horse colt called Simon, together with all my cattle being nine head and thirty head of sheep, together with all my stock of hogs amounting to 45 head, also my wagon and gearing and forming utensils, also my household and kitchen furniture. No witnesses. Ack 30 May 1836 before Ake HENRY, deputy clerk, by Richard WILLIAMS Sr., the bargainer. 13 June 1836.

866. (3:189-90) Jesse KERR to Joseph H. PRICHARD: 7 Mar 1834, $300, 92 ac on waters of Nine Mile Creek, adj James HENRY and Robert HAMMILL, Thomas RANKIN, heirs of John HENRY, decd, and John POLAN, being part of a Grant to Michal REAGAN, "having reference to Michal REAGAN Grant for its bearings and conditional line recorded in the last will and testament of REAGAN, between Allen STRAIN and wife and Polly REAGAN." Wit: Will WILLIAMSON, Samuel TULLOCH. 13 Jun 1836.

867. (3:190-91) Thomas CONNER, Sr. to Alferd Burton CONNER, son of Rubin CONNER: 6 Feb 1836, for "natural love and affection" and for the better maintainence and support of Alferd Berton CONNER, 52 ac in Cades Cove adj Thomas DAVIS, Ruben CONNER, to include the dwelling where Ruben CONNER now lives, William TIPTON's old line, cor to a 4 ac tract Thomas CONNER purchased of Jane TIPTON. Wit: John COLLIS, Thomas (X) DAVIS. 30 Jun 1836.

868. (3:192-93) Thomas CONNER, Sr. to Nancy BRIANT: 20 Feb 1836,"a parcel of land that was left out of [his] will, it including the house and buildings and one sow and pig... this I give to her during her lifetime on condition she .. puts it to her use, and this property at her death to be divided equal between Ruben CONNER and James CONNOR. Thomas CONNER, Jr. and Reuben CONNER are to see

that this goes to her use". Wit: John COLLIS, Thomas (X) DAVIS. 30 Jun 1836.

869. (3:193) Thomas CONNER, Sr. to Thomas CONNER, Jr.: 9 Feb 1836, for natural love and affection, one negro woman named RACHEL and her child HENRY supposed to be in Birk Co., North Carolina. Wit: John COLLIS, Thomas (X) DAVIS. 30 June 1836.

870. (3:194) Benjamin UNDERWOOD to Samuel HENERY and son: 30 June 1836, $75, 3 head of horses, 1 bay mare, 1 clay bank mare, 1 sorrell horse, 4 head of cattle, 35 head of hogs, 1 loom, 1 cart, 1 spinning wheel. UNDERWOOD shall pay HENRY and sons the sum of $75 within 12 months for redemption of the property. Sig: Benjamin (X) UNDERWOOD. Wit: P. Nelson MORONY, James CASTEEL. 2 July 1836.

871. (3:195-96) Will WALLACE, Sheriff, to Thomas ELIOTT: 20 Jun 1836, 100 ac on waters of Crooked Creek adj Henry LONG, David CUPP, and others. Public sale 1 Feb 1834 at which Daniel D. FOUTE became the purchaser for $15, to satisfy judgment issued by Circuit Court of Blount County on 20 Nov 1833 in favor of the State of TN against Jacob ELLIOTT. Thomas ELLIOTT, being the son of Jacob ELLIOTT, came forward on 29 Dec 1835 and claimed the right and privilege to redeem the land according to law by paying the full of amount of FOUTE's bid with ten percent interest together with the balance that was due and owing, amounting to the sum of $62.13. Land was part of Grant #829 to Henry THOMAS, adj Jacob NIMAN and David CUPP, Margaret THOMAS, Black HUS, Martin ROREX, Henry LONG..."I ..sell and convey all the right that Sarah ELLIOTT had in the tract..at the time [it] was levied upon..and do warrant [it] against the right or claim of Sarah ELLIOTT." Wit: Thomas WHITE, W. W. WALLACE. 4 July 1836.

872. (3:197) John KIDD and Mary KIDD, his wife, to (my brother) Zephaniah HARRIS: 2 May 1836, $55, all [my] claim and interest in all the lands formerly belonging to my father in Blount County. Sig: John (X) KIDD, Mary (X) KIDD. Wit: Joseph HARRIS, Lewis (X) KIDD. 2 July 1836.

873. (3:197-98) Joseph HARRIS to my brother Zephaniah HARRIS: 29 Apr 1836, $55, my claim in the land formerly belonging to my father in Blount Co. Wit: Jackson (X) STINET, James KIDD. 2 July 1836.

874. (3:198) William J.J. MINOR/MORROW and George D. EDGAR to Samuel PRATER of Knox Co.: 4 July 1836, $500, six negro slaves, to wit: CHOE aged about 35 years and his five children, CHARLES, NANCY, POLLY, JIM and EPHRAIM...being the same negros that the SWAN (sic) have a suit pending about in the Chancery Court in Monroe County. Wit: Anderson HILL, Hugh D. HALE. Ack before Moses M. SWAN, Clerk of Knox County Court, on 4 July 1836. 5 July 1836.

875. (3:199-200) Elizabeth HARRIS to Donald McINTOSH of Knox Co.: 3 Jun 1836, $35, lot #10 in the division of Benjamin HARRIS real estate as made by commissioners appointed by order of Blount County Court apportioning said deceased's lands amongst his heirs containing in all 24 ac. Wit: John GODDARD, Thomas J. TIPTON. Ack 4 July 1836 by witnesses before Moses M. SWAN, clerk of Knox Co. Court. 4 July 1836.

876. (3:200-01) Montgomery McTEER (first party) to Ferdinand A. PARHAM, trustee (second party) and William WALLACE of Blount County and Samuel McCAMMON of Knox Co. (third party): 2 Jul 1836, three lots in Maryville, #53 on Main St. and 91 and 102 being back lots, which McTEER purchased of Elexander McNUTT; also all the cabinet maker's tools and mechanic's tools of every kind, supposed to be worth $200, also all his stock of lumber, supposed to be worth $100, all his household and kitchen furniture consisting of bed beaurow, tables, etc. and various articles "two (sic) tedious to mention." McTEER procured a loan of $300 from the Union Bank at Knoxville, for which WALLACE and McCAMMON are his security, dated 14 Jun 1836 and due six month after date. McTEER is to keep possession of the property and use such parts or all of lumber if he desires to do so in his line of business. Wit: Ake HENRY, Alexander WALLACE. 20 July 1836.

877. (3:202) David EDMONDSON to George BELL of Washington Co.: 7 Sep 1833, $600, 186 ac on waters of Baker's Creek, part of a Grant to James LOGAN, adj William EWING. Wit: John EAKIN, John B. BELL. 20 Jul 1836.

878. (3:203) Zephaniah HARRIS to Donald McINTOSH of Knox Co: 2 July 1836, $70, lot #3 containing 25 ac in the schedule of the commissioners apptd by order of Blount County Court to make partitition of the real estate of Benjamin HARRIS, decd, containing 362 ac, among the heirs, which land was deeded and conveyed to me or relinquished in my favor by Joseph HARRIS. Also lot #5 containing 25 ac, adj the widow's dower, relinquished by Mary KIDD and John KIDD to me. Wit: Elizabeth HARRIS, Joseph HARRIS. 21 July 1836.

879. (3:204) Zephaniah HARRIS to Donal McINTOSH of Knox Co: 2 July 1836, $80, all my title in and to negroes ALLECH and NANCE, being the only slaves now belonging to Benjamin HARRIS, decd, estate. Wit: Elizabeth HARRIS, Joseph HARRIS. 21 July 1836.

880. (3:204-05) John JONES to Robert EAGLETON: "Whereas John JONES has purchased a sorrel mare from Robert EAGLETON for the present campaign against the Creek Indians, for which he is to pay...EAGLETON the sum of $67, and to secure the same...JONES conveys to EAGLETON the sorrel mare, which is to be and remain his property...reserving to myself the right and privilege of riding the sorrell mare in the present campaign, and should ...the mare die or be lost in the service and anything should be received of or from the general government for the same...EAGLETON is to draw and receive it...I constitute Robert EAGLETON my lawful attorney for that purpose...be it further understood that [JONES] has enrolled in Capt. Benjamin CUNNINGHAM's company of Mounted Volunteers for a six months tour of duty in the service of the United States...do appoint Robert EAGLETON my lawful atty in fact for me and in my name to draw and receive from the paymaster or any other person authorized by the general government to pay the mounted volunteers such money as may be due me for my services...2 July 1836." Sig: John (X) JONES. Wit: Will WALLACE, J. J. WALKER. 4 Aug 1836.

881. (3:206-07) Thomas CALDWELL to John RODDY: 1836, $132.50, 18 ac on waters of Little River adj CALDWELL's occupant survey. Wit: Jonathan THORP, Beren HADDOX. 6 Aug 1836.

882. (3:207-08) Jesse ROGERS to James DAVIS: 11 Jul 1836, $100, 35 ac on waters of Ellejoy Creek. Sig: Jesse (X) ROGERS. Wit: Joseph BROWN, William McTEER. 7 Aug 1836.

883. (3:208-09) John IRVIN/IRWIN of Mecklinburg Co., NC, to the Reverend Darius H. HOYT of Blount Co.: 30 Aug 1836, $130, 77 ac on waters of Pistol Creek, adj Hugh WEAR, James DONOHOO, John HANNA, Robert GAUT. Wit: Will WALLACE, Wm. TOOL. 7 Aug 1836.

884. (3:209-10) James TALLENT, Jr. to Samuel HENRY and Son: 15 Aug 1836, $30.75, 1 man's saddle and bridle, 2 head of cattle, 2 beds and furniture, 2 ovens, 1 pot, 1 skillet, 2 plows, 1 pair geese, 1 table. TALLENT to pay HENRY and Sons $30.75 within 12 months for redemption of property. Sig: James (X) TALLENT. Wit: Eliju? (X) LONGALLAN?, Ake HENRY. 29 Aug 1836.

885. (3:210-11) William LOWERY (first party), Jesse KERR, Jr. (second party) to Jesse KERR, Sr. (third party), trustee: 14 May 1836, LOWERY has borrowed from Jesse KERR, Sr. $500 for which he executed a promissory note on 30 Mar 1836, due 1 May 1837, for which Jesse KERR, Jr. is trustee; negro man named RUSSELL aged 27 yrs now in the possession of Jesse KERR, Sr. Wit: Newlon WILSON, P. W. HENRY, John C. LOGAN. 30 Aug 1836.

886. (3:211-12) John J. HANER to John HENDERSON: 5 Sep 1836, $200, 60 ac on waters of Holston River, adj Bowling John HENDERSON, cor to J. J. HANER...a conditional line is between land conveyed by John and Bowling BROOKS to John HENDERSON. Wit: John HACKNEY, Sr., John TUCK. 8 Sep 1836.

887. (3:213-14) Caswell HALL, Sr. to William HEISKELL of Monroe Co.: 10 Dec 1835, $2,000, 108 ac on Little Tennessee River, adj the great road in the fourth line of the original survey made for Hugh KELSO, James HALL's old plantation, Robert WEAR, cor to land bought by HALL from James BADGETT, Sr. Also a tract on

bank of Little Tennessee River adj KELSO's survey, cor to above tract, being the tract bought by HALL from James BADGET Sr. of 125 ac, including the ferry landing. Wit: John H. CRAIG, Wm. SERVINER?, Edwin HEISKELL. 10 Sep 1836.

888. (3:214-15) Robert NEAL to D. D. FOUTE: 8 Sep 1835, $50, 50 ac on headwaters of Six Mile Creek granted to NEAL on 10 Dec 1825. Wit: Nathaniel RAGAN, Jeremiah HAMMONTREE, Robert DELZELL. 10 Sep 1836.

889. (3:215-16) Peter FRENCH of Knox Co. to James DAVIS: 6 Sep 1833, $300, 80 ac on waters of Ellejoy Creek, adj George HADDAN, John WILLIAMS. Sig: Peter (X) FRENCH. Wit: N. JEFFERS, M. ANDERSON, Wm. DAVIS, J. C. BOGLE. 11 Sep 1836.

890. (3:217-18) James COPE to Elexander COOK: 12 Sep 1836, $600, 80 ac on Nine Mile Creek adj Charles HENRY, John HANNA, John STONE; part of Grant #1610 to George COPE. Another parcel of 16 ac adj John HANNAH part of Grant #1441 to Charles HENRY. Another tract of 40 ac late Entry #508 dated 20 Oct 1827 granted to James COPE, cor to David KERR's 100 ac entry, adj James McTEER's occupant survey. Wit: William WALLACE, J. J. WALKER. 13 Sep 1836.

891. (3:218-19) Peter FRENCH of Knox Co. to James DAVIS: 6 Sep 1833, $100, 43 ac on waters of Ellejoy Creek, adj John RHEA, Mathew BOGLE, David CUSACK, THORPE, Peter FRENCH, Jr. Sig: Peter (X) FRENCH. Wit: M. ANDERSON, J. C. BOGLE, N. JEFFERS, Wm. DAVIS. 13 Sep 1836.

892. (3:220-21) James DAVIS, Sr. to William DAVIS, Sr. [in one place he is referred to as Jr.]: 6 Oct 1833, $10, 40 ac on the waters of the dry fork, cor to a conditional line between John W. DAVIS and William DAVIS. Sig: James (X) DAVIS. Wit: Hugh BOGLE, James H. BLACK. 17 Sep 1836.

893.   (4:1) Agreement between Montgomery McTEER and a committee of the County Court for transcription of about 600 deeds for the sum of 25 cents per deed...working at the rate of six deeds for each working day and to commence the work immediately. 20 Dec 1855.

894.   (4:2) John FREEMAN to Campbell WALLACE: $350, negro boy named JACK about 33 yrs old.   18 Dec 1830. Wit: Sam WALLACE, William R. BARTON. 10 Jan 1831.

895.   (4:2-3) Jonathan TRIPPET to Christian BEST: 9 Nov 1823, $970, 310 ac on Nine Mile Creek, adj John POLAND, James McCOLLUM, James HENRY, part of Grant #799 to TRIPPET assignee of John COWAN dated 23 Nov 1809.   Wit: Samuel HAMELL, Wm. HARRIS, Wm. GARNER. Proven at court Dec 1829 by HAMILL and HARRIS. 1 Apr 1830.

896.   (4:3-5) William WALLACE, Sheriff to James LOGAN: 23 Mar 1830, $300, 518 ac on waters of Cloyd's Creek, Grant #2491 to John GLASS, assignee of James LOGAN dated 3 Aug 1812, surveyed 22 July 1807, adj Edward DIXSON, MONTGOMERY, JOHNSON, ORR, Sam JOHNSTON, WILLSON, Sam DIXON, John WOODY. Public sale 31 Oct 1821 by Charles DONAHOO, then sheriff, to satisfy judgment obtained by James LOGAN against John GLASS for $391.37. "DONAHOO [has] gone out of office and removed out of the county not having executed any deed for the land." Wit: Jacob F. FOUTE, John GOULD. 3 Apr 1830.

897. (4:5-6) Samuel STEELE to David A. STEELE of Montgomery Co. AL: 10 Nov 1829, $200, 69 ac lying on the Gray Ridge, part of land located by Jesse JAMES, Sr., decd, adj Robert HARRISON, agreeable to the line of the deed of conveyance given by Jesse JAMES, Jr., now owner of the residue of the tract located by Jesse JAMES, Sr. Samuel STEELE is to have the use of the plantation until his death. Wit: John STEEL, Benjamin FORD. Proven at court March 1830 by

Benjamin FORD who stated that John STEEL, the other witness, is not now an inhabitant of the state. 5 Apr 1830.

898. (4:6-7) John NEALY of Knox Co. to William TOOL: 8 Apr 1829, in order to secure payment of following debts to TOOL: one note of $24, another $37, another $31.25, due to TOOL by accounts amounting in the whole to $92.25; one black horse 10 yrs old 16 high, 17 head of cattle, 21 head of hogs, 5 stand of bees, 50 head of geese, three feather beds and furniture, one loom and wheel containing 30 yards, two shovel plows and one bar shear plow, two pair of hawes and chains, one hundred bushels of corn, one man's saddle. Wit: James RODGERS. 24 Apr 1830.

899. (4:7-8) William FAGG to William TOOL: 15 Mar 1830, $350, a house and lot #114 in Maryville. Wit: Wm. A. SPENCER, Andrew McCULLEY. 26 Apr 1830.

900. (4:8) William C. NORWOOD to Daniel D. FOUTE: (day omitted) Feb 1830, $300, 106 ac adj William HARRIS, John DUNCAN, R. GAUTT, John WILKINSON, James DONOHOO, David CUP. Wit: Samuel PRIDE, William TOOLE. 27 Apr 1830.

901. (4:9) Deed of Release, TRUSTEES OF EAST TENNESSEE COLLEGE to Citizens South of French Broad and Holston: [copied in its entirety; some punctuation has been added] "In pursuance of an act passed at the state session of the 18th General Assembly of state of Tennessee on 31 December 1829 entitled An Act to settle the controversy between the colleges and academies and the citizens south of French Broad and Holston and west of Big Pigeon Rivers: Trustees of East Tennessee College, being desirous to settle the controversy, rejoice in the prospect of the complete discharge and release from the demands of the Literary Institutions recited in the Act and particularly as it is in our power to co-operate in effecting it, now consistently with our duties as Trustees of East Tennesse College altho we see in the Act of Assembly some ambiguity in regard to the interests of the institutions concerned, yet we feel assured that it was intended that East Tennessee College should have one half the land proposed to be granted in the first section of the before recited Act. At the same time we hereby protest against any thing in the said act or in this deed

contained from being construed to operate as a release to the State from its obligation to pay to this institution the balance of its portion of the Congressional donation. We hold it bound in equity and good conscience to make good to this institution the donation of the General Government and relying on the Legislature hereafter to provide for the more extensive usefulness of this literary institution. We cheerfully comply with the provisions of the Act of Assembly.

Therefore it is understood by the Board of Trustees of East Tennessee College at Knoxville in their legal capacity that they do make sign seal and deliver to the Secretary of State on behalf of the Citizens South of French Broad and Holston and west of Big Pigeon river a deed of release and quit claims as follows viz:

The Board of Trustees of EAST TENNESSEE COLLEGE at Knoxville in pursuance of the Act of Assembly above referred to have released, discharged, and by these presents do release and discharge and forever quit claim to the Secretary of State in behalf of the Citizens South of French Broad and Holston and west of Big Pigeon rivers all judgments, debts, dues, demands, claims, rents, issues, proffits (sic) or suits of any kind character or description whatever, either in law or equity and also all rights that may have been acquired through or under the sale of any of the lands in said section of country and which may have been bid off either directly or indirectly for its benefit by the Treasurer of East Tennessee. In testimony whereof the Board of Trustees direct the same to be signed by the President of the Board and countersigned by the Secretary and the Seal of the Board be affixed thereto at Knoxville, this 20 day of April 1830. Sig: William PARK, President Pro. Tem. of the Board of Trustees of East Tennessee College." W. B. A. RAMSEY, Secretary. Registered 28 Apr 1830.

902. (4:10) Thomas HIX to James THOMPSON: 22 Mar 1830, $400, 123 ac on Ellejoy Creek, adj John F. GARNER, John DUNLAP. Surveyed January 1, 1807. Wit: Sam HENRY, Alexander LOGAN. 28 Apr 1830.

903. (4:11-12) John McMAHON to Alexander COOK, Trustee for the use of James McMAHON: 6 May 1828, [consideration] a debt of

$245.39 owing to James McMahon by John McMahon, 90 ac on waters of Nine Mile Creek, cor with James McMahon, adj DAVIS, RUSH. John McMahon to make payment of $245.39 with lawful interest within two years from the date hereof. Wit: Samuel COPE, Newton WILLIAMS. 29 Apr 1830.

904. (4:12-13) Samuel THOMPSON to Ephraim SAWTELL: 27 Feb 1828, $213, 241 ac on waters of Crooked Creek, part of a tract granted to Samuel Thompson, adj David WHITE, cor to parcel sold by Thompson to Michael TEAFATELLER, heirs of William GLASS. Wit: A. EARLY, Isaac YEAROUT. 29 Apr 1830.

905. (4:13) Heirs of James COOK, decd, to James McMAHON: 28 Jan 1822, $192, 128 ac on waters of Nine Mile Creek, a part of a whole tract held by the heirs which descended to them by heirship, adj William DAVIS, Joseph COOK, including the free continuance of the dam now erected. Sig: Wm. COOK, Alexander COOK, I. A. WRIGHT, Anny Belinda WRIGHT, Elizabeth COOK, James COOK, John McMAHON, Jane McMAHON, Joseph COOK, Robert SLOAN, Margaret (X) SLOAN. Wit: Elijah ELLIS, William HARRIS to all but Sloan's wife 17 Mar 1829, Wm. GARNER to all but Sloan's wife, James HENRY and Samuel HENRY witness as to Sloan's wife. 4 May 1830. Proven at court March 1829.

906. (4:14-15) Heirs of James COOK to John McMAHON: 28 Jan 1822, $400.49, 90 ac on waters of Nine Mile Creek, cor with James McMahon on south side of creek, crossing the creek through the mouth of Machine branch, DAVIS, RUSH, Widow's dower. [excepting the free use of the dam to Thomas WALLACE]. Sig: Wm. COOK, Elizabeth COOK, James COOK, J. A. WRIGHT, Ann Celia WRIGHT, Alexander COOK, James McMAHON, Mary McMAHON, Joseph COOK, Robert SLOAN, Margaret (X) SLOAN. Wit: Chas. REEVES, Wm. GARNER, James HENRY, Samuel HENRY. 4 May 1830.

907. (4:15) John MONTGOMERY to Alexander KENNEDY: 24 Feb 1830, "whereas many years ago, the particular time not now recollected, Andrew KENNEDY..made me a bill of sale of his black man ABEL to secure the payment of a debt he owed me, said bill of

sale being lost or mislaid, whereas Andrew KENNEDY has since honestly paid and fully satisfied me as to the amount of the debt and..Andrew has directed me to transfer the right of said negro to his son Alexander KENNEDY..."   Wit: John MONTGOMERY, Jr., Samuel WERE. 17 May 1830.

908. (4:16) Thomas HENDERSON to Major BEAVORS: 7 Nov 1818, $700, 106 ac on waters of Pistol Creek, cor to John WOODS and Jacob DANFORTH, adj Josiah PAYNE, David OWENS, John GARDNER, KING AND MONTGOMERY, Jacob DANFORTH. Wit: Charles DONOHOO, David S. S. BURKE. 17 May 1830.

909. (4:16-17) Major BEAVORS to Thomas HENDERSON: 7 Nov 1818, $500, 89 ac on Pistol Creek, cor to Gideon BLACKBURN, adj WOODS, Robert McNUTT. BEAVORS is not to be responsible or to warrant the tract against claims of Josiah DANFORTH, and HENDERSON is to pay the State installments due. Wit: Charles DONOHOO, David S. S. BURKE. 17 May 1830.

910. (4:17-18) Henry BOND to Francis SHAW: 19 Sep 1829, $500, 136 ac in Hickory Valley, part of two tracts formerly owned by Nicholas STEPHENSON, near to Thomas SIMPSON, cor to original survey, cor to Henry BOND's land and Nicholas STEPHENSON's line, adj Hollingsworth STEPHENSON, decd. Sig: Henry (X) BOND. Wit: Wm. GRIFFITHS, Samuel LEWIS. 17 May 1830.

911. (4:18-19) James LOGAN (first party) to John WILSON, trustee, (second party) for Samuel HENRY (third party): 1 Jun 1829, 194 ac whereon LOGAN now lives; one sorrel horse and one sorrel mare and one wagon; LOGAN has in debt to Samuel HENRY his promisory note now due for cash amounting to $181.31. LOGAN to pay before 1 Feb 1830. Wits: Alfred COWAN, James HENRY. 18 May 1830.

912. (4:19-20) Lot ROGERS to James DAVIS: 20 Mar 1830, $150, 73 ac adj late entry of ROGERS, Vincent ROGERS, Samuel PICKENS or Larkin BOLLING. Sig: Lot (X) ROGERS. Wit: Vincent ROGERS, Jesse ROGERS. 19 May 1830.

913. (4:20-21) William TOOLE to William WALLACE. 16 Aug 1829, $100, lot #81 in Maryville. Wit: Wm. H. THOMPSON, Campbell WALLACE. 19 May 1830.

914. (4:21-22) Samuel LOVE and William TOOLE to William WALLACE: 16 Aug 1829, $800, lot #33 in Maryville which had been granted heretofore to Miles and David CUNNINGHAM by the state of TN. Wit: Campbell WALLACE, W. H. THOMPSON. 19 May 1830.

915. (4:22-23) George CALDWELL to William CARPENTER of Washington Co., VA: 4 June 1823, $400, 164 ac, the land where CALDWELL now lives, adj John CALDWELL, John McCULLOCH, William LOWRY. Wit: John M. LOWRY, William LOWRY. Sig: George (X) CALDWELL. Proven at court Mar 1830 by William LOWRY who says that John M. LOWRY is now dead. 20 May 1830.

916. (4:23-24) John TAYLOR to William HENDRIFF: 9 July 1828, $100, 91 ac on waters of Little River, adj Elizabeth COULTER. Surveyed 27 May 1826. Wit: John COLTER, Alexander S. COLTER. 20 May 1830.

917. (4:24-25) William HARPER to Enoch WATERS: 22 Mar 1830, $300, 62 ac on Crooked Creek, cor George BERRY, adj heirs of William REAGAN, "above the head of the spring..dividing spring and crossing the creek"..LOWRY. Wit: William HENDRIX, Josias GAMBLE. 24 May 1830.

918. (4:25-26) Eli TIPTON to Enoch WATERS: 18 Nov 1829, $300, 72 ac on waters of Hesse Creek in Miller's Cove, part of Grant #2423 to Mashac TIPTON, on a conditional line between Meshac TIPTON and Eli TIPTON, adj James TIPTON. Sig: Eli (X) TIPTON. Wit: Wm. HENDRIX, Green (X) TARFER. 24 May 1830.

919. (4:26-27) Thomas K. WYLEY to James WYLEY: 16 Nov 1829, $2200, 405 ac Granted to John CASTEEL in three different grants and all joining together on Tennessee River adj James WYLY, Samuel DOUTHET. Second title #10881 adj original survey of John CASTEEL and Samuel DOUTHET, 150 ac. Title #10880 adj CASTEEL's 150 ac entry, 50 ac, granted to John CASTEEL by #172.

Wit: George (X) BROWN, C. K. WYLY. Ack at court Feb 1830 by George BROWN who says that C. K. WYLY is not now an inhabitant of this state. 7 June 1830.

920. (4:27-28) John CASTEEL to Thomas K. WYLY: 10 Sep 1828, $2000, 500 ac on Little Tennessee River, cor James WYLY, original Grant #171 to CASTEEL, also to include Grant #10880 and #10881, and intended to include all and every part of the land ceded by grants and to include the land where CASTEEL now lives. Wit: James WYLY, Elisha WILLIAMS. Ack at Sept 1829 court by James WYLY who says that WILLIAMS is not now an inhabitant of the state. 8 Jun 1830.

921. (4:28-29) Will WALLACE, Sheriff, to Jacob F. FOUTE: 2 Aug 1828, $15, 60 ac near the Big Spring adj Alexander HENDERSON, Bolling JOHNSTON; public sale 2 Aug 1823 to satisfy judgment in favor of David PARKINS against Samuel FRAZIER for $16.28. Wit: James BERRY, S. E. A. B. ANDERSON. 9 Jun 1830.

922. (4:29-30) John NORWOOD to John S. BURNETT: 7 May 1821, $300, 106 ac on waters of east fork of Pistol Creek, cor William HARRIS, Jno. DUNCAN, Robert GAUTT, WILKINSON and James DONOHOO, David CUP. Wit: Azariah SHELTON, William FAGG. 9 June 1830.

923. (4:30-31) Alexander HUMPHREYS to Samuel HUMPHREYS: 10 Jan 1830, "agreement to divide their property as fully explained by a will made by Samuel as it respects horses, cattle, sheep, etc., with the land also provided their father William HUMPHREYS make a good and sufficient title to the land they now live on...Alexander is to pay to the child of Samuel, Louise Emeline HUMPHREYS when she shall come of age, $400 in land or money, the difference between the place they now live on and the one they purchased from Cyrus HUMPHREYS which Alexander has given up this day unto Samuel and which Samuel has willed to the support of his wife during her widowhood and to his child before named, and all the farming tools, wagon harness, etc. [are] given unto Alexander and he is to furnish the widow and child 400 weight of meat yearly, the three horses willed to Emaline, Alexander is to have the management of and do with them to

the best advantage for the child's use. Alexander agrees to furnish Samuel's family 15 bushels of wheat yearly provided there is any grows." Wit: Joseph JONES, Jac. W. HAIR. 9 Jun 1830.

924. (4:31-32) William GAULT, Esqr. to Abijah CONGER, John GAULT and Robert CALDWELL, as a school committee: 8 Mar 1830, $1.00, a tract (ac not stated) on the headwaters of Baker's Creek adj the lands of A. CONGER and Robert CALDWELL being the 4th corner of GAULT's survey.   Wit: Allen STRAIN, Wm. B. McCAMPBELL. 9 Jun 1830.

925. (4:32-33) Landon Carter MACLIN (first party), James WILSON (second party) and Daniel D. FOUTE, trustee (third party): 29 Dec 1829, MACLIN is indebted to WILSON on note of $85.87 dated 30 Dec 1829 due one day after date and for securing payment MACLIN conveys to FOUTE for the benefit of WILSON, a negro girl slave NANCY aged about 23 years. Wit: John SAFFLE, William KEITH. 9 Jul 1830.

926. (4:33-34) John FREEMAN (first party), Daniel D. FOUTE (second party) and James WILSON (third party): 19 Nov 1829, FREEMAN is indebted to WILSON by note dated 19 Nov 1829 and due one day after date for $638.14 for which FOUTE is security; lot #63 in Maryville at intersection of Main street and an alley, adj lot #62 belonging to Campbell WALLACE, whereon FREEMAN now lives. FREEMAN to pay his debt to WILSON on or before 1 July next. Wit: John SAFFELL, William KEITH. 9 July 1830.

927. (4:34-36) William THOMPSON (first party) to Daniel D. FOUTE (second party) and James WILSON (third party): 26 Dec 1829, THOMPSON is indebted to WILSON for $1409.80 by note dated the same day of this trust, for which FOUTE is security; 404 ac on Little River, cor to George EWING, cor to George BERRY, adj George CALDWELL.   Also, the following negroes: POLLY, supposed to be between twenty and thirty years old; BETSY, about 20 years old or upwards; POLLY ANN, ten yrs old; HENRY, about ten or twelve yrs old and MILINDA about 5 or six yrs old. THOMPSON to pay debt to WILSON with legal interest and costs before 1 Jan 1831. Wit: William KEITH, John SAFFELL. 13 July 1830.

928. (4:36-37) Edward CAWOOD to William WILSON: 16 July 1825, $750, 167 ac on waters of Sinking Creek, being part of Grant #393 to Moses CAWOOD. Wit: John CARSON, Joseph CARSON. 14 July 1830.

929. (4:37) Benjamin D. CLIFT of Monroe Co. to Philip HENSON: 7 Nov 1827, $250, 50 ac, part of grant to Mark LOVE, adj EDEN's line, William JAMES. Wit: John DOYL, Milton BRADBERRY, Alford JACOBS. 16 July 1830.

930. (4:38) Philip HENSON and Polly HENSON to James WILSON: 18 Apr 1830, $40, 50 ac, part of tract granted to Mark LOVE, adj EDEN's line, William JAMES. Wit: John SAFFELL, William KEITH. 20 July 1830.

931. (4:38-39) Conrad EASTERLEY (first party) to Jesse THOMPSON (second party), James WILSON (third party) and WILSON AND SAFFELL (fourth party): 2 Mar 1830, EASTERLY is indebted to WILSON by note executed by Conrad EASTERLY and George W. MURRY for $101.58 on 18 Mar 1830 due one day after date, also one note to WILSON AND SAFFLE amounting to $18.59 dated 18 Mar 1830 due one day after date, for which THOMPSON is security; 217 ac, a tract of land purchased of Joseph...(name omitted) on waters of Nine Mile Creek, adj John TEDFORD, "COOK's other tract". EASTERLY to pay debt on or before 1 March 1831. Wit: John HENRY, Henry RODDY.

932. (4:40-41) William THOMPSON (first party) to Daniel D. FOUTE (second party) and James WILSON (third party): 27 Apr 1830, on 26 Dec 1829 THOMPSON sold to FOUTE by deed in trust for the benefit of WILSON a tract of 404 ac on Little River. THOMPSON has since become further indebted to WILSON for $316.43 by note dated the same day of this deed. To secure WILSON in payment therefor, THOMPSON conveys to FOUTE the land and the following articles of personal property: one bay horse about 11 yrs old, one bay mare about same age, one sorrel colt about two yrs old, 16 head of cattle (one yoke of steers, one red and white and one black and white, four muley cows, and ten stock cattle heifers and steers) and farming tools: two barshares, three shovels, one bull tongue and

coulter plows, four pair of gears, two iron toothed harrows, two broad axes, two hand axes, two tenon saws, one crosscut saw, one stove, one brace and bits, one set chisels and gouges, one set of wagon hub augurs, one set common augers, two set hub bands, six feather beds, under beds, furniture and six bedsteads and cords, one book case, one cupboard, one bureau, one falling leaf table and two small walnut tables, two set windsor chairs, one set split bottom chairs, and one set of cupboard furniture, one big pot and some small pots and ovens and skillets, six drawing knives, one foot adze, and various other tools, about 20 head of hogs (two sows and pigs), five barrows and one rifle gun. THOMPSON to pay WILSON $316.43 secured in this deed in addition to the sum of $1409.08 secured in the deed of trust referred to on or before 1 Jan 1831. Wit: William KEITH, John SAFFELL. 21 July 1830.

933. (4:41-42) Spencer BLANKENSHIP of Monroe Co. to Samuel JONES: 18 Apr 1826, $100, vacant land entered at 12-1/2 cents per acre, adj William McCULLEY, land originally surveyed for A. LOGAN, original survey for A. FOSTER, Francis JONES, William BAKER. Wit: William HENDERSON, Peter (X) SMITHSON. 24 July 1830.

934. (4:42-43) Spencer BLANKENSHIP of Monroe Co. to Samuel JONES: 15 Apr 1826, $115, 15 ac on waters of Gallaher's Creek, cor to Wm. BAKER and Robert McCULLEY near the east fork of Gallaher's Creek.   Wit: William HENDERSON, Peter (X) SMITHSON. 24 July 1830.

935. (4:43) Joseph ALEXANDER, John B. CUSICK, Robert B. YOUNG to Daniel D. FOUTE: 19 Feb 1829, $3.37, Quit Claim to "our claim in and to our undivided interest of an 81 ac tract of land joining the Yellow Springs tract." Wit: J. McGHEE, Daniel McCULLOCH. 26 July 1830.

936. (4:43-44) Jesse THOMPSON to Daniel D. FOUTE: 28 June 1830, $700, lots #2, 3, 46, 47, 48 in town of Maryville; lot #2 adj lot #1 whereon Rev. Isaac ANDERSON now lives. Lots #46, 47, 48 adj each other on which John A. AIKEN now lives. All of the five lots

have been for some time in the possession of FOUTE and are now occupied by John A. AIKEN. Wit: Will B. MARTIN. 26 July 1830.

937. (4:44-45) Lot ROGERS to Jesse DEAN: 18 Feb 1828, $300, 50 ac on waters of Ellejoy Creek. Sig: Lot (X) ROGERS. Wit: Sam PICKENS, William SHAMBLIN. 4 Aug 1830.

938. (4:45-47) Jacob DANFORTH and Mary DANFORTH, his wife, of Augusta, Richmond Co., GA, to Josiah F. DANFORTH: 25 June 1825, $500, 10 ac on Pistol Creek adj town of Maryville, corner to KING AND MONTGOMERY on northwest side of town, adj the Commons. Wit: Chas. T. PHELPS, W. N. THOMAS, Justice of the Peace. 30 Aug 1830.

939. (4:47-48) Miller FRANCIS, Treasurer of East Tennessee and succesor in office to Mathew NELSON, late Treasurer of East Tennessee, to John WRIGHT, now of Roane Co., TN: 2 Nov 1829, NELSON by virtue of an Act of General Assembly passed on 16 Nov 1823 entitled an act for relief of the citizens..to appropriate the monies due from said citizens for their land...sold among others, on the 20th and 21st days of July 1825, a tract of land Grant #1026 to David LOVELESS containing 37 ac... to satisfy the amount due and payable on said tract of land.. to John WRIGHT, by his agent William TOOL, for $5.31, that being more than the said NELSON was authorized to bid or offer for the tract. Wit: Will B. REESE, Jac F. FOUTE. 30 Aug 1830.

940. (4:48-49) William DON to Hughs BURKE: 4 Sep 1829, $250, part of Grant #942 to Jesse WALLACE containing 100 ac, adj Samuel THOMPSON, Abram WALLIS. Sig: William (X) DON. Wit: David P. ROWAN, James A. ROWAN. 30 Aug 1830.

941. (4:49-50) Joseph HAIR, John BRUCK, Nathaniel and Mariah MORRISON, Eliza HAIR of Blount Co., Adam and Sarah HUFFMAN of Roane Co., Jacob W. HAIR of Blount, Isaac M. HAIR of Blount, John and Rachel RUBEL? of Washington Co. to William GRIFFITH: 8 Jan 1828, $1175, 7286 ac on Cloyd's Creek, adj WALKER's line, Josiah JOHNSTON. Land formerly belonging to Isaac HAIR, decd, which land was left to us by will. Sig: Joseph HAIR. John (X) BRUCK. Eliza (X) HAIR. Adam (X) HUFFMAN.

Sarah (X) HUFFMAN. Nathaniel and Mariah MORRISON. Jac W. HAIR. Isaac M. HAIR. John G. RUBEL and Rachel RUBEL his wife by their attorney William BAYS. Wit: John GRIFFITHS, Samuel LEWIS, Jac W. HAIR. 9 Sep 1830.

942. (4:50) Baldwin H. TAYLER of Monroe Co., to Baldwin HARLE of Jefferson Co.: 17 Oct 1829, $33, my right...as heir of David MILLER, decd, of an undivided share ..the one-eleventh part of the one half of a tract Grant #1126 to David MILLER dated 16 May 1810, containing 383 ac, 135 ac of which had been conveyed away by MILLER in his life time. Also my undivided share or the one-eleventh part of the one half of a certain tract in Hiwassee District granted to the heirs of David MILLER by Grant #7089 dated 24 May 1822 containing 221 ac. Wit: Isaac M. MOORE, Leonard HARLE. 10 Sep 1830.

943. (4:51) Henry FINGER to William C. NORWOOD: 1 Aug 1829, $350, 106 ac on waters of the east fork of Pistol Creek, being Grant #1371 to John HANNAH's son, cor to William HARRIS, adj John DUNCAN, Robert GAUTT, John WILKINSON and James DONOHOO, David CUPP. Sig: Henry (X) FINGER. Wit: Danl. D. FOUTE, Nelson WRIGHT. 11 Sep 1830.

944. (4:52) Danl. D. FOUTE, Clerk & Master of Circuit Court, to Jesse KERR: 28 April 1830, $200, 91 ac on waters of Nine Mile Creek, adj James HENRY, Robert HAMELL, James HIGGINS, John BERRY. Public Sale 18 July 1827. On 1 Jan 1827 by the decree of the circuit court, it was ordered that the tract of land mentioned in the pleadings in the cause of Jesse KERR against John HENRY and others..should be sold. Wit: W. B. MARTIN, J. A. AIKEN. 28 Sep 1830.

945. (4:52-53) Danl. D. FOUTE, Clerk and Master in Equity of the Circuit Court sitting in Chancery Court, to Jesse KERR: 28 Apr 1830, $270, on 31 Jan 1827 by the decree of the Circuit Court sitting in Chancery, lot #66 in Maryville mentioned in the pleadings in the cause Thomas GARNER against John S. BURNET, James R. DANFORTH, John W. DANFORTH, Josiah F. DANFORTH, Matthew W.

McGHEE and William LOWRY was ordered to be sold. Public Sale 2 Apr 1827. Wit: W. B. MARTIN, J. A. AIKEN. 28 Sep 1830.

946. (4:53-54) Decree of the Supreme Court (Knoxville), Mary R. WALLACE by her Guardian Wm. McCLUNG vs Mathew WALLACE and Andrew HENDERSON, Admins: July-Aug term 1829. The Arbitrators appointed to determine this cause..award title to the whole tract of land in dispute be vested out of Mathew WALLACE and vested in Mary R. WALLACE in fee. Land was originally granted to Moses CAWOOD, contains about 179 ac on Baker's Creek, adj John RIDEN, cor to A. MALCOM. Mathew WALLACE to pay $124.43, the balance of the rents and profits of said land in his hands unaccounted for, to William McCLUNG, guardian, and $101.96 personal estate and WALLACE to pay costs of this cause. Sig: Hu BROWN, Clerk of the Supreme Court of Errors and Appeals of Knoxville, 16 Sept 1829. 8 Oct 1830.

947. (4:54-56) James McCALMAN and wife Betsy, formerly Betsy SCOTT, to John and William Alexander SCOTT: 22 Nov 1825, $1.00, James SCOTT died seized and possessed of the following tracts of land, having verbally expressed it to be his will that William A. and John SCOTT should inherit from him the same; John and William relinquish to James and Betsy their claim to the ninth part...of the estate of James SCOTT, decd, [two] tracts of 683 ac adj each other on Baker's Creek, cor to Robert BOYD and James EDMONSTON, adj William MOORE, John GAUTT, Joseph GLENN, Thomas McCLERKIN, Bartley McGHEE, John EWING. Granted to James SCOTT on 11 May 1830 containing 635 ac. The other tract was conveyed to James SCOTT by Alexander WILSON on 9 May 1825 containing 45 ac adj tract above. Sig: James McCALMAN. Betsy (X) McCALMAN. Wit: Joseph HENDERSON, John TEDFORD. Betsy was examined privately by John GOULD and William TOOL, two members of the court. 11 Oct 1830.

948. (4-56) Jesse KERR, quit claim to William ASHER: 14 Jan 1829, 114 ac on waters of Nine Mile Creek adj William DAVIS and others, which land was sold by Charles DONOHOO, Sheriff, [to KERR]. "I have transferred all my right to William ASHER in consequence of ASHER buying the land of Joseph COOK and COOK transferred my

obligation to ASHER". Wit: William DAVIS. David (X) KERR. 13 Oct 1830.

949.   (4:57) Danl. D. FOUTE to William TOOL: Sept 1830, [consideration] two saddles; lot #116 in Maryville, lying near the town spring. Wit: Leonard WOOD, John FURGUSON. 14 Oct 1830.

950.   (4:57-58) William WALLACE, Sheriff, to Daniel D. FOUTE: 27 Sep 1830, $12.25; Public sale 1820 (date omitted) by Sheriff Charles DONOHOO, lot #115 in Maryville, to satisfy judgment for $55.25 with interest from 12 Jun 1819 plus $5.27 costs in favor of James and Ignatius WILSON against Andrew AGNEW. DONOHOO [has] gone out of office and removed out of the county. Wit: James HENRY, Leonard WOOD. 14 Oct 1830.

951.   (4:58-59) Michael McNELLY to William McCAMY: 19 Feb 1820, $400, 93 ac on waters of Crooked Creek, adj William GLASS. Wit: Jeffry JOHNSON, Charles McNELLY. Ack at March court 1822. 15 Oct 1830.

952.   (4:59) John LOWRY to David RUSSELL: 28 Dec 1830 (sic), $55, a tract containing two roods and two square chains near the town of Maryville bounded east by Mathew McGHEE, south by James TURK, west by lands of Sam LOVE, and North by the main road leading from Maryville to Tennessee River, adj LOVE's corner on the edge of the Great road to Tellico. Wit: Pryor LEA, John F. GILLESPY. Ack at court Dec 1822 and certified for registration 27 Jan 1823 by Jac. F. Foute, Clerk. Reg 15 Oct 1830.

953.   (4:60) Abraham UTTER to William UTTER: 13 July 1822, $200, 29 ac on Baker's Creek. Wit: Robert R. YOUNG, Jacob (X) HUFFMAN. 15 Oct 1830.

954.   (4:61) John LICKENS to Robert MORRIS: 24 Jan 1821, $500, 76 ac on waters of Baker's Creek, cor to Robert RICHEY, part of 311 ac Grant #1273 to David RICHEY. 23 May 1810. Wit: Will?/Webb? BARNHILL, Terrence CONNER. 15 Oct 1830.

955. (4:61-62) John SHARP of Sevier Co. to David WHITE: 24 Jun 1816, $600, 192 ac on Brown's fork of Crooked Creek. Wit: J. MONTGOMERY, Banner SHIELDS. 18 Oct 1830.

956. (4:63) John EWING to James STRAIN: 20 December 1822, $300, 248 ac on waters of Baker's Creek, cor to James SCOTT and Robert BOYD, adj McGHEE, John CALDWELL's beginning corner, CALDWELL and FORD's corner, part of a tract granted to John EWING. Wit: John DUNLAP, William EWING. Sig: John (X) EWING. 18 Oct 1830.

957. (4:64-65) James BOYD, Joseph McMURRY, John M. McMURRY, Polly McMURRY, John SIMS, Archibald McMURRY, Fanny McMURRY, Boyd McMURRY, Henderson McMURRY, Nancy McMURRY all of Blount Co., William E. CRESSWELL of (omitted) to William McMURRY of Blount Co.: 21 Dec 1816, $120, 139 ac adj James SIMS. Wit: James SIMMS, Charles KIRKPATRICK. 17 May 1817.

958. (4:65) Jesse WALLACE to Samuel W. WALLACE: 17 Aug 1830, $100, negro boy CHARLES, aged about 5 yrs, slave for life. Wit: John F. GILLESPY, Joseph J. WALKER. 25 Oct 1830.

959. (4:66) Jesse WALLACE to Campbell WALLACE: 17 Aug 1830, $1,000, six slaves: negro woman HANNAH aged about 50 yrs, negro woman named FRANKY aged about 35 yrs, boy THOMAS aged about 15, girl named ELIZA about 11 yrs, girl HARRIET about 9 yrs and girl MAHALY about two yrs. Wit: John F. GILLESPY, Joseph J. WALKER. 25 Oct 1830.

960. (4:66-67) John FREEMAN to Abram WALLACE: 20 Aug 1830, $400, negro girl named SYNTHENY aged about 19 yrs, girl named ANN, about 3 yrs. Wit: Joseph J. WALKER, Campbell WALLACE. 29 Oct 1830.

961. (4:67) William WALLACE, Sheriff, to John B. ROGERS: 7 Jun 1830, $66, "By virtue of an execution from the Supreme court at Sparta at the instance of the state against the goods...of John B. THOMPSON, negro boy named THOMPSON, aged about 19 yrs." Wit: Josiah JOHNSTON. 29 Nov 1830.

962.   (4:67-68) John McGHEE of Monroe Co. to Campbell
WALLACE: 15 Sep 1830, $1175, lot #62 in town of Maryville, adj
the court house lot, the front street and the Village Hotel lot, being the
house formerly occupied by McGHEE AND BROTHERS, then by
BERRY AND WALLACE, and now by WALLACE AND JACOBS
as a store house. Wit: John F. GILLESPY, I. GILLESPY. 29 Oct
1830.

963.   (4:68-69) Jenny OWENS, executrix of David OWENS, decd, to
Isaac ANDERSON: 13 Apr 1830, $300, 205 ac on waters of Pistol
Creek, adj KING AND MONTGOMERY, cor John GARDNER, adj
Gideon BLACKBURN, Robert McNUTT, John McNEELY, David
EAGLETON, William WALLACE. Grant #1197. "Excepting one-
fifth part of the parcel, to wit 41 ac, it being the part devised to me by
will of David OWENS, adj William WALLACE, KING AND
MONTGOMERY, including the spring, the houses and the barn.
Granting to ANDERSON free access to the spring doing as little
damage as may be to the part hereby reserved to Jenny OWENS." Sig:
Jenny (X) OWENS. Wit: Latten W. DUNLAP, Will WALLACE,
S.E.H.B. ANDERSON. 30 Oct 1830.

964. (4:70) Landon C. MACLIN of Gibson Co.to Jacob F. FOUTE:
15 Sep 1830, $480, negro woman LUCINDA aged 19 yrs and her
child JAMES aged 2 yrs, both of yellow complexion. Wit: Daniel D.
FOUTE, Wm. M. LOWRY. 30 Oct 1830.

965. (4:70-71) John GILLESPY to Arthur B. CAMPBELL: 6 Aug
1830, $300, negro woman TEMPERANCE about 35 yrs, negro boy
slave aged 11 months named Adam PUSTOW. Wit: Will WALLACE,
Campbell WALLACE. 1 Nov 1830.

966.   (4:71-72) Josiah F. DANFORTH, atty for James R.
DANFORTH, to Leonard WOOD: 9 Sept 1830, $475, 342 ac on
waters of Pistol Creek, adj Thomas TURK, John WOODS, Bartley
McGHEE, John LOWRY, Abraham YEAROUT, James McCALLEN,
being Grant #6136 to John THORNBERRY. Wit: William TOOL,
Daniel D. FOUTE. 1 Nov 1830.

967.   (4:72-73) Michael BOWERMAN of Ohio to Henry
BOWERMAN: 24 Jun 1815, $450, 253 ac on Holston River, being

tract formerly belonging to Peter BOWERMAN, decd, adj Washington ALLEN. Wit: Pelrone BOWERMAN, Elizabeth (X) BOWERMAN. Proven in court 22 July 1817. 8 Nov 1830.

968. (4:73) James HALL to Thomas CROWDER: 20 Oct 1829, $1,000, two negro men, each 20 yrs of age, EVERETT and CHARLES. Wit: Wm. HENRY, Caswell HALL. 21 Nov 1830.

969. (4:73-74) Daniel BONINE to Michael BOWERMAN: 27 Jan 1815, $1500, 386 ac tract on Walker's Mill Creek whereon he now lives, adj Alexander HENDERSON, Peter BOWERMAN, John LOWE. Wit: Josiah PATTY, Jesse JAMES. Proved at court 1 Oct 1817. 8 Nov 1830.

970. (4: 74-75) James TIPTON to John HENDRIX and Elijah HATCHER: 25 Dec 1829, $100, 124 ac surveyed 8 Nov 1826, Grant #13999, on waters of Hesse's Creek in Miller's Cove, adj Nathan FARMER, Thomas DAVIS, TIPTON, HATCHER. Sig: James (X) TIPTON. Wit: Daniel D. FOUTE, John TEDFORD. 9 Nov 1830.

971. (4:75-76) Henry BOND to Samuel WINTERS: 26 Sep 1827, $500, 109 ac, adj WINTERS, TURNER's heirs, William GRIFFITHS. Sig: Henry (X) BOND. Wit: Wm. GRIFFITHS, Josiah JOHNSON. 9 Nov 1830.

972. (4:76-77) John GILLESPIE to Barton L., Henry and Robert WARREN: 5 Sep 1829, $300, 182 ac, part of a tract granted to James HOUSTON, James, John and Robert GILLESPIE, adj William WALLACE, Samuel RANKIN, Abraham HEARTSELL. Wit: W. WALLACE, Abraham HEARTSELL. Ack Dec 1829 court. 9 Nov 1830.

973. (4:77-78) Samuel CLARK of Lincoln Co. to heirs of Robert MAXWILL, decd [Sarah MAXWELL, wife of Robert; Jane LOE formerly Jane MAXVILLE, Susannah SHARP, formerly Susannah MAXVILLE; Sarah FURGUSON, formerly Sarah MAXVILLE; Elizabeth R. MAXVILLE and Melinda MAXVILLE]: 14 Dec 1829, $500, 92 ac derived by descent from Thomas CLARK, decd, on waters of Pistol Creek, adj James CLARK, David HUME, upon which

Sarah MAXVILLE now lives. Wit: Eleven HITCH, James CLARK.
9 Nov 1830.

974. (4:78-79) Henderson LEA to James LEA: 25 Sep 1830, $300,
negro man named ALEXANDER. Wit: Elbert F. MERCER, Joseph
BLACK. 21 Nov 1830.

975. (4:79) James A. McCLURE to Randolph KIDD: 9 Sep 1830,
$450, 285 ac, being Grant #1108 to John McCLURE, adj Charles
McCLURE, Josiah PAYNE, Richard CHANDLER. Wit: Alexander
RICE, Daniel D. FOUTE. 21 Nov 1830.

976. (4:79-80) James BADGETT, Sr. to James BADGETT, Jr.: 26
November 1822, $1,000, negroes ROBIN and his wife CLARY, three
children FRIDAY, ANDREW, MARY MARTHA. Wit: Will
DONCARLOS, James (X) FORESTER. 29 Nov 1830.

977.   (4-80-82) Heirs of Alexander McCULLOCH [Robert
EAGLETON and Elizabeth J. EAGLETON formerly Elizabeth
McCULLOCH, Robert McCULLOCH of Blount County; John
McCULLOCH, Thomas McCULLOCH, Alexander EAGLETON and
Jane EAGLETON formerly Jane McCULLOCH, and Samuel EWING
and Mary EWING his wife, formerly Mary McCULLOCH, of Indiana]
to David HUME: date omitted 1830, $800, 150 ac on Little River,
derived by descent from Alexander McCULLOCH, decd. Wit:
Alexander SHARP, James CLARK, James BEAR, Ewing
ALEXANDER. Ack in Vigo Co., IN, Circuit Court 10 Apr 1828. 21
Nov 1830.

978. (4:82-83) John B. RODGERS to Elijah WALKER: 7 June 1830,
$200, negro boy THOMAS. Wit: Will WALLACE. 29 Nov 1830.

979. (4:83) Eli RICHEY to James BADGETT, Sr.: 17 July 1828,
$600, 123 ac on Tennessee River, adj Hugh KELSOE, Thomas
CROWDER. Wit: D. McGAUGHY, James SLOAN. 22 Nov 1830.

980. (4:83-84) Henry McCRAY to William BRADBURY: 10 Feb
1830, $10, 13 ac on the dividing line between the lands of William
BURTON and the land McCRAY now owns, adj Gilbert
BLANKENSHIP, part of the tract which McCRAY bought of Jacob

HOLLINGSWORTH.   Wit: Paten   (X)   LANE,   Jacob HOLLINGSWORTH. 22 Nov 1830.

981.   (4:84-85) Jacob HOLLINGSWORTH to Henry McCRAY: 8 Feb 1830, $200, 62 ac on waters of Gallaher's Creek, on which Jacob HOLLINGSWORTH now lives, part of a tract originally granted to Alexander FORSTER adj James WILSON and the heirs of Ignatius WILSON, decd, Gilbert BLANKENSHIP.   Wit: William BRADBURY, Wm. BURTON. 22 Nov 1830.

982.   (4:85) Shelton HARRIS of Orange Co., IN, to Andrew HARRIS: 14 Sept 1829, $144.75, "all the right, title, claim and interest that I have in and to two boys and one girl and the land formerly belonging to my father". Wit: Eleven HITCH. 22 Nov 1830.

983.   (4:85-86) Thomas CROWDER to James HALL, Sr.: 10 Oct 1829, $1200, 187 ac on the great road in fourth line of original survey made for Hugh KELSOE, adj James HALL, the river bank, Robert WEAR, BADGET. Wit: Wm. HENRY, Caswell HALL.   22 Nov 1830.

984.   (4:86-87) James BADGETT to Caswell HALL: 27 Sep 1830, $500, 125 ac on Little River, adj Hugh KELSOE, Thomas CROWDER now James HALL, Sr. Witnesses omitted. 22 Nov 1830.

985.   (4:87-88) Lott ROGERS to James DAVIS: 24 Aug 1830, $150, 25 ac on waters of Ellejoy Creek, adj Vincent ROGERS, DAVIS' own land. Wit: John (X) WHITE, Henry ORMAN. 29 Nov 1830.

986.   (4:88-89) Evan EMBREE of Monroe Co. to Sarah ALLEN: 16 Feb 1829, $8, 83 ac on waters of Gallaher's Creek, adj Samuel JONES, WALKER, the heirs of ALLEN, Aron HACKNEY. Wit: John JONES, Samuel JONES. 29 Nov 1830.

987.   (4:89) John FREEMAN to Jessee F. BUNKER: 20 Apr 1830, $300, negro boy DICK. Wit: James SINGLETON. 4 January 1830.

988.   (4:89-90) John WOOD to Moses SCRUGGS: 5 Apr 1830, $200, 89 ac on waters of Baker's Creek, cor Brice BLAIR and Wm.

GRAY, adj John BEATY, John MILLER, Wm. BEASLY. Wit: John RIDEN, Jr., Marvel DUNCAN. 30 Nov 1830.

989. (4:90-91) James GILLESPIE to Benjamin PRATER of Roane Co.: 27 Feb 1830, $600, 160 ac on the river below Low's Ferry, cor James GILLESPIE and James McILHERON, Sr. where McILHERON now lives. Wit: A. ISH, Nelson WRIGHT, John HOUSTON. 30 Nov 1830.

990. (4:91) James GILLESPIE to Benjamin PRATER of Roane Co.: 27 Feb 1830, $600, 64 ac, "being a certain island in the Holston River known as Scott's Island, which is the first island in Holston River below Captain BIRD's old ferry and the first island above Abraham LOW's Ferry." Wit: A. ISH, Nelson WRIGHT, John HOUSTON. 30 Nov 1830.

991. (4:91-92) Nathaniel HARRIS to Jesse F. BUNKER: 9 Mar 1830, no consideration stated, negro boy named JOHN about 21 yrs of age. Wit: Randolph KIDD, Zephaniah (X) HARRIS. 4 Jan 1831.

992. (4:92) Harvey N. WILSON of Monroe Co. to James CONNER: 19 Mar 1830, $57, 40 ac on waters of Baker's Creek, cor Alexander McCOLLUM, survey made for Hugh KELSOE, FARMER's line. Wit: John BIGGS, John CARSON. 30 Nov 1830.

993. (4:93) John WOOD to Robert WOOD: 5 Apr 1830, $300, 70 ac on waters of Baker's Creek, adj Samuel COWAN, William BEASLY, being part of original survey made for John MILLER. Wit: John RIDER, Jr., Marvel DUNCAN. 30 Nov 1830.

994. (4:93-94) James HENDERSON to William SCOTT: 17 Nov 1826, $400, 143 ac on Pistol Creek being held by the right of occupancy and preemption and being part of 173 ac granted to Robert HENDERSON and by him conveyed to Jesse BUCKLEY and by him to Elias DEBUSK and by him to HENDERSON, cor William SIMONS, adj Hezekiah PASSEY, Daniel YEAROUT, Andrew CUMMINGS, Susan?/Jason? McCARTY, Robert LOVE, Thomas HUNTER. Wit: Alexander McKEE, Robert LOVE. Ack at court Sept 1828 by witnesses. 30 Nov 1830.

995. (4:94-95) John HALL to William WILLIAMSON: 21 July 1830, $300, 131 ac on waters of Nine Mile Creek, Grant #1797 to James GILMORE, cor to James MONTGOMERY, Hugh MONTGOMERY and William ARMSTRONG, adj John HAMMERSLY, Abraham UTTER. Sig: John (X) HALL. Wit: Samuel HAMMELL, Robert HAMEL. 1 Nov 1830.

996. (4:95-96) Jesse BUTLER of Monroe Co. to John HAMMONTREE: 23 Nov 1829, $400, 173 ac on waters of Baker's Creek, cor to Brice BLAIR and Samuel COWAN. Wit: Philip HAMMONTREE, Hugh HAMMONTREE. 1 Dec 1830.

997. (4:96-97) William McTEER and James BOYD, executors of William BOYD, decd, to John McGAUGHY of Sevier Co.: 28 Sep 1830, public sale 22 Dec 1828, $600, 264 ac on waters of Nails Creek, cor KIRKPATRICK and James BOYD, adj James McCLURG, SKEEN's old corner. Wit: William KENDRIFF, James UPTON. 1 Dec 1830.

998. (4:97-98) Isaac YEAROUT to William EARLY: 27 Sep 1830, $300, 114 ac on waters of Pistol Creek being part of Grant #176 to John EDMISTON and by him conveyed to John MILLER; cor John WILKINSON, adj Mary PASEY, PAULEY, HENDERSON, William JACKSON, Samuel MAJORS, decd, Andrew YOUNG. Wit: Robert HOUSTON, Alexander STEWART. 3 Dec 1830.

999. (4:98-99) John S. DUFF (first party) to Daniel D. FOUTE (second party) and James TRUNDLE (third party): 6 Jul 1829, a parcel on which DUFF now lives on road from Maryville to Little River, adj John CALDWELL, John McCULLEY, William LOWRY's old survey. DUFF is indebted to TRUNDLE by notes: $100 cash bearing date 21 May 1829, due 21 March next; one note dated 6 July 1829 for $50, due 21 Mar next; note for 100 bushels of corn dated 21 March 1829 due 15 Nov next; one note for 25 bushels of corn due 15 Nov next and dated 6 July 1829. FOUTE is security for DUFF. Wit: Alexander RICE, Daniel McCULLOCH. Proved at June 1830 court by Alexander RICE, who said that Daniel McCULLOCH is not an inhabitant of this state. 25 Dec 1830.

1000. (4:99-100) Benjamin S. ADAMS to Jeffrey JOHNSON: 13 Dec 1828, $700, 180 ac on waters of Nails Creek, cor HARDING and NIEMAN, HAFLEY, N. FARMER, A. PHILIPS. Wit: William KEITH, Daniel D. FOUTE. 25 Dec 1830.

1001. (4:100-01) Daniel D. FOUTE to Benjamin S. ADAMS: 13 Dec 1828, 182 ac on waters of Nails Creek, cor to Peter WHEELER and NEYMAN, adj C. HAFLEY, N. FARMER, A. PHILIPS, HARDIN. On 10 Mar 1828 ADAMS conveyed this tract to FOUTE as trustee to secure payment of certain monies to Jeffry JOHNSON. ADAMS has paid the sums owed to JOHNSON and FOUTE returns property to ADAMS. Wit: Jeffry JOHNSON, William KEITH. 27 Dec 1830.

1002. (4:101-02) James L. WARREN to James SINGLETON: Jan 1826, $300, 24 ac on waters of Holston River, part of Grant #9711 to James L. WARREN, cor John SINGLETON and Samuel GEORGE. Wit: Edward GEORGE, Sr., Edward GEORGE, Jr. Ack at court Dec 1827. 27 Dec 1830.

1003. (4:102-03) William McKAMY to Mathew H. BOGLE: 27 Jun 1827, $25, 100 ac on waters of Ellejoy Creek, cor Joseph TIPTON, adj T. McBARNEY, BOYD, Mathew H. BOGLE, A. BOGLE, James TIPTON. Sig: William (X) McKAMY. Wit: Danl. D. FOUTE, Will B. REESE. 27 Dec 1830.

1004. (4:103-04) John WILSON, Sr. to Thomas WEAR: 7 Oct 1822, $200, 41 ac on waters of Baker's Creek, part of 63 ac granted to John WILSON, adj David EDINGTON, Charles LOGAN, Thomas ROACK, Thomas WEIR, Thomas MONTGOMERY. Wit: Alexander CARSON, David CARSON. Ack Dec 1826 court. 27 Dec 1830.

1005. (4:104-05) William F. ADAMS to Milton BRADBURY: 12 Mar 1824, $300, 127 ac on waters of Gallaher's Creek, part of Grant #2478 to Alexander FORESTER. Sig: William (X) ADAMS. Wit: William BROWN, Ben. D. CLIFT. Proven Dec 1826 court. 27 Dec 1830.

1006. (4:105-06) William WALLACE, Sheriff, to Philmore GREEN: 27 Dec 1830, $3.00, public sale 20 June 1830 to satisfy judgment for $60.06 recovered by GREEN against Augustine BOWERS, six ac on waters of Ellejoy Creek adj Philmore GREEN, William DAVIS and others [not named]. No witnesses. 6 Jan 1831.

1007. (4:106-07) William WALLACE, Sheriff, to Philmore GREEN: 29 Dec 1830, $105, Public Sale 22 March 1827 to satisfy judgments which GREEN recovered against Augustine BOWERS, issued on 15 and 16 Jan 1827, to satisfy the sums of $84.65 with interest from 23 Oct 1826 with $5.55 costs; $59.16 with interest from 23 Oct 1826 and $5.55 costs, and $67 with interest from 21 Oct 1826 with $5.50 costs; two tracts containing 153 ac on waters of Ellejoy Creek, Grant #2458 to Philmore GREEN assignee of Jacob MOORE, the other tract containing 86 ac joining the other tract and the land of William DAVIS. GREEN bid $100 for the tracts containing 153 ac, and $5 for the tract containing 86 ac. 7 Jan 1831.

1008. (4:108) Alexander HENDERSON and John PICKENS, execrs of Francis HENDERSON, decd, to James McCALMON: 15 Oct 1826, $600, 94 ac on waters of Gallaher's Creek, part of the place McCALMON now lives on. Wit: John McTEER, Landon McCALMON. 10 Jan 1831.

1009. (4:108-09) Alexander B. GAMBLE to William TOOLE: 22 Oct 1830, $900, 361 ac, Grant #972 to Johnathan TRIPPETT on 8 May 1810, cor to Richard TROTTER, adj Joseph TEDFORD, Thomas MAXWELL, Joseph ALEXANDER, Andrew YOUNG, Elias DEBUSK. Wit: Joseph A. B. WILKINSON, Daniel D. FOUTE. 10 Jan 1831.

1010. (4:109-10) James and John GILLESPIE to William McILHERON: 4 Apr 1829, $300, 96 ac on Holston River, the tracts surveyed for Patrick BEARD and a piece of vacant land entered by John GILLESPIE, beginning on a cliff of the river bank, cor to survey made for James now belonging to McILHERON. Wit: James McILHERON, John McILHERON. 12 Jan 1831.

1011. (4:111-12) John CROMWELL (first party), Abraham UTTER (second party) to Jesse KERR (third party): 19 Feb 1830, 100 ac on waters of Baker's Creek adj lands of Robert THOMPSON and Nathaniel HARRISON, John HALL, and others [not named]; part of a 212 ac Grant to Abraham UTTER on 7 June 1809. CROMWELL has executed his promissory note to KERR for $91.00 in par money dated this 19th day of Feb 1830 due one day after date. If CROMWELL shall pay interest of the note at the end of every six months then the sale of land is not to come for the term of two years from this date. Wit: John GOULD, R. THOMPSON. Proven at Sept 1830 court by GOULD and THOMPSON. 19 Jan 1831.

1012. (4:112-13) Isaac CAMPBELL to Samuel GEORGE: 6 Aug 1828, $1,000, the undivided one half of 152 ac on Little River, Grant #2335 to Thomas McCULLOCH, cor to Alexander McCULLOCH, adj Thomas CLARK, Eleven HITCH, Pistol Creek. Wit: Jacob F.FOUTE, Robert M. ANDERSON. 19 Jan 1831.

1013. (4:113-14) James MOORE to "James JONES, son of Johnston": 10 Feb 1828, $600, 135 ac on Gallaher's Creek, cor to Samuel DICKEY. Three-quarters of an acre "that he sold off said tract for the use of the QUAKER MEETING HOUSE" is excepted. Wit: John JONES, Enos ELLIS. Proved at Dec 1830 court by witnesses. 25 Jan 1831.

1014. (4:114) Samuel and Robert HAMILL to John HALL: 16 Mar 1829, $300, 130 ac claimed and held by right of occupancy and preemption, Grant #1797 to James GILMORE, cor to James MONTGOMERY, Hugh MONTGOMERY and William ARMSTRONG, adj John HAMMERSLY, Abraham UTTER. Wit: Daniel (X) DELANY, William (X) HARRISON. Ack Sept court 1830. 26 Jan 1831.

1015. (4:115) Jacob F. FOUTE, trustee of C. M. NORWOOD, to James N. HAYDEN: 16 Apr 1830, "on 29 July 1826 NORWOOD executed a deed of trust to FOUTE for certain lots and land in Maryville as security for Francis and John IRWIN, and John IRWIN and William DAVIDSON and John IRWIN of North Carolina for himself and as partner and agent of Francis IRWIN and William DAVIDSON, authorizing FOUTE to release and quit claim to land therein mentioned on conditions which have been complied with. NORWOOD has sold to James N. HAYDEN one acre of land, part of the said tracts for $100, and NORWOOD requires FOUTE to convey the land. The one ac is part of the same purchased of Samuel M.

GAUT by NORWOOD and conveyed to FOUTE as trustee, adj Commons of Maryville, B. McGHEE's cor." Wit: Wm. M. LOWRY, James BERRY. 31 Jan 1831.

1016. (4:116) Moses SCRUGGS to John WOOD of Grainger Co.: 14 Oct 1825, $400, 89 ac on waters of Baker's Creek, cor Brice BLAIR and William GRAY, adj John BEATY, John MILLER, William BEASLEY, William GRAY. Wit: Berry ABERNATHY, Sylvester COBB. Ack at June 1830 court. 31 Jan 1831.

1017. (4:116-17) Moses SCRUGGS to John WOOD of Grainger Co.: 14 Oct 1824, $400, 70 ac on waters of Baker's Creek, adj the Great road, Samuel COWAN, William BEASLEY, part of original survey made for John MILLER. Wit: Berry ABERNATHY, Sylvester COBB. Ack June court 1829. 31 Jan 1831.

1018. (4:117-18) John ADAMSON of Jefferson Co. to Jesse HAMMER: 9 Mar 1826, $133, 44 ac in the Hickory Valley, part of occupant survey made for David PINKLES, adj Henry BOND, Leroy NOBLES, Samuel WINTERS. Wit: James JONES, Isaac ADAMSON. 31 Jan 1831. Proven at court June 1829.

1019. (4:118-19) William TIPTON to Isaac TIPTON of Carter Co.: 10 Apr 1822, $1500, 426 ac in Hiwassee District in Cades Cove on waters of Tennessee River, part of Grant #6731 to William TIPTON dated 23 Mar 1821, adj Mary LINVILE. Wit: Jos. CALLAWAY, Nath. HENDRIX. Proven at Circuit Court January 1831 by witnesses. 11 Feb 1831.

1020. (4:119-20) Campbell WALLACE to James WHITE of Abingdon, VA: 27 Jan 1831, $3500, 330 ac on waters of Pistol Creek, part of original Grant to William AYLETT, cor James WEAR. Wit: Will WALLACE, James H. GILLESPIE. 18 Feb 1831.

1021. (4:120-21) Campbell WALLACE to James WHITE of Abingdon, VA: 27 Jan 1830, $1500, 175 ac, part of Grant #780 to Banner SHIELDS, adj Michael GOODLINK. Wit: Will WALLACE, James H. Gillespie. 18 Feb 1831.

1022.   (4:121-22) William WALLACE, Sheriff, to Thomas
BLACKBURN: 10 Jun 1829, 232 ac property of Robert ALLEN.
Public sale 29 Dec 1828, when Daniel D. FOUTE purchased the
property for $10.75, to satisfy judgment recovered on 29 Mar 1828
by Valentine HOOKER/HOOKES? against ALLEN for $145.69 debt
and $9.30 costs. WALLACE made application on 20 Jan 1829 to
redeem the tract from FOUTE, he being a creditor of ALLEN, and on
20 Jan 1829 redeemed the tract of land according to law...Thomas
BLACKBURN being [also] a lawful creditor of ALLEN claimed the
right of redemption...and [BLACKBURN] redeemed the tract of land
on 29 Mar 1829 of WALLACE. For the purpose of saving the cost
and expense of a multiplicity of deeds of conveyance, FOUTE has
authorized WALLACE to make the deed to BLACKBURN. Wit:
Campbell WALLACE, John S. BERRY. 1 Mar 1831.

1023.   (4:123) James R. DANFORTH of the city of Augusta,
Richmond Co., GA, to Josiah F. DANFORTH: 28 June 1828, power
of atty to convey a certain tract of land within one mile of Maryville.
Wit: Samuel HALE, Justice of the Inferior Court, Richmond Co.

1024.   (4:124) Trustees of PORTER ACADEMY to the Citizens
South of French Broad and Holston: 3 Sep 1830, "whereas by an act
of the General Assembly of the State of Tennessee entitled an Act to
settle the controversy between the colleges and academies and the
citizens south of French Broad and Holston and west of Big Pigeon
Rivers," passed at Nashville on 31 Dec 1829, provision is made for the
benefit of said Institutions upon condition that they shall in their
corporate capacity ...make such deed as is required...[to] forever
acquit, discharge and release the Citizens residing south of French
Broad and Holston and west of Big Pigeon Rivers..from all judgments,
debts,   dues,   etc...of   any   character,   kind,   or   description
whatever...which the said Academy may have ...against said Citizens...
quit claim and release to said Citizens all...right the Academy may have
acquired by, through or under the sale of any of the land". Sig: James
GILLESPIE, President pro tem of the Board of Trustees of Porter
Academy. James BERRY, Clerk. Recorded 1 Oct 1830 by Thos. H.
FLETCHER, Secretary of State. 10 Mar 1831.

1025. (4:124-26) Jacob F. FOUTE to Elders of NEW PROVIDENCE CHURCH [Samuel THOMPSON, Thomas HUNTER, William GILLESPIE, William EWING, David DELZELL, Andrew EARLY, John EAGLETON, Robert TEDFORD, Robert HOOKE]: 25 July 1828; on 29 July 1826, Caleb M. NORWOOD conveyed in trust to FOUTE certain town lots and tracts of land for the benefit and security of Francis and John IRWIN, John IRWIN and William DAVIDSON and John IRWIN of North Carolina, and ..John IRWIN for himself and as the partner and agent of Francis IRWIN and William DAVIDSON, authorized and permitted FOUTE to release and quit claim to a certain tract of land therein mentioned on conditions which have been complied with, and..NORWOOD has sold to the Elders four ac of land, part of one of said tracts, for the sum of $125...and has requested FOUTE to convey to Mr. EARLY or the Congregation the four acres of land lying west of the Meeting House..being the same purchased of Sam M. GAUTT by NORWOOD, beginning at a stake on the commons of the Town of Maryville four feet in advance of the line of the north west side of the Main Street, B. McGHEE's corner...adj Gideon BLACKBURN, containing five acres more or less, excepting and reserving one ac thereof lying on the end of the tract joining the Commons, that being heretofore sold to James N. HAYDEN and is to be divided from the said four acres hereby intended to be conveyed to the Elders, so as to include one ac and the shop and building of James N. HAYDEN. Wit: S.E.H.B. ANDERSON, Wm. M. LOWRY. Ack at court Dec 1829. 16 Mar 1831.

1026. (4:126) Josiah F. DANFORTH to William GAULT, Jr.: 16 Feb 1828, $100, lot #79 in town of Maryville. Wit: Danl. D. FOUTE, Abram WALLACE. 25 Mar 1831.

1027. (4:126-27) John CALDWELL to Alexander SHARP: 7 Mar 1831, $600, 280 ac on waters of Little River, one half of Grant #1718 to John CALDWELL, cor to Robert CHANDLER. Wit: Adison SHARP, Danl D. FOUTE. 28 Mar 1831.

1028. (4:127-30) James BERRY and Jacob F. FOUTE (first party) to Thomas L. WILLIAMS of Knox Co. (second party) and William F. and Alexander MURDOCK of Baltimore, MD (third party): 30 Dec

1830, BERRY and FOUTE are indebted to MURDOCK(s) by note dated 3 Dec 1829 due nine months after date for $3,049.55 and also by a note due 15 Feb 1832 for $502.16, for which WILLIAMS is security; 10 ac adj town of Maryville on Pistol Creek, purchased by BERRY and FOUTE of Josiah F. DANFORTH on 6 Jan 1829, on which BERRY and FOUTE have built a merchant Grist Mill, etc. called MORELAND MILLS; also, lots #82 and 83 conveyed by John McGHEE to FOUTE on 25 Sep 1827; lots #384 and #109 conveyed by James BERRY to FOUTE on 8 Oct 1827; lot #40, conveyed by William W. BERRY to James BERRY on south side of Main Street of Maryville on which stands a white painted framed house now occupied by Doctor Samuel PRIDE. BERRY and FOUTE to pay debts before 15 Feb 1832. Wit: Jo JOHNSTON, Wm. M. LOWRY. Proven at court March 1831 by Joseph JOHNSTON, who stated that William LOWRY is not now a resident of this state. 5 Apr 1831.

1029. (4:130-31) James HALL, Sr. to Caswell HALL: 10 Feb 1831, $1200, 181 ac adj Great Road in the fourth line of original survey made for Hugh KELSOE, adj James HALL, Sr., Little Tennessee River, cor to Robert WEAR, Caswell HALL. Wit: Darby RAGAN, Nathaniel RAGAN. 4 Apr 1831.

1030. (4:131-32) John B. CUSICK to Daniel D. FOUTE: 9 Feb 1829, $1600, 8 ac on Pistol Creek, Grant #1538 to CUSICK, adj Commons of Maryville, cor with John LOWRY now the Seminary tract, McGHEE, John MONTGOMERY. Wit: James H. GILLESPIE, John SAFFELL. Proven by witnesses June 1830 court, 12 Apr 1831.

1031. (4:132-33) Leonard WOOD to James N. HAYDEN: 28 Mar 1831, $650, 342 ac on waters of Pistol Creek, adj Thomas TURK, John WOODS, Barclay McGHEE, John LOWRY, Abraham YEAROUT, James McCALLEN, being Grant #6136 to John THORNBERRY. Witnessess omitted. 27 Apr 1831.

1032. (4:133-34) William WALLACE to Daniel D. FOUTE: 6 Dec 1830, $1,000, 240 ac on the great road from Maryville to Little River and on the waters of Pistol Creek, part of Grant #748 to Samuel McGAUGHY, adj Pat EDINGTON, KING and MONTGOMERY, J.

P. SMITH, John WOODS, D. CALDWELL.   Wit: Wm. A. SPENCER, John WILSON. 13 Apr 1831.

1033. (4:134-35) William McKAMY to Daniel D. FOUTE: 15 Jan 1830, $400, two tracts, one of 93 ac adj FOUTE's Currier place, John KEY, George BERRY; the other of 66 ac joining first tract. Sig: Will (X) McKAMY. Wit: Will WALLACE, John WILSON. 13 Apr 1831.

1034. (4:135-38) Will WALLACE, Sheriff, to Daniel D. FOUTE: 29 Mar 1831, $37.50, public sale 4 Oct 1828 to satisfy judgments recovered against John NORWOOD as follows: By Samuel HENRY for $70.31 plus $9.20 costs, 25 Jun 1828. Elem TATE, $3.20 plus costs, 24 Feb 1827. CURTIS for $9.31 plus costs, 5 Jan 1828. Richard LANNING, 23 Dec 1822, $8.82. Robert H. BINE, 24 Feb 1821 for $56.73 and costs. John DUN, 3 Dec 1824, $13.45 and costs. John CHANDLER for A. THOMAS, 19 Feb 1828, for $6.08 and costs. "There being no personal property of NORWOOD's to be found...clear of incumbrances and adverse claiming on which to levy,"...111 ac adj D. WHITE, WHITEHEAD's cor, KING; also an undivided interest in another tract of 160 ac in Hiwassee District known by the Yellow Spring place, entered in the name of John NORWOOD and James BERRY as lot #39; also NORWOOD's undivided interest in another tract of 80 ac joining the Yellow Spring tract entered in the name of NORWOOD, John B. CUSICK, Joseph ALEXANDER and Robert YOUNG. FOUTE bid $15.50 for the first tract of 111 ac and $21 for defendant's interest in second tract, $1.00 for defendant's interest in the third tract. Wit: Lewis RENEAU, Pryor LEA. 14 Apr 1831.

1035. (4:137-38) Edward MITCHEL to William A. SPENCER: 26 Mar 1831, $3,000, lots #14, 15, 16 in Maryville in the first range of back lots, now in possession of SPENCER. Lots 14 and 15 joining each other on which a Tanyard is situated, bounded on the east by lot #13 owned by C. M. NORWOOD, on the south by the commons of the town, on the west by a cross alley, and on the North by a Main Street, and lot #16 bounded on the east by the said cross alley, on south by Commons, on west by lot #17 owned by John SHARP, and on north by the said back street. MITCHEL also "transfers the liberty of conveying water in pipes from the spring formerly owned by James

TURK in the same manner as he hath liberty from the said TURK".
Wit: Daniel K. SPENCER, Martin SLATERY. 15 Apr 1831.

1036. (4:138-39) Abijah CONGER to John JACKSON: 20 Feb 1831,
$300, 103 ac on Pistol Creek, adj the Creek, cor to Andrew
CUMMINGS, Patrick CULTON, a tract granted to Adam
DINSMORE assignee of John B. CUSICK. Wit: James CULTON,
David CONGER. 27 Apr 1831.

1037. (4:139-40) Daniel D. FOUTE (first party), William WALLACE
(second party) to Campbell WALLACE (third party): 6 Dec 1830,
240 ac on the great road leading from Maryville to Little River and on
waters of Pistol Creek, part of Grant #748 to Samuel McGAUGHY,
cor James EDINGTON, KING and MONTGOMERY, Josiah P.
SMITH, John WOODS, David CALDWELL. FOUTE is liable for
note for $100 in current bank notes due 1 Aug 1831, another for $100
due 1 Aug 1831 and one note for $100 due 1 Aug 1833, another for
$100 due 6 Dec 1830, another for $100 due 6 Dec 1832 and one other
for $219 due 6 Dec 1831 payable in leather, another for $250 payable
in leather on 6 Dec 1832. FOUTE to pay the obligations plus interest
on or before 1 Aug 1833. Wit: Wm. A. SPENCER, John WILSON.
27 Apr 1831.

1038.   (4:140-41) Thomas SUTHERLAND and Anna G.
SUTHERLAND, his wife, one heir of William HENRY, decd, of
Anderson Co. to James HENRY: 27 Jan 1826, $300, 501 ac of land
and one other tract of 220 ac on waters of Little River and Ellejoy
Creek. The tract of 501 ac surveyed 22 Dec 1805 was Grant #2366,
the other surveyed 6 Jan 1801, Grant #2565, both belonging and
granted to the heirs of James HENRY, decd. Quit claim as heirs of
William HENRY, decd, and also the part that may descend to us at the
death of Jane HENRY, the wife of James HENRY, decd. Wit: John
CHILES, Michael CLARDY. Proven in Anderson Co. Court by
witnesses Jan 1831. 4 May 1831.

1039. (4:142) Josias G. HENRY and Hugh HENRY to James
HENRY: 21 May 1828, $650, 65 ac on Little River, being the
undivided share of two tracts of land granted to the heirs of James

HENRY, decd, and our share of said land as heirs of William HENRY, decd. Wit: A. B. GAMBLE, John GAMBLE. 4 May 1831.

1040. (4:142-43) James DAVIS to George DAVIS: 26 Mar 1830, $400, 192 ac adj the creek (not identified), the 11th cor of original survey of 344 ac made for "said TIPTON" (sic). Witnesses omitted. 6 May 1831.

1041. (4:143-44) James DAVIS to George DAVIS: 26 Mar 1831, $200, 5 ac on waters of Ellejoy Creek, cor to Benjamin TIPTON's original survey, adj Adam GRAVES. Witnesses omitted. 6 May 1831.

1042. (4:144-45) Zepheniah HARRIS to "my brother-in-law" Thomas J. TIPTON: 7 May 1831, Quit claim to 35 ac of land... my undivided interest in and to all the land formerly (word omitted) to my father in the county of Blount..it being for a consideration of $140 paid on 7 May 1830." Wit: Andrew HARRIS, Jabes THURMAN. Witnesses omitted.

1043. (4:145-46) Adam KOUNTS to James JULIAN: 29 Jan 1831, $479, 179 ac on waters of Ellejoy Creek, cor William CUMMINS, adj James DUNLAP. Wit: D. D. FOUTE, Henry LAMON. 7 May 1831.

1044. (4:146-47) John COOK to Archibald SLOAN: 10 Sep 1816, $125, "a piece of land on COOK's property and part being one- sixth of a tract formerly held by John SLOAN, decd, and descending to COOK as heir at law". Wit: James SLOAN, Robert SLOAN. 29 May 1831.

1045. (4:147) David CARSON, Blount Co., and Milton Henderson CARSON, Caldwell Co., KY, to John THOMPSON: 2 Feb 1831, $285, 95 ac cor to John THOMPSON on James HAMMONTREE's line. Wit: John CUNNINGHAM, Alexander CARSON, Joseph CARSON. 5 Jun 1831.

1046. (4:147-48) William HENDERSON to Levi PARKINS: 8 Oct 1830, $900, 149 ac on waters of Holston River, cor to Alexander LOGAN, being a tract conveyed from Isham BLANKENSHIP to

HENDERSON in 1826. Wit: John HACKNEY, Enos ELLIS. 6 June 1831.

1047. (4:148-49) David WILLIAMS to Samuel C. WILLIAMS: 26 Jan 1829, $606, 229 ac on Holston River, adj BRIANT, John STALEY, Jesse MITCHELL. Wit: John STALEY, W. B. WILLIAMS. Proven by witnesses Mar 1831 court. 6 June 1831.

1048. (4:149-50) Mark MARTIN and John MARTIN of Blount Co. and Holden MARTIN of McMinn Co. to Armstead CARPENTER: 17 Sep 1828, $250, 86 ac in Hickory Valley, cor Jacob HUSE, adj Daniel DURHAM, Samuel WINTERS, Nicholas STEPHENSON. Sig: Mark MARTIN. Holden MARTIN. John (X) MARTIN. Wit: Robert SLOAN, Jac W. HAIR. 6 Jun 1831.

1049. (4:150-51) Joseph HAIR to John STALEY: 28 Mar 1831, $150, 88 ac being part of an entry made by Jesse MITCHELL, including an entry made by Mathew SULLENS, cor to the 150 ac entry made by MITCHELL, adj STALEY, S. C. WILLIAMS. Wit: D. D. FOUTE, James M. BUSSELL. 7 Jun 1831.

1050. (4:151-52) Jesse MITCHELL to Joseph HAIR: 16 Nov 1827, $225, 88 ac, part of an entry made by MITCHELL and part of occupant survey made for Benjamin PRATER including an entry made by Mathew SULLENS, cor to 150 ac entry made by MITCHELL, adj John STALEY, D. WILLIAMS. Wit: Wm. GRIFFITH, Jac W. HAIR. Proven by witnesses Mar 1831 court. 7 Jun 1831.

1051. (4:152) Samuel CLOUD to James W. BUSSELL: 28 Mar 1831. $20, 36 ac, being an entry made by CLOUD, cor to occupant survey made for Benjamin PRATER. Wit: D. D. FOUTE, Henry LAMON. 7 Jun 1831.

1052. (4:152-53) John RIDER, Sr. to John RIDER, Jr.: 6 Feb 1828, $350, 132 ac on Baker's Creek, cor John McGHEE, adj James SLOAN, John BEATY. Wit: John WOOD, Samuel THOMPSON. Sig: John (X) RIDER. Proven by one witness at June 1829 court and further proven Sep 1831 by Samuel THOMPSON. 7 Jun 1831.

1053. (4:153-54) Samuel GOLD (first party) to James W. LOGAN (second party) for John GOLD (third party): 4 Dec 1830, $340, 200 ac originally granted to William STEWART and conveyed to Samuel CARGO and from CARGO to Andrew COWAN, from COWAN to Samuel GOLD; also one good horse, one sorrel mare and two sorrell colts, ten head of cattle, nine head of sheep, fourteen head of hogs, one wagon and gears, household and kitchen furniture consisting of two beds and furniture, cupboard, tables, chairs, pots, ovens, etc.; also crop of corn (suppose three hundred bushels). Samuel GOLD has received of John GOLD $100 in hand "and is justly due him one hundred dollars in current money for two years service, and John GOLD stands as security for $140 more. LOGAN is security. Samuel to pay John before 1 Jan 1833 the sum of $340 current money. Wit: And. COWAN, Alfred COWAN. Ack at March 1831 court for 200 ac of land and various articles of personal property. 9 Jun 1831.

1054. (4:154-55) John McALLISTER to Daniel MOORE: 16 Aug 1822, $500, 124 ac on waters of Baker's Creek, part of 277 ac granted #280 to Samuel SCOTT, adj GREER, UTTER. Wit: Isaac ELDER, James MOORE. Proven at Mar 1831 court by MOORE, who stated that ELDER is now dead. 14 Jun 1831.

1055. (4:155-56) Morris MITCHELL of Roane Co. to James W. BUSSELL: 26 Mar 1831, $350, 75 ac on Holston River, adj J. W. BUSSELL on north, John STALEY on south. Wit: John STALEY, Samuel CLOUD. 14 Jun 1831.

1056. (4:156-57) Benjamin CUNNINGHAM to Jonathan BROWN: 3 July 1830, $150, 152 ac on waters of Little River, cor Shadrick MOORE, McCALLIE. Wit: Jesse BROWN, Joseph BROWN. 14 Jun 1831.

1057. (4:157-58) Samuel COWAN and George EWING and James EWING to James H. GILLESPY: 23 Jan 1828, $300, town lot #65 in Maryville. Wit: James GILLESPY, J. C. EWING. Proved Mar 1831 court by James GILLESPEY and John C. EWING. 6 July 1831.

1058. (4:158-59) William MERRIOTT of Roane Co. to Francis SHAW: 3 Sep 1830, $70, 150 ac on waters of Holston River, cor James JONES, cor Samuel BOND, adj David WILLIAMS. Sig:

William (X) MERRIOTT. Wit: William GRIFFITH, John BROOKE, Josiah JOHNSTON. 6 Jul 1831.

1059. (4:159-60) John FREEMAN to William TOOL: 6 Apr 1831, $225, two lots #68 on Main Street in Maryville, adj Thomas HENDERSON's lot #67 on east, by Alex McGHEE's lot #69 on west, and on north by a back alley; also lot #77. Wit: Julius C. FAGG, Thomas L. LUCKETT. 6 July 1831.

1060. (4:160-61) Samuel SLOAN to Archibald SLOAN of St. Clair Co., AL: 30 May 1830, $125, 36 ac, being the one sixth part of an undivided tract of land granted to John SLOAN, decd, adj James COPE, Richard WILLIAMS, David CARR and others. Land descended to Samuel SLOAN as one of the legal heirs and representatives of John SLOAN, decd. Wit: John M. COOK, James TEDFORD. 6 July 1831.

1061. (4:161) Mathew W. McGHEE to John FREEMAN: 31 Dec 1830, $225, two lots #68 and #77 in Maryville adj Thomas HENDERSON, Alexander McGHEE. Wit: Samuel WALLACE, Robert HOUSTON. 6 July 1831.

1062. (4:162) Charles DONOHOO, Sheriff, to Samuel GEORGE: 1 Apr 1824, $5, public sale 16 Feb 1822, levied on as the property of Gabriel MORGAN, lands upon which MORGAN then lived, to satisfy a judgment recovered against him on 16 Feb 1822 by Samuel GEORGE and Isaac CAMPBELL. Wit: Daniel D. FOUTE, William WALLACE. 6 Jul 1831.

1063. (4:162-63) Bennet JAMES of Lawrence Co. to Robert GALLAHER: 27 Jun 1831, $500, 94 ac on Little Tennessee River adj Robert and GREENWAY. Sig: Bennet JAMES by Wm. GRIFFITTS his Attorney. Wit: Will WALLACE, Leroy NOBLE. 6 July 1831.

1064. (4:163-64) John NORWOOD (first party), Daniel D. FOUTE (second party) to James BERRY and William W. BERRY and Jacob F. FOUTE (third party): 8 Sep 1827, NORWOOD is indebted to James BERRY for $400 and to William W. BERRY by note dated 12 July 1826 for $75 payable in hauling as therein specified, and is also indebted to Wm. W. BERRY and Jacob F. FOUTE under the firm of

BERRY AND FOUTE for two notes, one for $100 dated 30 Dec 1826, the other for $1.71 dated 8 Sep 1827. D. D. FOUTE is security. One blue painted wagon, six pair of gears, wagon cover, halter chains, feed troughs and all the apparatus belonging thereto, also two black horses and one sorrel horse, 12 feather beds with all their covering and furniture, 14 bedsteds, one bureau, one side board, 8 tables, 30 chairs and all the kitchen furniture belonging to NORWOOD, two red cows. Wit: Thomas J. FOUTE, Josiah F. DANFORTH. 18 July 1831.

1065. (4:165) James DAVIS to Vincent ROGERS: 24 Feb 1831, $125, 60 ac, adj ROGERS' occupant survey. Wit: Jesse ROGERS, Martin HARMAN. 3 May 1831.

1066. (4:165-66) James DAVIS to Jesse ROGERS: 24 Feb 1831, $10, 10 ac of the original survey of 73 ac made for DAVIS, on the Rocky Branch. Wit: Martin HARMAN, George SMITH. 9 Aug 1831.

1067. (4:166-67) James DAVIS to Jesse ROGERS: 14 Dec 1830, $135, 50 ac on waters of Ellejoy Creek, adj Larkin BOWLING. Wit: Vincent (X) ROGERS, Martin (X) ORMAN. 9 Aug 1831.

1068. (4:167-68) James DAVIS to Vincent ROGERS: 24 Feb 1831, $75, 25 ac on waters of Ellejoy Creek, adj ROGERS' occupant survey, a rocky branch, crossing a spring branch. Wit: Jesse (X) ROGERS, Martin ORMAN. 9 Aug 1831.

1069. (4:219-20) William GREEN to James KEE: 17 Oct 1831, "in consideration of the natural love and affection for KEE and also for the further consideration of an obligation bond by James KEE given to William GREEN for the support and maintenance of GREEN and his present wife during their natural life", 97 ac on waters of Holston River, whereon GREEN now lives, adj the survey made for Michael CASTATOR now John REAGAN's, adj George MOORE, Shadrack HICKS, Peter KEE, Jacob COPPENBARGER. Sig: William (X) GREEN. Wit: William COLEBURN, Jasper BRIGHT. 10 Apr 1832.

1070. (4:220-21) James and John GILLESPIE to John WRIGHT of Roane Co.: 20 Oct 1830, $799.50, 256 ac on Holston River, Grant

#37 to James, John, and Robert GILLESPIE. [Description includes: "to a stake and double stump by Indian graves."]   Wit: Will WALLACE, Samuel WALLACE. 23 Apr 1832.

1071. (4:221-22) John GILLESPIE to John WRIGHT of Roane Co.: 20 Oct 1830, $120.50, 241 ac on Holston River, cor to survey made for James, John and Robert GILLESPIE, GIBSON, RUSSELL, cor to survey made for William GILLESPIE, adj John HICKLAND. Wit: Will WALLACE, Samuel WALLACE. 23 Apr 1832.

1072. (4:223) Daniel D. FOUTE to John FREEMAN: 3 Jan 1831, "Whereas on 19 Nov 1829 John FREEMAN of Maryville sold to me in trust for the purpose of securing James WILSON for payment of $638.14, lot #63 in Maryville, and FREEMAN has paid WILSON the debt..". Wit: Robert HOUSTON, Campbell W. GILLESPY. 24 Apr 1832.

1073. (4:223-24) John FREEMAN to James CARSON of Monroe Co.: 30 Jun 1831, $2000, a house and lot #63 in Maryville, now occupied by FREEMAN, being the same property occupied by Jesse WALLACE, together with all the houses, out houses, stables and appurtenances. Wit: Peter (X) BRICKY, John RANSBARGER. 24 Apr 1832.

1074. (4:224-25) James CARSON of Monroe Co. to Campbell and James H. GILLESPY: 3 Jan 1832, $1400, a house and lot now occupied by John FREEMAN and formerly by Jesse WALLACE. Wit: Will WALLACE, John A. AIKEN. 25 Apr 1832.

1075. (4:225-26) Jonathan ANDERSON by his atty in fact Samuel HENDERSON to William CAMPBELL: 26 June 1819, $450, 180 ac on waters of Crooked Creek, cor Thomas WALLACE, HOUSTON, Jacob THOMAS, the tract originally Grant #1695 to Robert BELL. Wit: John WILKINSON, Robert REYNOLDS. 26 Apr 1832.

1076. (4:226-27) Elizabeth THOMPSON to son Jesse THOMPSON: 12 Dec 1831, in consideration of natural love and affection, all that undivided parcel of land devised and left to me by my husband Andrew THOMPSON, decd, in his Last Will and Testament; 437 ac on the road from Maryville to Knoxville, cor to James TRUNDLE, adj James

P. MONTGOMERY and Jane OWENS, adj Isaac ANDERSON and James WHITE, Robert EAGLETON, John ARMBRISTER; "provided that Jesse THOMPSON shall allow me to use, keep and enjoy the lands with the rents, profits, etc. during my natural life without yielding anything for the same." Sig: Elizabeth (X) THOMPSON. Wit: William KEITH, James McANDERSON. 27 Apr 1832.

1077. (4:228) James McWILLIAMS to Henry LOGAN: 26 Mar 1832, $500, 232 ac on headwaters of Gallaher's Creek, part of the Big Spring Tract, cor HANLEY, PAUL?, LOGAN, EDMONDSON. Wit: Abijah CONGER, Sam WEAR. 27 Apr 1832.

1078. (4:229) Jonathan TIPTON of Monroe Co. to John TALMAGE of Clark Co., GA: 1 Mar 1831, $1035, 237 ac on headwaters of Baker's Creek, part of tract Granted by State of TN, cor Hugh B. LEEPER, William McCAMPBELL. Wit: Alex WAYER, Lorenzo D. TIPTON, John F. GILLESPEY, Robert M. ANDERSON. 27 Apr 1832.

1079. (4:230) Heirs of John COOK, decd, to Archibald SLOAN of St. Clair Co., AL: 1 Jun 1831, $125, 38 ac on waters of Nine Mile Creek being one sixth part of a tract that was Grant #161 to John SLOAN, which descended to Margaret COOK, widow of John COOK, decd, as one of the heirs of John SLOAN, decd, and to Mary COOK, Ann COOK, John M. COOK and Sarah COOK as heirs of John COOK, decd; adj James COPE, Richard WILLIAMS, Daniel BAN/BAR? and others. Sig: Margaret, Mary and Ann COOK signed (X). Wit: Alexander COOK, Samuel SLOAN. 27 Apr 1832.

1080. (4:231) William FAGG to Hughs BURK: 29 Sep 1830, $737.50, 200 ac on waters of Crooked Creek, part of Grants #958 and 942 to Jesse and Abram WALLACE, adj Thomas WALLACE, cor to DUNN, Jesse WALLACE, Samuel ROWAN. Wit: Campbell WALLACE, J. Harvey ROWAN. 1 May 1832.

1081. (4:232-33) Jonathan TRIPPETT to David W. TEDFORD: 3 Nov 1831, $100, one ac on waters of Pistol Creek, on the old line between TRIPPETT and Joseph TEDFORD, decd, near the [mill] race, adj John HOUSTON. Wit: Robert HOUSTON, William HARRIS. 1 May 1832.

1082. (4:233) James STEVENSON to John STEVENSON: 23 Dec 1830, $200, 70 ac in Tuckaleechee Cove on north side of Little River, adj Jacob McGHEE, John HEADERICK, Robert BATY. Wit: James QUIETT, William HEADERICK. 8 May 1832.

1083. (4:234) William CORLEY to Edward GOURLEY: 23 Feb 1832, $7.00, 1-1/4 ac on waters of Holston River, part of a survey made for the heirs of John CHAMBERLAIN, decd, cor to CORLEY and GOURLY on the original line between CORLEY and Robert YOUNG, near the branch. Wit: Hugh TORBETT, William HASKEW. 8 May 1832.

1084. (4:234-35) Henry WHITTENBARGER, Sr. to Edward GOURLEY: 15 Aug 1827, $700, 172 ac on both sides of the Great Road leading from Maryville to TOWNSEND's Ferry, adj Samuel SAFFELL, Henry WHITTENBARGER, Jr. Sig: Henry (X) WHITTENBARGER. Wit: Josiah PATTY, Matthew WHITTENBARGER. 8 May 1832.

1085. (4:236-37) Josiah PATTY to Edward GOURLEY: 23 Apr 1827, $240, 121 ac in two tracts, on both sides of the road leading from Maryville to TOWNSEND's ferry on Holston River, including the occupant grant to PATTY for 63 ac and the Grant to PATTY by virtue of an Entry made thereon in the Entry Taker's Office for Blount County for 58 ac, "and on the first mentioned grant of 63 ac, there is a certain demand which the state has against the tract called installments which GOURLEY is to pay." Cor to Henry WHITTENBARGER's occupant survey now belonging to Matthew WHITTENBARGER, cor to John COX's survey now belonging to VANPELT and others, J. BOGLE, Charles H. WARREN, William CORLEY. Wit: J. P. SMITH, W. COX. 9 May 1832.

1086. (4:237-38) Stephen PLUMLEE, Sr. to Stephen J. PLUMLEE, Jr.: 11 May 1830, natural love and affection...for his son, 100 ac on waters of Little River, part of a Grant to James CLARK, including the land where Stephen J. PLUMLEE now lives. Wit: James GILLESPY, William C. GILLESPY. 9 May 1832.

1087. (4:238-39) John BLAIR to Charles COLTER: 20 Jan 1832, $300, 34 ac in Miller's Cove on south side of Little River, adj J.

COLTER. Wit: John HENDRIX, Wm. LOVE. Sig: John (X) BLAIR. 9 May 1832.

1088. (4:239-40) John RODDY to Gabriel CORLEY: 7 Mar 1832, $100, 10 ac on the waters of a branch of Little River, part of Grant #819. Wit: Sevier WHEELER, Jonathan THARP. 9 May 1832.

1089. (4:240) Robert EVERETT to James EVERETT: 15 Dec 1825, natural love and affection..for his son; 50 ac on waters of Crooked Creek, "on a line of Robert Everett running in a square for complement". Wit: John REAGAN, Moses GAMBLE. At County Court March 1832 John REAGAN and Alex B. GAMBLE stated that Moses GAMBLE is now deceased. 9 May 1832.

1090. (4:241) Robert EVERETT to James EVERETT: 1 Feb 1826, $50, 50 ac, part of Grant #1669 to Robert, on waters of Crooked Creek, on the original line, "leaving out my spring". Wit: John REAGAN, Moses GAMBLE. 9 May 1832.

1091. (4:242-43) William DAVIS and Sarah DAVIS, his wife, to Jacob BIRD of Greene Co.: 12 Mar 1829, $500, 120 ac in Tuckaleechee Cove on north side of Little River. Sig: Wm. (X) DAVIS, Sarah (X) DAVIS. Wit: Levi DUNN, Philip DAVIS. Privy examination of Sarah taken by Hugh TORBITT and William McTEER, Justices of the Court of Pleas and Quarter Sessions. 10 May 1832.

1092. (4:242) Alexander M. CARSON to Robert THOMPSON: 15 Sep 1830, $100, 22 ac on waters of Baker's Creek, formerly part of a tract of John WILLSON but now belongs to heirs of Thomas WEAR, decd, adj WEAR's old tract, MONTGOMERY's and LOGAN's. Wit: Joseph CARSON, David THOMPSON. 22 May 1832.

1093. (4:244) Cary TUCK to John HENDERSON: 17 Nov 1830, $150, 30 ac on waters of Gallaher's Creek, part of a grant to Samuel DICKE, adj Joseph JOHNSON, Benjamin MATHIS, John HACKNEY. Sig: Care (X) TUCK. Wit: Wm. GRIFFITTS, Jac W HAIR. 22 May 1832.

1094.   (4:245)   John P. MONTGOMERY and James
MONTGOMERY to Robert THOMPSON: 21 Jan 1830, $160, 55 ac
on waters of Baker's Creek, adj John P. MONTGOMERY and
Andrew COLE, cor to John TAYLOR. Sig: J. P. MONTGOMERY,
executor of the estate of Thos. MONTGOMERY, decd; James (X)
MONTGOMERY. Wit: John THOMPSON, David THOMPSON. 22
May 1832.

1095. (4:245-46) Jesse KERR/CARR to Robert THOMPSON: 5
Mar 1832, $300, 100 ac on waters of Baker's Creek, cor Robert
THOMPSON and Jesse CARR, adj tract that THOMPSON purchased
of Daniel MOORE, adj heirs of David THOMPSON, decd, cor on the
big road.   Wit: Maclin CARR, David THOMPSON, John
THOMPSON. Sig: Jesse KERR. 22 May 1832.

1096. (4:246-47) Samuel SHAW to Elias BRIANT: 24 Mar 1832,
$250, 100 ac on south side of Holston River, adj the river. Wit: D. D.
FOUTE, Leroy NOBLE. 23 May 1832.

1097. (4:247-48) Peter BRAKEBILL to James THOMPSON: 27 Mar
1830, $300, 195 ac, being a tract granted to BRAKEBILL, on waters
of Ellejoy Creek, adj William GAY, Alexander RANEY, James
THOMPSON, William UPTON, BOGLE, Samuel BOGLE.   Wit:
Joseph RAMSEY, Alexander LOGAN. 23 May 1832.

1098. (4:248-49) Willoughby ROGERS to James DAVIS: 23 Nov
1831, $100, 62 ac on waters of Ellejoy Creek, adj David ORMAND,
Shadrack ROGERS. Sig: Willowby (X) ROGERS. Wit: Vincent (X)
ROGERS, William JOHNSON. 23 May 1832.

1099. (4:249-50) Henry WHITTENBARGER to Josiah PATTY: 20
Sep 1829, $122, 26 ac on waters of Lackey's Creek including the fork
of the creek, being a part of tract whereon WHITTENBARGER now
lives, beginning on a line of the survey made for John JOHNSON, cor
Alexander PATTERSON, Samuel ROAN.   Sig: Henry (X)
WHITTENBARGER. Wit: John NORWOOD, Robert CARSON,
William MAXWELL. 23 May 1832.

1100. (4:251-52) Josiah PATTY, Henry WHITTENBERGER Sr.,
Henry WHITTENBERGER, Jr. to Matthew WHITTENBERGER: 8

Apr 1829, $1200, 231 ac on waters of Holston River, adj Samuel SAFFELL, Nathaniel COX, Josiah PATTY, WHITTENBERGER, Sr., WHITTENBERGER, Jr.   Sig: Josiah PATTY. Henry (X) WHITTENBERGER, Sr. Henry WHITTENBERGER. Wit: William WHITTENBERGER, Peggy WHITTENBERGER. 23 May 1832.

1101. (4:252-53) William L. McMAHON and Ann C. McMAHON to James McMAHON: 22 July 1831, $50, 128 ac, all their claim and interest in a certain tract of land which descended to them by heirship, being part of the estate of their grandfather James COOK, decd, it being the part whereon James McMAHON now lives on the waters of Nine Mile Creek. Wit: Michael HUFFSTETLER, Joseph KIZER. 1 June 1832.

1102. (4-253-55) John CUMMINS (first party) to Daniel D. FOUTE (second party) and James BERRY and Jacob F. FOUTE trading as BERRY AND FOUTE: 31 Oct 1831, CUMMINS is indebted to BERRY AND FOUTE by note dated and due 5 May 1830 for $54.35, also by note dated 9 July 1831 due one day after date for $133.08; also by note dated and due same day as these presents for $26.09, for which Daniel D. FOUTE is security; one cross cut saw, three hand saws, one broad axe, three falling axes, two hand axes, seven augurs, one brace and bitts, etc., all the wagon maker's tools and all the timber and materials for wagon making business now on hand and belonging to CUMMINS.   Also lot #72 on Main St., Maryville, where CUMMINS' shop now stands, and lot #73 in the rear of #72 on back alley and back street; also two tracts of land, one containing 6 ac on McTeer's Mill Creek, adj Samuel BOGLE's spring branch; another of 30 ac adj John WILLIAMS, Richard WILLIAMS. CUMMINS to pay within three months from date.   Wit: Wm. M. LOWRY, Jo. JOHNSTON. 1 June 1832.

1103.   (4:255-56) George W. MONTGOMERY and William MONTGOMERY of Monroe Co. to Jesse KERR: 16 Dec 1828, $400, 46 ac on waters of Cloyd's Creek, being part of Grant #1294 to Samuel JOHNSTON for 172 ac. Wit: Isaac WRIGHT, John GOLD. Proved at court March 1832 by Isaac WRIGHT, who said that John GOLD is not now an inhabitant of this state, as he believes. 1 June 1832.

1104. (4:256-57) Abraham UTTER to Jesse KERR: 29 Aug 1830, $1536, 324 ac on waters of Baker's Creek, cor John CARSON, adj Samuel HANDLEY, John CARSON, John BLACK, William MOORE, Samuel THOMPSON, Samuel SCOTT. Wit: John WILSON, Jesse KERR, Jr. Proven by witnesses Dec 1831. 1 Jun 1832.

1105. (4:257) James W. LEA (first party) to Jesse KERR, Jr. and Jesse KERR, Sr.: 10 Sep 1831, LEA has this day become indebted to KERR, Sr. for $400, due twelve months after date, for which KERR, Jr. is security; a negro boy named ALEX about 20 yrs of age. Wit: Albert G. WEAR, William KERR, John SPRADLIN. 2 June 1832.

1106. (4:258-59) Abraham UTTER to Jesse KERR/CARR, Sr.: 29 Aug 1831, $100, 138 ac on waters of Baker's Creek, being one undivided moiety of 277 ac, cor Abraham UTTER, adj Samuel THOMPSON, Arthur GREER?. Wit: John WILSON, Jesse CARR, Jr. 2 Jun 1832.

1107. (4:259-60) William TAYLOR to Hugh HENRY: 21 May 1828, $50, 50 ac near Little River, adj William DONALDSON, Isaiah THOMPSON, Samuel HENRY, Henry and Hugh CRAIG. Sig: William (X) TAYLOR. Wit: James HENRY, Jr. Saml HENRY. Proven Dec 1831 by witnesses. 12 Jun 1832.

1108. (4:260-61) James DAVIS to William DAVIS: 30 Sep 1831, $10, 20 ac on waters of Ellejoy Creek, adj road leading from John TIPTON's to James DAVIS, Sr., Adam GRAVES. Wit: James (X) DAVIS, William DAVIS. 12 Jun 1832.

1109.   (4:261-62) William HUMPHREYS to Alexander HUMPHREYS: 1 Mar 1830, for natural love and affection [for] his son, 378 ac in Hickory Valley. Sig: William (X) HUMPHREYS. Wit: James HUMPHREYS, Hugh TORBET. Proven by TORBET Sept 1831 and James HUMPHREYS Mar 1832. 12 Jun 1832.

1110. (4:262-63) Hugh HENRY to William REAGAN: 29 Aug 1829, $144, two tracts, one of 128 ac, the other 16 ac, the latter being my part of the undivided land lying back of James HENRY, both pieces being near Little River. The former cor to land originally granted to John GIBSON, adj JULIAN, ROGERS, HARVEY's heirs, John F. GARNER, William TAYLOR, DONALDSON, cor Isaiah THOMPSON. Wit: Ake HENRY, D. D. FOUTE. 12 Jun 1832.

1111. (4:263-64) Joseph McMURRY to Hugh REED of Sevier Co.: 11 June 1831, $90, 99 ac on waters of Nails Creek, adj Samuel McMURRY. Wit: Hugh BOGLE, James BOYD. 12 June 1832.

1112. (4:265-66) Joseph McMURRY to Hugh REED of Sevier Co.: 11 Jun 1831, $20, 18 ac on waters of Nails Creek, adj David HICKY, McMURRY, Grant #311 to William E. CRESSWELL and conveyed by him to Joseph McMURRY. Wit: Hugh BOGLE, James BOYD. 13 Jun 1832.

1113. (4:266-67) Joseph McMURRAY to Hugh REED of Sevier Co.: 11 Jun 1831, $30, 32 ac on waters of Nails Creek, adj McMURRY's occupant survey, Robert REED's entry. Wit: Hugh BOGLE, James BOYD. 13 June 1832.

1114. (4:267-68) Joseph McMURRY to Hugh REED of Sevier Co.: 11 Jun 1831, $50, 50 ac on waters of Nails Creek. Wit: Hugh BOGLE, James BOYD. 13 Jun 1832.

1115. (4:268-69) Benjamin ALEXANDER to Nathaniel COX: 26 Sep 1826, $700, 130 ac on Holston River, part of occupant survey made for John RANKIN, cor to survey made for heirs of Cornelius BOGARD, adj Samuel U? RANKIN. Wit: Josiah PATTY, A. B. CAMPBELL. Proven by CAMPBELL Dec 1831 and by PATTY Mar 1832. 27 Jun 1832.

1116. (4:269-70) John SMITH to Frederick EMMITT, Peter SNIDER, George SNIDER, George KAYLOR, Isaac HEART, Trustees of the METHODIST EPISCOPAL CHURCH IN AMERICA: 2 Aug 1831, gift, one ac on south side of Little River in Tuckaleechee Cove at the mouth of a branch. Sig: John (X) SMITH. Wit: Josias GAMBLE, Vance WALKER. 27 Jun 1832.

1117. (4:271) William CUMMINS to Elizabeth CUMMINS: 17 Mar 1831, $20, 7 ac on waters of Ellejoy Creek, cor to Wm. CUMMINS, Jr.'s original tract, adj W. CUMMINS, Sr.'s 50 ac entry. Sig: William

(X) CUMMINS. Wit: William McTEER, Saml BOGLE.   25 Jun 1832.

1118. (4:272-73) Daniel D. FOUTE (first party) to James WILSON (second party) and Joseph R. HENDERSON (third party): 9 Jun 1832, WILSON is security for FOUTE on four notes to Thomas HENDERSON executed on 5 Feb 1829 for $100 each, payable $100 on 1 Sep 1829, $100 1 Sep 1830 upon which there is a credit of $27, 8 Jun 1832, the third payable 1 Sep 1831 and the fourth payable on 1 Sep 1832, which notes are unpaid and assigned by Thomas HENDERSON to Joseph R. HENDERSON on 8 Jun 1832; lot #37 in Maryville, being the corner lot on which the Clerk's Office now stands. FOUTE is to pay the notes within nine months from date. Wit: Jac F FOUTE, Hedges T. CONGER. 29 Jun 1832.

1119. (4:173-74) James BERRY and Jacob F. FOUTE (first party), Daniel D. FOUTE (second party) and Thomas ANDERSON of Monroe Co. and Richard MEREDITH of Roane Co. (third party): 19 July 1831, "BERRY and FOUTE wish to obtain a loan of $3,000 from some banking institution at Nashville (The United States Bank if practicable) using the name of BERRY and FOUTE as drawers, and to obtain the names of HENDERSON and MEREDITH together with Danl. D. FOUTE as Indorsers, and to secure [them] against any liability or loss"...lots #55, 56, 57 in Maryville whereon James BERRY now lives; negro slaves ARCH aged 23 yrs, REUBEN aged 40 yrs, HARRIET the Elder aged 28 yrs and her four children SALLY, 10 yrs; NELSON 8 yrs; FRANCIS 2 yrs, and an infant WILLIAM JEFFERSON; HARRIET the younger aged 18 yrs and her three children ALEXANDER, 3 yrs, and LAFAYETTE and ADDISON. Jacob FOUTE conveys lots #82, 83, 84, 109, 110 in Maryville, on which FOUTE now lives and on which the stables stand. Also 260 ac which were Grant #2385 dated 29 June 1812 to Robert GAUTT. Also a negro man named JAMES, aged about 29 yrs, and a negro girl named PATTY aged about 17 yrs and her child ALLEN aged about 2 yrs, and a mulatto slave named LUCINDA aged about 12 yrs. Wit: Wm. M. LOWRY, Ro. McNUTT, Reuben L. CATES, Julius C. FAGG. 29 June 1832.

1120. (4:275-76) Miller FRANCIS, Treasurer of East Tennessee and successor in office to Mathew NELSON, to Samuel HENRY: 3 Apr 1832, $33, "NELSON by virtue of..an act of the General Assembly of Tennessee passed at Murfreesborough 15 Nov 1823 entitled an Act for the relief of the citizens residing in the district of country South of French Broad and Holston and between the rivers Big Pigeon and Tennessee and to appropriate the money due from said citizens for those lands..after having given four weeks notice by publication in the KNOXVILLE REGISTER"..[sold] on 21 July 1825, amongst others, 99 ac on Little River, Grant #1008 to John SNIDER, for payments due the State and unpaid. Lands adj the heirs of James HENRY, Samuel WALKER. Wit: Saml. R. RODGERS, James HAIR, James HENRY, Jr. 30 Jun 1832.

1121. (4:276-77) Stokely D. SWAGGERTY to James HENRY of William: 3 Mar 1832, $20, 99 ac on Little River, adj James HENRY, Samuel WALKER. Wit: Josias GAMBLE, A. B. GAMBLE. 6 Jul 1832.

1122. (4:277-78) William WALLACE, Sheriff, to William TOOLE: 13 Jan 1832, $12.60, 247 ac on waters of Gallaher's Creek, property of the heirs of Terrence CONNER, decd, being part of Grant #137 to Terrence CONNER adj William, Michael BOWERMAN and William S. KING. Public sale 25 Sep 1830, for taxes for 1827 and 1827 (sic). Wit: W. B. MARTIN, Sam WALLACE. 6 Jul 1832.

1123. (4:279) John FREEMAN (first party) to Daniel D. FOUTE (second party) and WILSON and SAFFELL: 21 May 1832; FREEMAN is indebted to WILSON & SAFFELL for $337.98 by noted dated 21 May 1832 and due one day after date, for which FOUTE is security; two negro boys, JACK aged 9 yrs and BLOUNT aged 6 yrs. FREEMAN to pay the debt by 20 June next. Wit: William KEITH, Joseph WILKINSON. 12 July 1832.

1124. (4:280-81) Miller FRANCIS, Treasurer of East Tennessee, to Samuel HENRY: 3 Apr 1832; $18.27, public sale 20 July 1825, for installments due the State and unpaid on Grant #1708 to Henry BAIN, 136 ac in Miller's Cove on waters of Hesse Creek, adj Richard

DAVIS. Wit: Saml. R. RODGERS, James HENRY, Jr., James HAIR.
12 July 1832.

1125. (4:281-82) Miller FRANCIS, Treasurer of East Tennessee, to
Samuel HENRY: 3 Apr 1832, $109.66, public sale 21 July 1825 by
virtue of an Act of the General Assembly on 15 Nov 1823 [for unpaid
installments due the state], 332 ac on waters of Nails Creek, cor
Warner MARTIN. Wit: Saml. R. RODGERS, James HENRY, Jr.,
James HAIR. 12 July 1832.

1126. (4:283-85) Miller FRANCIS, Treasurer of East Tennessee, to
Samuel HENRY: 3 Apr 1832, $16.38, by virtue of Act of 19 Nov
1823 [for unpaid installments due the state] public sale 21 July 1825,
121 ac on Little River, Grant #2539 to John HESS, cor BAINTER?.
Wit: Saml. R. RODGERS, James HENRY, Jr., James HAIR. 12 July
1832.

1127. (4:285) James BERRY to James TRUNDLE: 19 Jan 1832,
$900, negroes HARRIET aged about 30 yrs and her daughter SALLY
aged about twelve and her son NELSON aged about ten years, her
daughter FRANCES about three years and her son WILLIAM
JEFFERSON aged about ten months. Wit: Daniel D. FOUTE, Wm.
M. LOWREY. 13 July 1832.

1128. (4:286-87) Jane RUSSELL, Robert A. RUSSELL, Hance
RUSSELL, Robert CALDWELL and Siby his wife and Elizabeth
RUSSELL to William TOOL: 29 Feb 1832, $350, 9 ac on waters of
Pistol Creek, whereon Reuben L. CATES now lives, adj the
Commons of Maryville, adj TOOL, CURTIS. Wit: Reuben L. CATES,
Andrew McCLAIN. 13 July 1832.

1129. (4:287-88) William HENDRIF to Samuel WALKER: 1 Mar
1832, $20, 91 ac on waters of Little River, adj James TAYLOR,
Elizabeth COLTER, Wit: W. B. WILLIAMS, Robert (X) McGILL.
14 July 1832.

1130. (4:288-89) William HENDRIF to Samuel WALKER: 24 Jan
1832, $500, 87 ac on Little River, adj Josiah WALKER. Wit: Vance
WALKER, Robert (X) McGILL. 14 July 1832.

1131. (4:289-90) William BARNHILL, Sr. (first party) to Moses SCRUGGS (second party) and Nathaniel RAGAN (third party): 1 Feb 1832, $107.73 for goods, wares and merchandise sold and advanced to BARNHILL by RAGAN at the store in Morganton, for which SCRUGGS is security; one bay horse six years old and one black cow with a white face, one heifer two years old, one bureau, one cupboard and furniture, one gallon pot, one hundred bushels of corn, one sow and six pigs, one feather bed, bedsted and bedding, one thousand bundles of fodder. BARNHILL to pay RAGAN the sum of $107.73 in three notes, one $42, one $40, one $25.73 all dated the second day of Jan 1832, on or before 15 Nov next. Wit: Darby RAGAN, Jeremiah (X) HAMMONTREE. 16 July 1832.

1132. (4:290-91) William GRIFFITTS to William and Margaret JONES: 29 Dec 1829, $240, 140 ac on waters of Gallaher's Creek, adj John HANNAH now in possession of Uriah HENSHAW, Alexander FORD. Wit: James JONES, Samuel LEWIS. 16 July 1832.

1133. (4:291-92) John F. GARNER to Andrew PEERY: 13 Apr 1832, $15, 2 ac on Ellejoy Creek. Wit: A. B. GAMBLE, William McTEER. 16 July 1832.

1134. (4:292-93) James GILLESPEY to Samuel COWAN: 14 Oct 1817, $250, all my right, etc. in and to a tract [of 337 ac] on waters of Pistol Creek granted to Thomas and Alexander McCOLLOCH, assignees of Samuel McCOLLOCH and conveyed by Thomas and Alexander McCOLLOCH to COWAN and myself. Wit: John F. GILLESPY, Wm. C. GILLESPY. Proven June 1832 court. 17 July 1832.

1135. (4:293-94) Thomas McCOLLOCH and Alexander McCOLLOCH to James GILLESPY and Samuel COWAN: 5 Feb 1813, for "a valuable consideration", 337 ac on waters of Pistol Creek, cor Samuel CLARK and David OGLESBY, Thomas McCOLLOCH, John THORNBURY, John CLAYTON. Surveyed 15 July 1807 for Samuel McCOLLOCH and Granted to Thomas and Alexander McCOLLOCH as assigness of Samuel, being part of said grant. Wit: Jesse WALLACE, Jesse THOMPSON, William WALLACE. Proven at June 1832 court by witnesses. 18 July 1832.

1136. (4:294-95) Mitchell READ (first party) to Daniel D. FOUTE (second party) and Jacob F. FOUTE (third party): 1 Feb 1832, REED is indebted to Jac F. FOUTE by note dated 17 Apr 1830 for 100 bushels of good sound merchantable corn to be delivered at his crib in Maryville on 15 Nov 1830; also by note dated 17 Apr 1830 for $35 in two months after date, payable in a good four horse wagon. Also by note dated and due 17 Apr 1830 for $10.30, for which Daniel D. FOUTE is security. [Conveys] the whole of his crop of corn except one fourth thereof, one thousand bundles of fodder, two beds, bedsteds and furniture, one black cow and calf, one barshare, one shutt? and one bull tongue plow, two pair gears, one small flax wheel, one big wheel, two ovens, two pots, one set wagon maker's tools, nine head hogs some pigs, one rifle gun, one walnut cupboard. REED to retain possession of property until a sale is required but should not dispose of it nor remove it out of Blount County. Sig: Mitchell READ. Wit: James BERRY, Augustus M. FOUTE. 17 July 1832.

1137. (4:295-97) Samuel STEELE (first party), Samuel PRIDE (second party) and James BERRY and Jacob F. FOUTE (third party), all of Maryville: 26 Jun 1832, STEELE is indebted to BERRY and FOUTE by note given on settlement dated and due on 8 Feb 1828 for $95.38; note 22 Dec 1831 for $369.67; note 26 Mar 1832 for $7.50, for which PRIDE is security; 234 ac whereon STEELE now lives and part of tract originally granted to John McKEE, Sr., cor J. B. LAPSLEY and David and Wm. EDMONSON, adj Jo. McCONNELL. STEELE to pay within 3 months from this date with interest. Wit: Wm. B. MARTIN, Wm. M. LOWREY. 11 July 1832.

1138. (4:297) Erastus TIPPET of Rhea Co. to Daniel McKINSEY: 23 Sept 1811, $40, 12 ac adj William BARNES, Daniel McKINSEY, Moses HUGHS. Wit: Wm. LOWREY, Jr., J. GARDNER. 23 Sep 1811.

1139. (4:297-98) Benjamin WATKINS to Samuel WEAR: 7 Aug 1832, "Whereas the General Assembly of Tennessee on 7 Jan 1830 passed an act entitled An Act to provide for certain children, and whereas I, Benjamin WATKINS, am entitled to the benefit of said act,"..nominate Samuel WEIR my lawful attorney to lay down on any one of the general plans of either of the surveyors, South and West of the Congressional Reservation lines, any quantity of land not exceeding 200 ac for each of my three children. Wit: David McKAMY, Robert HOUSTON, justices of the peace for Blount County. 13 Aug 1832.

1140. (4:298-99) Daniel D. FOUTE to Campbell WALLACE: 14 July 1832 on 19 July 1831 James BERRY and Jacob F. FOUTE executed a deed of trust to Daniel D. FOUTE as trustee for the benefit of Thomas HENDERSON and Richard MEREDITH as indorsers, and FOUTE amongst other things conveyed five lots in Maryville, and whereas MEREDITH is released from and now is no longer liable as indorser for BERRY and FOUTE, and whereas Jacob FOUTE has sold and conveyed the five lots to Campbell WALLACE for 1600 bushels of salt at Saltville, Virginia, and whereas Thomas HENDERSON by his deed dated 8 June 1832 approved of the sale and covenanted so soon as the order of Jacob F. FOUTE on Col. James WHITE for 1600 bushels of salt should be accepted that he, HENDERSON, would quit claim all right to the five lots, and whereas I have the evidence of T. M. ROPP, clerk and agent for James WHITE at Saltville, VA, dated 23 Jun 1832 and of Joseph R. HENDERSON, agent of said HENDERSON dated 3 July 1832, that the said order in favor of Thomas HENDERSON was accepted and passed to his credit on the books of James WHITE at Saltville, VA...release and transfer lots #82, 83, 84, 104 and 105 in Marvyille. Wit: J. J. WALKER, Hiram HARTSILL. 20 Aug 1832.

1141. (4:299-301) James BERRY and Jacob F. FOUTE (first party), Samuel PRIDE (second party) to Thomas HENDERSON of Monroe County and Daniel D. FOUTE (third party):   8 Jun 1832, HENDERSON and Daniel D. FOUTE are indorsers for BERRY and Jacob F. FOUTE to the Branch Bank of the United States at Nashville on two notes, ones for $2225, the other for $5367, both now under protests..for which HENDERSON and D.D. FOUTE require further indemnity for their liability...convey to Samuel PRIDE as trustee..850 barrels of salt at the following places: 30 barrels to Samuel H. EWING, 25 barrels at Benjamin MAXWELL's pond creek, 30 barrels at John N. ROBINSON's, 55 barrels at GAMBLE and CRAWLEY's, 28 barrels at Charles TALIAFERRO's, all on sale; also 128 barrels at LENOIR's ferry, all in Roane Co., TN, the said 128 barrels at

LENOIR's ferry to be distributed to Col. MEREDITH and other places in the hands of solvent persons for sale; also 19 barrels in hands of J.C. and A. BOGLE, 14 barrels in hands of John McLEAN, Esq., 22 barrels in hands of Joseph DUNCAN, Esq., 53 barrels in hands of GRIFFITHS and STANDFIELD, all on sale; also 50 barrels at Maryville and about 113 barrels at GILLESPIE's Warehouse and stored at Capt. W. WALLACE, all in Blount Co., the salt at Maryville GILLESPIE's Warehouse and Captain WALLACE's to be removed and distributed to suitable markets and placed in the hands of solvent persons if it cannot be advantageously disposed of where it is. Also 80 barrels of salt in hands of Peter REAGAN, Esq. Ten barrels in the hand of Hugh GODDARD. 47 in the hand of Jacob PEARSON, 48 barrels in the hand of UPTON and CALDWELL, 14 barrels in the hand of Jonathan DOUGLASS, 30 barrels in the hand of Silas PERRY, 15 barrels in the hands of Jonathan DAVIS, Esq, all on sale in Monroe Co. Also 20 barrels in the hands of SHIRLEY and SPEAR of (word omitted); also 30 barrels stored in the warehouse at GARDENHIRE's or BLAIR's old ferry in Roane Co. Jacob FOUTE also sells of his own estate and individual property: one negro woman called LUCINDA aged about 20 years and her child JAMES aged about three years now in Sommerville, Tenn. Also one yoke of oxen and one ox wagon, one cart, two cows, one dining and pair of circular tables, one china press, two bureaus, four beds, bedsteds and furniture, one clothes press, two wash stands and dozen chairs, and all household and kitchen furniture belonging to him, also his library of books, maps, etc. consisting of law works, scientific library and miscellaneous books. Wit: Wm. M. LOWREY, Spencer JARNAGIN. 3 Sep 1832.

1142. (4:301-02) Thomas HENDERSON to Jacob F. FOUTE: 8 Jun 1832, whereas on 19 July 1831 James BERRY and Jacob F. FOUTE executed a deed of trust to Daniel D. FOUTE for the benefit of Thomas HENDERSON and Richard MEREDITH as endorsers..for a negro woman named PATTY and her child ALLEN, also five lots in Maryville, #82, 83, 84, 104, and 105, and whereas Jacob F. FOUTE has sold PATTY and ALLEN to Andrew C. MONTGOMERY and has executed this day a deed of trust to Doctor Samuel PRIDE as trustee for the benefit of Thomas HENDERSON and Daniel D. FOUTE as endorsers...and has conveyed a negro woman named

LUCINDA and her child JAMES in the room and stead of said PATTY and ALLEN, and had sold the said lots to Campbell WALLACE, and executed an order on Col. James WHITE for 1600 bushels of salt at Saltville, VA...Thomas HENDERSON releases and quit claims to the negro woman PATTY and her child ALLEN to Jacob F. FOUTE. Wit: Hedges T. CONGER, Asa M. CARPENTER. 3 Sep 1832.

1143.   (4:302-03) John HARVEY to William REAGAN: 10 Apr 1832, $10, 6 ac on Little River.   Wit: Robert WEAR, Thomas KEEBLE. 11 Sep 1832. Certified by Daniel D. FOUTE, Clerk, by H. T. CONGER, Deputy Clerk.

1144.   (4:303) Jacob F. FOUTE to Andrew C. MONTGOMERY: 20 July 1832, $450, a negro girl slave named PATTY and her male child named ALLEN, [who were] sold on or about 10 Dec 1831 and FOUTE now having received the consideration therefor.   PATTY about 22 years old, her son ALLEN having died since the aforesaid sale and delivery to MONTGOMERY. Wit: John MONTGOMERY, Orestus HAYS, Saml. PRIDE. 11 Sep 1832.

1145.   (4:304-05) Thomas SPRADLING (first party), Jesse KERR (second party) and Abijah CONGER (third party): 23 July 1832, SPRADLIN has executed his promissory note for $100 to Jesse KERR to be paid on or before 25 July 1833 with interest, for which CONGER is security; several tracts of land all totalling 385 ac, one tract whereon SPRADLING now lives containing 95 ac; also one tract adj it of 50 ac, being part of a Grant to James SCHRIMPSHER and conveyed by him to SPRADLIN; one other tract adj the above for 40 ac and one other tract Granted to SPRADLIN by Entry #374 dated 19 Jan 1826 containing 200 ac.   Wit: Wm. B. McCAMPBELL, David CONGER, William EARLY. 12 Sep 1832.

1146.   (4:305-06) John CARSON to Jesse KERR: 25 Nov 1829, $400, 62 ac on waters of Cloyd's Creek, cor George MONTGOMERY and Samuel JOHNSON, adj Samuel DICKSON, James LOGAN. Wit: A. UTTER, David KERR, Jr. 12 Sep 1832.

1147.   (4:306-07) John S. DUFF to Jesse THOMPSON: 19 May 1832, $500, 164 ac by the side of the road corner to the original survey granted by State of Tennessee, adj tract formerly owned by John CALDWELL, John McCOLLOCH, William LOWREY's former property. Wit: Daniel D. FOUTE, James TRUNDLE. 12 Sep 1832.

1148. (4:307-08) William CARPENTER of Washington Co., VA, to John S. DUFF: 7 May 1832, $425, 164 ac cor to survey granted to George CALDWELL, adj John CALDWELL, John McCOLLOCH, William LOWREY. Wit: John NORWOOD, William (X) MASON. 12 Sep 1832.

1149. (4:308-09) James McCONNELL to John McNABB: 18 Feb 1832, $70, 14 ac tract lying in the south corner of the tract on which McNABB now lives, adj Absolom McNABB and Isom ADAMS. Wit: Robert L. McNABB, Joseph B. LOGAN. 13 Sep 1832.

1150. (4:309) David CALDWELL of Monroe Co. to James BERRY and Jacob F. FOUTE: 12 Aug 1829, $550, lot #65 on Main Street in Maryville, adj the lot on which Dr. Jos. H. GILLESPY now lives and separated by a cross alley from the tavern now occupied by John FREEMAN. Wit: Robert McNUTT, Will LOWREY. Proven at court June 1830 by Robert McNUTT, who stated that William LOWREY is not now an inhabitant of this state. 17 Sep 1832.

1151. (4:310-11) Mathew H. BOGLE to William McTEER: 5 Sep 1830, $500, 114 ac on waters of Ellejoy Creek. Wit: Hugh BOGLE, John TIPTON. 24 Sep 1832.

1152. (4:311) Stephen KERRICK to George HADDON, Jr.: 11 Oct 1831, $200, negro woman named TEEN, 18 or 19 years old. Wit: Mansfield ANDERSON. 24 Sep 1832.

1153. (4:311-12) George HADDON Jr. to John McNELLY: 18 Nov 1830, $150, 130 ac on waters of Ellejoy Creek, on south end of a conditional line made by George HADDEN, Sr. and Peter FRENCH. Wit: James BERRY, Daniel D. FOUTE. 25 Sep 1832.

1154. (4:312-13) Thomas PAINE to Moses SCRUGGS: 10 Jan 1826, $1235, 160 ac on Tennessee River and Baker's Creek, cor to warehouse lot on the river bank in Morganton, adj Eli RITCHEY formerly Richard DEARMOND's, granted to Hugh KELSO on 25

May 1800, which tract of 463 ac has since been divided into three separate tracts, adj HALL, LOWRY, cor formerly Wyly LASETER, A. COBLE, including a part of another Grant of land to H. KELSOE. Wit: James DOUGLASS, Jacob FULKERSON, Joseph DUNCAN. Proven at court Sep 1832 by DOUGLASS. 2 Oct 1832.

1155. (4:313-14) John HOUSTON to Martin ROREX: 4 Oct 1831, $1200, 360 ac on Pistol Creek, adj Samuel HOUSTON. Wit: William M. ROREX, John HOUSTON. 2 Oct 1832.

1156. (4:315) Seth ADAMSON to Samuel JONES: 8 Sep 1830, $550, 138 ac on west fork of Gallaher's Creek, cor Robert McCULLY, Isaac WHITE. Wit: James JONES, Absolom SPARKS. 3 Oct 1832.

1157. (4:316) Seth ADAMSON to Samuel JONES: 8 Sep 1830, $50, 50 ac on waters of Cherokee Creek, cor S. McCAMMON, adj HACKNEY's heirs. Wit: James JONES, Absolom SPARKS. 3 Oct 1832.

1158. (4:317) Samuel D. WARREN to John STALEY: 22 Sep 1832, $50, 200 ac being an entry #333 made by WARREN, cor to Jesse MITCHEL's 150 ac entry then with S. WILLIAMS entry, adj W. B. LENOIR. Wit: Leeroy NOBLE, M. G. MAUPIN. 3 Oct 1832.

1159. (4:317-18) Jonathan TRIPPETT to Jonathan T.[Trippett] HARRIS: 14 Aug 1832, $2000, 205 ac on waters of Pistol Creek, part of a 411 ac tract. Wit: Robt. HOUSTON, Thomas BELL. 3 Oct 1832.

1160. (4:318-19) James BERRY and Jacob F. FOUTE to Thomas WHITE: 15 Sep 1832, $500, in discharge of our bond for Title dated 10 Jan 1832, lot #65 in Maryville on Main St. adj lot on which Dr. James H. GILLESPY now lives and separated by a cross alley from the Tavern now occupied by Mrstrs (sic) Jane OWENS, being the same conveyed by David CALDWELL to BERRY and FOUTE on 25 Aug 1829. Wit: Asa M. CARPENTER, Samuel Jo or Jr.? AIKEN, Will WALLACE. 3 Oct 1832.

1161. (4:319-20) Wilson NORTON to Robert HOUSTON: 7 Sep 1832, $480, 120 ac on waters of Nails Creek, adj KIRKPATRICK, James BOYD. Wit: Andrew BOGLE, Jr., Samuel M. CRESWELL. 4 Oct 1832.

1162. (4:320-21) Daniel D. FOUTE to William H. STRAIN: 31 May 1832, $200, lot #48 in Maryville, whereon Strain now works his smith shop, except the smith shop which FOUTE formerly sold to Brittain GERRARD. GARRARD is to have liberty to move unless STRAIN and him agree otherwise. Wit: Hedges T. CONGER, William A. SPENCER. 5 Oct 1832.

1163. (4:321-22) James HOUSTON to Alexander McNUTT: 8 May 1832, $1200, 384 ac on waters of Pistol Creek, adj the road leading to RANKIN's ferry at the west end of the Bridge on Pistol Creek cor to James HOUSTON, departing from the road...below the spring..adj McGHEE..EBBET's? line, WEAR. Wit: Jac F. FOUTE, Wm. B. MARTIN. 5 Oct 1832.

1164. (4:322-23) Polly INMAN and William INMAN to Robert THOMPSON: 28 May 1832, $225, a tract on waters of Baker's Creek, adj on southeast by William ILES, on northeast by Joseph LOGAN, on northwest by Alexander CARSON, and on southwest by William McCLUNG and John THOMPSON, "it being the land bequeathed to Polly Inman and her heirs of her own body begotten" by Thomas WEIR, decd. Sig: Polly (X) INMAN. William INMAN. Wit: Robert THOMPSON, John THOMPSON, Lazarus INMAN. 5 Oct 1832.

1165. (4:323-25) Heirs of James SMITH, decd, to Thomas JONES: 24 Sep 1832, $1,000, 640 ac on waters of Little Tennessee River in Cades Cove. Heirs are John SMITH, William SMITH, Sarah FOLKER, Henry SMITH. Sig: William SMITH. John (X) SMITH. Henry SMITH. William FELK. John (X) DAVIS. Delaney (X) DAVIS. Attest: A. FINE, Justice of Peace for Cocke County; William SMITH, Jared B. MILLSAPS, Jane (X) BOTSTON, Jared B. MILLSAPS. Proven Sep 1832 court by Peter BRICKY and Will SMITH. Robert HOUSTON & Samuel HAMILL, Esqrs., were appointed commissioners to take privy examination of Delany DAVIS,

who reported that she signed the deed of her own free will. 6 Oct
1832.

1166. (4:325-26) George EWING and James EWING to William
EWING: 30 Mar 1832, two (word omitted) dollars, 39 ac on Little
River, cor Robert PORTER, adj John EWING. Wit: William
THOMPSON, R. P. McCOLLOCH. 8 Oct 1832.

1167. (4:326-27) James BERRY and Jacob F. FOUTE to Henry
RODDY: 15 Sep 1832, on 15 Oct 1827 Berry and Foute purchased at
Sheriff's Sale two tracts of land, one of 95 ac and the other 50 ac, sold
as property of James HARRIS; on 17 Feb 1831 Henry RODDY,
claiming to be a creditor of James HARRIS and desiring to redeem
and repurchase the land, and BERRY and FOUTE being willing to
take the amount of their bid at Sheriff's Sale and the amount of their
judgment and claims against HARRIS with the interest then due
thereon, agreed to receive the same..RODDY has this date paid the
sum of $117.85. Wit: Samuel J. AIKEN, Asa M. CARPENTER. 8
Oct 1832.

1168. (4:327-28) John C. GUNN of Knoxville, TN, and Michael
SMITH of Maryville: 25 Sep 1832, $2,000 paid by delivery of goods,
wares and merchandise now on hand and belonging to Smith in his
store in Maryville, Agreement to transfer of copyright, the sole and
exclusive right of vending, selling and printing for sale within the state
of Mississippi a medical work entitled Gunn's Domestic Medicine or
Poor Man's Friend, the copyright of which, according to act of
Congress, is secured to GUNN by the certificate of William C.
MYNATT, Clerk of the Circuit Court for the District of East
Tennessee, dated (date omitted). SMITH shall not sell said work in
any other state within the US except in the state of Miss. Wit: Jac. F.
FOUTE, John LOWREY, James HAIR. 9 Oct 1832.

1169. (4:328-29) William WALLACE, Sheriff, to James BERRY and
Jacob F. FOUTE: 1 Sep 1832, $42, 145 ac total in two tracts of land
of James HARRIS, the old tract 95 ac and the late entry 50 ac adj the
land of Will WHEELER, Andrew McBATH, Tobler VINYARD, and
James RHEA. Levied on 18 June 1829, by James HENRY, deputy
sheriff. Public sale 15 Oct 1829 to satisfy judgments issued against

James HARRIS in favor of John DEARMOND, James L. PORTER, Mathew NELSON, William MONTGOMERY, Isaac TIPTON. Wit: Andrew McCLAIN, Asa M. CARPENTER. 2 Oct 1832.

1170. (4:329-30) Daniel BOWERS to Robert DELZELL and David DELZELL: 28 Sep 1811, $500, 216 ac on waters of Nine Mile Creek, cor Jacob TIMBERMAN, adj Mathew TIMBERMAN. Wit: John WILKINSON, Edward BUCHANAN. Proven Sep 1832 court by Will WALLACE who said he is well acquainted with the handwriting of John WILKINSON, a witness, and believes the signature to be his, and WILKINSON is now dead. Proved July 1832 by Edward BUCHANAN. 9 Oct 1832.

1171. (4:331) John WILKINSON to Caleb M. NORWOOD: 25 Feb 1826, $131 paid by John NORWOOD as atty in fact for Caleb M. NORWOOD, 77 ac on waters of Pistol Creek, cor Hugh WEAR, James DONOHOO, John HANNA, Robert GAUTT. CALEB to pay all Government demands due from and after 1 Apr 1824 and also any redemption money and costs that may be due in consequence of a sale thereof by the Treasurer of East Tenn. Wit: Stephen A. HALE, Jr., Samuel E. SHERRILL. 10 Oct 1832.

1172. (4:332) Obediah BOAZ to Caleb M. NORWOOD, both of Maryville: 7 Feb 1826, $1800, two lots #13 and #35, on Main Street cor to lot #36 belonging to J. B. CUSICK. Wit: Reuben L. CATES, Alexander RICE. 11 Oct 1832.

1173. (4:332-33) Moses SCRUGGS to James ALLEN of Claiborne Co.: 24 Mar 1822, $300, three lots in Morganton, adj Porter St. Wit: Marvel DUNCAN, Edmund WAYMAN. 10 Dec 1832.

1174. (4:333-34) Susannah ROGERS and Willoughby ROGERS to James DAVIS: 3 Nov 1831, $250, 45 ac on waters of Ellejoy Creek, adj Shadrack ROGERS. Sig: Susannah (X) ROGERS. Willoughby (X) ROGERS. Wit: Vincent (X) ROGERS, William JOHNSON, Jesse (X) ROGERS. 2 Jan 1833.

1175. (4:334-35) James DAVIS to Vincent ROGERS: 28 Aug 1832, $10, 27 ac on waters of Ellejoy Creek. Wit: Shadrick (X) ROGERS. Martin ORMAN. 2 Jan 1833.

1176. (4:335-36) James DAVIS to Vincent ROGERS: 21 Sep 1832, $10, 11 ac on waters of Ellejoy Creek. Wit: Shadrick (X) ROGERS. Martin ORMAN. 3 Jan 1833.

1177. (4:336) Powell WILLIAMS of Roane Co. (first party) to Jesse HENDRICKSON and James McWILLIAMS: 14 Aug 1832, WILLIAMS has this day purchased of McWILLIAMS 225 ac, being the same whereon McWilliams now lives including the Big Spring, and has executed his notes to him as follows: one for $200 due 1 Oct next, one for $300 due 1 March 1836; to secure the payment of these notes WILLIAMS conveys to HENDRICKSON the above land in trust. Wit: A. S. LENOIR, Wm. B. LENOIR. 4 Jan 1832.

1178. (4:337) James CRAWFORD to William A. CRAWFORD: 17 Feb 1831, $360, 50 ac, part of a grant to James CRAWFORD, adj James COCHRAN. Wit: John JONES, George A. CRAWFORD. Proven by witnesses Dec 1832 court. 4 Jan 1833.

1179. (4:337-38) Joshua W. WARREN and Notley WARREN to James SINGLETON: 29 Sep 1832, $455, 146 ac. Wit: John P. KERR, Hugh L. W. SINGLETON. 4 Jan 1833.

1180. (4:338-39) Johnston JONES to [son] Samuel JONES: 17th day of the sixth month, 1829, $45, 95 ac on Holston River, adj Benjamin MILLS, Thomas LEWIS. Wit: James JONES, Henry LEWIS. Proven by witneses Dec 1832 court. 4 Jan 1833.

1181. (4:339-40) Johnston JONES to [son] Samuel JONES: 17th day of sixth month, 1829, $5, 17 ac on Holston River, cor to original survey made for John SHADLE. A spring in the bank of the river near the beginning corner is excepted for the use of Henry LEWIS. Wit: James JONES, Henry LEWIS. Proven by witnesses at Dec 1832 court. 5 Jan 1832.

1182. (4:340) William BROWN to Joseph McREYNOLDS: 22 Nov 1832, BROWN is largely indebted to McREYNOLDS, and in consideration of the sum of $200 paid by McREYNOLDS, 50 ac and one cow, one bay mare, 13 head of hogs, 2 beds and furniture, 3 head of sheep, 2 plows, one set of gears and 600 bundles of fodder, one mattock, one cutting box and knife, one pair of truckly (sic) and water barrel, seven head of geese, one hoe, one iron wedge, two clevises (sic) two singletrees, one saddle and bridle. Witnesses omitted. 5 Jan 1833.

1183. (4:341) John McGAUGHY of Sevier Co. to James BOYD: 2 July 1832, $500, 145 ac on waters of Nails Creek, cor NORTON, adj James BOYD, James McGAUGHY. Wit: William BOYD, Wilson NORTON. 5 Jan 1833.

1184. (4:341-42) Joseph BLACK of Anderson Co. to Jincy BLACK: 20 May or August [both months are shown] 1832, $250, 85 ac on waters of Ellejoy Creek, cor James McNEILY and Jincy BLACK. Wit: James H. BLACK, Mansfield ANDERSON. Proven by witnesses Dec 1832 court. 7 Jan 1833.

1185. (4:342-43) John EAKIN to William EAKIN: 24 Dec 1832, $300, 164 ac on Tennessee River cor Valentine MAYO. Wit: Jac F. FOUTE, James HAIR. 7 Jan 1833.

1186. (4:343-45) Agreement between Hannah LOGAN, John M. LOGAN and Alexander LOGAN: 10 Dec 1832, John M. LOGAN forever renounces all his claim to a part of land settled to him at his mother's death and sells all his right, etc. to a certain part of his land described, to Alexander LOGAN, and in consideration of $12 paid to him and also in consideration of his now getting possession of the rest of the place, being about 100 ac, with the house and everything thereunto belonging...except the orchard or that part of the fruit thereof which Hannah LOGAN may think fit to make use of, not exceeding one half, together with the use of the hot house or drying house with wood for drying fruit so long as she may live, the land thus sold lying in the upper end of the place or on the east end of the old line from the beginning, containing together, with some that was sold off before, about 134 ac. Alexander LOGAN agrees that Hannah LOGAN shall have that part of the land lying west of the main hollow leading from Thomas McHENRY's through Alexander's land, [to] the conditional line between him and John, to hold during her lifetime, at her death to belong to Alexander. Alexander agrees to keep up a sufficient fence around the cleared land belonging to Hannah, in consideration of which she renounces all her right or claim to the part of her land lying west of the conditional line above named with the exception of half the orchard, being about 100 ac of land, on the waters of Little River. Land is the estate of David LOGAN, decd [relationship not stated]. Wit: Joseph RAMSEY, George MORE. 7 Jan 1833.

1187. (4:345) John TEDFORD to Mathew HANNAH: 21 Sep 1831, $500, 130 ac on headwaters of Nine Mile Creek, opposite David HAMMIL's house on the 3d line of the old survey. Wit: Robert DELZELL, Andrew L. ANDERSON. 8 Jan 1833.

1188. (4:346) Berry ABERNATHY to Harvey GREENAWAY: 7 May 1832 $20, 116 ac cor ROBBINET, cor to occpt survey made for Henry FRANKS, near Jarrett JAMES' entry, cor WOODEN's entry in a line by TURK's. Wit: Marvel DUNCAN, James BLACK. 8 Jan 1833.

1189. (4:346-47) Allen STRAIN to John FOWLER: 20 Feb 1832, $80, 42 ac on waters of Baker's Creek, adj John MEANS. Wit: David McKAMY, John MORRIS. 8 Jan 1833.

1190. (4:347-48) Johnston JONES to Henry LEWIS: 17th day of sixth month, 1829, $5, 12 ac on Holston River, adj Benjamin MILLS, John SHADDLE. LEWIS to have use of the spring immediately below the elm on the bank of the river. Wit: James JONES, Samuel JONES. 9 Jan 1832.

1191. (4:348-49) John CROMWELL [in trust] to Samuel HENRY: 28 Feb 1832, $120, 100 ac on waters of Baker's Creek, being part of a 220 ac tract Granted to Abraham UTTER on 17 June 1809, adj Robert THOMPSON. CROMWELL is to pay $120 to HENRY in the space of three years, for which amount HENRY holds CROMWELL's note. Wt: John M. RANKIN, John B. HALE. 12 Jan 1833.

1192. (4:349-50) Jonathan T. HARRIS to Jonathan TRIPPETT: 26 Oct 1832, $1200, part of 411 ac on waters of Pistol Creek. Wit: Robert HOUSTON, Wm. HARRIS. 14 Jan 1833.

1193. (4:350-52) Heirs of Joseph TEDFORD to Jonathan TRIPPETT: 3 Nov 1831, $100, two tracts on waters of Pistol Creek containing one acre, adj Joseph TEDFORD's grant, the old line between Jonathan TRIPPETT and Joseph TEDFORD, decd. Heirs named are Polly TEDFORD, Nancy TEDFORD, Robert TEDFORD, James TEDFORD, John TEDFORD, David TEDFORD, Erskine TEDFORD, Eleanor TEDFORD, Peggy Jane TEDFORD. [A note preceding signatures of John N. TEDFORD, Nancy TEDFORD, and James TEDFORD reads: "Signed on the fifth December 1852." (sic)] Wit: Robert HOUSTON, Thomas McCOLLOCH, Robert HENDERSON. 15 Jan 1833.

1194. (4:352) Jesse KERR to William WILLIAMSON: 28 Jun 1831, $500, 175 ac on a branch of Nine Mile Creek, which includes 35 ac of a tract granted to John WALLACE and conveyed to KERR. Wit: James A. WILLIAMSON, Lafayette WILLIAMSON. 17 Jan 1833.

1195. (4:353 Archer JOHNSON to Gilbert BLANKENSHIP: 5 Dec 1831, $1250, 145 ac on Tennessee River. Wit: James McCALMON, Moses H. HUGHS. 17 Jan 1833.

1196. (4:354) Archibald SLOAN and James McTEER to James McWILLIAMS: 28 Sep 1832, $360, 640 ac located in the name of Robert McTEER in the Western District in Madison County which warrant was laid by Samuel WILSON, Surveyor, and he was to have one fifth part in the land for locating it. By the Last Will and Testament of Robert McTEER he left the balance of the tract to four of his children: Margaret SLOAN and Janet McTEER being two of them. William SLOAN, husband of Margaret SLOAN, by his Last Will and Testament left Margaret's interest to Archibald SLOAN. Janet McTEER is deceased, and James McTEER, husband of Janet, sells to McWILLIAMS...our interests in a tract of land lying in Madison County, Western District in Tennessee near Mount Pinson, Warrant #31, issued by Archibald ROAN on 9 July 1808. Wit: Samuel HAMIL, John WILSON. 18 Jan 1833.

1197. (4:353-54) James McWILLIAMS to Powell WILLIAMS of Roane Co.: 14 Aug 1832, $1,000, 225 ac, part of a tract of 572 ac of land lying about 8 miles from Maryville, and including the Big Spring, which was Grant #2538 to William GRAY, adj Jesse HENDRICKSON, Henry LOGAN, McWILLIAMS, Samuel WEAR and David WEAR, Samuel McCULLEY, John HARRIS, except between two and three acres on which the SECEDER MEETING HOUSE stands as conveyed to them by William GRAY. Wit: Jesse HENDRICKSON, A. S. LENOIR, Wm. B. LENOIR. 21 Jan 1833.

1198. (4:356-57) Archer JOHNSON to Gilbert BLANKINSHIP: 5 Nov 1831, $1250, 241 ac on Tennessee River, adj Robert HUGHES, John FRANKS, Valentine MAYO, Holbert McCLURE. Wit: James McCALMON, Moses W. HUGHS. 21 Jan 1835.

1199. (4:357-58) James COOK to Moses W. McMAHON: 14 Feb 1832, $260, 112 ac on waters of Nine Mile Creek, adj the forge tract and Samuel HENRY, Samuel COPE. Wit: A. CONGER, James McMAHON. 22 Jan 1833.

1200. (4:358-59) James HENRY, Sr. to Nicholas NORTON: 26 Feb 1831, $2,400, 232 ac on Crooked Creek, part of Grant to Charles and William REGAN, cor to William McKAMY. Excepted is the dower of the Widow Leah REGAN and the state claim. Wit: A. GAMBLE, Ake HENRY. 22 Jan 1833.

1201. (4:359-60) James SHADDEN to Charles K. SHADDEN and Thomas SHADDEN (in trust): 17 Apr 1832, "in consideration of the trust and confidence in Thomas and Charles reposed," and also for consideration of $5 paid to James, all interest in a tract on which Darby REGAN now lives containing 65 ac. James SHADDEN is indebted to Jesse KERR and others, for which debt Thomas and Charles are indorsers for the Bank of the State of Tennessee. Wit: John EAKIN, William EAKIN. 22 Jan 1833.

1202. (4:360-61) James McNUTT to James GILLESPY: 28 Mar 1832, McNUTT is indebted by a promissory note in favour of William WALLACE for $170, bearing date with these presents and due one day after date, for which GILLESPY is security; the wagon I now own, two working oxen, two bay mares, one three years old, the other ten or twelve years old, one sorrel horse, two years old. Wit: John F. GILLESPY. 22 Jan 1833.

1203. (4:361) James McNUTT to [daughters] Jane McNUTT, Elizabeth F. McNUTT and Mary McNUTT: 28 Mar 1832, "for natural love and affection and in consideration of their industry and service in supporting my family", all my household and kitchen furniture, including my large washing kettle, also two side saddles. Wit: John F. GILLESPY. 17 Jan 1833.

1204. (4:361-62) William WALLACE to Solomon D. JACOBS of Knox Co.: 17 Jan 1833, $500, a negro slave HARRY, about 29 or 30 years old, sound and healthy. Wit: Campbell WALLACE, Wilson L. TRUNDLE. 8 Feb 1833.

1205. (4:362) Campbell WALLACE to Samuel WALLACE: 2 Oct 1832, $700, a negro girl slave aged about 12 years named ELIZA, two negro slaves female children named MAHALA aged about 4 years old, MARIAH aged about 2 years old. Wit: Will WALLACE, J. J. WALKER. 12 Feb 1833.

1206. (4:362-63) William TURK to Will WALLACE: 17 Jan 1833, $5, two and a half ac on waters of Pistol Creek, cor Thomas TURK. Wit: Samuel WALLACE, Campbell WALLACE. 13 Feb 1833.

1207. (4:363-64) William THOMPSON to William WALLACE: 28 Jan 1833, $884, an undivided moiety and interest (one-half) in 152 ac on waters of Little River and Pistol Creek, being Grant #2335 to Thomas McCOLLOCH, cor Alexander McCOLLOCH, Thomas CLARK. Wit: J. C. FAGG, Campbell WALLACE.13 Feb 1833.

1208. (4:364-66) Thomas TURK to William WALLACE: 5 Sep 1832, $2700, one tract of 444 ac on waters of Pistol Creek, being Grant #722 to William AYLETT, adj Miles and David CUNNINGHAM and John McCULLY, Felix KENNEDY, James TEDFORD, William HOUSTON, James WEAR, land sold by A. WEAR to William AYLETT, and another tract of 235 ac adj the above, on the west fork of Pistol Creek that was Grant #721 to William AYLETT, adj James WEAR, Cornelius ALEXANDER, J. McCULLY, Miles and David CUNNINGHAM. Excepted is a tract conveyed on 28 Mar 1832 from Thomas TURK and Hiram K. TURK to Dread J. FREEMAN and another piece containing 125 ac, which was part of a Grant to Banner SHIELDS and conveyed to FREEMAN on 28 Mar 1823. Wit: Samuel WALLACE, William TURK, Jesse WALLACE. 14 Feb 1833.

1209. (4:366-67) Thomas L. WILLIAMS of Knoxville to Campbell WALLACE of Maryville: 6 Feb 1833; on 13 Dec 1830 James BERRY and Jacob F. FOUTE executed a deed of trust to WILLIAMS to secure a debt due from them to Wm. F. and Alexander MURDOCK of Baltimore, and conveyed in trust lots #82 and 83 conveyed by John McGHEE to Jacob F. FOUTE on 25 Sep 1827; also lots #84, 104 and 105 conveyed by BERRY to FOUTE by deed on 8 Oct 1827. The debts mentioned in the deed of trust are fully and completely paid, and Jacob F. FOUTE has informed WILLIAMS that he has sold said lots to Campbell WALLACE and requested him to quit claim the lots to WALLACE. Wit: James HENRY, A. B. GAMBLE. 15 Feb 1833.

1210. (4:367-68) Daniel D. FOUTE to Darius HOYT: 7 May 1832, $160, lots #2 and #3 in Maryville, adj lot #1 owned by Isaac ANDERSON and lot #4 in possession of Mr. McCRACKEN. Possession to be given at the expiration of John A. AIKEN's present year renting. Wit: Jacob F. FOUTE, James BERRY. 15 Feb 1833.

1211. (4:368-69) John P. MONTGOMERY to John THOMPSON: 30 Aug 1832, $680, 250 ac on waters of Baker's Creek, cor Joseph LOGAN, beside the big road, cor Robert THOMPSON's fence. Wit: John THOMPSON, Sr., David THOMPSON. 15 Feb 1833.

1212. (4:369-70) Heirs of Robert MAXWELL to James THOMPSON: 29 Dec 1829, $300, 90 ac on waters of Pistol Creek adj James THOMPSON, James CLARK, David HUME, and others. Heirs named are: Sarah MAXVILLE, wife of Robert MAXVILLE, decd, Thomas LOWE and Jane LOWE formerly Jane MAXWELL, Alexander SHARP and Susannah his wife, formerly Susan MAXVILLE, and Elizabeth MAXVILLE and Melinda MAXVILLE (all of Blount Co.), James FURGUSON and Sarah his wife, formerly Sarah MAXWELL, of Sevier Co. Sig: Sarah FURGUSON and Jane LOWE signed with "marks". Wit: James CLARK, Stephen KENDRICK, Charles N. GEORGE, Eleazur M. KELSO. Privy examination of Jane LOWE, Susan SHARP and Sarah FURGUSON was taken by Eleven HITCH and James GILLESPY, Esqrs. Reg Blount County, 5 May 1831. Reg Sevier Co. 6 Jun 1831.

1213. (4:371) D. D. FOUTE as trustee for James TRUNDLE to John S. DUFF: 19 May 1832; on 6 July 1829 John S. DUFF executed a deed of trust for 164 ac to secure payment to TRUNDLE of certain monies, which debts have been paid; quit claim to land so deeded. Wit: James CUSICK, Jessee THOMPSON. 11 Feb 1833.

1214. (4:371-74) James BERRY (first party) trust to Samuel PRIDE (second party) and Nancy B. McCHESNEY, John SHARP, John COX, William PUGH, Elijah WALKER, Joseph BOGLE, Michael SMITH, William ANDERSON Esqr., James MAXWELL, John WOODS, Isaac

YEAROUT and James BIDDLE, all of Blount County (John SHARP excepted, who is of Sevier Co.): 8 Sep 1831, BERRY is indebted to Nancy B. McCHESNEY by note dated 15 Sep 1829 for $600 due one day after date thereof; to John SHARP by note dated 8 Sep 1826 for $1,015, the whole amount of the interest on the sum paid up to 16 June 1832; to John COX by note 20 Aug 1832 for $484; to William PUGH by note dated 15 Mar 1832 for $600; to Elijah WALKER by note dated 19 Feb 1831 for the balance of $350 due from date to the payment made stopping the interest of their date and leaving the balance of principal; to Joseph BOGLE by note dated June 1832 for $300; to Michael SMITH by note dated 12 May 1832 for $120; to William ANDERSON Esqr by note dated 12 May 1832 for $202; to Thomas MAXWELL by note for $200; to John WOODS by note dated 12 May 1832 for $266; to Isaac YEAROUT by noted dated 12 May 1832 for $188, and to James BIDDLE by note dated 12 Aug 1832 for $165. Samuel PRIDE is security for above debts; 430 ac on waters of Pistol Creek, whereon BERRY formerly lived and held under conveyance to him by Samuel STEELE, Samuel BLACKBURN and Samuel WEIR, adj John MONTGOMERY, decd, James TRUNDLE, D. D. FOUTE, James WILSON, Jacob F. FOUTE and Matthew W. McGHEE; [also conveys] one blue painted wagon, one low wheeled wagon, one ox cart, six pair of harness, one yoke black oxen, one yoke or pair spotted oxen, four milk cows, one roan horse about 6 yrs old, one sorrel horse about 4 yrs old got of D. D. FOUTE, one grey horse about 5 yrs old, two mules got of J. B. HOUSTON, and one carriage or carryall and harness; also household furniture: one secretary and book case with the library of books contained therein, one china press with the furniture therein, one clock and case, two bureaus, seven beds, bedsteads and furniture, one clothes press, one set of falling leaf tables, four small tables, four looking glasses, one settee, one dozen Windsor chairs, one dozen split bottom chairs, together with a variety of kitchen furniture. BERRY is to pay the above notes within twenty four months with interest. BERRY is to retain in his possession and have use of the property. Wit: Daniel D. FOUTE, Jacob F. FOUTE. 19 Feb 1833.

1215.   (4:374-75) Heirs of Ephraim BRABSON, decd, late of Washington Co. to Alexander CAMPBELL: $500, 50 ac in Washington Co. on both sides of a little branch of Little Limestone Creek adj Daniel BOGLE, Stephen BROWN, John ALLEN and Jacob BROWN. Heirs named are: Thomas BRABSON, John BRABSON, Charles COLLIN and Margaret COLLIN his wife formerly Margaret BRABSON, John JOHNSON and Elizabeth his wife formerly Elizabeth BRABSON, William THOMPSON for himself and for John THOMPSON, a minor; James THOMPSON, Dutton LANE and Nancy his wife, formerly Nancy THOMPSON, Peter SWATZELL and Charity his wife, formerly Charity THOMPSON, Jane THOMPSON and Robert BRABSON. Sig: Nancy (X) LANE. [Not all heirs signed] 21 Feb 1833.

1216. (4:375-76) John T. ATKINS (first party) to Daniel D. FOUTE (second party) and Samuel PRIDE and Daniel D. FOUTE: 7 Mar 1833, PRIDE and FOUTE are indorsers of a note dated 9 Feb 1833 to the Bank of the State of Tennessee at the Agency of Blount County for $218 and due 88 days thereafter; to indemnify them, ATKINS conveys four feather beds, bedsteads and furniture, one old book case, one bureau, four tables, two of which are falling leaf, three pots, to ovens, one dozen chairs six of which are Windsor, the others split bottom, one chest of drawers, one cow, some cupboard furniture and water rails and two sets of dog-irons and one wooden clock. ATKINS to retain possession of property unless sale is necessary. Sig: John T. (X) ATKINS. Wit: Joseph D. FOUTE, William TOOLE. 8 Mar 1833.

1217. (4:377) Jesse F. BUNKER to Nathaniel HARRIS: 9 Mar 1830, negro woman and child named MARY and HARRIET, the former about 17 yrs of age, the latter about ten months. Wit: Zephemiah HARRIS, Randolph (X) KIDD. 9 Mar 1833.

1218.   (4:377-78) James and Ignatius WILSON to James CRAWFORD: 29 July 1821, on 7 Feb 1820 CRAWFORD made a deed of conveyance for 256 ac and CRAWFORD has refunded and repaid to the WILSONS the consideration mentioned in that deed, [and] WILSONs quit claim to CRAWFORD all title. Wit: Hiram H. TURK, Terrance CONNER. 1 Oct 1822.

1219. (4:378-79) James HENRY, trust to James McCALLON for John DUNLAP: 16 Mar 1833; Henry is indebted to DUNLAP for $50 and DUNLAP has "went security" for HENRY to Alexander KENNEDY for $140; two stills and all the vessels belonging to the distillery, 50 head of hogs, the first choice in the stock. HENRY to pay debt on demand. Wit: William DUNLAP, Daniel D. FOUTE. Sig: James HENRY, John DUNLAP, James McCALLON. 1 Apr 1833.

1220.   (4:379) Betsy MAXWELL and Executors of John MAXWELL, decd, to David CARR: 4 Mar 1833, $4, 17 ac, it being the fourth part of 71 ac of land that Hugh FURGUSON sold to James OLIVER, Granted to William WOOD, adj William MILLER. Sig: Betsy (X) MAXWELL, Thomas MAXWELL. Wit: Wm. COOPER, Archibald MAXWELL.   Proven at Circuit Court Mar 1833 by witnesses who say that they are acquainted with "Eliza" MAXWELL and Thomas MAXWELL. 2 Apr 1833.

1221.   (4:380) Jacob TEAFATELLER (first party) to Daniel D. FOUTE (second party) and James TRUNDLE (third party): 21 Dec 1831, TEAFATELLER is indebted to TRUNDLE for one note for 13 bushels of shelled corn due 25 Dec 1825 dated 27 Oct 1825; another note dated 15 Mar 1829 for $22, one other dated 21 Dec 1831 for $25, for which FOUTE is security; two black cows, two sows, seven shoats, one black mare about 13 yrs old, 100 bushels of corn, one thousand bundles of fodder, one stack of hay. Wit: Ben PRIVETT, John B. WEBSTER. Sig: Jacob (X) TEAFATELLER. 2 Apr 1833.

1222.   (4:381) Jacob TEAFATELLER (first party) to James TRUNDLE (second party) and Daniel D. FOUTE (third party): 25 March 1833, TEAFATELLER is indebted to TRUNDLE for one note dated 1 Jan 1833 for $10.88, another for 6 bushels of corn dated 25 Mar 1833, another dated 25 Mar 1833 for $5, for which FOUTE is security; one blind bay horse about 12 years old, 15 head of hogs. Sig: Jacob (X) TEAFATELLER.   Wit: J. A. AIKEN, Wilson L. TRUNDLE. 3 Apr 1833.

1223.   (4:382) Ambrose COX to Joseph VANPELT: 25 Feb 1833, $130, 18 ac cor to VANPELT near the spring.   Wit: Michael BRIGHT, Robert WEAR. 5 Apr 1833.

1224.   (4:382-85) Joseph VANPELT (first party) to Daniel D. FOUTE (second party) and James WILSON (third party): 27 Feb 1833, VANPELT is indebted to WILSON for $202.25 on a note dated 27 Feb 1833 and due one day thereafter for which FOUTE is security; several tracts on waters of Holston River, one tract of 111 ac being part of land granted to John COX adj Henry WHITTENBERGER Sr. and others, called the dry land tract, adj a piece previously sold to Henry WHITTENBERGER, Jr. by Philip FORSTER.   Another tract of 18 ac cor to above tract.   Personal Property: one grey mare about 12 yrs old, one yoke of oxen, ten head of sheep, 40 head of hogs, one loom, one corner cupboard, one bureau, two chests, 7 Windsor chairs, one clock, four beds, bedsteads and furniture.   VANPELT to pay debts within twelve months.   Wit: Joseph WILKINSON, John SAFFELL. 8 Apr 1833.

1225. (4:385) John McGHEE of Monroe Co. to James N. HAYDEN: 7 Feb 1833, $100, lot #72 in Maryville adj the commons on the west and lots owned by Samuel LOVE on the east; being the same lot on which John CUMMINS erected a wagon maker's shop and dwelling house in which CUMMINS now lives. Wit: Jac. F. FOUTE, John CUMMINS. 8 Apr 1833.

1226. (4:386-87) James N. HAYDEN, agent of John CUMMINS, trust to Daniel D. FOUTE: 11 Feb 1833, HAYDEN as the agent and for the use and benefit of John CUMMINS purchased lot #72 in Maryville from John McGHEE, who executed his deed on 7 Feb 1833. HAYDEN delivered to Jacob F. FOUTE his note dated 7 Feb 1833, due months after date, for $100, the amount of purchase. McGHEE being indebted that sum to FOUTE and requiring the note to be given to FOUTE, it was agreed that HAYDEN should execute a deed of trust for the lot for the benefit of Jacob F. FOUTE to secure him the payment of $100. On 31 Oct 1831 CUMMINS issued a deed of trust to Daniel D. FOUTE for the benefit of James BERRY and Jacob F. FOUTE. CUMMINGS to pay the $100 to Jacob F. FOUTE. Wit: S. J. BLACKWELL, Joseph D. FOUTE. Certified for registration 4 Apr 1833 by Jacob F. FOUTE, Clerk, by his deputy J. D. FOUTE. 9 Apr 1833.

1227. (4:388) James BERRY to Samuel PRIDE: 25 Mar 1833, $1,000, lot #44 in Maryville, on south side of Main Street and adj lot # (omitted) belonging to the Directors of the SOUTHERN AND WESTERN THEOLOGICAL SEMINARY, being the lot whereon PRIDE has for some time past and now resides. Wit: Hugh B. LEEPER, M. W. LEGG. 9 Apr 1833.

1228. (4:389-90) Thomas L. WILLIAMS of Knoxville, Knox Co., to Samuel PRIDE: 15 Feb 1833; on 30 Dec 1830 James BERRY and Jacob F. FOUTE executed a deed of trust to WILLIAMS to secure debts due from them to William F. and Alexander MURDOCK of Baltimore, MD, for lot #40, the same conveyed to BERRY by William W. BERRY, on south side of Main Street of Maryville on which stands a white house, then and now occupied by Dr. Samuel PRIDE; conveyed and intended as security for the one fourth part of a debt. BERRY has fully paid his debt and has sold the lot to Samuel PRIDE and requires WILLIAMS to release it to PRIDE. Wit: James HAIR, J. A. AIKEN, Jac. F. FOUTE. 9 Apr 1833.

1229. (4:390-91) Henry WHITTENBERGER, Sr. to Samuel SAFFELL: 10 Apr 1829, $800, 197 ac on waters of Holston River, part of 461 ac Granted to WHITTENBERGER, cor to WHITTENBERGER and Abraham HAMILTON, cor Matthew WHITTENBERGER, Henry WHITTENBERGER, Jr., Edward GOURLEY. Sig: Henry (X) WHITTENBERGER. Wit: Josiah PATTY, Matthew WHITTENBERGER. 10 Apr 1833.

1230. (4:391-92) John CUMMINS (first party) to Samuel PRIDE (second party) for William GAULT (third party): 20 Mar 1833, CUMMINS is indebted to GAULT for $2.00 by note dated 22 Jan

1833 payable on 1 Feb next, also for $6.00 by note dated 15 Dec 1832 to be paid on 1 Mar 1833, and note dated 20 Mar 1833 payable one day after date for $30.00, for which PRIDE is security; two carryall wagons, one set of harness for a one-horse carryall, one china press, one bureau, one clock and one dining table. CUMMINS to retain possession until sale is required. Wit: J. D. FOUTE, Augustus M. FOUTE. 16 Apr 1833.

1231. (4:392-94) Charles N. GEORGE (first party) to Mathew HANNAH (second party) for Joseph NOLLEN and Michael BEST (third party): 5 Apr 1833; HANNAH is security for GEORGE on debt to NOLLEN for $107 due by note and also $18.69 due by note and also a further sum of (omitted) dollars, the price of making and painting a good new wagonbed; also BEST became the security of GEORGE on two notes to David KERR for $81.50. [Conveys in trust] 5 horses, one bald chesnut sorrel mare and colt, one pale sorrel mare, one bay gelding and one bay horse colt; also 6 head of cattle, 33 head of hogs and 7 head of sheep; also five feather beds and furniture, one cupboard, one bureau, 6 Windsor chairs and three chests, one trunk, 800 weight of bacon and six split bottom chairs, two tubes, and all my cooking utensils and all other household and kitchen furniture; also all my farming utensils, to wit: ploughs, hoes, mattocks, plough gears and harrows, and also one hundred bushels of corn. Wit: Wm. B. MARTIN . 17 Apr 1833.

1232. (4:394-95) James HARRIS to William HARRIS: 6 Mar 1833, $100, 50 ac granted to James HARRIS by Entry #113. Wit: Alexander (X) RODDY, Gideon B. RODDY. 18 Apr 1833.

1233. (4:395-96) William WALLACE, Sheriff, to Joseph TUCK: 26 Mar 1833, $9.08, 100 ac in Hickory Valley adj George COOK, Berry ABERNATHY, the heirs of GREENAWAY; public sale 27 Aug 1831 as property of Elizabeth WOODEN for taxes amounting to ninety three cents due for 1828 and 1829. Wit: Sam WALLACE, J. J. WALKER. 19 Apr 1833.

1234. (4:396-97) Robert MINNIS to John WILSON in trust for Samuel MINNIS: 9 Apr 1833, 75 ac, part of the tract whereon Robert MINNIS now lives; one grey mare, 9 sheep, 10 hogs, 2 cows and all the household furniture of Robert, also the crop of wheat he has now growing.   Samuel MINNIS holds a book account against Robert MINNIS amounting to $50.   Robert to pay before 1 May 1836. Wit: David McKAMY, Robert W. CALDWELL. 22 Apr 1833.

1235. (4:397-99) William WALLACE, Sheriff, to William TUCK: 20 Mar 1833, $9.24, 117 ac in Hickory Valley adj Thomas CARTWRIGHT, George COOK, Bennett JAMES, Jacob (name omitted). Public sale 27 Aug 1831 for taxes for 1828 and 1829, amounting to $1.10 for the two years, returned in the name of Elizabeth WOODEN. Wit: Sam WALLACE, J. J. WALKER. 22 Apr 1833.

1236. (4:399-401) Charles N. GEORGE (first party) to Matthew HANNAH (second party) and James WILSON and John SAFFELL (third party): 5 Apr 1833, GEORGE is indebted to WILSON and SAFFELL for one note due 30 Oct 1832 for $37.75; another for $164.71 due 29 Nov 1831; another assigned by William McCAMY to and for $10 due 25 Dec 1831, for which HANNAH is security. [Conveys] parcels of land: 141 ac whereon Joseph NOLLEN now lives and conveyed by William ANDERSON to GEORGE, adj Michael BEST, John GLASS, Elizabeth MAXWELL, and Philip MERONEY and others; also the undivided half of lot #14 of 80 ac of land and the undivided half of lot #15 of 160 ac, and of lot #13 for 80 ac, #11 for 80 ac, and lot #10 for 160 ac, and lot #12 for 160 ac, lot #44 for 160 ac, all being on "the flat of Chilhowee Mountain" in the Hiwassee District, the land whereon Richard ROBERTS now lives. Wit: Jos.? WILKINSON, Wm. B. MARTIN. 23 Apr 1833.

1237. (4:401-02) James BERRY and Jacob F. FOUTE of Maryville and Thomas L. WILLIAMS of Knox County to James WHITE of Abingdon, Washington Co., VA: 15 Feb 1833; on 30 Dec 1830 BERRY and FOUTE executed a deed of trust to WILLIAMS for 10 ac of land on Pistol Creek, adj the town of Maryville, being the same purchased of Josiah F. DANFORTH on 26 Feb 1829, to secure debts due to William F. and Alexander MURDOCK, merchants of Baltimore, MD. On the said tract BERRY and FOUTE have built a Merchant Grist Mill, called MORELAND MILLS. On 27 Jan 1831 James BERRY and Jacob F. FOUTE sold the lands, mills, etc. to

James WHITE and agreed to make a sufficient deed for the same by 15 Jan 1832 for the price of $6,000 payable as provided in agreement. The debts due to MURDOCK are now fully paid and the provisions of the deed complied with, and BERRY and FOUTE require WILLIAMS to release and convey the land, Mills, etc. to WHITE for the sum of $6,000. Land adj KING AND MONTGOMERY. Wit: James HAIR, J. A. AIKEN, D. D. FOUTE, Joseph D. FOUTE. 23 Apr 1833.

1238. (4:403) John NORWOOD (first party) to Jesse THOMPSON (second party) and Jacob F. FOUTE (third party): 26 Jan 1833, NORWOOD is indebted to FOUTE for $17 cash, this day loaned and advanced to NORWOOD, and also by note for $103.75 dated 21 Jan 1829 for which THOMPSON is security. [Conveys] 200 pounds of nails now in the lumber room of WILSON & SAFFELL, one black horse about 10 yrs old, one flat boat 12 feet wide 42 feet long now lying at Gillespie's Landing on Holston River; also a thousand feet of plank and lumber now on the kiln and at SAFFELL's saw mill. NORWOOD to pay within three months from this date. Wit: Thomas GARDINER. 24 Apr 1833.

1239. (4:404) Henry RODDY to William HARRIS, Jonathan THARP, and Bevin HADDOX: 28 Jan 1833, $144, two tracts of land, one 95 ac, the other 50 ac, sold as the property of James HARRIS at Sheriff's Sale on 1 Sep 1832 to BERRY and FOUTE and redeemed by RODDY for $149. Wit: Alexander (X) RODDY, Joel THARP. 24 Apr 1833.

1240. (4:405) James WEAR and Hugh WEAR to Robert McREYNOLDS: 2 Mar 1833, $170, 76 ac on Crooked Creek, being Grant #605 to Hugh WEAR, adj Samuel WEAR, James McGINLEY. Wit: Robert HOUSTON, John WILSON. 24 Apr 1833.

1241. (4:406) John F. GILLESPY of Monroe Co., atty in fact of William HOUSTON of Haywood Co., to William HUDGEONS: 14 Mar 1833, $300, a negro man named WILL, age 48 yrs. Wit: Benjamin F. (illegible), George (X) CARTER. 25 Apr 1833.

1242. (4:406-07) Loid HITCH to William HARRIS: 10 Nov 1827, $300, 5 ac, part of Grant #1384 to Lucas HOOD. Sig: Loid (X)

HITCH. Wit: Isaac TIPTON, Jonathan THARP, Nathaniel HARRIS. Proven at court by THARP and HARRIS Apr 1833. 25 Apr 1833.

1243. (4:407-09) William WALLACE, Sheriff, to Robert SHIELDS of Sevier Co.: 26 Mar 1833, $70, 170 ac on north side of Little River in Tuckaleechee Cove, adj lands of Robert McMURRY (now BIRD's Land), SAILOR's land. Public sale 25 June 1831 to satisfy judgment for $55.50 recovered on 30 Jan 1828 by Jacob McGHEE against Christopher F. WINDER rendered by Alexander B. GAMBLE, a Justice of the Peace for Blount County, who has since resigned. Samuel HENRY was high bidder and he has ordered WALLACE to make a deed to SHIELDS. Wit: Daniel D. FOUTE, Saml. R. RODGERS. 26 Apr 1833.

1244. (4:409-10) Joseph HENDERSON to Bowling and John BROOKS: 8 Oct 1830, $800, 221 ac on waters of Holston River. Wit: John TEDFORD, Levi PERKINS, Thomas JONES. 26 Apr 1833.

1245. (4:410-11) Andrew VAUGHT to Thompson BRYANT: 20 Dec 1832, $200, 86 ac on Nine Mile Creek, original Grant #976 to VAUGHT, adj Reuben CHARLES, Silas GEORGE, William LOGAN. Wit: Andrew COWAN, Leroy S. THOMPSON. Sig: Andrew (X) VAUGHT. 29 Apr 1833.

1246. (4:411-12) James and John GILLESPIE to Samuel SAFFELL: 25 June 1830, $300, 81 ac which GILLESPIEs purchased of William YOUNG, near the waters of Holston River, adj Ambrose COX. Wit: Abraham HEARTSELL, M. M. HOUSTON. Proven at court Apr 1833 by HEARTSILL, who said that Mathew M. HOUSTON, the other witness, is not a resident of the state. 1 May 1833.

1247. (4:413) Robert SHIELDS to John HUSKY, both of Sevier Co.: 26 Mar 1833, $500, 170 ac in Tuckaleechee Cove, adj Robert McMURRY, SAILOR?. Wit: Lewis RENEAU, Samuel HENRY. 2 May 1833.

1248. (4:414) Daniel D. FOUTE to John SAFFELL: 28 Dec 1832, $400, two lots #46 and #47 in Maryville, adj lot #48 now occupied by William STRAIN and also lot #45 now occupied by Brittain GARRARD; the same lots conveyed to FOUTE by Jesse

THOMPSON and now occupied by Col. John AIKEN. Wit: James WILSON, Joseph WILKINSON. 6 May 1833.

1249. (4:415-16) John SCOTT and William A. SCOTT to Jonathan TRIPPET: 4 Feb 1826, $1200, 169 ac on Baker's Creek, part of occupant surveys made for James SCOTT and Joseph GLENN, adj John SCOTT, Joseph GLENN. Wit: Adrian BALL, Andrew MILLER. Proven at court by MILLER, who said that Adrian BALL is not now an inhabitant of the state. 6 May 1833.

1250. (4:416-17) Andrew COLTER of Blount Co. and John and Jesse JAMES of Monroe Co. to Alexander S. COLTER: 2 Feb 1833, $500, two tracts, one containing 189 ac, the other 114 ac, first tract cor to Robert LEATHERDALE, adj John ORR, Mark LOVE, William JAMES; the other cor to James CULTON and Robert LEATHERDALE, adj John B. CUSICK, Patrick CULTON and E. BURNET. Wit: Wm. BELUE, Wm. JAMES. 8 May 1833.

1251. (4:418) Nancy HARRIS, widow of John B. HARRIS, to Thomas L. UPTON: 29 Oct 1828, $300, 100 ac on the headwaters of Baker's Creek, part of Grant #2194 to Wm. HAMIL and conveyed to Robert and James STRAIN, adj Isaac YEAROUT, Thomas MAXWELL. Sig: Nancy (X) HARRIS. Wit: Lewis RICE, Joseph WILSON. 9 Mar 1831. [M. McTEER, the Transcriber, appended the following note at the end of the above deed: "This deed was torn from its place in the original book and not noticed for some time, hence it is placed here out of its regular order."]

1252. (4:419) Charles DONOHOO of Monroe Co. to John HUTSELL: 13 Nov 1826, $250, 175 ac on east fork of Pistol Creek, being the west side of a tract granted to James DONOHOO by Grant #1766 dated 16 June 1800, adj John DUNCAN, Josiah F. DANFORTH, John WILKINSON, Hugh WEAR. Wit: John NORWOOD, Jos. DONOHOO. 9 Mar 1831. [Note by M. McTEER, Transcriber: "This deed was torn from its place in the original book and not noticed for some time, hence it is placed here, out of its regular order."]

INDEX

As a convenience for the researcher, *EACH DEED* is *SEQUENTIALLY NUMBERED* and *INDEXED* by *DEED NUMBER*, not the page on which the deed appears.

NOTE: INDEX REFERENCES DEEDS, NOT PAGE NUMBERS

ANDERSON (Continued) 1076, 1078, 1119, 1152, 1184, 1187, 1210, 1214, 1236

ANDREW (slave)   117, 976

ANN (slave)   960

ANNEY (slave)   392

ARCH (slave)   1119

ARCHY (slave)   536

ARMBRISTER   1076

ARMSTRONG   61,   100, 142, 154, 267, 387, 720, 829, 995, 1014

ASHER   710, 948

ASLER   110

ATKINS   1216

AULD   420

AUSTIN   666, 861

AYLET   674

AYLETT   13,   118,   364, 373, 431, 467, 577, 1020, 1208

BADGET   887, 983

BADGETT   416,   419,   627, 682, 707, 720, 887, 976, 979, 984

BAILEY (slave)   578

BAILY   33

BAIN   534, 1124

BAINTER   1126

BAIRD   39

BAIRD/BARD   39

BAKER   233, 529, 544, 606, 933, 934

Baker's Creek   28,   70,   93, 102, 109, 113, 115, 118, 125, 149, 157, 191, 200, 217, 220, 243, 265, 266,

Baker's Creek (Continued) 276, 290, 293, 294, 295, 296, 309, 311, 322, 338, 341, 346, 359, 417, 434, 435, 442, 450, 458, 467, 481, 502, 508, 509, 515, 517, 518, 521, 525, 528, 532, 560, 580, 601, 602, 631, 634, 635, 644, 651, 652, 689, 738, 741, 742, 743, 744, 780, 781, 786, 804, 824, 840, 851, 877, 924, 946, 947, 953, 954, 956, 988, 992, 993, 996, 1004, 1011, 1016, 1017, 1052, 1054, 1078, 1092, 1094, 1095, 1104, 1106, 1154, 1164, 1189, 1191, 1211, 1249, 1251

BALEY   813

BALL   86, 635, 652, 1249

BAN/BAR   1079

BARNARD   234, 235, 238

BARNES   237, 629, 1138

BARNETT   84

BARNETT/BURNETT 184

BARNHILL   338, 434, 435, 580, 954, 1131

BARTLET   386, 391

BARTLETT   402, 469, 582, 591, 707, 720

BARTON   894

BASHEAR   606

BASHERS   542

BASS   727, 728

BATENY   157

BATES   31, 32, 37

NOTE: INDEX REFERS TO DEEDS, NOT PAGE NUMBERS

NOTE: INDEX REFERENCES DEEDS, NOT PAGE NUMBERS

NOTE: INDEX REFERS TO DEEDS, NOT PAGE NUMBERS

NOTE: INDEX REFERENCES DEEDS, NOT PAGE NUMBERS

NOTE: INDEX REFERS TO DEEDS, NOT PAGE NUMBERS

NOTE: INDEX REFERENCES DEEDS, NOT PAGE NUMBERS

CONDRAN   362
CONGER   481, 563, 689,
 690, 924, 1036, 1077, 1118,
 1142, 1143, 1145, 1162,
 1199
CONLEY   175
CONNALLY   14
CONNATSER   67
CONNEL   509
CONNER   88, 89, 162, 234,
 276, 286, 287, 389, 428,
 430, 450, 451, 762, 867,
 868, 869, 954, 992, 1122,
 1218
CONNEY   762
CONNOR   868
COOK   110, 136, 211, 236,
 237, 253, 305, 360, 361,
 381, 464, 468, 503, 630,
 704, 710, 890, 903, 905,
 906, 931, 948, 1044, 1060,
 1079, 1101, 1199, 1233,
 1235
COOKE   646, 710
COOP   56
COOPER   226, 370, 505,
 544, 551, 565, 603, 604,
 646, 782, 783, 1220
COPE   504, 556, 583, 780,
 781, 890, 903, 1060, 1079,
 1199
COPELAND   192, 569, 773,
 800, 805
COPERBURGER   297
COPLAND   421, 569, 570,
 573
COPPENBARGER   1069

COPPENBURGER   263
COPPOCK   41, 570, 678, 679
CORDEAL   624
CORLEY   17, 198, 324,
 844, 1083, 1085, 1088
COSNER   147
COSTNER/CARTER   173
COTHER   813
COULBURN   198
COULDWELL   16, 19, 35,
 82, 87, 122, 126, 127, 141,
 188, 290, 592, 662, 746,
 751, 752
COULSEN   41
COULTER   164, 348, 349,
 350, 476, 764, 770, 777,
 794, 916
COUNDRY   688
COURRIER   139, 140
COWAN   28, 123, 169,
 188, 272, 337, 356, 371,
 403, 436, 517, 553, 562,
 589, 610, 648, 654, 693,
 708, 772, 895, 911, 993,
 996, 1017, 1053, 1057,
 1134, 1135, 1245
COWEN   288
COWN   281
COX   29, 169, 178, 242,
 354, 406, 407, 412, 575,
 763, 777, 778, 780, 781,
 791, 798, 812, 816, 817,
 833, 1085, 1100, 1115,
 1214, 1223, 1224, 1246
CRAFORD   208
CRAFT   732
CRAGE   292, 430

NOTE: INDEX REFERS TO DEEDS, NOT PAGE NUMBERS

NOTE: INDEX REFERENCES DEEDS, NOT PAGE NUMBERS

DAVIS (Continued) 790, 803, 816, 856, 863, 867, 868, 869, 882, 889, 891, 892, 903, 905, 906, 912, 948, 970, 985, 1006, 1007, 1040, 1041, 1065, 1066, 1067, 1068, 1091, 1098, 1108, 1124, 1141, 1165, 1174, 1175, 1176

DAVISON   72, 438, 574

DEAN   716, 937

DEARMOND   109, 171, 226, 277, 396, 523, 592, 638, 695, 696, 697, 699, 745, 746, 850, 852, 1154, 1169

DEAVIES   543

DeBUSK   64, 313, 474, 994, 1009

DELANY   1014

DELOZIER   256, 499, 727, 728

DELY (slave)   675

DELZELL   42, 327, 328, 790, 825, 858, 888, 1025, 1170, 1187

DENNING/DEMMING 121

DENTEN   86

DEVER   216, 453

DEVINE   338

DICK (slave)   987

DICKE   1093

DICKEY   1013

DICKSEN   346, 511

DICKSON   367, 554, 1146

DINSMORE   95, 1036

DIXON   417, 691, 724, 896

DIXSEN   5

DIXSON   402, 415, 417, 896

DOBSON   243, 534, 607

DODD   367

DON   940

DONAHOO   134, 288, 381, 574, 725, 896

DONALDSON   766, 771, 1107, 1110

DONALSON   587

DONCARLAS   416, 419, 685, 715

DONCARLOS   976

DONELSON   387

DONOHOO   11, 14, 15, 19, 23, 26, 27, 34, 61, 62, 84, 85, 101, 102, 126, 135, 136, 168, 173, 179, 190, 192, 196, 207, 221, 226, 253, 284, 286, 335, 344, 370, 373, 450, 725, 883, 900, 908, 909, 922, 943, 948, 950, 1062, 1171, 1252

DORKAS (slave)   345

DOUGLASS   84, 356, 654, 1141, 1154

DOUGLESS   144, 654, 665

DOUTHET   919

DOWNEY   86

DOWNS   561, 622

DOYEL   448

DOYL   929

DUFF   752, 999, 1147, 1148, 1213

DUGLESS   144

DUN   161, 668, 1034

DUNCAN   11, 30, 205, 210,

NOTE: INDEX REFERS TO DEEDS, NOT PAGE NUMBERS

NOTE: INDEX REFERENCES DEEDS, NOT PAGE NUMBERS

Ellejoy Creek (Continued) 1097,
    1098, 1108, 1117, 1133,
    1151, 1153, 1174, 1175,
    1176, 1184
ELLENER (slave)   329
ELLIOT   135, 435, 486, 519
ELLIOTT   486, 538, 797,
    847, 871
ELLIS   64, 126, 343, 344,
    345, 567, 778, 905, 1013,
    1046
EMBREE   986
EMET   545, 546, 550
EMMENSON   103, 187
EMMERSEN   226, 227, 388,
    390
EMMERSEN/EMMENSEN 185
EMMERSON   200, 224, 246,
    268, 315, 330, 331, 332
EMMESON   104
EMMITT   1116
EMMONSON   488
EMMUNSEN   94
EPHRAIM (slave)   874
ETHERTON   658
EVANS   380, 835
EVERETT   54, 66, 495, 496,
    1089, 1090
EVERETT (slave)   968
EWIN   290
EWING   17, 35, 81, 122, 212,
    290, 291, 293, 294, 320,
    340, 387, 428, 441, 481,
    483, 510, 528, 572, 605,
    637, 638, 644, 652, 732,
    735, 751, 778, 820, 825,
    877, 927, 947, 956, 977,

EWING   (Continued)   1025,
    1057, 1141, 1166
FAGALA   807
FAGELA/FAGALA   180, 181
FAGG   223, 238, 450, 594,
    711, 721, 777, 796, 853,
    899, 922, 1059, 1080, 1119,
    1207
FALKER   271
FALKERTH   615
FALKNER   519, 764
FANY (slave)   306
FARMER   172, 336, 723,
    970, 992, 1000, 1001
FARR   216
FELK   1165
FEMSTER/FOSTER   155
FERBY (slave)   811
FERGUSEN   367, 664
FERGUSON   468, 505, 506,
    864
FINDELEY   678
FINDLEY   58
FINDLY   14, 274
FINE   1165
FINGER   574, 943
FINLEY   14, 326, 540
FINOL   694
FIRE/FARR   39
FLETCHER   1024
FLOOD   264
FOLKER   1165
FORD   44, 290, 293, 409,
    543, 573, 800, 805, 897,
    956, 1132
FORESTER   137, 324, 402,
    976, 1005

NOTE: INDEX REFERS TO DEEDS, NOT PAGE NUMBERS

NOTE: INDEX REFERENCES DEEDS, NOT PAGE NUMBERS

NOTE: INDEX REFERS TO DEEDS, NOT PAGE NUMBERS

NOTE: INDEX REFERENCES DEEDS, NOT PAGE NUMBERS

NOTE: INDEX REFERS TO DEEDS, NOT PAGE NUMBERS

NOTE: INDEX REFERENCES DEEDS, NOT PAGE NUMBERS

NOTE: INDEX REFERS TO DEEDS, NOT PAGE NUMBERS

NOTE: INDEX REFERENCES DEEDS, NOT PAGE NUMBERS

NOTE: INDEX REFERS TO DEEDS, NOT PAGE NUMBERS

NOTE: INDEX REFERENCES DEEDS, NOT PAGE NUMBERS

KERR (Continued) 866, 885,
890, 944, 945, 948, 1011,
1095, 1103, 1104, 1105,
1145, 1146, 1179, 1194,
1201, 1231
KERR/CARR   1095, 1106
KERRICK   1152
KEY   658, 758, 805, 830,
1033
KEYS   141, 758, 846
KIDD   823, 872, 873, 878,
975, 991, 1217
KIDEL   682
KILBURN   103, 124, 732,
735, 736
KINARD   319
KINCANNEN   252
KINCANNON   40,   195,
241, 692, 729
KING   14, 19, 62, 127, 199,
222, 223, 280, 281, 287,
388, 490, 584, 594, 661,
662, 669, 747, 812, 826,
828, 1032, 1034, 1037, 1122
KING AND MONTGOMERY
251, 303, 908, 938,
963, 1237
KIRKPATRICK   318,   366,
384, 507, 587, 957, 997,
1161
KIRLY   453
KITCHEN(S)   83
KITCHENS   721
KITHCART   612
KIZER   1101
KNARD   433
KNIGHT   723, 820

KOUNS   189
KOUNTS   1043
LACKEY   99,   175,   217,
391, 413, 625
Lackey's Creek   1, 29, 45,
242, 263, 270, 271, 297,
354, 406, 407, 412, 437,
607, 625, 632, 798, 854,
1099
LACKY   163, 239
LACY   801
LAFAYETTE (slave)   1119
LAIN   151, 172
LAMBERT   359, 460, 539,
714
LAMON   657, 739, 1043,
1051
LAMON/LAYMON   748
LANDER   491
LANDERS   595
LANE   153, 310, 347, 980,
1215
LANE/LOVE   451
LANGFORD   538
LANKFORD   766
LANNING   1034
LAPSELY   118
LAPSLEY   149, 378, 467,
1137
LAPSLY   502
LARKINS   300
LASETER   28, 243, 1154
LASSATER   28
LASSETER   109, 266, 359,
413
LATTAMORE   264
LAYMON   748

NOTE: INDEX REFERS TO DEEDS, NOT PAGE NUMBERS

NOTE: INDEX REFERENCES DEEDS, NOT PAGE NUMBERS

NOTE: INDEX REFERS TO DEEDS, NOT PAGE NUMBERS

NOTE: INDEX REFERENCES DEEDS, NOT PAGE NUMBERS

NOTE: INDEX REFERS TO DEEDS, NOT PAGE NUMBERS

NOTE: INDEX REFERENCES DEEDS, NOT PAGE NUMBERS

NOTE: INDEX REFERS TO DEEDS, NOT PAGE NUMBERS

NOTE: INDEX REFERENCES DEEDS, NOT PAGE NUMBERS

NOTE: INDEX REFERS TO DEEDS, NOT PAGE NUMBERS

NOTE: INDEX REFERENCES DEEDS, NOT PAGE NUMBERS

NOTE: INDEX REFERS TO DEEDS, NOT PAGE NUMBERS

NOTE: INDEX REFERENCES DEEDS, NOT PAGE NUMBERS

NOTE: INDEX REFERS TO DEEDS, NOT PAGE NUMBERS

NOTE: INDEX REFERENCES DEEDS, NOT PAGE NUMBERS

SCHRIMPSHER   1145
SCHRIMSHER   27
SCOTT   149, 197, 311, 340,
    376, 515, 554, 564, 572,
    634, 635, 649, 652, 790,
    815, 829, 836, 947, 956,
    994, 1054, 1104, 1249
Scott's Island   990
SCROGGS   135, 517, 518,
    806
SCRUGGS   379, 651, 656,
    988, 1016, 1017, 1131,
    1154, 1173
SECEDER MEETING HOUSE
    1197
SERVINER   887
SHADDEN   58, 379, 408,
    422, 1201
SHADDING   326
SHADDING/SHADDEN651
SHADDLE   1190
SHADELLE   616
SHADLE   43, 567, 647,
    1181
SHADOE/SHADLE   44
SHAMBLIN   668, 937
SHANK   341
SHARP   47, 73, 84, 132, 167,
    179, 252, 325, 429, 441,
    529, 754, 807, 835, 955,
    973, 977, 1027, 1035, 1212,
    1214
SHAW   30, 43, 44, 116, 117,
    128, 137, 147, 148, 249,
    341, 526, 681, 714, 805,
    910, 1058, 1096
SHEFFY (slave)   287

SHELTON   26, 49, 59, 74,
    84, 119, 135, 136, 179, 191,
    192, 199, 370, 488, 922
SHERREL   279, 283
SHERRELL   234, 339, 628,
    669
SHERRILL   1171
SHIELDS   274, 279, 363,
    423, 432, 576, 673, 677,
    714, 955, 1021, 1208, 1243,
    1247
SHIRLEY   1141
SHROYER   82, 229
SHUGART   207
SILVIA (slave)   317
SIMENS   327
SIMERLY   75, 770, 788
SIMINS   274
SIMINS/SIMMS   393
SIMMERMAN   299, 862
SIMMONAIN   299
SIMMONS   459
SIMMS   384, 394, 957
SIMONS   327, 328, 346,
    370, 994
SIMONS/SIMS   589
SIMPSON   177, 236, 261,
    910
SIMS   298, 318, 477, 807,
    957
SINGLETON   549, 759, 776,
    858, 987, 1002, 1179
Sinking Creek   278, 370, 375,
    490, 714, 724, 928
Six Mile Creek   9, 42, 232,
    233, 529, 551, 785, 808,
    835, 888

NOTE: INDEX REFERS TO DEEDS, NOT PAGE NUMBERS

NOTE: INDEX REFERENCES DEEDS, NOT PAGE NUMBERS

NOTE: INDEX REFERS TO DEEDS, NOT PAGE NUMBERS

NOTE: INDEX REFERENCES DEEDS, NOT PAGE NUMBERS

TUCK (Continued) 1233, 1235
Tuckaleechee Cove   72, 228,
    398, 399, 400, 438, 537,
    545, 546, 550, 769, 836,
    1082, 1091, 1116, 1243,
    1247
TUCKER   24, 70
TULLOCH   73, 525, 602,
    741, 866
TULLOCK   179
TURK   13, 25, 64, 90, 105,
    107, 124, 221, 224, 225,
    226, 314, 333, 363, 364,
    376, 389, 390, 423, 429,
    456, 470, 574, 576, 577,
    578, 585, 658, 677, 679,
    708, 952, 966, 1031, 1035,
    1188, 1206, 1208, 1218
TURNER   971
UNDERWOOD   693, 870
UPTON   78, 649, 653, 661,
    743, 997, 1097, 1141, 1251
URIAH/WACH (slave) 267
UTTER   142, 154, 346, 515,
    602, 631, 644, 824, 953,
    995, 1011, 1014, 1054,
    1104, 1106, 1146, 1191
VANCE   113, 231, 331, 479,
    706, 807, 831
VANPELT   175, 1085, 1223,
    1224
VARNER   93
VAUGHT   183, 335, 617,
    1245
VAUGT   61
VAUT   483, 608
VICKS   80

VILET (slave)   666
VINEYARD   821, 822
VINYARD   422, 507, 821,
    822, 1169
VIVENE   264
WAKER   66
WALKER   10, 36, 38, 98,
    116, 146, 147, 162, 176,
    181, 247, 349, 350, 358,
    415, 543, 550, 570, 574,
    681, 703, 794, 821, 836,
    861, 880, 890, 941, 958,
    959, 960, 978, 986, 1116,
    1120, 1121, 1129, 1130,
    1140, 1205, 1214, 1233,
    1235
Walker's Mill Creek   162, 969
WALLACE   11, 17, 35, 65,
    71, 91, 93, 99, 100, 121,
    124, 127, 134, 135, 141,
    154, 198, 200, 257, 277,
    291, 292, 312, 322, 324,
    326, 333, 348, 351, 360,
    361, 369, 375, 388, 410,
    414, 421, 437, 445, 450,
    456, 457, 458, 470, 485,
    486, 487, 491, 525, 529,
    536, 553, 557, 560, 561,
    562, 565, 571, 585, 592,
    598, 601, 602, 610, 619,
    621, 624, 625, 645, 651,
    656, 658, 660, 662, 663,
    664, 665, 666, 673, 674,
    675, 680, 709, 725, 730,
    732, 753, 754, 769, 774,
    786, 788, 790, 794, 795,
    809, 810, 818, 827, 836,

NOTE: INDEX REFERS TO DEEDS, NOT PAGE NUMBERS

NOTE: INDEX REFERENCES DEEDS, NOT PAGE NUMBERS

WHIGHT   87
WHITE   35, 47, 66, 122, 159,
    252, 273, 308, 367, 426,
    488, 495, 496, 871, 904,
    955, 985, 1020, 1021, 1034,
    1076, 1140, 1142, 1156,
    1160, 1237
WHITEHEAD   785, 835,
    1034
WHITTENBARGER   297,
    863, 1084, 1085, 1099
WHITTENBERGER   1100,
    1224, 1229
WHITTENBURGER   1,   29,
    354, 575
WICK   632
WILBOURN   362
WILBURN   362
WILCOX   603
WILKENSON   752
WILKINSON   11, 12, 51, 55,
    81, 104, 108, 119, 120, 121,
    124, 126, 169, 208, 225,
    234, 258, 269, 270, 272,
    301, 315, 339, 360, 374,
    444, 485, 489, 551, 574,
    594, 900, 922, 943, 998,
    1009, 1075, 1123, 1170,
    1171, 1224, 1236, 1248,
    1252
WILL (slave)   1241
WILLIAM (slave)   225, 578
WILLIAM JEFFERSON (slave)
    1119, 1127
WILLIAMS   6, 10, 40, 93,
    189, 193, 195, 197, 234,
    267, 268, 322, 339, 443,

WILLIAMS (Continued)   480,
    499, 503, 504, 511, 514,
    524, 531, 556, 582, 583,
    617, 630, 639, 646, 681,
    783, 791, 810, 829, 838,
    865, 889, 903, 920, 1028,
    1047, 1049, 1050, 1058,
    1060, 1079, 1102, 1129,
    1158, 1177, 1197, 1209,
    1228, 1237
WILLIAMSON   69,   100,
    349, 365, 754, 866, 995,
    1194
WILLIS   108
WILLSON   293, 896, 1092
WILSON   7, 55, 120, 141,
    166, 168, 190, 208, 209,
    223, 234, 267, 281, 282,
    283, 284, 286, 287, 290,
    294, 298, 304, 311, 339,
    341, 347, 348, 374, 389,
    390, 410, 415, 417, 458,
    503, 504, 525, 541, 556,
    623, 630, 647, 741, 743,
    747, 765, 774, 780, 789,
    791, 798, 804, 811, 816,
    817, 819, 857, 859, 885,
    911, 925, 926, 927, 928,
    930, 931, 932, 947, 950,
    981, 992, 1004, 1032, 1033,
    1037, 1072, 1104, 1106,
    1118, 1123, 1196, 1214,
    1218, 1224, 1234, 1236,
    1240, 1248, 1251
WILSON & SAFFELL 1238
WILSON AND SAFFELL 857,
    931

NOTE: INDEX REFERS TO DEEDS, NOT PAGE NUMBERS

NOTE: INDEX REFERENCES DEEDS, NOT PAGE NUMBERS